普通高等教育“十三五”精品规划教材
本教材由上海财经大学浙江学院发展基金资助出版

国际贸易实务

（双语版）

姜艳艳 主编

上海财经大学出版社

本教材由上海财经大学浙江学院发展基金资助出版

图书在版编目(CIP)数据

国际贸易实务:双语版/姜艳艳主编. -上海:上海财经大学出版社,2018.11
(普通高等教育"十三五"精品规划教材)
ISBN 978-7-5642-3083-8/F·3083

Ⅰ.①国… Ⅱ.①姜… Ⅲ.①国际贸易-贸易实务-双语教学-高等学校-教材-双、英 Ⅳ.①F740.4

中国版本图书馆 CIP 数据核字(2018)第 177193 号

□ 责任编辑 石兴凤
□ 书籍设计 张克瑶

国际贸易实务
(双语版)
姜艳艳 主编

上海财经大学出版社出版发行
(上海市中山北一路 369 号 邮编 200083)
网 址:http://www.sufep.com
电子邮箱:webmaster @ sufep.com
全国新华书店经销
上海华教印务有限公司印刷装订
2018 年 11 月第 1 版 2018 年 11 月第 1 次印刷

710mm×1000mm 1/16 25.5 印张 444 千字
印数:0 001-3 000 定价:56.00 元

前　言

随着全球化进程的加速，中国加入 WTO；“一带一路”大战略的提出，中国成为世界第一大贸易国。我国与世界各国的经济贸易往来越来越密切，这需要大量的既有良好的外语语言能力，又掌握国际贸易专业知识的复合型人才，这对高校在人才培养方面提出了挑战。为此本书编写的出发点就是让学生能够将外语语言能力与专业知识有机地结合，融会贯通，培养适应国际化需要的国际贸易专业人才。

本教材采取了英汉对照的方式，介绍了《国际贸易实务》这门课的内容。本书包括国际贸易合同中的各项交易条件及应注意的问题，进出口交易磋商、订立合同和履行合同等一系列必要的知识点。内容涵盖面广泛、深入浅出，图表、样本示例丰富，注重理论与实践相结合，使读者能够用英语掌握系统的专业知识，熟练地进行进出口业务的操作。全书共分 12 章，每章包括 3 个部分。第一部分是课文。该部分用中英文系统地阐述了国际贸易业务内容。第二部分是专业术语解释。该部分对英文术语代表的国际贸易业务含义进行了中文解释。第三部分是练习题。该部分可以加深读者对国际贸易业务知识的理解，以便灵活运用。

本书共分为 12 章，其中第 1、2 章由姜艳艳编写；第 3、4 章由王巧红编写；第 5、6 章由刘靖思编写；第 7、8 章由盛乐编写；第 9、10 章由叶文洁编写；第 11、12 章由丁瑾编写。

本书可作为高校经管类学生的教材，也可以作为从事外贸工作的商务人士的参考书。编者在编写过程中参阅了国内外很多相关著作和教材，国外很多专家和学者也帮忙做了语言校对，在此表示衷心的感谢！由于编者水平和学识有限，难免有差错和疏漏的地方，敬请高校同仁和读者批评指正。

Contents

目　录

Chapter 1

A Brief Introduction to International Trade

Part A Text

International trade, also called foreign trade, world trade or overseas trade, is the worldwide exchange of products across national boundaries. Products refer to goods and services. Services are found in areas such as transportation, tourism, banking, advertising, construction, retailing, wholesaling and mass communications. International trade includes import and export trade operations.

Section One Reasons for International Trade

For instance, if you live in Brazil and want a computer, you have to buy it from abroad; if you live in England and want to drink coffee, you have to buy it from abroad. Why is international trade necessary? Why can't people be self-sufficient on the goods and services produced in their own countries? This is due to several reasons.

1. Different Endowments

The different distribution of the world's resources. Some countries or regions are abundant in natural resources; while other nations' reserves are scarce or nonexistent. For example, the Middle East countries have vast oil deposit but less in of the resources; Democratic people's Republic of Korea has many minerals such as coal, nickel, copper, aluminum, etc. whereas Japan lacks many minerals. Thus, to obtain these through trading is an absolute necessity.

The different climate and terrain can affect a nation's cultivation of some agricultural products. For instance, Brazil enjoys a favorable climate to grow coffee plants, while the United States does not grow coffee. As a result, the United States has to import coffee. On the other hand, the climate and terrain of west America are ideal for planting wheat. The large quantity of wheat enables America to export to other countries.

The different level of technology and capital resources can determine what a nation is able to produce and trade with other nations. The developed countries are rich in capital resources, so they can concentrate on producing many technology-intensive products such as computers, aircrafts, etc. However, the developing countries lacking capital resources can hardly manufacture simple products. For example, Japan uses its technology and capital resources more efficiently in producing automobiles compared to other countries.

2. Benefits Acquisition

It has been found that a country benefits more by producing goods it can make most cheaply and buying those goods that other countries produce at a lower cost. This is often explained by the *theory of comparative advantage*, also called the *comparative cost theory*, which was developed by a famous English, David Ricardo in the nineteenth century. The Ricardian model uses the concepts of *opportunity cost* and *comparative advantage*. The *opportunity cost* of producing goods A is measured by the units of goods B that are *not* produced as a result. Comparative advantage has directed countries to specialize in particular products and to mass-produce. The US has a comparative advantage in computer production: it uses its resources more efficiently in producing computers compared to other uses; Ecuador has a comparative advantage in rose production, suppose that initially Ecuador produces roses and the US produces computers, both countries can be better off.

3. Risk Avoidance

Companies usually prefer to avoid fluctuations in their sales and profits; so they seek out foreign markets as a means to spread the risks and changes. Some movie companies have to plan year long sales for children's films because the summer vacation period (the main season for children's films attendance) varies between the northern and southern hemispheres. These companies have also taken advantage of the fact that the timing of product life cycle differs among countries. Thus while sales decrease in one country that is experiencing recession, they increase in another that is undergoing recovery. Finally, by depending on exporting the same product or component to different countries, a company may be able to avoid the full impact in any country that might be brought about, for example, by a strike, anti-dumping and anti-circumvention measures etc..

4. Economies of Scale

Another reason for international trade is *economies of scale*. If all factors of production double then the output the will double more, increasing returns to scale or economies of scale. This implies that the cost per unit of the output falls as a firm or industry increases its output . In a word, larger is more efficient. There are two types of economies of scale. External economies of scale which occurs when the cost per unit of output depends on the *size of the industry*. For example, a larger industry allows for more efficient provision of services or equipment to firms in the industry, it does not imply imperfect competition. *Internal economies of scale* occur when the cost per unit of output depends on the *size of a firm*, such as auto industry internal economies of scale result in an imperfectly competitive market. Economies of scale are achieved through a larger order book and better utilization of company resource, especially in the areas of production, design and so on. To realize economies of scale, sales must be big enough, and are limited by the number of people in a firm's products and services and by customers' capacity to make purchases. Since the number of people and degree of their purchasing power are much higher for the world as a whole than for a single country, firms may increase their sales through international trade. Ordinarily higher sales means higher profits.

Section Two Differences between International Trade and Domestic Trade

Both international trade and domestic trade are the exchange of commodities and service. There are also some differences between international trade and domestic trade. In particular, these differences include cultural problems, laws and customs, risks and information. Foreign traders must be aware of these differences because they often bring about troubles in international trade.

(1) There are many cultures just as there are people on earth. When companies do business overseas, they come in contact with people from different cultures. They often speak different languages and have their own particular customs and manners. For Japanese people, however, no business begins until after a great deal of informal conversation and tea drinking is done. While for Americans, they may immediately bring out their charts and cases for the first sales presentation. Therefore, in international trade, business people should be on the alert against different local customs and business norms.

(2) In international trade, what laws, customs, regulations and international rules should be used is very important. As these rules and regulations varies from country to country and international rules adopted by some countries may not be accepted by other countries. Before a specific transaction, two parties must come to an agreement on the laws and customs applied into the contract.

(3) Risks levels might be higher in international market than that in domestic market. The risks include political risks of the imposition of restrictions on imports, etc.; commercial risks of market failure; foreign partners not abiding by the contract and transportation risks; financial risks of exchange rates. These exchange rates change every day and are constantly updated in banks and foreign exchange offices around the world. Suppose a UK importer must pay a certain amount of Euros in 60 days to a German exporter for some equipment. This transaction leaves the UK firm open to substantial exchange rate risk because during those 60 days, the pounds may depreciate relatively to the Euro, forcing the UK firm to suffer from the loss of a large

amount of pounds in that case. So a good trader needs to be cautious about various risks in international trade and learn to avoid them.

(4) Compared to domestic trade, it is more difficult for dealers in international trade to get the necessary information of a particular firm in a foreign country. Control and communication systems are normally more complex for foreign operations than for domestic operations. It is also far more difficult to observe and monitor trends and activities in foreign countries.

Section Three Problems Concerning International Trade

1. Factors of Trade Volume

(1) The size of an economy is directly related to the volume of imports and exports. A large economy produces many goods and services, and therefore can make big exports and generates high income, and therefore can demand big imports. Size is measured by the *gross domestic product* (GDP).

(2) *Distance* between markets influences transportation costs and therefore the cost of imports and exports is affected.

(3) *Cultural affinity*: if two countries have cultural ties, it is likely that they also have strong economic ties.

(4) *Geography*: ocean harbors and lack of mountain barriers make transportation and trade easier.

2. Composition of Trade

(1) Today, most of the volume of trade is in manufactured products such as automobiles, computers, clothing and machinery.

(2) Services such as shipping, insurance, legal fees and spending by tourists account for 20% of the volume of trade.

(3) Mineral products (e.g., petroleum, coal, copper) and agricultural products are a relatively small part of trade.

(4) Developing countries, or low and middle-income countries, have also

changed the composition of their trade.

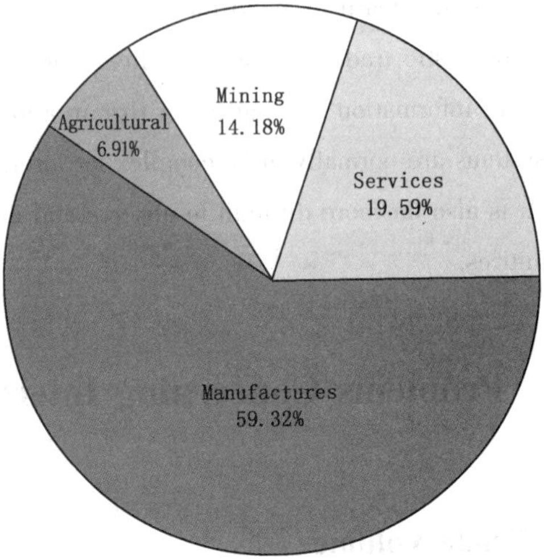

Source: World Trade Organization.

Fig. 1-1 Composition of Trade

——In 2001, about 65% of exports from developing countries were manufactured products, and only 10% of exports were agricultural products.

——In 1960, about 58% of exports from developing countries were agricultural products and only 12% of exports were manufactured products.

3. Trade Barriers

Trade barriers, like walls between feuding neighbors, are usually imposed unilaterally by one country acting on its own to limit the amount of foreign products available to local producers from foreign competition and allow them time to improve productivity. For example, even if it is not efficient for the US to manufacture cars, it may be in its national interest to do so and restrict trade. For the following reasons:

(1) Self-sufficiency in the event of war.

(2) Maintain production capabilities and know-how in the case a new technology makes them competitive again.

(3) Cannot compensate or retrain laid off workers of the auto industry.

(4) Free trade may transmit know-how to other countries, enabling them to manufacture cars on their own.

Section Four Learning Objectives

(1) Learn the course nature and content

(2) Be familiar with the relevant laws and practices applicable to international trade

(3) Master the basic procedures of import and export

(4) Study clauses of the contract

Sample of contract

中 艺 华 昌 进 出 口 公 司

CHINA HUA CHANG IMPORT & EXPORT CORPORATION

Foreign Trade Building No.200 Zhanqian Road, Nanchang, China

售 货 确 认 书

SALES CONFIRMATION

编号
No. JXHC009
日期
Date: MAY.8, 2003

买方
Buyers: CHK CORPORATION LTD.
10D.W.Rupasingbe Mawatba, Nugegooa, Srilanka

兹经买卖双方同意按下列条款成交:

The undersigned Sellers and Buyers have agreed to close the following transaction according to the terms and conditions stipulated below:

1.

货号 Art. No.	品名及规格 Description	数量 Quantity	单价 Unit Price	金额 Amount
	Ladies' Velvet Gowns		CIF Colombo	
ESA163	Size: L Color: White	400 DOZ	USD30.00/DOZ	USD12 000.00
ESA164	Size: M Color: Black	500 DOZ	USD28.00/DOZ	USD14 000.00
ESA165	Size: S Color: Red	600 DOZ	USD26.00/DOZ	USD15 600.00
	Total:	1 500DOZ		USD41 600.00

数量及总值均得有　%的增减,由卖方决定

With more or less　% both in amount and quantity allowed at the Sellers' option

总值

2. Total Value: Say US Dollars Forty One Thousand And Six Hundred Only

包装

3. Packing: At The Sellers' Option

装运期

4. Time of Shipment: Latest Date of Shipment 2003/08/31; Partial Shipment Prohibited And Transshipment Allowed

装运口岸和目的地

5. Loading Port & Destination: From Chinese Port To Colombo, Srilanka

保险

6. Insurance: To Be Covered By the Sellers For 110% of the Invoice Value Against All Risks And War Risk As Per CIC

付款条件

7. Terms of Payment: L/C SIGHT

装运标记

8. Shipping Mark:

C.H.K
123
COLOMBO
C/NO.1-160

备注

9. Remarks:

卖方
The Sellers
李健明

买方
The Buyers
Charles Brown

Part B　Key Terms

International trade　国际贸易

Endowments　要素禀赋

Theory of comparative advantage　比较优势理论

Opportunity cost　机会成本

External economies of scale　外部规模经济

Internal economies of scale 内部规模经济

Gross Domestic Product(GDP) 国内生产总值

Trade Barriers 贸易壁垒

Part C Exercises

Ⅰ. Answer the following questions

1. What is international trade?
2. Why does international trade happen?
3. What is external economies of scale?
4. What are the differences between international trade and domestic trade?
5. What is trade barrier?

Ⅱ. Case & Analysis

Case: A British businessman (A) makes an offer to a federal German businessman (B) on May 3rd to sell a certain number of goods. B is in the receipt of this offer on May 4th, and make a complete answer to accept the offer on the morning of May 4th. After A sends the offer, he finds the commodity prices upward, hence he cabled B to withdraw the offer in the afternoon of May 5th. It is on the morning of May 6th that A receives the acceptance from B.

Question: (1) According to the British law, is it legal for A to withdraw the offer? (2) If the case is applied to the CISG, do both sides exist contract relationships?

Analysis: (1) According to the British law, it is illegal for businessman A to withdraw the offer. According to the British law: an acceptance once sent out, it is effective immediately, and in this case B makes a promise on the morning of May 4th, the contract between them has come into effect.

(2) According to the CISG, both parties have the contract relationships. According to the CISG, an offer can be withdrawn before the offeree advises the commitment. However, in this case, B has made a commitment before A makes the withdrawal advice. So A cannot withdraw. The commitment made by B has come into effect when it reaches A on the afternoon of May 8th. The contract is formed.

第一章

国际贸易简介

国际贸易,又称对外贸易、世界贸易或海外贸易,是指跨越国界交换产品的行为。这里的产品包括商品和服务。服务是指交通运输业、旅游业、银行业、广告业、建筑业、零售业、批发业和大众传媒业。国际贸易包括进口业务和出口业务。

第一节　国际贸易产生的原因

如果你住在巴西想买计算机,则你必须从海外买;如果你住在英格兰想喝咖啡,则你也得从海外买。为什么进行国际贸易是必要的?为什么人们不能在自己的国家实现产品和服务的自给自足?这里有以下原因:

1. 不同的资源禀赋

世界上的资源是分布不均的,一些国家或地区自然资源非常丰富,而另外一些国家或地区存量稀少甚至没有。举例来说,中东国家有大量的石油储备,其他的几乎没有;朝鲜有很多矿产品,如煤、镍、铜和铝等;而日本却缺少这些矿产品。因此,要想获得这些矿产品,就必须通过国际贸易。

不同的气候和土壤会影响一个国家农产品的种植。举例来说,巴西的气候非常适宜种植咖啡,而美国却不能种植咖啡,结果就是美国必须进口咖啡。而另一方面,美国西部的气候和土壤却十分适合种植小麦,美国生产的小麦量非常之大,以至于经常可以出口到其他国家。

不同的技术水平和资本资源可以决定一个国家是否能够生产及与其他国家进行交易。发达国家的资本资源是十分丰富的，能够专注生产许多技术密集型产品，如计算机和航天产品等；而发展中国家由于缺乏资本资源，只能局限于生产和制造一些简单的产品，如与其他国家相比，日本利用技术水平和资本资源可以更有效地生产汽车。

2. 追求效益

人们发现，如果一个国家只生产低成本的产品，而其他国家购买这些产品，那么这比该国自己生产所有的产品要划算。对于这一点，人们常用比较优势理论来解释。比较优势理论也叫比较成本理论，是由英国著名经济学家大卫·李嘉图在 19 世纪发展而来的。大卫·李嘉图的模型采用了机会成本和比较优势理论，指生产 A 的机会成本是用不生产 B 的收益来衡量的。比较优势理论指导国家专门生产某类具有优势的产品并大规模地生产。美国在利用资源生产计算机方面更加有效率，厄瓜多尔在生产玫瑰花方面具有比较优势。假设厄瓜多尔只生产玫瑰花，美国只生产计算机，这两个国家则会更加富裕。

3. 风险规避

为了尽量避免销售量和利润剧烈波动，公司通常会寻找海外市场分散这种风险和防止变动出现。由于南北半球学校放暑假的时间不同（此时为放映儿童电影的主要时间），一些电影公司将对其年度销售计划做精心策划。其他许多公司则利用各个国家的产品生命周期的不同，对其生产量与销售量进行调整。这样，当一国经济萧条而引起销量减少时，在另一国则可因经济复苏而使销量增加。最后，依靠进口不同国家市场销售的同一产品或配件，公司就可避免一国产品的价格波动或由于采取贸易措施而带来的损失，比如由罢工、反倾销和反规避等措施引起的上述情况。

4. 规模经济

另外一个产生国际贸易的原因就是规模经济。如果所有的生产要素加倍，那么产出会更多，规模或规模经济的回报会增长，这意味着随着公司或产业产出的增多，产品的单位成本会下降。简而言之，量大意味着更加有效率。这里有两种规模经济。当单位成本的产出取决于整个产业的大小的时候，称之为外部规模经济。举个例子，整个行业规模的扩大会让一个公司产生更多有效的服务或设备,这并不意味着会产生不完全竞争。当单位成本的产出取决于一个公司的规模的时候,称之为内部规模经济。举个例子,当汽车业出现规模经济的时候,会导致不完全竞争。规模经济通过大量的订单和有效地利用公司资源来达到,尤其是在生产和设计领域等。为了实现规模经济,销售额必须足够大才行,但是一个公司的产品和服务的销售额受到消费者数量和消费者购买能力的限制,而全世界的消费者的数量和购买能力都比单一国家大得多,公司就会寻求国际贸易来增加销售额,通常来讲,更高的销售额意味着更高的利润。

第二节　国际贸易与国内贸易的区别

国际贸易和国内贸易都是产品和服务的交易。但是国际贸易和国内贸易仍然存在着一些区别,尤其是在文化、法律和惯例、风险和信息方面。外贸从业人员必须注意这些差别,因为这些差别经常会给国际贸易带来麻烦。

(1)这个世界上的文化跟人口一样多。当公司从事海外贸易的时候,它们要同具有不同文化的人们打交道。他们说着不同的语言并有着他们特有的文化和习俗。对于日本人来说,只有在愉快的非正式交谈和喝完茶之后才能进行交易;而对于美国人来说,就会马上直接拿出各种表格和案例进行第一笔交易的演讲。因此对于国际贸易从业人员来说,要特别关注当地不同的习俗和交易准则。

(2)在国际贸易中,要使用什么样的法律、惯例、法规和国际规则是非常重要的。因为国家与国家之间,这些法规和法令有很大的不同。对于有些国际法规,有些国家是接受的,而有些国家是不接受的。所以在具体交易前,双方就合同适用的法律和惯例必须达成一致。

(3)国际市场上进行交易的风险也高于国内市场。这些风险包括政治风险,如各国实施的进口限制措施等;各种市场失败的商业风险;国外交易伙伴不履行合同的风险和运输途中的风险;还有金融汇率风险。这些汇率每天都在变化,并在全世界的各银行和外汇管理局进行更新发布。假设英国的一个进口商跟德国的一个出口商做了一笔有关设备的交易,英国的进口商要在 60 天之后付给德国的出口商一定数量的欧元。这笔交易会使英国公司面临着很大的外汇风险,因为在这 60 天内,英镑兑欧元可能会贬值,在那种情况下,英国公司就会被迫损失一大笔英镑。所以一个好的外贸从业人员对国际贸易中的各种风险都要保持敏感度并设法规避。

(4)与国内贸易相比,对于国际贸易从业人员来说,获得有关国外公司的必要信息是非常困难的。控制和信息沟通系统通常比国内更加复杂,在别的国家进行观察与监督趋势和活动也变得更加有难度。

第三节　国际贸易中的一些问题

1. 影响国家之间贸易量的一些因素

(1)经济规模的大小直接决定了进口量与出口量。一个大的经济体能够生产很多的商品和提供很多的服务,所以能够大量地出口,以获得较多的收入,同样也就能够对进口有大的需求。经济体大小是用国内生产总值来衡量的。

(2)国际市场之间的距离影响了运输成本,也就影响了进口和出口的成本。

(3)文化的亲密度。如果两个国家有着很深的文化渊源,那么这两个国家也倾向于有很多的经济联系。

(4)地理位置。一个国家如果是海港国家,没有那么多的山脉阻碍交通,那么这个国家跟别国进行贸易也就容易得多。

2. 世界贸易结构

(1)当今时代,贸易量最大的是生产制造品,如汽车、计算机、服装和机器。

(2)服务像海运、保险、法律咨询费和旅游的花费占到整个贸易量的20%。

(3)矿产品(如石油、煤、铜)和农产品在贸易中占的比重相对较小。

(4)发展中国家或者低收入和中等收入国家的贸易结构也在变化:

——2001年,发展中国家工业制成品占总出口的65%,农产品只占10%。

——1960年,发展中国家农产品占总出口的58%,工业制成品的出口只占12%。

3. 国际贸易壁垒

国际贸易壁垒,就像长期不和的两个国家之间的一面墙一样,经常是一个国家单方面实施的,目的是限制国外产品进入国内市场的数量,以确保本土的生产商远离外国厂商的竞争,给他们时间去提高生产率。举个例子,即使美国

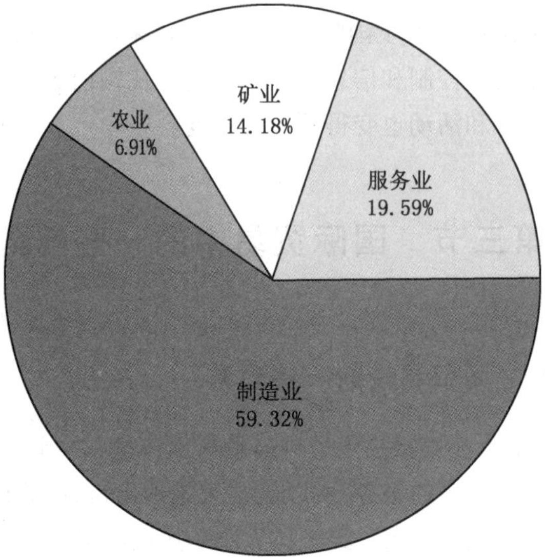

资料来源:World Trade Organization.

图1-1　贸易结构

在生产汽车方面没有效率,但是为了国家的利益,美国也会去限制汽车贸易,具体有以下原因:

(1)一旦发生战争的时候,可以自给自足。

(2)保持生产能力和生产诀窍,这样的新技术一旦产生,就会使美国再次具有竞争能力。

(3)以保障从事汽车业的工人留在产业内,如果汽车业的工人失业,补偿则将难以支付。

(4)自由贸易将会使生产诀窍泄露出去,而其他国家将会开始自己生产。

第四节　课程学习目标

1. 学习课程的本质和内容
2. 学习和熟悉国际贸易中的相关法律和惯例
3. 掌握进口和出口的流程
4. 学习合同条款

合同样本

中 艺 华 昌 进 出 口 公 司

CHINA HUA CHANG IMPORT & EXPORT CORPORATION

Foreign Trade Building No.200 Zhanqian Road, Nanchang, China

售 货 确 认 书

SALES CONFIRMATION

编号
No. JXHC009
日期
Date: MAY 8, 2003

买方
Buyers: CHK CORPORATION LTD.
10D.W.Rupasingbe Mawatba, Nugegooa, Srilanka

兹经买卖双方同意按下列条款成交:

The undersigned Sellers and Buyers have agreed to close the following transaction according to the terms and conditions stipulated below:

1.

货 号 Art. No.	品名及规格 Description	数 量 Quantity	单 价 Unit Price	金 额 Amount
	Ladies' Velvet Gowns		CIF Colombo	
ESA163	Size: L　Color: White	400 DOZ	USD30.00/DOZ	USD12 000.00
ESA164	Size: M　Color: Black	500 DOZ	USD28.00/DOZ	USD14 000.00
ESA165	Size: S　Color: Red	600 DOZ	USD26.00/DOZ	USD15 600.00
	Total:	1 500DOZ		USD41 600.00

数量及总值均得有　%的增减,由卖方决定

With more or less　% both in amount and quantity allowed at the Sellers' option

总值

2. Total Value: Say US Dollars Forty One Thousand And Six Hundred Only

包装

3. Packing: At The Sellers' Option

装运期

4. Time of Shipment: Latest Date of Shipment 2003/08/31; Partial Shipment Prohibited And Transshipment Allowed

装运口岸和目的地

5.Loading Port & Destination: From Chinese Port To Colombo, Srilanka

保险

6.Insurance: To Be Covered By the Sellers For 110% of the Invoice Value Against All Risks And War Risk As Per CIC

付款条件

7. Terms of Payment: L/C SIGHT

装运标记　　C.H.K

123

8.Shipping Mark:　　COLOMBO

C/NO.1-160

备注

9.Remarks:

卖方	买方
The Sellers	The Buyers
李健明	Charles Brown

Chapter 2

Terms of Commodity

Part A Text

Section One   Name of Commodity

Name of commodity is a conception and appellation which can make products different from others. It somehow can show the natures, uses and functions of products. In international trade, name of commodity is the first clause in the main body of contract. Name of commodity is very important, because it concerns the rights and obligations of the buyer and the seller. If the goods delivered by the seller are not in accordance with the agreed name of commodity in the contract, which the buyer can reserve the right to cancel the contract, which it belongs to fundamental breach of contract. Therefore, name of commodity should be clearly and precisely stipulated in the contract as it is the main condition in a transaction. There are some points for attention in stipulating name of commodity clause:

1. Using Specific Name of Commodity in the Contract

Name of commodity should be stipulated in the contract specifically, avoiding too general, for example, "Younger Suit" is a specific name, but "suit" is a too general name, which cannot be stipulated in the contract like that. You should also take care not to add unnecessary adjectives such as "elegant" or "beautiful" before suit.

2. Using Mutually Recognized Commodity Name

In international trade, it often happens, that the same product in different countries has different names. Most of commodities in the export trade usually have their own standard names in different countries. It is important to be careful about the names of commodity so that misunderstanding can be avoided. Here are two examples: Americans use "elevator" while the English use "lifts"; Americans use "sofa" while the English use "couch". Chinese foreign trade companies must pay special attention to this problem because we have suffered a lot losses on the ignorance of this issue.

3. Choose Appropriate Name of Commodity

If the stipulation of the description has little influence on the properties of the subject matter, we should choose and utilize appropriate commodity names in terms of lowering costs and reducing tariffs. Take "Car Model" for example. The tariff is much lower when it is listed as "Car Model (for children)".

4. Using Good Translation Name of Commodity

We should give the product a proper translation name when the product is exported to other countries, which should take local language, culture, customs and hobbies into consideration. For example, Coca-cola Company has successfully translate its drinks' name into Chinese in China, Chinese people like "ke kou ke le" very much, since it symbolizes tasty and enjoyment. Speaking of Chinese products, brand name "hai xin" was translated into "Hisense", which is also a good example.

Section Two Quality of Commodity

The quality of goods refers to the combination of the intrinsic attributes and outer form or shape of the goods. The former includes the physical, mechanical, biological and natural properties and chemical compositions of goods. While the latter includes shape, structure, color, flavors or style of the goods. Quality is very important in international trade, it is also the major terms of contract. If the seller deliver the quality of goods which do not conform to the contract, the buyer will be entitled to cancel the contract and claim for the damages.

1. Methods of Stipulating Quality of Commodity

(1) Sale by sample

Sale by sample refers to the transaction method which is done by the sample agreed by both the buyer and seller. The sample refers to a small quantity of a product, often taken out from a whole lot of consignment or specially designed and processed by the production or user department. This method is used when the goods is not standard, such as certain arts and crafts products, local specialty, light industrial products, etc. Sale by sample can be classified into the following types:

- Sale by the seller's sample

In this case, the sample is supplied by the seller. While sending the samples to the buyer, the seller should keep "duplicate samples" for delivery, evidence when handling quality disputes arising between the seller and buyer.

- Sale by the buyer's sample

In this case, the sample is supplied by the buyer. It is very difficult to supply the goods with exactly the same quality as shown in the sample. In order to take the initiative and avoid risks, the seller may reproduce the buyer's sample and send it back to the buyer for confirmation, called "return sample" or "counter sample". If the buyer accepts this sample, then sale by buyer's sample is changed into sale by seller's sample.

- There is another sample, the reference sample, which is in order to promote and propagate the products, there can be many differences between the reference sample and the physical products. A reference sample should be marked clearly with "for reference only" to avoid future disputes. Reference sample is not considered as the basis of delivery. While the sample is the legal basis of delivery, that means the sample shall be treated as an integral part of this contract, the quality of the goods delivered shall conform with the sample.

(2) Sale by Description

In international trade, most commodities are suitable to sale by description which can be classified into the following types:

- Sale by specification

The specification of the goods refers to certain main indicators which indicate the quality of the goods, such as moisture, content, purity, size etc. Such a method which seller and buyer use the specification to determine the quality of goods is called "sale by specification". For example, the Chinese peanut, the moisture content is not higher than 13%, the broken particles is not higher than 5%, oil content is not lower than 45%.

- Sale by grade

The grade of the goods refers to the different grades classification of the commodity of same kind which is indicated by number, signs and words, such as Grade A, Grade B, Grade C; Grade 1, Grade 2, Grade 3…

- Sale by standard

The standard refers to the specifications or grades which are stipulated and announced by the government or the chambers of commerce, trade associations, commercial organizations, etc. In case of sale by standard, it is important to quote the edition of commodity standard, because the standard of a commodity is subject to change or amendment, e.g. Tetracycline HCL Tablets (Sugar Coated) 250g. B.P. 1973.

For international agricultural products, FAQ (fair average quality) is commonly employed. FAQ refers to the average quality level of the commodity in international trade within a certain period of time.

- Sale by brand name or trade mark

Some well-known brands and trade marks represent high and reliable quality and they are well known by the customers in international markets. When we use the trade mark and brand name to indicate the quality of goods, it is called sale by brand name or trade mark. For example, "Colgate Toothpaste", "BMW Automobile", etc.

- Sale by name of origin

Some goods, such as certain agricultural products subject to the influence of natural conditions and traditional production techniques, have enjoyed a good reputation for a long time. As for these products, the place of origin may well indicate their qualities. These goods can be sold by name of origin. For example, "Jingdezhen Porcelain", "Peking Roast Duck", "Jinhua Ham", etc..

- Sale by specifications and illustrations

The quality of some machines, instruments, electronic appliances and large-size equipment which have complicated structure cannot be described by merely specifications or brand. Thus, the specific descriptions of these products in detail are required to indicate the structure, material, performance as well as method of operation. If necessary, pictures, drawings and diagrams, etc. should also be provided.

2. Quality Latitude

Errors are inevitable in agricultural products, industrial raw materials or some products of light industry, quality latitude is usually stipulated in the sales contract. Quality latitude means permissible range of the goods delivered by the seller which may be that agreed on between the seller and the buyer beforehand. For example, "Yam-dyed Gingham Width 41/42", "Grey Duck Feather down content 18%, allowing 1% more or less", "admixture (max) 1%". Goods delivered by seller are qualified, Within the range of latitude, but the price can be increased or decreased according to the degree of the latitude. For example, China Sesame, Moisture (max) 8%; Admixture (max) 2%; Oil Content 52% basis. Should the oil content of the goods actually shipped be 1% higher or lower, the price will be accordingly increased or decreased by 1%, and any fraction will be proportionally calculated. Sometimes, price adjustment is not needed if the latitude is within certain limit.

Quality Tolerance is a special type of quality latitude, since the latitude is recognized by trade or industrial association. For example, the quality tolerance of watches is 1 seconds within 2 days.

3. Example of Quality Clauses in Contract

(1) Quality: by sample No.J0812 man's jeans, submitted by the seller on July 25. The quality of the delivered goods shall be about equal to the sample.

(2) Plush toys, quality as per Seller's sample No. 121015 submitted on Oct. 15th, 2012.

(3) Flower' brand color-pen, 12 colors with the buyer's packing card.

Section Three Quantity of Goods

Quantity clause is also one of the necessary conditions for the conclusion of a sales contract. The seller should deliver the quantity of goods in conformity with that in the contract. According to *United Nations Convention on Contract for Sale of Goods*, to deliver goods by the agreed amount is a fundamental obligation of the seller. If the quantity delivered is more than quantity agreed upon, the buyer may reject delivery of the excess quantity, or take delivery of all, or part of the excess quantity, but he must pay for it at the contract rate.

1. Measurement Units

Because different countries have different systems on calculating units such as length, capacity and weight, the units of measurement vary form a country to another, it is very important for international trader to know the units of measurement in different systems and the way how they are converted into another. The Metric System (the International System), the British System and U.S. System are commonly used in the world. Usually the International System is adopted in China. The commonly used measurement units are as follows:

(1) Weight

Kilogram (kg.); metric ton (m/t); long ton (l/t); short ton (s/t); gram (g.); pound (lb.); ounce (oz.). They are usually used for raw materials, agricultural products such as raw chemicals, cotton, grains and minerals.

(2) Number

Piece (pc.); package (pkg.); pair; set' dozen (doz.); gross (gr.); ream (m.); roll; case; bale; drum. These are usually used for industrial products and general products such as stationery, paper, toys, vehicles and live animals.

(3) Length

Meter (m); centimeter (cm); foot (ft); yard (yd); kilometer; mile, etc. These are usually used for textile products, metal cords, electric wires, ropes and so on.

(4) Area

Square yard (yd^2); square meter(m^2); square foot (ft^2), etc. These are usually used for glass, leatherwear and textile products such as cloth, carpets, plastic sheet, leather, and floor.

(5) Volume

Cubic meter (m^3); cubic foot (ft^3); cubic yard (yd^3), etc. These are usually used for woods, natural gases, etc.

(6) Capacity

Liter (L.); gallon (gal.); bushel (bu.), etc. These are usually used for grains, liquid cargo, alcohol, oils, etc.

The choice of the unit of measurement should be in accordance with the nature of the goods.

2. Methods of Calculating Weight

(1) By Gross Weight

Gross weight means the weight of the commodity plus its tare or weight of packing. That is to say it refers to the net weight plus the package weight.

(2) Net Weight

Net weight is the actual weight of the commodity excluding the tare or the package weight. As for some commodities of relatively low value or similar value to packing such as agriculture products in gunny bag, the weight of the package can be ignored. This way of weight calculation is called "gross for net". It is customary for the seller to make payment by net weight.

(3) Theoretical Weight

Commodities with regular specifications and regular sizes, such as galvanized iron, tin plate and steel plate, as long as the specifications and sizes of such commodities are the same, the weight can be calculated by the total number of pieces. This method is called theoretical weight.

(4) Conditioned Weight

Conditioned weight refers to the scientifically dried weight of a certain commodity plus the standard moisture content of that commodity. It is commonly used for high economic value and with unsteady moisture content, such as raw silk and wool. A formula to calculate the conditioned weight of the product is shown as below:

$$\text{Conditioned Weight} = \frac{\text{actual weight} \times (1+\text{standard regaining rate of water})}{1+\text{actual regaining rate of water}}$$

$$= \text{Dried Weight} + \text{Standard Moisture}$$

The accepted international standard regaining water content is 11%.

3. More or Less Clause

For some bulk goods such as agricultural products and mineral products like corn, soybean, wheat, coal, etc., it is hard to make the actual delivery quantity conform to the contracted quantity owing to the characteristic of the commodity itself. Moreover, being influenced by natural conditions, packing patterns, and loading and unloading methods, the quantity of the goods delivered by the seller usually doesn't conform to the quantity exactly stipulated in the contract. In order to facilitate the processing of the contract, the seller and the buyer stipulate in a sales contract that the seller is allowed to deliver the goods within a certain percentage of more or less than the contracted quantity. This is usually referred to as the "more or less clause". As long as the quantity delivered by the seller is within the range, it is regarded as delivery in accordance with the contract. For example, Peanut, 50 metric tons with 3% more or less at the seller's potion. The delivery quantity range is within 51.5-48.5MTs. Some questions about more or less clause:

(1) Option for the range of more or less.

Generally, the seller is to decide the range of how much more or less in practice. It is also practical to allow the carrier to decide the quantity according to the capacity of shipping; under the FOB terms, it is the buyer who charter a liner to carry the goods, so the quantity range can be stipulated as buyer's option in the contract.

(2) Under the more or less clause, the payment for the over-load or under-load will be made according to the contract price or at the market price at the time of shipment.

(3) Such expressions as "about or approximate" should not be used in the contract because it may be given to ambiguous interpretations: some refer to 2% more or less, and some 5%, some 10%. According to *UCP600*, "about/ approximate" allows the quantity to be 10% more or less; for bulk goods, 5% more or less is allowed if the contract doesn't stipulate definitely the range of more or less.

4. Examples of Quantity Clause

(1) "Butterfly" brand bicycles, 1 200 sets delivery.

(2) Chinese sesame, 100 MTs, with 3% more or less at the seller's option.

(3) 1 000 dozens gloves. The seller has the option to load 5% more or less than the quantity contracted, each difference shall be settled at the contract price.

Section Four Packing of Goods

Packing is one of the most important problems in international business practice. If the goods are delivered not in the stipulated packing, the buyer is entitled to reject the goods; the captain will refuse to sign a clean bill of lading if any package is damaged and the seller will fail to get payment. In recent years, the significance of packing has been increasingly recognized, and it is regarded as a part of quality and competitive force in international market.

1. Types of Packing

Packing can be divided into three kinds when it is taken into consideration whether or not the cargo needs packing:

(1) Nude Cargo

Nude cargoes or nude packed commodities refer to those kinds of cargoes whose qualities are more stable and are shipped without any packages or in simple bundles. They are difficult to be packed or do not need any packing, such as steel products, timber, rubber, automobile, etc.

(2) Cargo in Bulk/Bulk Cargo

Cargo in bulk refers to goods which are shipped or even sold without packages on the conveyance in bulk, such as oil, ore, grain, coal, etc.

(3) Packed Cargo

Most of commodities in international trade need certain degree of packing during the shipping, storing, and sales process. Packed cargoes refer to cargo which needs shipping packing, marketing packing or both.

Packing can be divided into transport packing and sales packing according to the functions of the package.

(1) Transport Packing

Transport packing is also called giant packing or outer packing. It is used mainly to keep the goods safe, to facilitate the transportation, for storage, identification and count, to reduce freight and cut costs. It must be solid enough to prevent the goods from any damage during handling and transportation. On the basis of packing materials and packing methods, transport packing includes the following types:

——Single piece packing: cases, drums, bags, bale, cartons, etc.

——Collective packing: container, pallet, flexible container, etc.

In recent years, containers have been developing very quickly. Containers are a large metal case, of standard shape and size, for carrying goods by road, rail, sea or air. The most common used containers are the following two kinds:

TEU (Twenty-foot Equivalent Unit), 20 foot×8 foot×8 foot

FEU (Forty-foot Equivalent Unit), 40 foot×8 foot×8 foot

When calculating the circulating quantity of a container, we often take the 20-foot container as a measuring unit, i.e., TEU (Twenty-foot Equivalent Unit).

(2) Sales packing

Sales packing is contact with the commodity directly and will go into sales outlets with the product to meet the consumer. It is now universally recognized as a aid in selling household consumer goods especially in the supermarket, so it is sometimes called "a Silent Sales Man". To facilitate sales, there are different designed packages: hanging packaging, stacked packaging, portable packaging, easy-open packaging, spray packaging, set packaging, gift packaging and reusable packaging, and balloon packaging. Some questions about packing:

- Design of Packing

The design of packing should apply to the national habits and preferences of relevant countries so as to promote products. Different countries have different customs and cultures, so an international trade company should get to know the local customs and taboos during market research when going about designing the export packing. Otherwise, it can result in serious results. For example, British people hate elephant designs on the package; Japanese people like pine tree designs etc.

- Labels

We should pay attention to the regulations and stipulations regarding labels in the target countries, when attaching labels on the sales packaging. especially for food, medicine, and clothing. For example, the Swedish government stipulates that washing instructions must be printed on the label for clothing.

- Bar Code

A bar code on the packing is a group parallel strips with numbers, which are black and white and of different intervals. The bar code is a special code language read by the optical scanning device in order to input data into a computer. It contains such information as the name, specifications, origin and price of the product.

There are two bar code systems: the Universal Product Code (UPC) of the USA and the European Article Number (EAN) system. The European Article Number (EAN) system is commonly used throughout the world. In 1991, China took part in the International Article Number Association and was assigned the use of digits "690 -695". It means any product beginning with any of these digits is made in China.

2. Marking of Package

In order to facilitate the goods' transportation, storage, handover and identification, the marks are stenciled on the outside of the package. The uses of packing marks can be divided into three kinds: shipping marks, indicative marks and warning marks.

(1) Shipping Marks

Shipping marks are marks of simple designs, some letters, numbers and simple words on packages that serve as identification of the consignment in the process of transporting, loading and unloading, storage and handover in international trade.

International standard shipping marks suggested by the International Standard Organizations consists of :

——Initials or abbreviations of the consignee's name

——Reference number(contract number, order number, L/C number)

——Destination

——Packages number

For example:

ABCCO——收货人名称

SC9750——合同号码

LONDON——目的港

No.4 - 20——件号(顺序号和总件数)

(2) Indicative Marks

Indicative marks are simple, obvious design and words on the packages used to remind the relevant workers to pay attention when they load, unload, carry and store the goods.

(3) Warning Marks

Warning marks are also called dangerous marks or hazardous marks, They must be brushed/printed clearly and permanently on the outer shipping packing of the inflammable, explosive, poisonous, corrosive or radioactive goods, so as to give warnings to people concerned to take protective measures and to guarantee the good conditions of goods and the life security of people [See Fig. 2 - 1 Examples of (3) warning marks].

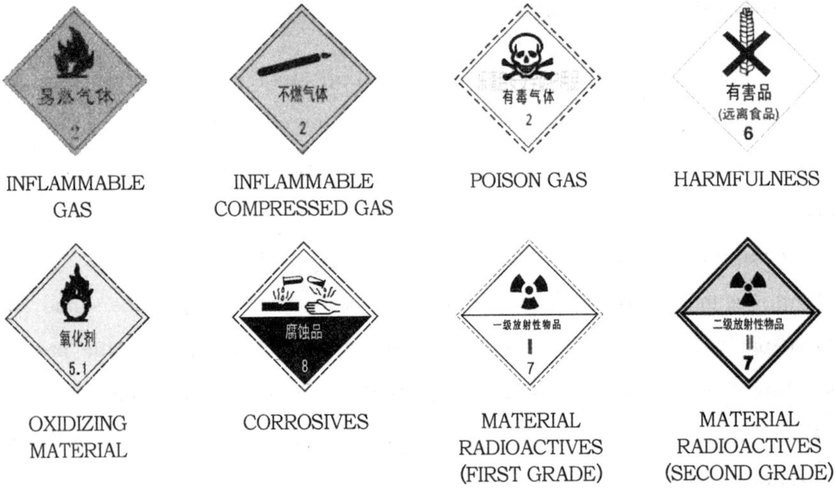

Fig. 2-1 Examples of (3) warning marks

3. Neutral Packing and OEM

Neutral packing means that there is no country of origin, or name and address of the manufacturer on the packing of the commodity. There are two types of neutral packing: neutral packing with designated brand and neutral packing without designated brand. There are two purposes for neutral packing: firstly, it is not necessary to print the place of origin for some raw materials; secondly, the exporters want to break down the tariff and non-tariff barriers of some countries, or avoid some political discriminations in the importing countries.

OEM is short for Original Equipment Manufacturer. It refers to a kind of international trade practice where seller use the brand name or trademark designated by buyers on their manufactured products.

This practice is popular internationally at present. Many transnational companies adopt OEM in order to take advantage of low labor cost in developing countries. China is called "the world's factory", because many Chinese factories manufacture the products with the buyer's brand name on them, but under the trade marks or brands, we print "Made in China".

It is advisable for seller to add a safeguard clause in the contract: "if the seller is charged with the infringement of industrial property by any third party, it has nothing to do with the seller."

In trade practice, the cost of packing is included in the contract price, unless the buyers have special requirements on the package.

4. Examples of Packing

(1) In wooden cases of 100 kgs net each.

(2) The goods shall be packaged in cartons of one set each, total 1 200 cartons.

(3) The tea under the contract should be packed in international standard tea boxes, 24 boxes on a pallet, 10 pallets in an FCL container. On the outer packaging please mark our initials SCC in a diamond, under which the port of destination and our order number should be stenciled.

Part B Key Terms

Fundamental breach 根本性违约

Counter sample 对等样品

Reference sample　参考样品
Sale by specification　凭规格买卖
Sale by grade　凭等级买卖
Sale by standard　凭标准买卖
Sale by brand name　凭品牌买卖
Sale by name of origin　凭原产地买卖
Sale by specifications and illustrations　凭说明书买卖
Quality latitude 品质机动幅度
Quality tolerance　品质公差
Gross weight　毛重
Net weight　净重
Gross for net　以毛做净
Theoretical weight　理论重量
Conditioned weight　公量
More or less clause　溢短装条款
Nude cargo　裸装货
Cargo in bulk/bulk cargo　散装货
Packed cargo　包装货
Container　集装箱
Bar code　条形码
Shipping marks　唛头
Indicative marks　指示性标志
Warning marks　警告性标志
Neutral packing　中性包装
Original equipment manufacturer　原始设备制造商

Part C　Exercises

Ⅰ. Answer the following questions

1. What points should be pay attention to in Stipulating Name of Commodity Clause?

2. What is the definition for quality?

3. Why should we marked "for reference only" on the reference sample?

4. What does "Sale by Description" usually include?

5. What is "gross for net"?

6. What is bar code?

7. What does the shipping mark of ISO generally contain?

8. What is indicative marks?

9. Why do the producers use neutral packing?

10. What does OEM stand for?

Ⅱ. Case & Analysis

1. A trade company of China exported a batch of cannabis to Germany. The sales contract specified as: moisture, 15% (max.); admixtures, 3% (max.). The exporter has sent the sample to the buyer before the transaction is concluded. So the exporter telephoned the buyer that the delivered goods are similar to the sample. Later signing the contract. The buyer inspected the goods after its arrival in Germany, and provide an inspection certificate stating that the quality of the goods is lower than that of the sample by 7%, and according to this, they claimed for 600 Euro as compensation against the losses. Could the exporter ignore the claim for the reason that the deal was not conducted based on sale by sample?

2. An exporter concluded a sales contract with a Japanese buyer. Both the contract and letter of credit stipulated that the apple should be grade three. But the exporter found the stock of apples of grade three out of stock just when the exporter arranged for shipment. So the exporter shipped the apples of grade two instead and noted on the invoice that "Apples of grade two sold at price of grade three". Do you think it is appropriate for the exporter to replace the goods by higher grade at the same price?

3. A trade company exported chemical raw materials. The total quantity is 500 metric tons. Both the contract and the credit stipulated the goods should be packaged in gunny bags. But when shipping the goods for delivery, the exporter found the quantity of goods packaged in gunny bags is only 450 metric tons, and then packaged the remaining 50 metric tons in plastic bags instead. Are there any problems in doing like this?

第二章

商品信息条款

第一节　商品名称

商品名称是指能使某种商品区别于其他商品的一种称呼或概念。商品的名称在一定程度上体现了商品的自然属性、用途以及主要的性能特征。在国际贸易中，商品名称是合同主体部分的第一条款。商品名称条款非常重要，因为它关系到买卖双方的权利和责任义务。如果卖方所交货物与合同中规定的名称不一致，买方有保留取消合同的权利，因为这属于严重违约。因此合同中的商品名称条款要规定得具体和精确，因为它是交易的主要条件。对于商品名称条款有以下注意事项：

1. 在合同条款中要使用具体的名称

合同条款中的名称要具体，避免太过笼统。举例来说，“雅戈尔西服”就是一个很具体的名字，而单独讲“西服”就太笼统，在合同中就不能这样规定。我们还应该注意不要在西服前面加不必要的形容词，如高雅的或漂亮的。

2. 使用双方认可的名字

在国际贸易中，对同一产品，不同的国家有不同的名字，大多数出口产品在不同的国家都有不同标准的名字，所以注意产品的名称问题是很重要的，以避免发生误解。这里有两个例子：对于电梯，美国用 elevator，而英国用 lifts；对于沙发，美国用 sofa，而英国用 couch。中国外贸公司对于产品名称问题尤其要注意，因为我们曾忽视了这个问题而遭受了巨大的损失。

3. 注意选择合适的商品名称

在不影响描述主体性质的情况下，我们应该选择和利用合适的名称来降低费用和关税。如“轿车模型”，如果我们把名字列为“轿车模型（儿童用）”就可以降低很多关税。

4. 使用合适的商品翻译名称

当产品出口到其他国家的时候，我们要给产品起一个合适的翻译名称，这个翻译名称要考虑当地的语言、文化、习俗和喜好。可口可乐公司成功地把它的饮料名字翻译成中文，因为中国人很喜欢“可口可乐”这个名字，它象征着可口和喜悦。说到中国公司的产品，品牌“海信”翻译成了“Hisense”，这也是一个很好的例子。

第二节　商品品质

商品品质是指商品内在属性与外观形态的综合。前者指商品的物理、机械、生物、自然特性和化学成分。而后者指商品的形状、结构、颜色、风味或者款式。商品品质在国际贸易中是非常重要的，它也是合同中主要的条款，如果卖方提供的商品品质不符合合同规定，买方有权利取消合同并且索赔损失。

1. 商品品质规定的方法

(1)凭样品买卖

凭样品买卖是指凭买卖双方都同意的样品作为交货品质依据的买卖方式。所谓样品，就是指能够代表一整批货物质量的实物，通常是指从一批货物中抽取出来或由生产和使用部门设计加工出来的、能够代表出售货物品质的少量实物。凭样品买卖的方法一般适用于难以标准化的商品，如工艺品、土特产品和轻工产品等。凭样品买卖可以分成以下三种类型：

- 凭卖方样品买卖

凭卖方样品买卖的情况下，样品由卖方提供。同时，卖方要自留“复样”，以备交货或处理品质纠纷时作核对之用。

- 凭买方样品买卖

凭买方样品买卖的情况下,样品由买方提供。由于很难生产出与样品一模一样的产品,为了主动避免风险,卖方会再加工一个买方样品,交回买方确认,这个样品被称为"回样"或者"对等样品"。买方如果接受这个样品,凭买方样品买卖就会变为凭卖方样品买卖。

- 还有一种样品被称为参考样品,目的是用来促销和宣传产品。参考样品和实际的商品可能会有差距和区别,所以参考样品一定要明确标识"仅供参考",以避免可能会出现纠纷。参考样品不是交货的依据,而样品却是交货的法律依据,这意味着样品是合同不可分割的一部分,所交货物应该与样品保持一致。

(2)凭说明买卖

在国际贸易中,大多数商品可以凭说明买卖,可以分为以下几类:

- 凭规格买卖

商品的规格是指一定的指标,这些指标能够反映商品的品质,如湿度、含量、纯度、尺寸等。这种买卖双方同意用规格来确定商品质量的方式被称为凭规格买卖。举个例子,中国花生,湿度不能高于13%,碎粒不超过5%,含油量不低于45%。

- 凭等级买卖

商品的等级是指同种类的商品用数字、符号、文字划分为不同的等级。例如,A级、B级、C级;一等、二等、三等……

- 凭标准买卖

标准是指由政府、商会、贸易协会、商业组织发布或规定的关于商品的规格或等级。当采用凭标准买卖的时候,指出采用的版本是非常重要的,因为产品的标准是通过修订不断变化的,如盐酸四环素糖衣片250毫克—— 按1973年版英国药典。

在国际贸易中,农产品的买卖经常会采用良好的平均品质。良好的平均品质是指在一定的时间段内国际贸易中商品的平均品质。

- 凭品牌或商标买卖

一些知名品牌和商标代表了高质量和可靠的商品品质,它们被消费者和国际市场所熟知。当我们用品牌或商标表示商品品质的时候被称为凭品牌或商标买卖,如高露洁牙膏、宝马汽车等。

- 凭原产地买卖

一些产品，像农产品，受自然气候和技术工艺的影响很大，因而长时间享有很高的声誉。对于这些产品，产地可以很好地表现它们的品质。这些产品可以凭原产地买卖，如景德镇瓷器、北京烤鸭、金华火腿等。

- 凭说明买卖

一些机器、仪器、电子电器、大型设备的结构非常复杂，不能只用规格或品牌去描述它们的品质，这类商品需要详细的说明来反映它们的结构、材料、功能以及操作方法。如果有必要的话，则还要配上图片、草图、图表等。

2. 品质机动幅度

在农产品、工业原材料、一些轻工业产品中，品质误差是不可难免的，在这些产品的合同中通常规定品质机动幅度条款。品质机动幅度是指买卖双方事先达成一致，同意卖方所交货物的品质变动范围。举个例子，“色织条格布　宽度　41-42”，“灰鸭毛　含绒量 18%，允许上下变动 1%”，“最大杂质含量为 1%”。只要卖方所交货物在品质机动幅度内就被认为是合格的，但是根据幅度的情况，价格可以进行相应的增减。举个例子，中国芝麻，水分（最高）8%；杂质（最高）2%；含油量以 52% 为基础。如实际装运货物的含油量增高或降低 1%，价格相应地增减 1%，不足整数部分，按比例计算。当然有时候在品质机动幅度内，价格不需要做调整。

品质公差是一种特殊的品质机动幅度，这个幅度是由贸易或工业行会认定的，如手表的品质公差为两天一秒钟。

3. 合同中品质条款举例

（1）男装牛仔裤，质量按卖方于 7 月 25 日提交的第 J0812 号样品，交货质量与样品质量须大致相同。

（2）长毛绒玩具，质量以卖方 2012 年 10 月 15 日提供的第 121015 号样品为准。

（3）花牌彩色笔，12 种颜色依照买方提供的包装卡。

第三节　商品的数量

数量条款是合同交易中非常必要的条款之一。卖方所交货物的数量应该与合同保持一致。根据《联合国货物销售合同公约》,卖方根据约定的数量交货是一项根本的义务。如果所交货物的数量超过约定的数量,买方有权拒收多交部分,也可以接受多交部分的全部或部分,但是必须按照合同支付货款。

1. 计量单位

由于各国度量衡制度不同,因而使用的计量单位也不同,如长度、容量和重量等。由于各国的计量单位不一样,了解不同度量衡制度中的计量单位和它们之间的换算对从事国际贸易的人员来说是非常重要的。现在世界上常用的三大度量衡制度为公制(国际单位制)、英制和美制。中国采用的是国际单位制。常用的单位举例如下:

(1)重量

公斤、公吨、长吨、短吨、克、磅、盎司。这些单位常用于原材料、农产品等,如化工原材料、棉花、谷物粮食和矿物产品等。

(2)个数

只、件、双、套、打、令、卷、箱、包、桶等。这些单位常用于工业制成品和一般杂货,如文具、纸张、玩具、车辆和活体动物等。

(3)长度

米、厘米、英尺、码、千米、英里等,这些单位常用于纺织品、金属绳索、电线、电缆等。

(4)面积

平方码、平方米、平方英尺等,这些单位常用于玻璃、皮革制品和纺织品,如布匹、毯子、塑料垫子、皮革和地板。

(5)体积

立方米、立方英尺、立方码,这些单位常用于木材、天然气等。

(6)容积

升、加仑、蒲式耳等,这些单位常用于谷物、流体货物、酒精、石油等。

选择单位的时候要依据货物的本质特点。

2. 计算重量的方法

(1)按毛重

毛重是指商品本身的重量加上皮重或包装物的重量,也就是商品净重加上包装物的总重量。

(2)净重

净重是指商品本身的实际重量,不包括包装物的重量。对于一些价值较低或者商品价值和包装价值相近的商品,如装在麻袋里的农产品,包装袋重量就会被忽略掉。这种计算重量的方法被称为“以毛做净”。卖方通常按净重支付货款。

(3)理论重量

某些有固定规格形状和尺寸的商品,如镀锌铁、马口铁、钢板等,只要规格一致、尺寸一致,就可以根据总件数来计算重量,这种方式就是理论重量。

(4)公量

公量是指用科学的方法抽出商品所含水分,再加上标准水分求得的重量。这种按公量计算的方法经常用于经济价值较大而水分含量极不稳定的商品,如丝绸、羊毛等。计算商品公量的公式如下:

$$公量=实际重量\times\frac{(1+标准回潮率)}{1+实际回潮率}=干量+标准含水重量$$

国际上规定的标准含水量为11%。

3. 溢短装条款

有些大宗农产品和矿产品如玉米、大豆、小麦、煤等,由于产品本身的性质特点,很难做到按照合同规定的数量进行交货。此外,由于受自然条件、包装方式、装卸货方法的影响,卖方所交货物往往很难与合同规定的数量保持一致。为了便于顺利履行合同,买卖双方在合同中同意卖方所交货物数量可在一定幅度内增减,这就是所谓的“溢短装条款”。只要交货的数量在幅度范围内,就认为是符合合同要求的。举个例子,50公吨花生,卖方可溢短装3%,由卖方选择。这个交货范围就是48.5~51.5公吨。关于溢短装的一些问题有:

(1)溢短装幅度范围的选择。

一般来说,由卖方决定实际溢短装的范围。由承运人根据船的承载情况来决定数量也是可以的;在FOB条件下成交的,由于是由买方租船来装载货物,也可以在合同中规定由买方来决定数量范围。

(2)在溢短装条款下,多装或少装的部分按照合同规定的价格计价,或者按照装船时的市场价格来计算价格。

(3)像“大约”这样的表达应该尽量避免,因为这样的表达会引起理解上的差异:有的理解为2%的差额幅度,有的理解为5%的上下幅度,有的理解为10%

的差额幅度。根据《跟单信用证统一惯例(UCP600)》规定,“大约”是指允许10%的差额幅度;对于散装货物来说,如果合同没有规定确切的溢短装条款,仍然允许5%的溢短装差额幅度。

4. 数量条款举例

(1)蝴蝶牌自行车,1 200 套。

(2)中国芝麻,100 公吨,溢短装 3%,由卖方选择。

(3)1 000 打手套,由卖方在合同规定的数量上按照 5%的浮动范围决定多装还是少装,差额部分按照合同价格结算。

第四节 商品包装

包装是国际贸易实践中最重要的问题之一。如果卖方所交货物的包装不符合合同规定,买方有权利拒收货物;如果货物包装有损坏,船长不会签发清洁提单,卖方就无法得到货款。近些年来,人们越来越认识到包装的重要性,它被看作质量的一部分和国际市场上重要的竞争手段。

1. 包装的类型

按照货物是否需要包装的角度,包装可以分为三类:

(1)裸装货

所谓裸装货,是指有些商品的品质比较稳定,没有任何包装或简单包装就可以运送的货物。这些货物很难包装或者不需要任何的包装,如钢材、木材、橡胶、车辆等。

(2)散装货

散装货是指未加任何包装、直接付运至销售的货物,例如石油、矿砂、煤炭、粮食等。

(3)包装货

大多数国际贸易货物都需要某种程度的包装,目的是用来运输、仓储和销售。所谓包装货,是指运输包装、销售包装或两者都需要的货物。

按照包装的作用不同,可以将包装分为运输包装和销售包装。

(1)运输包装

运输包装又称为大包装或外包装。它的主要作用是保护货物安全,以便于货物的运输、存储、识别和计数,减少运费,降低成本。它必须非常坚固,以保证货物在处理和运输途中避免被损坏。根据包装材料和包装方法,运输包装包括以下几类:

- 单件运输包装:箱、桶、袋、包、纸板箱等。
- 集合运输包装:集装箱、托盘、集装包和集装桶等。

近些年来,集装箱发展得非常迅速。集装箱是大的金属箱子,有着标准的形状和尺寸,通过公路、铁路、海运和空运来运输货物。现在最常用的有以下两类:

TEU (20 英尺单位),20 英尺×8 英尺×8 英尺

FEU (40 英尺单位),40 英尺×8 英尺×8 英尺

当计算集装箱流转量时,我们经常以 20 英尺规格的作为一个标准单位,也就是 TEU(20 英尺相当单位)。

(2)销售包装

销售包装直接接触商品,并且跟商品一起进入销售渠道与消费者见面,现在普遍认为销售包装有助于销售家用消费品,尤其是在超市里,所以被称为“无声的销售员”。为了便于销售,销售包装有很多不同的设计:挂式包装、堆叠式包装、便携式包装、易开式包装、喷嘴式包装、套装、礼品包装、复用包装、气球式包装。关于包装的一些问题有:

- 包装的设计

包装应该考虑相关国家的习惯和喜好,这样才能促进产品的销售。不同的国家有不同的习俗和文化,所以国际贸易公司在设计出口包装的时候,就要在市场调研中了解当地的文化习俗和禁忌;否则的话,会导致严重的后果。举个例子,英国讨厌大象的包装图案,日本人喜欢松树的包装图案。

- 标签

在往包装上贴标签的时候,我们要注意目标国家关于标签的法令法规,尤其是食品、机器、服装等。举个例子,瑞典政府规定服装上的标签必须印上洗涤方法。

- 条形码

条形码是一组黑白相间、粗细不等的平行条纹,下面带有数字。条形码是一种特殊的语言代码,用光电扫描设备输入数据到电脑上。它包含品名、规格、产地和价格这样的信息。

条形码系统有两种:一种是美国的世界产品代码,一种是欧洲的物品编码系统。世界上常用的是欧洲的物品编码系统。中国于1991年加入物品编码协会,协会分配给我们的编码是“690-695”。这意味着任何条形码以这三个数字开头的商品都是中国产的。

2. 包装标志

为了便于货物的运输、存储、交接和识别工作顺利进行,经常在外包装上印刷标志。根据标志的使用目的,可以划分为运输标志、指示性标志和警告性标志三类。

(1)运输标志

运输标志是印刷在包装上的标记,由一些简单的图案、字母、数字和文字组成,在国际贸易货物的运输、装卸、存储和交接过程中,用来识别货物。

国际化标准组织建议的国际标准运输标志包含以下几个部分:

- 收货人代号或缩写
- 参考号码(合同号、订单号或者信用证号)
- 目的地
- 件号

举例如下:

ABCCO——收货人名称

SC9750——合同号码

LONDON——目的港

No.4－20——件号(顺序号和总件数)

(2)指示性标志

指示性标志是在包装上印上简单的、明显的图案和文字,用来引起相关操作人员在装卸、搬运和存储货物时的注意。

(3)警告性标志

警告性标志又称为危险货物标志。它们是必须印刷在运输包装外面,表明各种危险品的标志,如易燃物品、易爆物品、有毒物品、腐蚀物品和放射性物品等,以示警告,使装卸、运输和保管人员按货物特性采取相应的防护措施,以保护物资和人身的安全(见图2-1)。

图 2-1　警告性标志示例(3)

3. 中性包装和贴牌生产

中性包装是包装上既不标明生产国,也不标明厂商的地名和名称的包装。中性包装有两种类型:带有指定品牌的和不带指定品牌的。中性的做法有两个目的:第一,有些原材料产品,是没有必要标明产地的;第二,出口商想打破某些进口国家和地区的关税或非关税壁垒,或者规避进口国的一些政治歧视。

OEM 是原始设备制造商的简称。它是指一种国际贸易实践,卖方在他们制造的产品上使用买方指定的品牌。

贴牌生产在国际贸易中很流行。许多跨国公司都会采用贴牌生产来利用发展中国家廉价的劳动力优势。中国被称为“世界的工厂”,因为中国许多工厂都在产品上使用买方指定的品牌名称,但是在品牌下面会印上“中国制造”。

在使用贴牌生产的时候,建议卖方在合同中订立保护性条款:“如果卖方遭到任何第三方关于侵犯知识产品的指控,均与卖方无关。”

在贸易实践中,包装的费用都包括在合同价格内,除非买方对包装有特殊的要求。

4. 包装条款示例

(1)用木箱装,每箱 100 公斤。

(2)每套货物都应该装在单独的纸板箱里,总共 1 200 箱。

(3)合同项下的茶叶应该装在国际贸易标准的茶盒子里,每24盒装一托盘,10个托盘装一个整箱。外包装要在一个菱形内标识缩写字母SCC,在下面刷上目的港和订单号。

Chapter 3

International Trade Terms and Customs

Part A Text

During the international business practice, the two parties are usually far away from each other and are separated by vast ocean. The international trade is very complicated, the seller and the buyer shall handle a series of formalities, including carrying out customs formalities for the goods, obtaining the import or export license, chartering a ship or booking shipping space, making insurance, asking for inspection etc., and pay for all kinds of charges and expense, such as freight, loading and unloading expenses, insurance premium, warehouse charges, duties and taxes, and other miscellaneous expenses. In other words, the seller and the buyer are not only enjoy the rights under the contract, but also should assume numerous obligations. Listing out all these problem for every transaction is time consuming and will diminish the trading efficiency. Businessmen from all over the world have created a series of trade terms after long time practice in world trading field. Simple English abbreviations are then used to represent main trading conditions explicitly. Transaction is completed once the mutual parties approve those regulated conditions. The business process is greatly simplified with these trade terms. They thus improve the efficiency and reduce the transaction cost.

Section One Definitions and Functions of International Trade Terms

1. Definition

Trade terms, also named price terms or price conditions, are abbreviations of letters or words specifying specific price composition and liabilities, cost and risk in the delivery of goods between the seller and the buyer. It covers two basic parts: first, trade terms indicate commodity price composition, for example, if the seller's quotation includes freight, insurance premium or discharge fee. FOB excludes freight and insurance fees which are paid by the buyer, and CIF is the opposite. Second, trade terms are specified terms concerning place or delivery, risks, obligations and costs during delivery of goods between the seller and the buyer.

2. Functions

Trade terms, which are used as unified and specific language for worldwide merchants, take shape gradually in international trade practice and greatly simplify dealing procedures, improve efficiency, promote the development of international trade and play significant roles in international trade. The main function of trade terms states as below:

(1) Trade terms clearly stipulated the risks, obligation and fees both for buyer and seller, it makes negotiation more easier, also save a lot of time for two parts.

(2) Trade terms also known as price conditions, each one contain different elements like freight, insurance premium or discharge fee, so the trade terms good for participant calculate the cost well.

(3) Trade terms provides a mechanism for resolving trade dispute.

3. Three Main International Rules on Trade Terms

As the quickly development of international trade, trade terms have been developed in international trade practice over many years to fit particular circumstances.

However, as different countries and areas might have different terms, misunderstandings and trade barriers occurred frequently. In order to clear up the confusion, some international organizations have made quite a few rules and explanations, which there are three main influential international rules on trade terms.

(1) Warsaw-Oxford Rules 1932

They are ruled for CIF contracts drafted at a conference of the international law association in Warsaw. In the mid-19th century, CIF has been widely applied in international trade, however, there were no unified explanations or rules on each party's obligations, misunderstanding and disputes frequently arose. International law association drafted and adopted rules for CIF contracts in the capital of Poland, Warsaw in 1928. After that, this rule was combined into 21 provisions in Oxford conference in 1932 and renamed as Warsaw-Oxford Rules 1932 used till now.

Warsaw-Oxford Rules state that these rules are not legally binding and are to both parties' option; once the rules are explicitly adopted, both parties shall be subject to them. In sales contract, the clauses could be different from the rules and each rule could be altered or added according to both parties agreement. If conflicts arise between the clauses and the rules, refer to the clauses. If the contract no relating clauses, refer to the rules.

Have to mention that, with the development of economy around the world and the change of the international trade circumstance, this rule almost no one to use it, but the Warsaw-Oxford Rules 1932 still exist and effective.

(2) Revised American Foreign Trade Definition 1941

The constitutors are Chamber of Commerce of the United State of America, American Importers Association (AIA) and national foreign trade council, etc.. At 1990, according to the developments of international trade practice, this rule has been revised for the newest, called Revised American Foreign Trade Definition 1990. It includes six terms, namely, EXW (Ex Works), FOB (Free on Board), FAS (Free Along Side), CFR (Cost and Freight), CIF (Cost, Insurance, Freight) and DEQ (Delivered Ex Quay). This rule mainly used in some North American and Latin American Countries.

(3) International Rules for the Interpretation of Trade Terms 2010 (*INCOTERMS* 2010)

International Rules for the Interpretation of Trade Terms 2010, we shortly called *INCOTERMS* 2010 as below, are the most widely used, most influential and the most important rules of international practices, it published by ICC (the International Chamber of Commerce), and all trade terms in this textbook are subject to it, totally including 11 trade terms. *INCOTERMS* was first created in 1936 and has been regularly updated for several times in order to keep pace of the development of the international trade. The latest version, *INCOTERMS* 2010 came into force on 1st January 2011. This is the seventh revision for *INCOTERMS*.

The three main international rules on trade terms mentioned above called international trade customs, it means they are not legislations or laws for all countries or areas, it become legally valid, and both parties are subject to it while both participants cite one international custom. Even if the contract does not indicate which custom the contract is subject to, the custom still has binding force. But if the sale contract clauses conflict with customs, the contract to be followed is as a basic principle. Therefore, it is better to clearly write down what trade terms and which international custom will be used on the sale contract in order to avoid any trade conflict in the future.

Section Two FOB, CFR and CIF

Under *INCOTERMS* 2010, there are totally have 11 trade terms, which is FOB, CFR, CIF, FCA, CPT, CIP, EXW, FAS, DAT, DAP and DDP. It made two groups by different shipping methods, FOB, CFR, CIF and FAS are suitable for sea and inland waterway transport only, other 7 trade terms are for any modes of transportation. Among above 11 trade terms, FOB, CFR and CIF are the most influential and most important, and they are most commonly used terms in the international trade practice. They are classified into one group as they are alike in characters from the below 5 aspects:

(1) They are sued for port-to-port waterway transportation.

(2) Place of delivery of the seller is on board a ship in the export country.

(3) The risks are transferred to the buyer once the seller delivers the goods on

board the vessel at the port of shipment.

(4) They are symbolic trade terms, it means the buying and selling of related documents instead of physical goods, in other words, the seller delivers the goods against documents and the buyer pay for the goods against the documents.

(5) Contracts signed under the above three terms are refer to shipment contracts, that means the seller is only responsible for punctual shipment and disregard when it arrives.

FOB

FOB, *Free On Board* (insert named of port of shipment) *INCOTERMS* 2010, it shall be followed by the name of port of shipment, e.g. FOB Shanghai.

This rule is to be used only for sea or inland waterway transport. *Free On Board* means that the seller delivers the goods on board the vessel nominated by the buyer at the named port of shipment or procures the goods already so delivered. The risk of loss of or damage to the goods passes when the goods are on board the vessel, and the buyer bears all costs from that moment onwards.

1. The Seller's Obligations

(1) General obligations of the seller

The seller must provide the goods and the commercial invoice in conformity with the contract of sale and any other evidence of conformity that may be required by the contract.

(2) Licenses, authorizations, security clearances and other formalities

The seller must obtain, at its own risk and expense, any export license or other official authorization and carry out all customs formalities necessary for the export of the goods.

(3) Contract of carriage and insurance

The seller has no obligation to the buyer to make a contract of carriage. The seller has no obligation to the buyer to make a contract of insurance. However, the seller must provide the buyer, at the buyer's request, risk, and expense (if any), with information that the buyer needs for obtaining insurance.

(4) Delivery

The seller must deliver the goods either by placing them on board the vessel nominated by the buyer at the loading point, if any, indicated by the buyer at the named port of shipment or by procuring the goods so delivered. In either case, the seller must deliver the goods on the agreed date or within the agreed period and in the manner customary at the port.

2. The Buyer's Obligations

(1) General obligations of the buyer

The buyer must pay the price of the goods as provided in the contract of sale.

(2) Licenses, authorizations, security clearances and other formalities

Where applicable, it is up to the buyer to obtain, at its own risk and expense, any import license or other official authorization and carry out all customs formalities for the import of the goods and for their transport through any country.

(3) Contract of carriage and insurance

The buyer must contract, at its own expense for the carriage of the goods from the named port of shipment. The buyer must make a contract of insurance after the goods delivered on board the ship from the port of shipment.

(4) Transfer of risks

All risks of loss of or damage to the goods transfer from the seller to the buyer when the goods have been delivered on board the ship.

Table 3-1　The obligation between the Buyer and Seller under the term of FOB

	Carriage	Insurance	Export clearance	Import clearance	Risk division	Mode of transport
Seller			√		On board the ship at the port of shipment	Sea or inland waterway transport
Buyer	√	√		√		

3. Some Points for Attention While Use the Term of FOB

(1) The transfer of the risks: the cancellation of the concept "cross the rail"

It is a historic practice before *INCOTERMS* 2010 to regard the rail as the boundary. However, some defects were found in practical application. And the meaning of it is obscure. *INCOTERMS* 2010 specified that the risk of loss of and damage to the goods passes when the goods are on board the vessel, and the buyer bears all costs from that moment onwards. It could be all engagement that both parties agree to regard boarding on ship as the boundary. The concept of "cross the rail" was cancelled thereafter.

(2) Link-up of vessel and goods

Because of the different obligations between two parts, the buyer cover the risks under FOB terms, the seller should notify the buyer the goods information promptly and correctly. Otherwise, if the buyer fails to cover the risks as a result of deferred notice by the seller and once accidents happen, the seller is responsible.

(3) Various explanation for FOB

The state for FOB above come from *INCOTERMS* 2010, but we should more carefully to use if the FOB terms from the Revised American Foreign Trade Definition 1990. In the Revised American Foreign Trade Definition 1990, the terms of FOB has 6 different statements, only the one named "FOB vessel" is the same explanation like *INCOTERMS* 2010.

CFR

CFR: *Cost and Freight* (insert named of port of destination) *INCOTERMS* 2010, it shall be followed by the name of port of destination, e.g. CFR New York.

This rule is to be used only for sea or inland waterway transport. *Cost and Freight* means that the seller delivers the goods on board the vessel or procures the goods already so delivered. The seller must contract for and pay the costs and freight necessary to bring the goods the named port of destination. The risk of loss of or damage to the goods passed when the goods are on board the vessel.

1. The sellers' obligations

(1) General obligation of the seller

The seller must provide the goods and the commercial invoice in conformity with the contract of sale and any other evidence of conformity that may be required by the contract.

(2) Licenses, authorizations, security clearances and other formalities

Where applicable, the seller must obtain, at its own risk and expense, any export license or other official authorization and carry out all customs formalities necessary for the export of the goods.

(3) Contract of carriage

The seller must contract or procure a contract for the carriage of the goods from the agreed point of delivery, if any, at the place of delivery to the named port of destination or, if agreed, any point at that port. The contract of carriage must be made on usual terms at the seller's expense and provide for carriage by the usual route in a vessel of the type normally used for the transport of the type of goods sold.

(4) Contract of insurance

The seller has no obligation to the buyer to make a contract of insurance. However, the seller must provide the buyer, at the buyer's request, risk, and expense (if any), with information that the buyer needs for obtaining insurance.

(5) Delivery

The seller must deliver the goods either by placing them on board the vessel or by procuring the goods so delivered. In either case, the seller must deliver the goods on the agreed date or within the agreed period and in the manner customary at the port.

2. The buyer's obligations

(1) General obligations of the buyer

The buyer must pay the price of the goods as provided in the contract of sale.

(2) Licenses, authorizations, security clearances and other formalities

Where applicable, it is up to the buyer to obtain, at its own risk and expense, any import license or other official authorization and carry out all customs formalities for the import of the goods and for their transport through any country.

(3) Contract of carriage and insurance

The buyer has no obligation to the seller to make a contract of carriage. The buyer must make a contract of insurance after the goods delivered on board the ship from the port of shipment.

(4) Transfer of risks

All risks of loss of or damage to the goods transfer from the seller to the buyer when the goods have been delivered on board the ship.

Table 3-2 The obligation between the Buyer and Seller under the term of CFR

	Carriage	Insurance	Export clearance	Import clearance	Risk division	Mode of transport
Seller	√		√		On board the ship at the port of shipment	Sea or inland waterway transport
Buyer		√		√		

3. Some points for attention while use the term of CFR

The term of CFR has two critical points, because risk passes and costs are transferred at different places.

While the contract will always specify a destination port, it might not specify the port of shipment, which is where risk passes to the buyer. If the shipment port is of particular interest to the buyer, the parties are well advised to identify it as precisely as possible in the contract.

The parties are well advised to identify as precisely as possible the point at the agreed port of destination, as the cost to that point are for the account of the seller. The seller is advised to procure contracts of carriage that match this choice precisely. If the seller incurs costs under its contract of carriage related to unloading at the specified point at the port of destination, the seller is not entitled to recover such cost from the buyer unless otherwise agreed between the parties.

CIF

CIF, *Cost Insurance and Freight* (insert named port of destination) *INCOTERMS* 2010, it shall be followed by the name of port of destination, e.g. CIF New York.

This rule is to be used only for sea or inland waterway transport. *Cost, Insurance and Freight* means that the seller delivers the goods on board the vessel or procures the goods already so delivered. The risk of loss of or damage to the goods passes when the goods are on board the vessel. The seller must contact for the pay the costs and freight necessary to bring the goods to the named port of destination. The seller also contract for insurance cover against the buyer's risk of loss of or damage to the goods during the carriage. The buyer should note that under CIF the seller is required to obtain insurance only on minimum cover. Should the buyer wish to have more insurance protection, it will need either to agree as much expressly with the seller or to make its own extra insurance arrangements.

1. The sellers' obligations

(1) General obligation of the seller

The seller must provide the goods and the commercial invoice in conformity with the contract of sale and any other evidence of conformity that may be required by the contract.

(2) Licenses, authorizations, security clearances and other formalities

Where applicable, the seller must obtain, at its own risk and expense, any export license or other official authorization and carry out all customs formalities necessary for the export of the goods.

(3) Contract of carriage

The seller must contract or procure a contract for the carriage of the goods from the agreed point of delivery, if any, at the place of delivery to the named port of destination or, if agreed, any point at that port. The contract of carriage must be made on usual terms at the seller's expense and provide for carriage by the usual route in a vessel of the type normally used for the transport of the type of goods sold.

(4) Contract of insurance

The seller must obtain, at its own expense, cargo insurance complying at least with the minimum cover provided by clauses.

(5) Delivery

The seller must deliver the goods either by placing them on board the vessel or by procuring the goods so delivered. In either case, the seller must deliver the goods on the agreed date or within the agreed period and in the manner customary at the port.

2. The buyer's obligations

(1) General obligations of the buyer

The buyer must pay the price of the goods as provided in the contract of sale.

(2) Licenses, authorizations, security clearances and other formalities

Where applicable, it is up to the buyer to obtain, at its own risk and expense, any import license or other official authorization and carry out all customs formalities for the import of the goods and for their transport through any country.

(3) Contract of carriage and insurance

The buyer has no obligation to the seller to make a contract of carriage. The buyer has no obligation to the seller to make a contract of insurance. However, the buyer must provide the seller, upon request, with any information necessary for the seller to procure any additional insurance requested by the buyer.

(4) Taking delivery

The buyer must take delivery of the goods when they have been delivered as required and receive them from the carrier at the named port of destination.

(5) Transfer of risks

All risks of loss of or damage to the goods transfer from the seller to the buyer when the goods have been delivered on board the ship.

Table 3-3 The obligation between the Buyer and Seller under the term of CIF

	Carriage	Insurance	Export clearance	Import clearance	Risk division	Mode of transport
Seller	√	√	√		On board the ship at the port of shipment	Sea or inland waterway transport
Buyer				√		

3. Some points for attention about CIF

(1) Booking shipping space by the seller

As *INCOTERMS* 2010 states, the seller is liable for shipping the goods with routine marine vessels. The buyer has no right to dominate the vessel age, vessel model or shipping company. The seller has the right to refuse the buyer' s requirement about vessel age, vessel shape and ship classification.

(2) Insurance coverage

As explained by *INCOTERMS* 2010, the seller acts for the buyer to cover insurance. If there is no stipulation on the contract, the lowest level of insurance could be covered, however, a higher level may be covered at the buyer' s requirement.

(3)Symbolic delivery

CIF is a typical symbolic delivery term and contracts under this term are shipment contract. As the same with FOB, place of delivery of CIF is port of shipment in export country but not port of destination.

Section Three FCA, CPT and CIP

The three trade terms FCA, CPT and CIP that we are going to mention are used when the exporter delivers the goods to the carrier and they have the same characters as following: They are suitable for any kinds of transport including marine cargo transportation; Place of shipment is in the exporting country; Risk is transferred at the point of delivery to the carrier in the exporting country; Contracts under these terms are shipment contract.

The nature of these three terms is the same as that of FOB, CFR and CIF. The difference between the two classifications is the mode of transport. FCA, CPT and CIP are applicable for all modes of transportation includes marine cargo transportation, and FOB, CFR and CIF for sea or inland waterway transport only.

FCA

FCA, *Free Carrier* (insert named place of delivery) *INCOTERMS* 2010. *Free Carrier* means that the seller delivers the goods to the carrier or another person nominated by the buyer at the seller's premises or another named place. The parties are well advised to specify as clearly as possible the point within the named place of delivery, as the risk passes to the buyer at that point. If the parties intend to deliver the goods at the seller's premises, they should identify the address of those premises as the named place of delivery. If, on the other hand, the parties intend the goods to be delivered at another place, they must identify a different specific place of delivery.

1. The Seller's Obligations

(1) The seller must provide the goods and the commercial invoice in conformity with the contract of sale and any other evidence of conformity that may be required

by the contract.

(2) Where applicable, the seller must obtain, at its own risk and expense, any export license or other official authorizations and carry out all customs formalities necessary for the export of the goods.

(3) The seller bears all risks of loss of or damage to the goods until they have been delivered to the carrier or another person nominated by the buyer.

2. The Buyer's Obligations

(1) The buyer must pay the price of the goods as provided in the contract of sale.

(2) Where applicable, it is up to the buyer to obtain, at its own risk and expense, any import license or other official authorization and carry out all customs formalities for the import of the goods and for their transport through any country.

(3) The buyer must contract at its own expense for the carriage of the goods from the named place of delivery, also its buyer's obligation to make a contract of insurance.

(4) The buyer bears all risks of loss of or damage to the goods from the time they have been delivered to the carrier.

3. Differences between FCA and FOB

Common points:

(1) The buyer is responsible for shipment and covering insurance and the contracted price does not include shipping charges or insurance premium.

(2) Port of loading is the place of delivery.

(3) Contracts under these two terms are shipment contracts but not sale contract.

Differences:

(1) FOB is used in port-to-port marine shipment; FCA could be used in all means of transport including marine shipment.

(2) Places of delivery for FOB is on board the ship at the port of loading, FCA is free carrier to a named place.

(3) Risks transfer when the goods are on board the vessel for FOB and when the

goods are delivered to the carrier for FCA.

(4) FOB is a symbolic delivery trade term.

CPT

CPT, *Carriage Paid To* (insert named place of destination) *INCOTERMS* 2010. *Carriage Paid To* means that the seller delivers the goods to the carrier or another person nominated by the seller at agreed place (if any such place is agreed between the parties) and that the seller must contract for and pay the costs of carriage necessary to bring the goods to the named place of destination. The risks are transferred to the buyer when the goods are delivered to the carrier in the exporting country, but the seller must arrange the goods to be transported to the destination. Also CPT requires the seller to clear the goods for export, however, the seller has no obligation to clear the goods for import, pay any import duty or carry out any import customs formalities.

1. The Seller's Obligations

(1) The seller must provide the goods and the commercial invoice in conformity with the contract of sale and any other evidence of conformity that may be required by the contract.

(2) Where applicable, the seller must obtain, at its own risk and expense, any export license or other official authorization and carry out all customs formalities necessary for the export of the goods.

(3) The seller must contract or procure a contract for the carriage of the goods from the agreed point of delivery, if any, at the place of delivery to the named port of destination or, if agreed, any point at that place.

(4) The seller has no obligation to the buyer to make a contract of insurance.

(5) The seller must deliver the goods by handing them over to the carrier on the agreed date or within the agreed period.

2. The Buyer's Obligations

(1) The buyer must pay the price of the goods as provided in the contract of sale.

(2) Where applicable, it is up to the buyer to obtain, at its own risk and expense, any import license or other official authorization and carry out all customs formalities for the import of the goods and for their transport through any country.

(3) The buyer has no obligation to the seller to make a contract of carriage. The buyer must make a contract of insurance after the goods delivered on board the ship from the port of shipment.

(4) All risks of loss of or damage to the goods transfer from the seller to the buyer when the goods have been handed to the carrier.

3. Some Points for Attention

(1) Risk Transfer

The seller delivers the goods to the carrier and pays the cost of carriage necessary to bring to goods to the destination; however, the seller bears risks until the goods are delivered to the carrier in the exporting country. As *INCOTERMS* 2010 explained, the buyer bears all risks and any other costs occurring after the goods have been so delivered. In multimodal transport, risks transfer to the buyer when the seller delivers the goods to the first carrier.

(2) Allocation of Obligation and Costs

The seller is responsible for the shipping charges to the destination. After he delivers the good to the carrier, the seller shall immediately notify the buyer for insurance covering and getting receipt of the goods in due time.

4. Differences between CFR and CPT

Common points:

(1) In both terms, the seller is obliged to arrange transport to the destination and bear related cost while the buyer covers insurance on himself.

(2) Contracts under both terms are shipment contracts.

Differences:

(1) CFR is used in port-to-port marine transport; CPT suits for all mode of transportation.

(2) Place of delivery of CFR is on board the ship in the port of shipment, and for CPT is in the exporting country to the carrier.

(3) Risks under CFR are transferred when the goods are on board the ship import of shipment in the exporting country, and under CPT risks are passed when the goods are delivered to the carrier in the exporting country.

CIP

CIP, *Carriage and Insurance Paid To* (insert named place of destination) *INCOTERMS* 2010. *Carriage and Insurance Paid To* means that the seller delivers the goods to the carrier or another person nominated by the seller at an agreed place and that the seller must contract for and pay the costs of carriage necessary to bring the goods to the named place of destination. The seller also contracts for insurance cover against the buyer's risk of loss of or damage to the goods during the carriage. The buyer should not that under CIP the seller is required to obtain insurance only on minimum cover. Should the buyer wish to have more insurance protection, it will need either to agree as much expressly with the seller or to make its own extra insurance arrangements. Also please note that the CIP term requires that seller to clear the goods for export.

1. The Sellers's Obligations

(1) The seller must provide the goods and the commercial invoice in conformity with the contract of sale and any other evidence of conformity that may be required by the contract.

(2) Where applicable, the seller must obtain, at its own risk and expense, any export license or other official authorization and carry out all customs formalities necessary for the export of the goods and for their transport through any country prior to delivery.

(3) The seller must contract or procure a contract for the carriage of the goods from the agreed point of delivery, if any, at the place of delivery to the named port of destination or, if agreed, any point at that port. The contract of carriage must be made on usual terms at the seller's expense and provide for carriage by the usual route. If a specific point is not agreed or is not determined by practice, the seller may select the point of delivery and the point at the named place of destination that best suit its purpose.

(4) The seller must obtain at its own expense cargo insurance complying at least with the minimum cover provided by clauses.

(5) The seller must deliver the goods by handing them over to the carrier on the agreed date or within the agreed period.

2. The Buyer's Obligations

(1) The buyer must pay the price of the goods as provided in the contract of sale.

(2) Where applicable, it is up to the buyer to obtain, at its own risk and expense, any import license or other official authorization and carry out all customs formalities for the import of the goods and for their transport through any country.

(3) The buyer has no obligation to the seller to make a contract of carriage. And the buyer has no obligation to the seller to make a contract of insurance. However, the buyer must provide the seller, upon request, with any information necessary for the seller to procure any additional insurance requested by the buyer.

(4) The buyer must take delivery of the goods when they have been delivered as required and receive them from the carrier at the named place of destination.

(5) All risks of loss of or damage to the goods transfer from the seller to the buyer when the goods have been handed to the carrier.

3. Comparison of CIF and CIP

Common points:

(1) The contracts price includes shipping charge and insurance premium and the seller arranges transport to port of the destination and pay for related shipping charges and insurance premium.

(2) Place of delivery is in the exporting country.

(3) Contracts under both terms are shipment contracts.

Differences:

(1) CIF is typically used in symbolic delivery, CIP is not a symbolic delivery if the ocean transport is not accepted.

(2) CIF is only suitable for ocean marine transport, CIP is used in multi-modal transport.

(3) Place of deliver for CIF is on board the ship in the port of shipment, and for CIP is to the carrier in the exporting country.

(4) Risks transfer when goods are on board the vessel for CIF, and for CIP risks transfer when the goods are delivered to the carrier.

(5) Insurance under CIF is purely ocean transport insurance, and insurance under CIP may not only involve transport insurance but also inland or airway insurance.

Section Four　Other Trade Terms

EXW

EXW, *EX Works* (insert named place of delivery) *INCOTERMS* 2010. This rule may be used irrespective of the mode of transport selected and may also be used where more than one mode of transport is employed.

Ex Works means that the seller delivers when it places the goods at the disposal of the buyer at the seller's premises or at another named place (i.e., works, factory, warehouses, etc.). The seller does not need to load the goods on any collecting vehicle, nor does it need to clear the goods for export, where such clearance is applicable.

This term impose on the seller the minimum obligations, costs and risks while the buyer obtains the goods at the lowest possible price. It is frequently used by any means of transport including multi-modal transport in both domestic trade and international trade. The buyer bears all costs and risks involved in taking the goods from the agreed point, and must pay all duties, taxes and other charges, as well as the costs of carrying out customs formalities payable upon export.

FAS

FAS, *Free Alongside Ship* (insert named port of shipment) *INCOTERMS* 2010. *Free Alongside Ship* means that the seller delivers when the goods are placed alongside the vessel (e.g., on a quay or a barge) nominated by the buyer at the named port of shipment. The risk of loss of or damage to the goods passes when the goods are alongside the ship, and the buyer bears all costs from that moment onwards. Please be noticed that the seller has to sue the barges to move the goods alongside the ship to make the delivery when the ship cannot be berthed. This rule is to be used only for sea or inland waterway transport.

1. The Seller's Obligation

(1) The seller must provide the goods and the commercial invoice in conformity with the contract of sale and any other evidence of conformity that may be required by the contract.

(2) Where applicable, the seller must obtain, at its own risk and expense, any export license or other official authorization and carry out all customs formalities necessary for the export of the goods.

(3) The seller has no obligation to the buyer to make a contract of carriage.

(4) The seller has no obligation to the buyer to make a contract of insurance. However, the seller must provide the buyer, at the buyer's request, risk, and expense (if any), with information that the buyer needs for obtaining insurance.

(5) The seller bears all risks of loss of or damage to the goods until they have been delivered to the carrier.

2. The Buyer's Obligations

(1) The buyer must pay the price of the goods as provided in the contract of sale.

(2) Where applicable, it is up to the buyer to obtain, at its own risk and expense, any import license or other official authorization and carry out all customs formalities for the import of the goods and for their transport through any country.

(3) The buyer must contract, at its own expense for the carriage of the goods from the named port of shipment.

(4) The buyer has no obligation to the seller to make a contract of insurance.

(5) The buyer bears all risks of loss of or damage to the goods when the carrier is taken over the goods.

3. Comparison of FOB and FAS

Common points:

(1) Both are used in port-to-port ocean marine transport.

(2) The buyer arranges transport, covers insurance and bears shipping charges and insurance premium.

Differences:

(1) FOB is used for symbolic delivery, FAS is used for physical delivery.

(2) Places of delivery for FOB is on board the ship and for FAS is alongside the ship.

(3) Risks transfer when the goods are on board the vessel for FOB and when the goods are alongside the ship for FAS.

(4) The seller is responsible for loading the goods for FOB and the seller is free from shipping charges for FAS.

4. Different Definition under American Trade Terms

(1) Under American Trade Terms, FAS is means free along side, in *INCOTERMS* 2010, FAS is free alongside ship.

(2) In America, FAS is used in any means of transportation.

(3) In *INCOTERMS* 2010, FAS is used in oceans marine transportation to be equivalent, word "vessel" must be added after FAS in American Trade Definition.

DAT

DAT, *Delivered At Terminal* (insert named terminal at port or place of destination) *INCOTERMS* 2010, this rule may be used for all modes of transportation.

Delivered At Terminal means that the seller delivers when the goods, once unloaded from the arriving means of transport, are placed at the disposal of the buyer at a named terminal at the named port or place of destination. "Terminal" includes any place, whether covered or not, such as a quay, warehouse, container yard or road, rail or air cargo terminal.

The seller bears all risks involved in bringing the goods to and unloading them at the terminal at the named port or place of destination. The parties are well advised to specify as clearly as possible the terminal and, if possible, a specific point within the terminal at the agreed port or place of destination, as the risks to that point are for the account of the seller. The seller is advised to procure a contract of carriage that matches this choice precisely.

Moreover, if the parties intend the seller to bear the risks and costs involved in transporting and handing the goods from the terminal to another place, then the DAP or DDP rules should be used (DAP and DDP will be placed as blow).

DAT requires must contract at its own expense for the carriage of the goods to the named terminal at the agreed port or place of destination, also this rule requires the seller to clear the goods for export, where applicable. However, the seller has no obligation to clear the goods for import, pay any import duty or carry out any import customs formalities.

The point for attention about DAT:

According to the *INCOTERMS* 2010 Rules, the transport terminal means any place regardless of whether the place is covered, such as a dock, a warehouse, a container yard or a road, a railway, an air cargo terminal. Both the buyer and seller are well advised to specify as clearly as possible the terminal and, if possible, a specific point within the terminal at the agreed port or place of destination, as the risks to that point are for the account of the seller. The seller is advised to procure a contract of carriage that matches this choice precisely.

DAP

DAP, *Delivered At Place* (insert named place of destination) *INCOTERMS* 2010, this rule may be used for all modes of transportation.

Delivered At Place means that the seller delivers when the goods are placed at the disposal of the buyer or the arriving means of transport ready for unloading at the named place of destination. The seller bears all risks involved in bringing the goods to the named place.

The parties are well advised to specific as clearly as possible the point within the agreed place of destination, as the risks to that point are for the account of the seller. The seller is advised to procure contracts of carriage that match this choice precisely. If the seller incurs costs under its contract of carriage related to unloading at the place of destination, the seller is not entitled to recover such cost from the buyer unless otherwise agreed between the parties.

DAP requires the seller to clear the goods for export, where applicable. However, the seller has no obligation to clear the goods for import, pay any import duty or carry out any import customs formalities. If the parties wish the seller to clear the goods for import, pay any import duty and carry out any import customs formalities, the DDP term should be used (DDP will be placed as below).

DDP

DDP, *Delivered Duty Paid* (insert named place of destination) *INCOTERMS* 2010, this rule may be used for all modes of transportation.

"*Delivered Duty Paid*" means that the seller delivers the goods when the goods are placed at the disposal of the buyer, cleared for import on the arriving means of transport ready for unloading at the named place of destination. The seller bears all the costs and risks involved in bringing the goods to the place of destination and has an obligation to clear the goods not only for export but also for import, to pay duty for both export and import and to carry out all customs formalities.

DDP represents the maximum obligation for the seller. The parties are well advised to specify as clearly as possible the point within the agreed place of destination, as the cost and risks to that point are for the account of the seller. The seller is advised to procure contracts of carry that match this choice precisely. If the seller incurs costs under its contract of carriage related to unloading at the place of destination, the seller is not entitled to recover such costs from the buyer unless otherwise agreed between the parties.

The parties are well advised not to use DDP if the seller is unable directly or indirectly to obtain import clearance. If the parties wish the buyer to bear all risks and costs of import clearance, the DAP rule should be used. Any VAT or other taxes payable upon import are for the seller's account unless expressly agreed otherwise in the sales contract.

Table 3-4 ***INCOTERMS* 2010 Rules**

Trade Terms	Full Name	Place of Delivery	Risks Transfer	Foreign Freight	Insurance Premium	Export Duty	Import Duty	Means of Transport
EXW	Ex Works	Named place	Delivered to the buyer	Buyer	Buyer	Buyer	Buyer	All modes
FCA	Free Carrier	Named place	Delivered to the Carrier	Buyer	Buyer	Seller	Buyer	All modes
FAS	Free Alongside Ship	Alongside ship at port of shipment	Alongside ship at port of shipment	Buyer	Buyer	Seller	Buyer	Sea and inland waterway
FOB	Free on Board	On board the ship	Delivered on board the vessel	Buyer	Buyer	Seller	Buyer	Sea and inland waterway
CFR	Cost and Freight	On board the ship	Delivered on board the vessel	Seller	Buyer	Seller	Buyer	Sea and inland waterway
CIF	Cost, Insurance and Freight	On board the ship	Delivered on board the vessel	Seller	Seller	Seller	Buyer	Sea and inland waterway
CPT	Carriage Paid to	To the carrier in export country	To the carrier	Seller	Buyer	Seller	Buyer	All modes
CIP	Carriage and Insurance Paid to	To the carrier in export country	To the carrier	Seller	Seller	Seller	Buyer	All modes
DAT	Delivered At Terminal	At named terminal at port or place of destination	Delivered at named terminal at port or place of destination	Seller	Seller	Seller	Buyer	All modes
DAP	Delivered At Place	At named place of destination	Delivered to buyer at named place of destination	Seller	Seller	Seller	Buyer	All modes
DDP	Delivered Duty Paid	At named place of destination	Delivered to buyer at named place of destination	Seller	Seller	Seller	Seller	All modes

Part B Key Terms

Trade terms 贸易术语

FOB

CFR

CIF

FCA

CPT

CIP

Physical delivery 实际交货

Symbolic delivery　象征性交货

International trade customs　国际贸易惯例

Transfer of risk　风险转移

Part C　Exercises

Ⅰ. Answer the following questions

1. What are trade terms?

2. What are the similarities and differences among FOB,CFR and CIF?

3. What are the differences between FOB and FCA?

4. What are the differences between CIF and CIP?

5. What are the differences between DAT and DAP?

6. What is symbolic delivery?

Ⅱ. Case & Analysis

Dispute about FOB term

The seller in China and the buyer in UK made a contract about barely seed under FOB term. In the contract,it was stipulated that the barley seed germination rate must be over 90%. Before shipment,the goods were tested by the seller and it was met the requirements. However, when the goods arrived at UK, the buyer had the goods tasted by his specified inspection organization,and the result showed that the barley seed germination rate was below 70%. As a result,the buyer refused to take the goods and lodged his claim for the losses. The seller refused the buyer' s requirements. The reason for the seller' s was that the goods had been tested before shipment. So the change of the quality of the goods happened during the transportation. According to *INCOTERMS* 2010,under FOB terms the obligation and the risks transfer to the buyer when the goods put on the ship by the seller. In this case,the buyer should be taken the risks because the quality change happening during the transportation. After several negotiations between the two parties,no agreement was reached. So the case was submitted for arbitration. When the arbitration tribunal tried the act, there were worm eggs attached to the gunny packing. It was because the worm eggs that damaged the germination during transportation,causing the low germination rate.

Question: who will take responsibilities for the result?

第三章

国际贸易术语

国际贸易的买卖双方分处两国,相距遥远。与国内贸易相比,国际贸易的复杂性显而易见。买卖双方在洽商交易、订立合同时,需要考虑诸多因素,例如买卖双方在什么地方、什么时间以什么样的方式办理交货;风险何时由卖方转移给买方;由哪方当事人负责办理货物的运输、保险以及检验、通关等手续。换言之,买卖双方既享受权利,也有必须要尽的义务。如果每笔交易都要对上述问题进行磋商,势必要耗费大量的时间和精力,降低国际贸易的效率,阻碍国际贸易的发展。在长期的国际贸易实践中,世界各国的商人逐渐形成了一套专门用于国际贸易货物买卖的术语,用简单的英文字母缩写或符号把主要的交易条件一目了然地表示出来,一旦对方同意即可成交,大大简化了交易程序,提高了交易的效率,降低了交易的成本。

第一节　国际贸易术语的定义及作用

1. 贸易术语的定义

贸易术语又称为贸易条件或价格条件,是指用几个英文字母缩写或符号来表示商品价格的构成,用来说明买卖双方的责任、费用和风险的划分等问题的专门用语。术语主要包含两层含义:第一层含义,贸易术语说明了商品价格的构成,比如说卖方所报的商品价格是否包含了运费、保费和装卸费等。例如,用术语 FOB 报价,说明价格不包含运费和保费,这些费用需要通过买方承担;而术语 CIF 则恰恰相反,卖方所报价格已经包含了运费和保险费。第二层含义,贸易术语是指买卖双方在货物交接过程中,关于交货地点、风险、责任和费用的划分问题的规定。

2. 贸易术语的作用

贸易术语作为全球商人的通用语言,在国际贸易发展中逐渐形成,很大程度上简化了处理程序,提高了效率,促进了国际贸易的发展,在交易中扮演着重要的角色,其作用主要表述如下:

(1)只要规定了按某种贸易术语成交,即明确了彼此在合同履行中所应承担的风险、责任和费用,大大节约了洽谈时间;

(2)贸易术语也可表示商品的价格构成,因此买卖双方确定价格时首先要考虑到术语中包含的价格构成,如运费、保险费及装卸费用等,有利于双方进行比价和加强成本核算;

(3)买卖双方在合同履行中出现贸易纠纷时,可以援引相关贸易术语的一般解释来处理,有利于妥善解决争端。

3. 有关贸易术语的三项主要国际规则

随着国际贸易的快速发展,为了适应国际新形势的变化,贸易术语也有了相应的改变。但是不同的国家和地区在使用贸易术语和相关规定时有着各自不同的解释和做法,这样一来,因为合同当事人对规则解释的不统一往往会造成买卖双方之间的误解、争议和诉讼,这既浪费了双方的时间和损害了双方的利益,同时也影响了国际贸易的发展。为了解决这一问题,一些国际组织制定了解释国际贸易术语的规则,这些规则在国际上被广泛采用。现行有较大影响力的国际贸易术语的惯例主要有以下三种:

(1)《1932 年华沙—牛津规则》

《1932 年华沙—牛津规则》是国际法协会专门为解释 CIF 术语合同而制定的。19 世纪中叶,CIF 术语在国际贸易中被广泛应用,但是各国之间没有对规则的统一解释,买卖双方之间因规则不明确而引起的误解和争议逐渐增多。国际法协会于 1928 年在华沙举行会议,制定了有关 CIF 买卖合同的统一规则,共包括 22 条。之后,在 1930 年的纽约会议、1931 年的巴黎会议和 1932 年的牛津会议上将此规则合并为 21 条进行了修改,更名为《1932 年华沙—牛津规则》,并沿用至今。

《1932 年华沙—牛津规则》规定买卖双方未明确在合同中规定采用此规则前不具有法律约束力。在销售合同中,只要双方当事人同意,合同条款可以与规则的规定不统一,可以改动或增加相关内容。一旦双方在执行合同过程中有任何纠纷,以合同条款为主;如果合同条款没有相关规定,则可根据贸易术语惯例来执行。

顺便提一下,虽然《1932 年华沙—牛津规则》一直存在并有效,但因其年代久远,相关规定不适应当今国际贸易的发展,实际上已经很少有人采用此规则。

(2)《1941 年美国对外贸易定义修订本》

该规则由美国商会、美国进口商协会、全国对外贸易协会等制定。1990 年,根据国际贸易形势发展的需要被修订,并命名为《1990 年美国对外贸易定义修订本》。该规则主要在北美和拉丁美洲国家使用。《1990 年美国对外贸易定义修订本》主要对以下 6 种贸易术语进行解释,分别为:

EXW(Ex Works)　原产地交货

FOB(Free on Board)　在运输工具上交货

FAS(Free Along Side)　在运输工具旁边交货

CFR(Cost and Freight)　成本加运费

CIF(Cost, Insurance, Freight)　成本、运费加保险费

DEQ(Delivered Ex Quay)　目的港码头交货

(3)《2010 年国际贸易术语解释通则》

《2010 年国际贸易术语解释通则》(以下简称为《2010 通则》),是国际上使用最广泛、最具影响力和最重要的规则。1936 年国际商会为了统一对各种贸易术语的解释而制定,后来根据国际贸易形势的发展经过了多次修订。《2010 通则》为第七次修改最新版本,于 2011 年 1 月 1 日起生效,修改后的通则主要包括 11 种贸易术语。

需要加以注意的是,以上提及的国际贸易术语属于国际贸易惯例,意思是说它不是一国或某地区的法律,不具有法律强制性。当买卖双方在合同中引用某项惯例时,该惯例即具有法律效力,对双方都有约束力,具有法律强制性。如果合同条款与惯例有冲突,以合同条款为准。因此买卖双方在订立合同时,为了避免贸易纠纷,条款必须明确、具体地表明用哪个贸易术语,术语援引自哪个惯例。

第二节　FOB、CFR 和 CIF 术语

在《2010 通则》中共提及 11 种不同的贸易术语,它们分别是 FOB, CFR, CIF, FCA, CPT, CIP, EXW, FAS, DAT, DAP 和 DDP。根据运输方式的不同,将这 11 种术语分成两组,第一组只适合于海运或内河运输,包括以下四种:FOB、CFR、CIF 和 FAS,其余 7 个被列为第二组,所有运输方式都适用。在当代国际贸易中,FOB、CFR 和 CIF 这三个术语是被提及最多、运用最广泛,同时也是最重要的术语。本书将这三个贸易术语放在一起来讨论,因为它们性质上是一样的,也有着共同的规律,具体可从以下五个方面来分析:

(1)这三个术语都只适用于港到港的海洋或内河运输;

(2)卖方的交货地点都是在装运港的船上;

(3)卖方只要在装运港将货物装上船就完成了交货义务,风险同时也转移给买方;

(4)这三个术语都属于象征性交货,意思是指卖方只要按期在约定地点完成装运,并向买方提交合同规定的相关单证就算完成了交货义务;

(5)三者签订的买卖合同都属于装运合同,换言之,卖方只管按时装运,不用管货物何时到达。

FOB 术语

FOB 是英文 Free on Board 的缩写,其后应注明《2010 通则》,是指装运港船上交货,后面跟着的是出口国指定装运港, 比如说 FOB Shanghai。

FOB 术语是国际贸易中常用的术语之一,只适用于海运或内河运输。装运港船上交货是指卖方将货物装运到买方指定的船上即完成交货责任,从此刻开始所有的费用及风险转移给买方。

1. 卖方的责任和义务

(1)卖方的一般义务

提供符合买卖合同的货物和商业发票,或与商业发票具有同等效力的电子信息,以及按合同规定需提供的证明货物符合合同的其他凭证。

(2)许可证、授权、安全许可证和其他手续

卖方承担货物在装运港装上船之前的一切费用和风险,取得所有出口许可证或其他官方授权,办理货物出口和在必要时从他国过境所需的一切海关手续。

(3)运输合同

卖方无订立运输合同的义务,但如果买方有要求,或按照商业习惯,在买方承担风险和费用的情况下,卖方也可以按照通常条件订立运输合同;同时运用此术语,卖方也无订立保险合同的义务,但如果买方要求,并在买方承担风险和费用的情况下,卖方必须向买方提供其办理保险所需的信息。

(4)交货规定

按照港口的惯常习惯,在规定的日期或期限内,在指定的装运港,将货物交至买方指定的船上。

2. 买方的责任和义务

(1)买方的一般义务

根据买卖合同规定受领货物并支付货款。

(2)许可证、授权、安全许可证和其他手续

买方自负风险和费用,取得进口许可证或其他官方批准证件,并且办理货物进口和从第三国过境运输所需的一切海关手续。

(3)运输合同

买方自费签订从指定装运港装运货物的运输合同,并将船名、装货地点和装货日期等相关信息及时通知卖方;买方负责订立货物保险合同。

(4)风险转移问题

买方承担货物在装运港上船之后发生的各种费用以及货物灭失或损坏的一切风险。

表 3-1　　在 FOB 下买卖双方的责任和义务

	Carriage	Insurance	Export clearance	Import clearance	Risk division	Mode of transport
Seller			√		On board the ship at the port of shipment	Sea or inland waterway transport
Buyer	√	√		√		

3. 使用 FOB 应注意的问题

(1)关于风险划分界限的变更

《2010 通则》之前的所有版本,FOB 是以装运港船舷作为划分风险的界限。"船舷为界"表明货物在装船时越过船舷之前的所有风险,包括在装船时货物跌落码头或海中所造成的损失,均由卖方承担。货物越过船舷装上船之后,包括在起航前和在运输过程中所发生的损坏和灭失,则由买方承担。但因为装货是一个连续的过程,按照"船舷为界"在运用中不甚科学且有很多缺陷,新的通则将风险划分改为以货物装上船为界。

(2)关于船货衔接的问题

在使用 FOB 术语的合同中,买卖双方承担着不同的责任,而此术语对于买方来说风险更大、责任更重,所以卖方在准备好货物后要及时通知买方,如果因为卖方的疏忽没有将相关信息及时通知买方的话,卖方将负有相应的责任。也就是说,如果买卖双方按 FOB 术语成交,对于装运期和装运港要慎重规定,签订合同之后,有关备货和派船事宜,双方要加强联系、密切配合,保证好船货衔接。

(3)关于个别国家对 FOB 的不同解释

以上有关 FOB 的解释都是按照国际商会《2010 通则》作出的,然而不同的国家和不同的管理对 FOB 的解释并不完全统一。比如,在北美和拉丁美洲等地区较常采用的《1990 年美国对外贸易定义修订本》中,FOB 的解释分为六种,只有在 FOB 和港名之间加上"船只"(vessel)字样的才与通则的解释一致,所以在运用 FOB 术语成交上要特别注意。

CFR 术语

CFR 是英文 Cost and Freight 的缩写,该术语是指成本加运费,后面跟着目的地港口名称,比如说 CFR New York。

CFR 术语只适用于海洋或内河运输,是指卖方负责租船或订舱,在合同规定的期限内将货物运送到指定装运港的船上,并支付将货物运送至目的地港口所需的运费。但当货物被放置到装运港的船上时,货物灭失或损坏的风险,以及装上船后发生的任何费用,都由卖方转移至买方。

1. 卖方的责任和义务

(1)卖方的一般义务

卖方必须按照销售合同和合同可能要求的任何其他合格证据提供货物和商业发票。

(2)许可证、授权、安全许可证和其他手续

卖方承担货物在装运港装上船之前的一切费用和风险,取得所有出口许可证或其他官方授权,办理货物出口和在必要时从他国过境所需的一切海关手续。

(3)运输合同

卖方必须在交付到指定目的港的交货地点(如果有的话)或在该港口的任何地点签订合同或采购货物运输合同(如果有的话)。运输合同必须按照通常的条款进行,费用由卖方承担,并规定用于运输所销售货物类型的惯常航线的船舶运输。

(4)保险合同

卖方无订立保险合同的义务,但如果买方要求卖方提供与货物相关的信息,卖方应给予协助。

(5)交货

在规定的日期或期限内,在装运港将货物交至船上。

2. 买方的责任和义务

(1)买方的一般义务

根据买卖合同规定受领货物并支付货款。

(2)许可证、授权、安全许可证和其他手续

买方自负风险和费用,取得进口许可证或其他官方批准证件,并且办理货物进口和从第三国过境运输所需的一切海关手续。

(3)运输和保险合同

买方没有义务让卖方订立运输合同,而买方必须在货物装运交付后才签订保险合同。

(4)风险转移

买方承担货物在装运港上船之后发生的各种费用以及货物灭失或损坏的一切风险。

表 3-2　　在 CFR 下买卖双方的责任和义务

	Carriage	Insurance	Export clearance	Import clearance	Risk division	Mode of transport
Seller	√		√		On board the ship at the port of shipment	Sea or inland waterway transport
Buyer		√		√		

3. 使用 CFR 术语应注意的问题

根据以上提及内容,因为 CFR 术语下费用和风险转移的地点不同,在使用该术语时需要注意两个关键点:

(1)虽然合同中通常都会规定目的港,但不一定会指定装运港,而装运港又是风险转移的地方,所以如果装运港对买方有特殊意义或有特别要求,建议在签订合同时明确指定装运港。

(2)由于卖方需要承担将货物运送至目的港的费用,特别建议买卖双方在合同中明确指定目的港的交付点,卖方最好取得完全符合该选择的运输合同。如果卖方按照运输合同在目的港的交付点发生了卸货等相关费用,除非双方另有规定,一般卖方无权向买方要求补偿此类费用。另外需要注意的是,卖方只需按时交货,而无须保证按时到货,所以在合同中卖方要避免订立到达时间。

CIF 术语

CIF 是英文 Cost, Insurance and Freight 的缩写,意思为"成本加保险费加运费",术语后面跟着指定目的地港口名称,比如说 CIF New York。

CIF 术语只适用于海运或内河运输,意思是指卖方自船上交货,货物灭失或损坏的风险在货物交到船上时转移给买方。卖方必须签订合同,支付必要的成本以及将货物运抵指定目的地港口的运费。卖方还必须签订保险合同并支付保险费,以防运输途中货物的灭失或损坏的风险。但买方应注意到,该术语只要求卖方投保最低限度的保险险别,如买方需要更高的保险险别,则需与卖方明确达成协议,或自行做出额外的保险安排。

1. 卖方的责任和义务

(1)卖方的一般义务

卖方必须在合同规定的装运期内将符合要求的货物运送到指定装运港船上，以及提供给买方合同所规定的相关文件。

(2)许可证、授权、安全许可证和其他手续

在适用情况下，卖方必须自担风险和费用，取得所有出口许可证或其他官方许可，并办理货物出口所需的一切海关手续。

(3)运输合同

自负费用，按照通常条件订立运输合同，将合同规定的货物用通常运输该项货物的那种类型的海轮，经惯常航线运至指定目的港。

(4)保险合同

卖方必须自负费用购买至少符合条款规定的最低金额的货物保险。

(5)交货

卖方必须在约定的日期或在约定的期限内以惯常的方式将货物放在船上。

2. 买方的责任和义务

(1)买方的一般义务

根据买卖合同规定受领货物并支付货款。

(2)许可证、授权、安全许可证和其他手续

买方自负风险和费用，取得进口许可证或其他官方批准证件，并且办理货物进口和从第三国过境运输所需的一切海关手续。

(3)运输和保险合同

买方无订立运输与保险合同的义务。但是如果卖方有要求，买方需提供给卖方订立保险合同的相关信息。

(4)收取货物

卖方按合同要求运输货物后，买方必须在指定目的港向承运人收取货物。

(5)风险转移

买方承担货物在装运港装上船之后发生的各种费用以及货物灭失或损坏的一切风险。

表 3-3 在 CIF 下买卖双方的责任和义务

	Carriage	Insurance	Export clearance	Import clearance	Risk division	Mode of transport
Seller	√	√	√		On board the ship at the port of shipment	Sea or inland waterway transport
Buyer				√		

3. 使用 CIF 应注意的问题

(1)卖方租船订舱问题

按照《2010 通则》的规定,卖方只负责将货物按照惯常线路用通常可提供装载该合同货物的海上航行船只即可。买方无权指定船龄、船型和船运公司,若买方有相关要求,卖方可以拒绝,除非合同中有另外的规定。

(2)保险险别问题

按照《2010 通则》解释,卖方还要为买方在运输途中货物的灭失或损坏风险办理保险。买方应注意,在 CIF 项下卖方仅需投保最低险别,如买方需要更多保险或更高险别,则需要与卖方达成协议,或自行做出额外的保险安排。

(3)象征性交货问题

CIF 是一种典型的象征性交货。与 FOB 一样,CIF 的交货地点是出口国的装运港而不是目的港。

第三节 FCA、CPT 和 CIP 术语

FCA、CPT、CIP 是指向承运人交货的贸易术语,它们都是在出口国货交承运人时使用,在性质上有以下几个共同点:第一,这三个贸易术语都适合于包括海运在内的任何一种运输方式;第二,这三个贸易术语卖方交货地点都是在出口国货交承运人;第三,这三个贸易术语的风险划分都是以出口国装运地货交承运人为界;第四,这三个贸易术语都是以出口国装运地为交货条件,签订的买卖合同都是装运合同。

这三个贸易术语与上一节我们提及的术语 FOB、CFR、CIF 在性质上很相近,唯一不同的是运输方式,FOB、CFR、CIF 只适合于海洋运输,而 FCA、CPT、

CIP 这三个术语适用于包括海运运输在内的任何一种运输方式。

FCA 术语

FCA 是英文 Free Carrier 的缩写，中文为“货交承运人”。该术语后面跟指定地点，适合于所有的运输方式。FCA 是指卖方在其所在地或其他指定地点将货物交给买方指定的承运人或其他人，并办理出口清关手续即完成交货。采用 FCA 术语时，建议双方尽可能详细地规定交货点，因为在该点风险将由卖方转移给买方。如果在卖方所在地交货，则应当明确卖方所在地为交货地点；若双方在其他地点交货，则必须明确不同的特定交货地点。

1. 卖方的责任和义务

（1）卖方必须根据合同要求，在规定时间内提交货物，并提供给买方相应的单据；

（2）卖方必须自负风险和费用，取得所需的出口许可证或其他官方授权，办理货物出口所需的一切海关手续；

（3）卖方承担货物灭失或损坏的一切风险，直至货物交付给承运人或买方指定的其他人为止。

2. 买方的责任和义务

（1）买方必须根据销售合同规定的货物价格支付货款；

（2）买方自负风险和费用，取得进口许可证或其他官方批准证件，并且办理货物进口和从第三国过境运输所需的一切海关手续；

（3）买方需签订货物运输合同并承担卖方货交承运人后的一切运费，并自行办理保险；

（4）买方负担卖方货交承运人后货物灭失和损坏的风险。

3. FCA 与 FOB 的异同点

相同点：

（1）FCA 和 FOB 术语都是由买方负责订立运输合同并支付运费，由买方买保险，所以在价格构成上都不包含运费和保费；

（2）这两个贸易术语都属于以出口国装运港（地）为交货条件；

（3）按这两个术语签订的买卖合同，都是装运合同，而不是销售合同。

不同点:

(1)FOB 只适用于港到港的海洋运输,FCA 适用于包括海运在内的所有运输方式;

(2)FOB 在装运港船上交货,FCA 在出口国指定的装运地货交承运人;

(3)FOB 是以装运港船上为界,FCA 以货交承运人为界;

(4)FOB 是象征性交货的贸易术语。

CPT 术语

CPT 是英文 Carriage Paid To 的缩写,后面跟目的地港口名称,中文意思为运费付至(目的地港口),其后面应注明《2010 年国际贸易术语解释通则》。按照 CPT 术语成交,卖方要在合同约定的日期或期限内,在规定的地点将货物交给指定的承运人或第一承运人,完成其交货任务。另外,卖方要自负费用订立货物运往目的地的运输合同,并承担运费。CPT 术语下卖方将货物交给承运人后所有的风险将转移给买方。CPT 还要求卖方办理出口货物的清关,但卖方没有义务清关货物进口、支付进口关税或办理任何进口海关手续。

1. 卖方的责任和义务

(1)卖方必须按照销售合同和合同可能要求的任何其他合格证据提供货物和商业发票;

(2)卖方承担货物在装运港装上船之前的一切费用和风险,取得所有出口许可证或其他官方授权,办理货物出口和在必要时从他国过境所需的一切海关手续;

(3)卖方需订立运输合同并支付将货物从指定装运港运至合同规定的目的港的运输费用;

(4)卖方对买方无订立保险合同的义务;

(5)卖方必须在规定的日期或期限内,在指定地点将货物交至承运人。

2. 买方的责任和义务

(1)买方必须根据买卖合同规定受领货物并支付货款;

(2)买方自负风险和费用,取得进口许可证或其他官方批准证件,并且办理货物进口和从第三国过境运输所需的一切海关手续;

(3)买方没有义务让卖方订立运输合同,而买方必须在货物装运交付后才

签订保险合同;

(4)买方承担货交承运人后发生的各种费用,以及货物灭失或损坏的一切风险。

3. 采用CPT术语需要注意的问题

(1)关于风险划分的界限。

按照CPT贸易术语,卖方要负责订立从装运地到指定目的地的运输合同,并承担运费;买卖双方的风险转移以在出口国货交承运人为界。按照《2010通则》的解释,货物自交货地点至目的地运输途中的风险由买方承担,卖方只承担货交承运人之前的风险。如果是在多式联运的情况下,卖方承担的风险在货交第一承运人时转移给买方。

(2)关于责任和费用划分的问题。

按照CPT贸易术语,卖方负责安排到目的地的运输费用。卖方将货物交给承运人之后,应向买方提供货物已运出的相关信息,以便于买方投保并在目的地受领货物。

4. CPT和CFR的异同点

相同点:

(1)以上两个贸易术语都是由卖方负责安排到目的地运输,并承担运费,由买方根据卖方提供的信息自行投保,承担保费;

(2)按这两个贸易术语签订的买卖合同都是装运合同。

不同点:

(1)CFR只适用于港到港的海洋运输,CPT适用于所有的运输方式;

(2)CFR下卖方在装运港船上交货,而CPT下在出口国货交承运人;

(3)CFR风险在出口国装运港货物装上船后转移至买方,而CPT以在出口国货交承运人为界风险转移给买方。

CIP术语

CIP是Carriage Insurance Paid To的缩写,中文译为"运费、保险费付至",术语后面跟指定目的地名称。该术语可适用于所有运输方式,包括多式联运。

CIP术语是指卖方将货物在双方约定的地点交给其指定的承运人或其他人即完成交货,卖方需要签订运输合同并支付将货物运至指定目的地所需的费用,要为在运输途中货物的灭失或损失签订保险合同,并支付保险费用。但需要注意的是,卖方只需要购买最低险别的保险,如买方想要投保更高的险别,需要双方在合同中约定,或买方支付最低险别之外的费用。另外,双方在 CIP 交货条件下,买方需要取得出口许可证或其他官方授权,办理货物出口和交货前从他国过境运输所需的一切海关手续并缴纳相关的费用。

1. 卖方的责任和义务

(1)卖方必须按照销售合同和合同可能要求的任何其他合格证据提供货物和商业发票;

(2)卖方自担风险和费用,取得出口许可证或其他官方许可的条件,并在需要办理海关手续时,办理货物出口所需的一切海关手续;

(3)自费订立按通常条件、通常路线及习惯方式将货物运至指定目的地约定地点的运输合同;如果合同中未规定具体地点,卖方可自行选定一个最合适的地点交货;

(4)卖方必须自负费用购买至少符合条款规定的最低金额的货物保险;

(5)卖方必须在约定的日期或在约定的期限内以惯常的方式将货物放在船上。

2. 买方的责任和义务

(1)根据买卖合同规定受领货物并支付货款;

(2)买方自负风险和费用,取得进口许可证或其他官方批准证件,并且办理货物进口和从第三国过境运输所需的一切海关手续;

(3)买方无订立运输合同与保险合同的义务。但是如果卖方有要求,买方需提供给卖方订立保险合同的相关信息;

(4)卖方按合同要求运输货物后,买方必须在指定目的地向承运人收取货物;

(5)买方承担货物交至承运人后发生的各种费用以及货物灭失或损坏的一切风险。

3. 术语 CIF 和 CIP 的区别

相同点:

(1)CIF 和 CIP 术语的价格构成中都包含了运费和保险费,卖方都要安排到目的地（港口）的运输，负责投保，支付相关的运费和保险费；

（2）CIF 和 CIP 术语下交货地点都是在出口国；

（3）CIF 和 CIP 术语下订立的买卖合同均为装运合同。

不同点：

（1）CIF 术语是典型的象征性交货，CIP 若不采用海运运输，则不属于象征性交货；

（2）CIF 只适合于海洋或内河运输，CIP 则适用于所有的运输方式；

（3）CIF 以在装运港装货物上船为界，CIP 以出口国装运地（包括装运港）货交承运人为界；

（4）CIF 下货物在船上时风险转移，而 CIP 下货物交付给承运人时风险转移；

（5）CIF 下的保险是纯海运保险，CIP 下的保险不仅涉及运输保险，还涉及内陆或航空保险。

第四节　其他贸易术语

EXW 术语

EXW 是英文 Ex Works 的缩写，意思为工厂交货（插入指定交货地点），其后应注明《2010 年通则》。不管所选择的运输方式如何，都可以使用该规则，并且也适用于多式联运。

EXW 是指在商品的产地或所在地交货，当卖方在合同约定的交货时间内在其所在地或其他指定地点，如工厂、仓库等，将合同规定的货物置于买方的处置之下时即完成交货。卖方不需要将货物装载到任何车辆上，也不需要负责货物的出口清关等。

EXW 是所有术语中卖方义务最少、买方义务最多的术语。EXW 经常被任何运输工具使用，包括国内贸易和国际贸易中的多式联运。买方应明白，若采用该术语，买方承担卖方交货后所有的风险及费用，甚至包括货物出口清关的所有手续及费用。另外，此术语对卖方来说相当于国内贸易。

FAS 术语

FAS 是英文 Free Alongside Ship 的缩写，意思为装运港船边交货(……术语后跟着指定装运港)，其后应注明《2010 通则》。此术语只适合海洋或内河运输。

FAS 是指当卖方在规定期限内将货物交到指定的装运港船边(例如，置于码头或驳船上)时即完成交货。买卖双方负担的风险和费用均以船边为界，买方必须承担自那时起货物灭失或损坏的一切风险。需要注意的是，当船舶不能停靠时，卖方必须使用驳船将货物移到船边以进行交货。

1. 卖方的责任和义务

(1)卖方必须按照销售合同和合同可能要求的任何其他合格证据提供货物和商业发票；

(2)卖方自负风险和费用，取得出口许可证或其他官方批准文件，并且办理货物出口所需的一切海关手续；

(3)卖方无订立运输合同的义务；

(4)卖方对买方无订立保险合同的义务，但如果买方有要求，并在买方承担风险和费用的情况下，卖方必须向买方提供其他办理保险所需的信息；

(5)卖方承担货交承运人前的所有风险和费用。

2. 买方的责任和义务

(1)接受卖方提供的有关单据，受领货物，并按合同规定支付货款；

(2)自负风险和费用，取得进口许可证或其他官方批准的证件，并且办理货物进口所需的海关手续，支付关税及其他相关费用；

(3)买方自费签订从指定装运港装运货物的运输合同，并将船名、装货地点和装货日期等相关信息及时通知卖方；

(4)买方无订立货物保险合同的义务；

(5)买方承担货交承运人后发生的各种费用以及货物灭失或损坏的一切风险。

3. FAS 和 FOB 的异同点

相同点：

(1)术语 FAS 和 FOB 都只应用于港到港海上运输;

(2)两者都是由买方安排运输、投保、承担运费和保险费。

不同点:

(1)FOB 属于象征性交货,而 FAS 属于实际交货;

(2)FOB 中卖方交货的地方在装运港船上,而 FAS 是在装运港船边;

(3)FOB 的风险划分是以卖方将货物放置到装运港船上为界,而 FAS 的风险划分则以装运港船边为界;

(4)FOB 中由卖方负责装船,而 FAS 中卖方不承担装船的费用。

4. 与美国对外贸易定义修订本项下定义的区别

(1)美国定义的 FAS 意思是指 along side, 而《2010 年通则》中的 FAS 是指 free alongside ship;

(2)因为定义不同,美国定义的 FAS 术语可在任何交通工具旁交货,所以此术语适用于包括海运在内的所有运输方式;

(3)若是想用《2010 年通则》中的 FAS,而惯例用的是美国修订本,可在美国定义的 FAS 后加上"vessel"字样,这样两者便具有相同意义。

DAT 术语

DAT 是英文 Delivered At Terminal 的缩写,意思为"运输终端交货",后面跟着指定港口或目的地的运输终端,应注明《2010 通则》。DAT 术语适用于所有运输方式,也可用于多式联运。

DAT 指卖方在合同中约定的日期或期限内将货物运到合同规定的港口或目的地的约定运输终端,并将货物从抵达的载货运输工具上卸下,交给买方处置时即完成交货。"运输终端"意味着任何地点,而不论该地点是否有遮盖,例如码头、仓库、集装箱堆场或公路、铁路、空运货站。

卖方承担将货物送至指定港口或目的地的运输终端并将其卸下这一期间的一切费用。由于卖方承担在特定地点交货前的风险,特别建议双方尽可能确切地约定运输终端,或如果可能的话,在约定港口或目的地的运输终端内的特定的点。建议卖方取得的运输合同应能与所做选择确切吻合。

此外,如果双方希望由卖方承担将货物由终端运输和搬运至另一地点的风险和费用,则应当使用 DAP 或 DDP 术语。

若适用,DAT 则要求卖方办理出口清关手续。但卖方无义务办理进口清关、支付任何进口税或办理任何进口清关手续。

使用 DAT 术语应注意的问题

根据《2010 通则》的解释,“运输终端”意味着任何地点,而不论该地点是否有遮盖,例如码头、仓库、集装箱堆场或公路、铁路、空运货站。为了避免不必要的纠纷,《2010 通则》建议买卖双方在订立买卖合同时尽可能地约定运输终端的名称和其具体位置,并且在运输合同中作出相应的规定。卖方订立的运输合同应能与所做选择确切吻合。

DAP 术语

DAP 为英文 Delivered At Place(named place of destination)的缩写,意思是指在目的地交货(插入指定目的地),其后应注明《2010 通则》,此术语适用于所有的运输方式。

DAP 术语是指卖方在合同约定的日期或期限内,将货物运到合同规定的目的地的约定地点,并将货物置于买方的控制之下,在卸货之前即完成交货。卖方承担将货物运送到指定地点的一切风险。

由于卖方承担在特定地点交货前的风险,特别建议双方尽可能清楚地订明指定的目的地内的交货点。建议卖方订立的运输合同应能与所做选择确切吻合。如果卖方按照运输合同在目的地发生了卸货费用,除非双方另有约定,卖方无权向买方要求偿付。

若适用,DAP 则要求卖方办理出口清关手续。但是卖方无义务办理进口清关、支付任何进口税或办理任何进口清关手续。如果双方希望卖方办理进口清关、支付所有进口关税,并办理所有进口海关手续,则应当使用 DDP 术语。

DDP 术语

DDP 是英文 Delivered Duty Paid(insert named place of destination)的缩写,意思为完税后交货(后面插入指定目的地),应注明《2010 通则》。该术语适用于所有的运输方式。

DDP 术语是指当卖方在指定目的地已办理进口清关手续,将在交货运输工具上尚未卸下的货物交予买方完成交货。卖方承担将货物运至目的地的一切风险和费用,并且有义务完成货物出口和进口清关,支付所有出口和进口的关税办理。

DDP 是所有术语中卖方承担责任、风险和费用最大的一种。由于卖方承担在特定地点交货前的风险和费用，特别建议双方尽可能清楚地订明在指定目的地内的交货点。建议卖方订立的运输合同应能与所做选择确切吻合。如果按照运输合同卖方在目的地发生了卸货费用，除非双方另有约定，卖方无权向买方索要。

如卖方不能直接或间接地完成进口清关，特别建议双方则不使用 DDP 术语。如果双方希望买方承担所有进口清关的风险和费用，则应使用 DAP 术语，除非买卖合同中另行明确规定，任何增值税或其他应付的进口税款由卖方承担。

表 3-4　　**《2010 通则》**

Trade Terms	Full Name	Place of Delivery	Risks Transfer	Foreign Freight	Insurance Premium	Export Duty	Import Duty	Means of Transport
EXW	Ex Works	Named place	Delivered to the buyer	Buyer	Buyer	Buyer	Buyer	All modes
FCA	Free Carrier	Named place	Delivered to the Carrier	Buyer	Buyer	Seller	Buyer	All modes
FAS	Free Along-side Ship	Alongside ship at port of shipment	Alongside ship at port of shipment	Buyer	Buyer	Seller	Buyer	Sea and inland waterway
FOB	Free on Board	On board the ship	Delivered on board the vessel	Buyer	Buyer	Seller	Buyer	Sea and inland waterway
CFR	Cost and Freight	On board the ship	Delivered on board the vessel	Seller	Buyer	Seller	Buyer	Sea and inland waterway
CIF	Cost, Insur-ance and Freight	On board the ship	Delivered on board the vessel	Seller	Seller	Seller	Buyer	Sea and inland waterway
CPT	Carriage Paid to	To the carrier in export country	To the carrier	Seller	Buyer	Seller	Buyer	All modes
CIP	Carriage and Insurance Paid to	To the carrier in export country	To the carrier	Seller	Seller	Seller	Buyer	All modes
DAT	Delivered At Terminal	At named terminal at port or place of destination	Delivered at named terminal at port or place of destination	Seller	Seller	Seller	Buyer	All modes
DAP	Delivered At Place	At named place of destination	Delivered to buyer at named place of destination	Seller	Seller	Seller	Buyer	All modes
DDP	Delivered Du-ty Paid	At named place of destination	Delivered to buyer at named place of destination	Seller	Seller	Seller	Seller	All modes

Chapter 4

Price of Commodity

Part A Text

In international trade practice, the terms of price are one of the most important terms of a contract, also the price of goods is the key to discuss between the buyer and the seller. Price is the amount of money that is needed to acquire some combination of a product and its accompanying services. So to understand the methods of pricing and reasonably establish the terms of price have significance on fulfilling mission of importing and exporting and improving economic benefits.

Section One Pricing Considerations

1. Pricing Principles

In international trade, the pricing for foreign markets is usually quite different compared to the domestic market. So before the price of import and export commodities is determined, there are three principles should be considered:

(1) According to the international market price level

On the basis of international market price level, adjust prices according to the exporter's specific purposes or the importer's requirements. International price is determined in the international market competition on the basis of international value of commodity, which can be accepted by both sides and will be the objective basis of importing and exporting commodity.

(2) To engage in country, regional policy pricing

Pricing should considering other countries' policies and regional rules in order to make the international trading conform to diplomacy.

(3) To combine the purpose of purchasing

Pricing should be in line with the international price. To considering the purpose of purchasing, the price can be a little higher or lower than the international price. Because the international market price is subject to the supply and demand, it is not so stable. Therefore, in order to make the right price of the goods, we should pay more attention to the ups and downs of the international market, make good prediction so as to avoid blindness of the making correct use of pricing.

2. Factors Consideration in Pricing

(1) Cost

To understand the cost structure of a product is often the first step in setting a price. From the factory workshop until the place of destination in the importing country, the internationally traded products may incur four categories of cost: products cost, sales cost, delivery cost and financing cost. As an exporter must has good knowledge of these costs for their own benefits.

(2) Anticipated profit

The expression of anticipated profit can be an absolute number, or a percentage. Many companies like to consider the profit as a percentage of the selling price, namely the profit margin. Normally, profit will have already been included in the domestic price, but if it is insufficient for the risk involved in selling abroad, an extra allowance for profit can be added.

(3) Capability of target market

Market capability refers to the consumption power, income level, and supply and demand relationship in the target market. Pricing strategy may be tailored to particular foreign markets. For lower per capita income markets, simplifying the product to reduce its selling price may be an answer for export. Products of higher quality, with more ornaments may be targeted developed countries. The international trader should also anticipate the specific segment potential customers. If the primary customers in a developing country are belong to the upperclass, a higher price might be feasible even if the average per capita income is low. In addition, the supply and demand relation in the foreign market is well worth measuring. Some products may create such a strong demand, such as popular goods like Nike shoes, that even low per capita income will not affect their selling price. Thus, traders should try to be aware of the consumption variety in target markets in export pricing.

(4) Terms of payment

The different payment terms has an impact on the financing and risk bearing situation of the traders. Exporters would provide favorable prices to encourage customers to accept the payment terms which will cause less or no financing stress and little risk. So different payment methods will affect the risk and cost for both parties. So the terms of payments can be used for barging.

(5) Other factors

Apart from the mentioned factors as above, there are some other factors also should be considered, for example, what kind of trade terms to be chosen to use, the quality of the goods or the quantity amount of products. Pricing is a complex activity always subject to many contingencies. International traders have to be aware of the dynamics in the market environment so that they will not miss any significant factor which might influence their pricing decision.

3. Pricing Methods

In the international business negotiation and contract conclusion, appropriate trade terms should be chosen to make reasonable price and favorable money of account. Detailed method of pricing should be included in the clause of price, and price adjustment clauses should also be added in the price term if necessary. In addition, commissions and discounts could be used as a flexible way of motivating the initiatives of the supplier and expanding the sales.

In international sales of goods, the following methods of pricing can be used.

(1) Fixed pricing

The seller delivers and the buyer accepts the commodities at a fixed price agreed by both parties. Neither party shall have the right to change the agreed price.

(2) Flexible pricing

The pricing time and the pricing method are specified in the price terms, for instance, "The price will be negotiated and decided by both parties 60 days before the shipment according to the international price level". Or only the pricing time is fixed, for instance, "To be priced on June 1st, 2017 by both parties".

(3) Partial fixed price and partial unfixed price

The parties concerned only fix the price for the commodities be delivered recently, and leave the price of commodities to be delivered in the long term open.

(4) Floating pricing

At the time of pricing, the price adjustment is also stipulated, for example, "If the concluded price for other buyer is 5% higher or lower than the contract price, both parties will negotiate to adjust the contract price for the quantity of the contract".

4. Selection of Money of Account

In international trade, the money of account can be use different countries' currency, for example, can be use the currency of the export country, the currency of the import country, or the currency of a third country agreed by both parties. As the change of the value of the selected currency may directly affect the financial interests of both parties, the parties concerned should choose the currency favorable to them during pricing. Theoretically, hard currency should be chosen for exports and soft currency for imports. In trade practice, however, the selection of money of account shall depend on the business practices and intentions of both parties. If unfavorable currency has to be adopted for the conclusion of a deal, the following two remedies may be taken: to make corresponding adjustment to the quotation according to the possible trend of the currency in the future and to get the price protected against the currency risks.

Section Two　Export Quotation and Cost Calculation

1. Price Components of Export Commodities

The price in international trade is composed of four indispensable parts: price currency, unite of measurement, unite value (price), trade terms. They typically look like the following expression:

USD200/piece CIF New York or FOB Shanghai EUR 100/set

It's up to the exporter if they put the trade term at the beginning or the end of the price.

But all terms should be followed by the name of an appropriate place as defined by the *INCOTERMS* 2010.

(1) Components of FOB, CFR and CIF

FOB price = Purchase Cost+ Domestic Cost+ Net Profit

CFR price = Purchase Cost+ Domestic Cost+ Overseas Freight+ Net Profit

CIF price = Purchase Cost+ Domestic Cost+ Overseas Freight+ Overseas Insurance+Net Profit

(2) Conversion of FOB, CFR and CIF

If FOB price is given, then we may get CFR and CIF price, Here is the formula:

CFR price = FOB+Overseas Freight

$$\text{CIF price} = \frac{\text{FOB+Overseas Freight}}{1-(\text{Insurance Percentage of Addition}\times\text{Premium Rate})}$$

If CIF price is given, then FOB and CFR price can be figured out as per the following formula:

FOB price = CIF × [1 − (Insurance Percentage of Adding × Premium Rate)] − Overseas Freight

CFR price = CIF×[1−(Insurance Percentage of Adding×Premium Rate)]

If CFR price is given, then, FOB and CIF price can also be calculated as per the formula as below:

FOB price = CFR − Overseas Freight

CIF price = CFR price/[1−(Insurance Percentage of Adding×Premium Rate)]

2. Export Exchange Cost

Export exchange cost of products refers to the amount of RMB required for a unit of foreign currency of certain export commodity. That means how much RMB can be exchanged for 1 US dollar, or the total RMB cost needed for exporting goods worthy of net 1 US dollar. Export exchange cost is an important index to show the profits and losses of the export business. If the exchange cost of export goods is lower than the foreign exchange rate of Bank of China, there will be profits, conversely, there will be losses.

Formula:

Export Exchange Cost = Total Export Cost (RMB)/Export Foreign Exchange Net Income (USD)

(1) Total export cost

Total export cost is composed of purchase cost, domestic cost and export tax, which means the total domestic cost paid by foreign trade enterprises for export commodities. The export cost price is calculated on the basis of total export cost, excluding any overseas cost.

Domestic cost includes circulation cost, processing fees, packaging fees, custodial fees (warehouse rental and fire insurance), domestic transportation cost (from warehouse to harbor), documents fees (inspection fees, notary fees, consular fees, certificate of origin and licensing fees, customs declaration fees, customs fees), freight (discount interest, loaded container cost, lifting cost and shipping fees), banking charges (discount interest and other charges) and postal fees.

(2) Export foreign exchange net income

Export foreign exchange net income comprises total export foreign exchange excluding labor cost and other non-trade foreign exchange (freight, insurance premiums, and banking charges), that means under FOB trade terms, the FOB price is export foreign exchange net income.

Export exchange cost is directly proportional to total export cost and inversely proportional to export exchange net income. Compared with foreign exchange rate of

BOC (Bank of China), the lower export exchange cost is, the more profits will be gained. For instance, in an export transaction, the export exchange cost is calculated as 6.03, while the foreign exchange rate is 6.25, this means every dollar gained will earn 0.22 RMB.

3. Profit and Loss Ratio of Export Commodities

Profit and loss ration ratio of export commodities demonstrates the ratio between the volume of export profit and total export cost. The volume of export profit indicates the balance between RMB net income of export sales and total export cost. If the balance is a positive number, it means making a profit, and vice-versa. The very ratio is perceived as an important index to measure the degree of export profit or loss. The formula as follow:

Profit and loss ratio of export commodities = (RMB Net Income of Export Sales - total Export Cost) / Total Export Cost × 100%

RMB Net Income of Export Sales = Foreign Exchange Sales FOB × Foreign Exchange Rate (Bid Price)

4. Foreign Exchange Earned through Export

Foreign exchange earned through export also called as Exchange Rate Appreciation, it is concluded by the ratio between certain difference calculated by export foreign exchange net income minus foreign exchange cost of raw materials and foreign exchange cost of raw materials. If the raw materials are made domestically, the FOB price is the foreign exchange cost of raw materials, if the raw material is imported, the foreign exchange cost of raw materials shall be calculated by CIF price. The ratio is universally adopted in imported materials processing and supplied materials processing to calculate exchange rate appreciation. The formula as following:

Foreign Exchange Earned through Export (Exchange Rate Appreciation) = (Export Foreign Exchange Net Income - Foreign Exchange Cost of Raw Materials) / Foreign Exchange Cost of Raw Materials × 100%

Through calculation of exchange rate appreciation, the profit of foreign exchange earned can be revealed, i.e. is raw materials export profitable or finished products export profitable.

Case: A trading company imports fabric to proceed to clothing at an amount of 100 000 Dollars for 20 000 garment in CIF terms (USD9/PC CIF HAMBURG per garment). The total freight is 8 000 Dollars, Premiums is 2 000 Dollars. Please calculate the exchange rate appreciation.

Exchange Rate Appreciation = (Export Foreign Exchange Net Income − Foreign Exchange Cost of Raw Materials)/Foreign Exchange Cost of Raw Materials × 100%

$$= (9\times 20\,000 - 8\,000 - 2\,000 - 100\,000)/100\,000 \times 100\%$$

$$= 70\%$$

Section Three Commission and Discount

If a price shown in the contract directly comes from the calculation of basic costs and profit, it is called a "net price". But sometimes the traders have to make some adjustments to the net price to achieve the goal of promoting sales. These adjustments include commission and discount.

1. Commission

(1) Definition

Commission is the remuneration for the agents who provide service for principals. During trading, commission is usually in the form of remuneration which either side of a trade provides to the middleman. For example, exporters pay commission to sales agents, or importers pay commission to purchase agents. Therefore, commission applies to the contract signed by the exporter/importer and the agents. Certain trading occurs through middlemen or agents who need to be paid commission. If the ratio of commission is defined, we call them the defined commission; otherwise, we call them undefined commission which agents may require from both sides.

A price which contains a proportion as commission payment is called a "price with commission". It can be defined as follows:

Labelled by word: e.g. USD 50/PC CIF NEW YORK, this price includes 5%

commission.

Using a capitalized “C” to indicate commission behind the trade terms:

e.g. CIFC 5 NEW YORK USD 50/PC.

Defined by number:e.g. USD 50/PC CIF NEW YORK,commission:USD 5/PC.

(2)Calculation of Commission

In the international trade,the calculation of commission in not a difficult problem,but it should be defined whether commission is calculated on the basis of FOB or CIF trade terms. It is more sensible to adopt FOB,which means that if the deal is finalized by CIF or any other terms,costs like ocean freight and insurance should be deducted before the commission is calculated,another words,the buyer or seller does not need to pay commission for the freight charges,insurance or other fees. However, it nevertheless cannot be accepted by agents and also incurs more trouble in calculating. It is conventional that CIF serves as the basis of commission's calculation in a CIF contract. If it is not clearly defined in the contract,it usually turns to the invoice.

Calculate the commission on the basis of the invoice value,the formula is as following:

Commission = Price with Commission × Commission Rate

For instance,if the price with commission is USD 100/pc,the commission rate is 3%,then the commission will be USD 3/pc.

Sometimes it occurs that during negotiation one needs to calculate the price including commission from a net price,then the formula will be:

Net Price = Price with Commission − Commission per Unit

= Price with Commission × (1 − Commission Rate)

Price with Commission = Net Price / (1 − Commission Rate)

e.g.:if net price is 100 USD/pc,the commission rate is 3%,then the price with commission will be USD 103.09/pc.

(3)Payment Methods of Commission

As for the payment methods of commission,it is made openly in most cases. It is indicated in the sales contract and normally paid after the transaction is completed. Either when the importer makes payment to the exporter through the middle person it is deducted directly,or after the exporter receives the full payment from the importer it is returned to the middle person from the exporter's account.

2. Discount (Rebate)

(1) Definition

Discount is aimed to motivate the initiatives of the buyer, which is provided by the seller as a concession in the contract. In China, discount is mainly used to take care of old customers or big customers, in order to ensure sales channels or expand foreign sales. In actual use, the seller should flexibly apply all kind of discounts according to different situations and customers.

The differentiation between the commission and the discount: commission are offered by the seller/buyer to the middle person, while discount are concessions provided by the seller.

For the discount, there are some types of discount (rebate) states as below:

Quantity Discount: discount offered if the amount buyers reach certain quantity;

Special Discount: discount offered for frequent client;

Turnover Bonus: bonus offered for client at the end of the year;

Defined discount: defined discount rate in a contract;

Undefined discount: not mentioned in a contract, but mentioned in other agreements.

(2) Defined Methods of Discount

In international trade, discounts usually have the following methods in the contract price clause:

Literally defined: it is usual that the discount rate should be defined literally in a pricing terms. For example, USD 1 000 per Ton CIF Hong Kong including 2% discount.

Defined by determined number: for instance, USD 1 000/mt less discount USD 5.00

(3) Calculation and Payment Methods of Discount

Discount can be calculated on the basis of turnover value or invoice value. The formula as follows:

Discount per unit = Original Price × Discount Rate

Net seller's Revenue = Original Price × (1 − Discount Rate)

e.g.: if original price is USD 50.00/pc CIF NEW YORK, discount rate is 3%, discount offered by the seller to buyer is USD 50.00×3% = USD 1.5, Net revenue of the seller is USD 50.00×(1−3%) = USD 48.50.

The payment method of discount can be offered directly during issuing; sellers remove the discount from the invoice value.

Part B Key Terms

Price 价格
Domestic cost 国内价格
Hard currency 硬币
Soft currency 软币
Overseas freight 国外运费
Insurance premium 保险费
Export exchange cost 出口换汇成本
Profit and loss ratio of export commodities 出口商品盈亏率
Foreign exchange earned through export 出口创汇率
Commission 佣金
Discount 折扣

Part C Exercises

Ⅰ. Answer the following questions

1. What is Export Foreign Exchange Net Income?
2. What is Export Exchange Cost?
3. What is Profit and Loss Ratio of Export Commodities?
4. What is foreign earned through export?

Ⅱ. Case & Analysis

An export company of China made an inquiry of a certain kind of export commodities to a French company. The French company quoted at 400 euro per metric ton on CIF Marseille basis, and the Chinese company internal control price of the commodity was RMB 2 978 Yuan per metric to FOB Shanghai. At that time, the Bank of China exchange rates for each of the purchase price of EUR 100 was RMB 938.12

Yuan, selling price of RMB 942.35 Yuan. The Chinese company has cash, and it can be sold out within the controllable price by the company itself. The goods would be transported from one Chinese port to the port of Hamburg, freight RMB 598 Yuan per metric ton and insurance RMB 102 Yuan per metric ton.

Question: Can the Chinese company accept the offer? Why?

第四章

商品的价格

在国际贸易货物买卖中,买卖双方对价格的讨论是能否达成交易的关键,因此价格条款是买卖合同中最重要的条款之一。价格是获得某种产品及其配套服务的组合所需的金额。正确掌握成交价格,合理采用各种作价方法,订立好相关的价格条款,贯彻国家的对外贸易政策,完成进出口任务和增加对外贸易利益对国家有重要意义。

第一节　成交价格的掌握

1. 作价原则

在国际贸易中,与国内贸易相比,确定进出口商品的成交价格非常复杂,为了做好此项工作,在买卖双方确定商品价格时,必须遵守以下原则:

(1)按照国际市场价格水平作价

国际市场价格是以商品的国际价值为基本,并在激烈的国际市场竞争中形成的,它是交易双方都能接受的价格,也是我们确定进出口商品价格的客观依据。因此,我国对外商品的进出口价格,通常都参照国际市场价格水平来确定。

(2)要结合国别、地区政策作价

为了使外贸配合外交,也为了和其他国家的友好交往,在参照国际市场价格水平的同时,也要适当考虑国别、地区政策,要在平等互利的基础上按照双方约定的比较优惠的价格成交。

(3)要结合购销意图

进出口商品价格在国际市场价格水平的基础上,可根据买卖双方的购销意图来适当调整成交价格,也就是说,进出口价格有时可以略高或略低于国际市场价格。因为国际市场价格受供求关系影响,并不稳定,因此,为了使货物的价格合适,我们应该注意国际市场的起伏,做好预测,避免盲目定价。

2. 影响定价的各种因素

(1)商品的成本

了解产品的成本结构往往是设定价格的第一步。产品从工厂生产完成到运送至进口国目的地的过程将会产生很多费用,比如产品的成本、销售费用、运输费用和金融核算费用等。出口商对成本较精准的核算是商品价格最重要的组成部分。

(2)可预期的利润

可预期利润可以是具体的金额,也可以是占销售额的百分比。在价格核算时,大部分的公司将销售价格的百分之几作为可预计收益。一般来说,产品的国内价格中已经包含了利润,但是如果外销的风险较大,出口商则可增加一部分特别利润。

(3)目标市场容量

定价策略可能适合特定的外国市场。商品出口目标国家的市场容量与一个国家的消费能力、收入水平及供需关系息息相关。定价策略可能适合特定的外国市场。对于平均收入水平比较低的国家,出口时应该降低商品的售价来刺激顾客的需求和消费;而对于高收入国家,出口商可以提供更多高质量的商品并提高售价来获取更多的利益。国际贸易商也应该预测具体的细分潜在客户。如果发展中国家的主要客户属于上层阶级,即使收入水平较低,也可能有更高的价格。除此之外,国外市场的供需关系对出口商也有较大的影响,需求高的商品如耐克鞋,出口商可以制定较高的价格,获取更大的收益;反之,若目标市场需求低,出口商可适当降低价格来刺激消费者购买。

(4)支付条件因素

买卖双方以什么样的支付方式成交将直接影响到商品的价格。出口商将提供有利的价格,鼓励客户接受付款条件,这样导致较少或没有融资压力,风险也很小。

(5)其他因素

除了上述提及的因素将影响到商品成交价格之外,其他的一些因素也会对商品价格产生影响,比如买卖双方选用的贸易术语,商品的质量或商品成交数量的多寡。定价是一项复杂的活动,总是受到许多突发事件的影响。对于出口商来说,要尽可能全面考虑相关因素,核算出比较有竞争力的出口商品的价格。

3. 作价方法

在进行国际贸易对外磋商交易和签订合同时,应采用适当的贸易术语和有利的计价货币来合理确定商品的价格。价格条款中应列明具体的作价办法,必要时订立价格调整条款,还可以灵活运用佣金和折扣,以调动采购商的积极性和扩大销路。

在国际买卖中,可采取下列几种作价办法:

(1)固定价格

买卖双方以约定价格交接货物和收付货款,任何一方无权要求对约定价格进行变更。

(2)暂不固定价格

在价格条款中明确规定定价的时间和作价方法。比如可以规定"在装船前60天按照国际市场价格水平,协商议定正式价格";或只规定作价时间,如"由双方在2017年6月1日商定价格"。

(3)价格部分固定,部分不固定

买卖双方只约定近期交货部分的价格,远期交货部分的价格可以等到交货前再商定。

(4)浮动价格

在规定价格的同时,还规定价格调整条款,比如,"如果卖方对其他客户的成交价高于或低于5%,对本合同的数量,双方协商调整价格"。

4. 计价货币的选择

在国际贸易中,可以有多种方式来选择计价的货币,可以是出口国家的货币,也可以是进口国家的货币或双方同意的第三国货币。由于计价货币的币值变化会直接影响到进出口双方的经济利益,因此买卖双方在确定价格时应注意选择对自己有利的计价货币。从理论上来说,出口时应选用硬币计价,进口时则应选择软币计价。但在实际业务中,以什么货币作为计价货币,还应视双方的交易习惯、经营意图而定。如果为达成交易而不得不采用对我方不利的货币，则可以采用以下两种补救方法：一是根据该种货币今后可能的变动幅度，相应地调整对外报价；二是争取订立保值条款，以避免计价货币汇率变动的风险。

第二节　国际贸易中出口报价计算和成本核算

1. 出口商品价格构成

在国际贸易中，出口商品单价由以下四个部分构成：计价货币、计量单位、单位金额和贸易术语。例如，USD200/piece CIF New York 或 FOB Shanghai EUR 100/set，出口商可以决定贸易术语放在最前面或最后面，但不管放置在哪里，都必须列明贸易术语的出处，如术语来源于《2010 通则》。

（1）三种主要贸易术语 FOB、CFR 和 CIF 的价格构成：

FOB 价=进货成本+国内费用+净利润

CFR 价=进货成本+国内费用+国外运费+净利润

CIF 价=进货成本+国内费用+国外运费+国外保险费+净利润

（2）FOB、CFR 和 CIF 三种贸易术语的换算

若我们掌握 FOB 价格，那么通过以下公式可以换算成 CFR 或 CIF 价格：

CFR 价=FOB 价+国外运费

CIF 价=（FOB 价+国外运费）/[1-（投保加成率×保险费率）]

若我们掌握的是 CIF 价格，那么通过以下公式可以换算成 FOB 价或 CFR 价：

FOB 价=CIF 价×[1-（投保加成率×保险费率）]-国外运费

CFR 价=CIF 价×[1-（投保加成率×保险费率）]

若我们掌握了 CFR 价格，那么我们通过以下公式可以换算成 FOB 价或 CIF 价：

FOB 价=CFR-国外运费

CIF 价=CFR 价/[1-（1+投保加成率×保险费率）]

2. 出口换汇成本

出口换汇成本是指某商品出口净收入一个单位的外汇所需要的人民币成本。一个单位的外汇通常以美元来计算，即某种商品的出口总成本与出口所得

的外汇净收入之比,得出用多少的人民币能够换取1美元。它是用来反映出口商品盈亏的一项重要指标。当出口商品换汇成本低于结汇时银行的外汇牌价,则表示出口有盈利;反之,则说明出口为亏损。计算公式为:

出口换汇成本=出口总成本(人民币)/ 出口外汇净收入(美元)

(1)出口总成本

出口总成本包括进货成本、国内所有费用和出口税,也就是外贸企业为出口商品支付的国内总成本。这是企业以出口总成本为基础计算出来的单位价格,并不涉及任何国外费用。

国内费用包括流通费用、加工整理费用、包装费用、保管费(仓库租金、火险等)、国内运输费用(仓库至码头)、各种证件费用(商检费、公证费、领事签证费、原产地证书费、许可证费用、报关单费及海关费用等)、装船费(贴现利息、集装箱费、起吊费和轮船费)、银行费用(贴现利息、手续费用)、邮电费等。

(2)出口外汇净收入

出口外汇净收入是指出口外汇总收入扣除劳务费用等非贸易外汇(运费、保险费、银行费用)后的收入,实际上,按FOB术语成交的价格就是出口外汇净收入。

出口换汇成本与出口总成本成正比,与出口外汇净收入成反比。与中国银行的外汇牌价相比,出口换汇成本越低,盈利就越多。例如,一笔出口贸易中,计算得出出口换汇成本为6.03,中行外汇牌价为6.25,那么意味着每收入1美元将盈利0.22元人民币。

3. 出口商品盈亏率

出口商品盈亏率是指出口盈亏额与出口总成本的比例,出口盈亏额是指出口销售的人民币净收入与出口总成本的差额。如果差额是正数,则为盈余;如果是负数,则为亏损。它是衡量出口盈亏程度的一项重要指标。计算公式为:

出口商品盈亏率=(出口销售的人民币净收入-出口总成本)/出口总成本×100%

出口销售的人民币净收入=外汇销售收入FOB价×外汇牌价(买入价)

4. 出口创汇率

出口创汇率又称外汇增值率,主要用来衡量加工贸易中进料加工业务经济效益的重要指标,用加工后的成品出口所取得的外汇净收入与进口的原材料所支出的外汇成本的比率来表示。如果原材料是国产的,则原材料的外汇成本可按该原料的 FOB 出口价计算;如果原材料是进口的,则按该原材料的 CIF 进口价计算外汇成本。通过计算这一指标,可以看出用成品出口的创汇情况,也反映出从原材料的进口到加工成成品出口这一整个过程中的增值情况。计算公式如下:

$$出口创汇率(外汇增值率)=\frac{成品出口外汇净收入-原材料外汇成本}{原材料外汇成本}\times 100\%$$

通过对外汇增值率的计算,可看出用成品出口的创汇情况,即出口原料有利还是出口成品有利。

[案例计算]

某外贸公司用 CIF 贸易术语进口布料 100 000 美元,加工成成衣20 000件,每件 USD9 /PC CIF HAMBURG,已知出口运费共计 8 000 美元,保险费共计 2 000美元,求该商品的出口创汇率。

解:出口创汇率=(成品出口外汇净收入- 原料外汇成本)/原料外汇成本×100%

$=(9\times 20\ 000-8\ 000-2\ 000-100\ 000)/100\ 000\times 100\%$

$=70\%$

该笔进料加工业务的出口创汇率或外汇增值率为 70%。

第三节　佣金和折扣

在进出口合同的价格条款中所规定的价格,可分为包含佣金和折扣的价格和不包含这两类因素的价格(称之为净价)。但有时交易者必须对净价进行一些调整才能达到促进销售的目的,这些调整包括佣金和折扣。

1. 佣金

(1)佣金的定义

佣金是指代理人或经纪人为委托人服务而收取的报酬。在货物买卖中,佣金常常表现为交易一方支付给中间商的报酬。例如,出口商支付佣金给销售代理人,或进口商支付佣金给采购代理人。因此,它适用于进出口商与代理人或佣金商签订的合同。有些交易是通过中间商、代理商进行的,这就要向其支付一定的酬金——佣金。凡货价中包含佣金的即为含佣金价。如明确规定佣金的百分比,则为明佣;如不标明百分比,甚至连"佣金"字样也不标示出来,则为暗佣,中间商两头签佣。

合同条款中包含佣金的价格称为"含佣价",通常有以下几种表达方法:

用文字说明:每件商品 50 美元,CIF 纽约,价格中包含 5%的佣金;

用英文字母 C 在术语中表示:每件商品 50 美元,CIF C 5 纽约;

用绝对数表示:每件支付佣金 5 美元。

(2)佣金的计算

在国际贸易中,计算佣金并不复杂,但是佣金是按照哪个贸易术语成交的要在合同中订明,比如说 FOB 价还是 CIF 价。通常来说,以 FOB 价来计算佣金对买卖双方比较有利,因为不需要支付国际运费、保险费等。但是以 FOB 价计算,中间商往往不同意。按照习惯做法,如 CIF 合同就按 CIF 总值作为佣金计算的基数,如果合同中未明确规定,通常按发票金额来计算。

以发票金额为计算佣金的基数,公式如下:

$$\text{佣金额}=\text{含佣价}\times\text{佣金率}$$

例如:某件商品含佣价为 100 美元,佣金率为 3%, 那么这件商品的佣金为 3 美元。

在国际贸易交易过程中,商品价格有时候为净价,那么只要知道佣金率,净价和含佣价之间可以自由转换,公式如下:

$$\text{净价}=\text{含佣价}-\text{单位货物佣金}=\text{含佣价}\times(1-\text{佣金率})$$

$$\text{含佣价}=\text{净价}/(1-\text{佣金率})$$

例:某商品净价为 100 美元,CIF 伦敦,佣金率为 3%,那么含佣价为:100 美元/(1-3%)= 103.09 美元。

(3)佣金的支付方式

对于佣金的支付方式,大多数情况下都有明确规定。一般来说,在销售合同中说明,通常在交易完成后支付。如果进口商通过中间商向出口商付款,中间商会将佣金直接扣除,或者如果出口商收到进口商的付款,则出口商将从收到的货款中把佣金支付给中间商。

2. 折扣

(1)折扣的定义

折扣是指在国际贸易中,为了调动买方的积极性,在合同中订明卖方按原价给买方一定百分比的减让。在我国的对外贸易中,使用折扣主要是为了照顾老客户或大客户，达到确保销售渠道、扩大对外销售等目的。而在实际使用中应该根据不同的情况,针对不同的客户，灵活运用各种折扣。

折扣和前面提及的佣金相似,两者的区别在于佣金是卖方/买方给第三者(中间商)的手续费,折扣则是卖方直接给予买方价格上的减让。

对于折扣,通常有以下几种:

数量折扣:买方达到一定的购买数量时卖方给予的折扣;

特殊折扣:给予购买比较频繁的客户的折扣;

年终折扣:在年底给予的折扣;

明扣:在合同中明确规定折扣率;

暗扣:合同中未提及折扣率,但在其他协议中有具体规定。

(2)折扣的表示方法

在国际贸易中,折扣通常在合同价格条款中有以下几种方法:

价格条款中用文字明确表示:比如,每吨 1 000 美元 CIF 香港,折扣为 2%;

用绝对数表示:比如,每公吨 1 000 美元,折扣 5 美元。

(3)折扣的计算与支付方式

折扣通常是以成交金额或发票金额为基础计算出来的,其计算公式如下:

单位货物折扣额=原价(或打折前的价格)×折扣率

卖方的实际收入=原价×(1-折扣率)

例如:某商品原价为 50.00 美元一件 CIF 纽约,折扣率为 3%,则卖方给买方的折扣为 USD50.00×3% = USD1.50,卖方的净收入为 USD50.00×(1-3%)= USD48.50。

折扣的付款方式可以在发货时直接提供,卖家可以从发票价值中取消折扣。

Chapter 5

International Cargo Transportation

Part A Text

In international trade, the sellers delivers the goods in exchange for the buyer's payment. It is the seller's basic duty to deliver the goods to the buyer or load the goods on the carrier as nominated at the time, place and with the mode of transport specified in the contract after signing it.

In common law, according to the cases over the past years, common law countries regard quality clauses, quantity clauses and time of delivery as the fundamentals of the contract. The consequences could be very serious once the rules are broken. Time of shipment and time of delivery are totally different concepts, but under FOB, CFR and CIF terms, the seller delivers the documents instead of the goods, which means, once the goods are delivered on board the ship or shipping conveyance at the loading port, the seller's duty to deliver goods is accomplished. The date indicated by the carrier on the shipping documents is the time of delivery and the place of shipment is rightly the place of delivery. That is to say, under CIF, FOB and CFR trade terms which indicate symbolic delivery, shipment just means delivery and time of shipment is rightly time of delivery.

Section One Methods of the Delivery

Basically transport is through land, air or water. On land we use trains, trucks, tractors, etc. to carry goods; In air, we find aeroplanes and helicopters to carry goods. Similarly, in water we find ships, steamers, etc. to carry goods. All these are known as various modes of transport. Carriage of goods can also take place by multimodal transport—a combination of the various modes of transport, etc..

1. Ocean Transport

Ocean transport here refers to movement of goods with the help of ships through sea or ocean waterways. It plays an important role in the development of international trade. For centuries, the ship has been the main instrument of commerce and communications between nations. Today, three-fourths of the trade among nations is transported by water. Water has long been considered the most economical form of mass transport.

Ocean transport has many advantages: It is a relatively economical mode of transport for bulky and heavy goods. It is a safe mode of transport with respect to occurrence of accidents. The cost of maintaining and constructing routes is very low as most of them are naturally made. However, ocean transport is slow, vulnerable to bad weather and less punctual if compared with road or air transport.

Depending on the amount of cargo, a number of options are open to the shipper (seller or buyer). If the cargo is insufficient to fill the entire cargo space of a ship, it is normal for the shipper to find a space on a liner service. If the amount of cargo is sufficient to take up a vessel's full carrying capacity, it is commonplace to charter a ship. Thus we are to discuss the two basic types of service in international ocean transportation: liner (berth) service and tramp (charter) service.

Liner Transport

A liner is a vessel with regular sailings and arrivals and sails on a fixed (regular) sailing route and calls at fixed (regular) base ports. It adopts a comparatively fixed timetable and charges at comparatively fixed rates. Liner transport is suitable for goods in small lots and high frequency. Most goods are transported through liner transport in international trade. We called the characteristics of liner transport is fixity, namely fixed routes, fixed ports of call, fixed dates and fixed rates. Responsibility: goods are subject to the loading and unloading by the liners and handling charges are already included in the freight. Liners and the consignor are free from handling charges, demur-rage charges and dispatch money. Liabilities, obligations and exemptions of liners and the shipper are all on the basis of the bill of lading issued by liners. In terms of goods with large transport volume and low value like grains, beans, mines and coals, the price is negotiated by both parties.

- Freight of Liners

Freight is the remuneration payable to the carrier for the carriage of goods. The freight paid for the carriage by a liner differs in the way of calculating from that paid under a charter party.

$Freight = Fb + \sum S$

Fb—Basic freight;

S—Surcharge.

The basic standards for calculating freight are stipulated as follows:

(1) According to gross weight in terms of WEIGHT TON (WT), i.e., weight ton, which is indicated by "W" in the tariff. Heavy cargo is usually charged on this basis. Internationally, besides MT (each equaling 1 000 kilos), British long tons and US short tons are also used nowadays. 1 MT is to be considered as 1 weight ton or one long ton (1 016kg) or one short ton (907.18kg).

(2) According to volume, i.e., measurement ton, which is indicated by "M" in the tariff. It is 40 cubic feet or one cubic meter that constitutes one measurement ton. Often light cargoes are charged on this basis.

(3) According to value of the cargo, i.e., a certain percentage of FOB price which is indicated by "A.V." (Ad Valorem) in the liner freight tariff. Usually a percentage between 1% and 4% is charged the value of such goods as gold, silver, precious stones, and valuable drawings and paintings.

(4) According to gross weight or volume, i.e., choosing the higher rate between the two, which indicated by "W/M" in the tariff.

(5) According to gross weight or volume or A.V., i.e., at the Discretion of the

Carrier, choosing the higher rate of the three, which is indicated by "W/M or A.V.". In this case, it is up to the carrier to decide to charge whichever of the three that produces the highest rate of freight.

(6) According to gross weight or volume, and then plus a certain percentage of A.V., which is indicated by "W/M plus A.V.".

(7) According to the number of the cargo. For example, a freight of so much is for one truck or one head of live animal.

(8) According to the temporary/interim or special agreement entered into between the ship-owner and the consignor.

- Based on different draftsmen, liner freight tariffs can be divided into four kinds:

(1) Shipping Conference Freight Tariff.

(2) Liner's Company Freight Tariff.

(3) Cargo Owner's Freight Tariff.

(4) Freight Tariff of Both Parties.

- The main surcharges are shown as follows:

(1) Heavy lift additional.

(2) Long length surcharge.

(3) Direct additional.

(4) Transshipment surcharge.

(5) Port congestion surcharge.

(6) Port surcharge.

(7) Bunker surcharge or bunker adjustment factor (BAF).

(8) Optional fees.

(9) Alternation of destination surcharge.

(10) Deviation surcharge.

In addition to the above-mentioned surcharges, ice surcharge, cleaning tank surcharge, currency adjustment factor, fumigation surcharge, etc. are something included.

- The way to calculate the freight

First, translate the English name of the commodity, find out the freight standard of calculating or the freight grade.

Second, find out the basic freight rate in the route freight tariff according to the grades and purpose sea route, the relative surcharges for the suitable route and basic port.

Third, the basic freight rate plus various additional surcharges is the freight per freight ton.

Freight per freight ton = the basic freight rate + rate of surcharge

Total freight amount = the freight ton of the goods × freight per freight ton

Shipping by Charter

Charter transport refers to a cargo ship not operating on regular routes and schedules. A ship may be hired wholly or just some shipping space for transportation. Contrary to a liner, a charter vessel does not follow a fixed route, freight rate or timetable and has no fixed ports of call. Charter vessels fall into three types: voyage charter, time charter and bare boat charter. This chapter focuses on voyage charter here because of its high relativity with export enterprises.

(1) Voyage Charter

Voyage charter is also named irregular charter, dividing into one-way charter, round-way charter and consecutive voyage charter according to the way of financing leasing. A voyage charter is the hire of a ship for the carriage of goods from one specified port to another, or for a round trip and is characterized by shipping low-value and bulk commodities like grains, coals, wood, and mines.

The freight calculation has two methods. By rate of freight, the total freight is determined by unit weight or size. By lump sum freight, the total freight is based on the entire ship.

Stipulations of loading and unloading cost. Loading and unloading costs are stipulated in the contract after negotiation and five methods are usually used to divide the expenses of loading and unloading:

- liner terms/gross terms/berth terms

The ship-owner bears loading and unloading cost.

- free in and out (FIO)

The ship-owner does not bear loading and unloading cost.

- free in (FI)

The ship-owner is only responsible for unloading cost.

- free out (FO)

The ship-owner is only responsible for loading cost.

- free in and out, stowed and trimmed (FIOST)

The ship-owner does not bear loading and unloading cost, not even bear the expenses of stowing and trimming.

In voyage charter transport, the lay time is directly related to the operating cycles and benefits of the ship-owner, so lay time should be stipulated in detail when both parties comes into a contract. If the charterer fails to finish loading the goods within the limited time resulting in extended staying time and trip time; it would increase expenses as well as decrease cycling rates for the ship-owner. So lay time stipulations are closely related to the benefits of both parties.

(2) Time Charter

The charterer charters the ship for a period of time during which the ship is deployed and managed by the charterer. What concerns the charterer most is the period, not the voyage. The chartering may be for a period of 1 year or of several years.

During the period of chartering, the ship is managed, deployed and used by the charterer. A series of work, such as loading, unloading, stowing and trimming and the so caused fuel expenses, port expenses, loading and unloading expenses, etc., should be borne by the charterer. The ship-owner should bear the wages and board expenses of the crew, and be responsible for seaworthiness during the period of chartering and the so-caused expenses and the vessel insurance premium.

(3) Demise Charter

Demise charter, is also called bare-boat charter, the charterer takes a lease of the entire ship for an agreed time. So demise charter belongs to time charter, but there are some differences: as to time charter, during the period of chartering, the shipowner provides the charterer with a crew, while as to bare-boat charter, the shipowner only provides the charterer with a bare-boat, the charterer employ the crew and pay the crew's wages and provisions, ship's maintenance and stores etc. by himself, apart from those expenses he is responsible for under the time charter.

2. Railway Transport

Railway transport is capable of attaining relatively high speeds with large quantities and is safe, at low cost, punctual, rather economical and less influence by weather. Railway transport falls into three kinds:

(1) Railway transport at home.

(2) International railway transport between two countries.

(3) International railway the rough transport.

According to the stipulations of the International Union of Railways, the International Railway Cargo Through Transport Agreement and the International Convention Concerning the Carriage of goods by Rail, the goods belonging to the export country may be transported directly to the place of destination as long as the carrier issues a railway bill of lading at the place of dispatch.

The main transport documents are the railway bill and its duplicate. The railway bill is the transportation contract and binding upon the consignee, the consignor and the railway department. The railway bill together with the goods is transported from the place of dispatch to the place of destination and then is delivered to the consignee after he has paid off the freight and other charges. The consignor may make exchange settlement with the bank against the duplicate of railway bill.

3. Air Transport

The advantages of air transport are high speed and quick transit, low risk of damage and pilferage with very competitive insurance, saving in packing cost, reducing amount of capital tied up in transit and so on; while the chief disadvantage is the limited capacity of air freight and over all dimensions of acceptable cargo together with weight restrictions. It is also subject to the influence of weather. However, it is suitable for those goods that are of time pressing, small quantity of cargoes but urgent need, light but precious. The air transport can be divided into the following kinds: scheduled air liner, charted carrier, consolidation, air express.

The airway bill, also called air consignment note, is a document or consignment note used for the carriage of goods by air supplied by the carrier to the consignor. An airway bill has the following features:

(1) It is a transport contract signed between the consignor/shipper and the carrier/airline.

(2) It is a receipt from the airline acknowledging the receipt of the consignment from the shipper.

(3) The airway bill is an internationally standardized document mostly printed in English and in the official language of the country of departure, which facilitates the on-carriage of goods going through 2 to 3 airlines in different countries to the final destination. Generally, there are usually 12 copies of each airway bill for distribution to the various parties, such as the shipper, consignee, issuing carrier, second carrier (if applicable), third carrier (if applicable), airport of destination, airport of departure, and extra copies for other purposes (if required). Copies 1, 2 and 3 are the originals.

The No.1 original airway bill is retained by the airline for filing and accounting purposes—for the carrier. This is signed by the consignor.

The No.2 original airway bill is to be carried with the consignment and delivered to the consignee at the destination—for the consignee. This is signed by the carrier, as well as the consignor, and is sent with the goods to the consignee.

The No.3 original airway bill is for the shipper, who may present it to the negotiating bank as a shipping document evidencing shipment having been made—for the consignor. This is signed by the carrier and sent back to the consignor.

4. Container Transport

With the expansion of international trade, the container service has become more and more popular. The use of container provides a highly efficient form for transport by ship, by road, by rail and by air, though its fullest benefits are felt in shipping, where costs may be reduced by as much as one half. Therefore, nowadays, it has become a very convenient and modern transport method in international practice. Containers are constructed of metal and of standard lengths, mostly ranging from ten to forty feet. The Intentional Standard Organization has made 3 series, 13 classes standard specifications from 1A to 3A, among which the mostly used is Type 1A (8 inches ×8 inches×40 inches), Type 1C (8 inches×8 inches×20 inches), and Type 1AA (8 inches×8.6 inches×40 inches).

Container transport falls into two kinds (methods of consignment): full container load (FCL) and less than container load (LCL). As for the consignment that reaches the demand of FCL, the vanning FCL is done either by the consignor himself or the carrier at the production side or the warehouse. Then it is sent to the container yard

(CY) for consolidation by the carrier. As for the consignment that does not reach the demand of a full container, we call it less than container, the vanning LCL is done by the consignor himself and then send the consignment to the container freight station (CFS) or inland container depot for consolidation by the carrier, who will piece together the goods according to the nature, destination, weight and so on in the container and then send it to the container yard.

5. International Combined Transport

International combined transport means the conveyance of cargo includes at least two modes of transport by which the goods are carried from the place of dispatch to destination on the basis of combined transport or a multimodal transport contract. Under this method, the container is used as an inter-medium which makes up of an international multimodal transport mode by sea, air and land.

It usually includes:

(1) Train-Air (or Truck-Air, or Ship-Air). The export goods are carried to Hong Kong by train or truck or ship and then loaded into airplanes at Hong Kong.

(2) Train-Ship. The export goods from Chinese interior provinces may also be transported to Hong Kong by railway for a transshipment to foreign ports by vessels.

(3) Container Transport/Containerized Traffic.

6. Land Bridge Transport

Land bridge transport is a mode of transport that connects the ocean transport on the two sides of the land by the railway and land which runs across the continent, i.e.. ship-train-ship. Land bridge transport use the container as a medium, so it has all advantages of container transport. There are three main land bridges in the world: American land bridge; Siberian land bridge; The New European-Asia land bridge.

7. Postal Transport

According to international trade practice, the seller fulfills the duty of delivery only if he delivers the parcel to the post office, pays off the postage, and gets the receipt. The post office is responsible for the delivery of the goods to the destination, and the consignee goes to the office for picking up his goods. Postal transport falls into two kinds regular mail and air mail.

This method is simple and convenient, and delivery is made simply when a receipt of the goods posted is obtained. It is a kind of international and "door-to-door" transport. According to the postal regulations of the world, the longest length of each parcel limits to one meter, and the weight under 20 kilograms. The restriction of the size and weight on the parcels limits the practicality of this mode, it is only suitable for exactitude instruments, machinery components, bullion ornaments, material medical and other small sized and precious goods.

8. Pipelines Transport

Pipelines transport is used for transporting commodities, such as crude oil and gases etc., long distances over land and under the sea. Rising fuel costs make pipelines an attractive economic alternative to other forms of transport in certain circumstances. Safety in transferring flammable commodities is another important consideration.

Section Two Shipping Documents

International trade attaches so great importance to shipping documents that, to a certain degree, it can be called trade of document, or "symbol of trade". This is because shipping documents represent the title to the goods. For example, under letter of credit, the buyer cannot take the delivery of the goods until he obtains the shipping documents; on the other hand, only if the seller releases the shipping documents can he receive the payment. What documents to be used and how to carefully and accurately complete them deserve our adequate attention. As a rule, every contract of sale stipulates the kinds of shipping documents required. Any slightest negligence in these documents might result in serious problems, which is not in frequent in practice. It is, therefore, imperative for both an exporter and an importer to abide by such stipulations. Generally, commercial invoice, bill of lading, insurance policy or certificate, packing list, and weight memo, etc., are called shipping documents. In addition, other documents required by the buyers and related to the matter of duty to be paid on the imported goods, sometimes, are also included in shipping documents. They are the proforma, consular invoice, certificate of origin, certificate of value, certificate of inspection. The commercial invoice, bill of lading and insurance policy constitute the chief shipping documents in international trade. They are in dispensable in almost every instance of export and import consignment. This unit mainly deals with bill of lading.

A bill of lading is a transportation document issued by an ocean carrier to a shipper with whom the carrier has entered into a contract for the carriage of goods. The bill of lading plays a vital role in international trade.

Three functions performed by the B/L: The B/L performed as a receipt for the goods, evidence of the contract of carriage and document of title to the goods.

(1) Receipt for the goods

The bill of lading acts as a receipt for the goods received. A bill of lading describes the goods put on board a vessel, stating the quantity, and their condition. The form itself is normally filled out in advance by the shipper, then, as the goods are loaded aboard the ship. The carrier will check to see that the goods loaded comply with the goods listed. The carrier, however, is responsible only to check for outward compliance—that is, that the labels comply and that the packages are not damaged. If all appear proper, the appropriate agent of the carrier will sign the bill and return it to the shipper.

(2) Evidence of the contract of carriage

The B/L is an evidence of the contract of carriage between the shipper and the carrier. The bill becomes conclusive evidence of the terms of the contract of carriage once it is negotiated to a good faith third party.

(3) Document of title to the goods

The named consignee or the holder of a bill of lading, provided he has received it in good faith through due negotiation, has a claim to title and, by surrendering the bill, to delivery of the goods. The carrier is under obligation to deliver the cargo only against an original bill of lading. If the carrier delivers goods without the production of a bill of lading, he will be liable in contract or in tort to the bill of lading holder.

Since possession of the bill of lading is regarded as good as possessing the goods, the buyer can sell the goods on while they are at sea to a third party by simply endorsing the bill of lading and delivering it to the third party. The third party, by becoming the holder, can demand delivery of the goods on arrival. Furthermore, as a document of title, the bill of lading also serves a vital function in providing for security, for example, in letter of credit transaction. It is this function of bill of lading as a document of title that makes the bill of lading a very important document in maritime trade.

But not all bills of lading are transferable. To impart transfer-ability to a bill of lading, it must be drafted as an order bill—that is, where the carrier is to deliver the goods to a named consignee or his order or assigns. It must be noted that bills of lading made out to named consignees, known as straight bills of lading, are not transferable.

There are a number of different types of bill of lading. The following lists those encountered the most often. The follow B/L is a combined transport B/L.

<table>
<tr><td colspan="2">Shipper
B/L NO. SHANGHAI CHEMICALS IMPORT AND EXPORT CORPORATION
16 JIANGYAN ROAD, SHANGHAI</td><td rowspan="3">B/L NO.
PACIFIC INTERNATION LINES (PTE) LTD
(Incorporated in Singapore)
COMBINED TRANSPORT BILL OF LADING
Received in apparent good order and condition except as otherwise noted the total number of container or other packages or units enumerated below for transportation from the place of receipt to the place of delivery subject to the terms hereof. One of the signed Bills of Lading must be surrendered duly endorsed in exchange for the Goods or delivery order. On presentation of this document (duly) Endorsed to the Carrier by or on behalf of the Holder, the rights and liabilities arising in accordance with the terms hereof shall (without prejudice to any rule of common law or statute rendering them binding on the Merchant) become binding in all respects between the Carrier and the Holder as though the contract evidenced hereby had been made between them.
SEE TERMS ON ORIGINAL B/L</td></tr>
<tr><td colspan="2">Consignee
TO ORDER OF COMMERCIAL BANK OF ETHIOPIA</td></tr>
<tr><td colspan="2">Notify Party
MAGIC INTERNATIONAL PLC
DEBRE ZEIT ROAD,
ADDIS ABABA ETHIOPIA</td></tr>
<tr><td>Vessel and Voyage Number
GUANG HANG V.312</td><td>Port of Loading
SHANGHAI</td><td>Port of Discharge
ASSAB</td></tr>
<tr><td>Place of Receipt</td><td>Place of Delivery</td><td>Number of Original Bs/L
THREE</td></tr>
</table>

<table>
<tr><th colspan="5">PARTICULARS AS DECLARED BY SHIPPER - CARRIER NOT RESPONSIBLE</th></tr>
<tr><td>Container Nos/Seal Nos.
Marks and/Numbers</td><td colspan="2">No. of Container/Packages/Description of Goods</td><td>Gross Weight
(Kilos)</td><td>Measurement
(cu-metres)</td></tr>
<tr><td>MAGIC INT'L PLC
P.O.BOX 147140
ADDIS ABABA
ETHIOPIA
VIA ASSAB</td><td>75PACKAGES</td><td>TRANSMISSION BELT

ON BOARD
AT SHANGHAI
ON GUANGHANG V.312
MARCH 19.2009</td><td>8820KGS</td><td>20CBM</td></tr>
<tr><td colspan="2" rowspan="4">FREIGHT & CHARGES
FREIGHT PREPAID
FREIGHT CHARGE:USD6574.00</td><td colspan="3">Number of Containers/Packages (in words)
SEVENTY FIVE PACKAGES ONLY</td></tr>
<tr><td colspan="3">Shipped on Board Date:
2009-3-19</td></tr>
<tr><td colspan="3">Place and Date of Issue:
SHANGHAI, MARCH 19, 2009</td></tr>
<tr><td colspan="3">In Witness Whereof this number of Original Bills of Lading stated Above all of the tenor and date one of which being accomplished the others to stand void.

for PACIFIC INTERNATIONAL LINES (PTE) LTD as Carrier</td></tr>
</table>

Fig. 5-1 Combined Transport B/L

1. Shipped(on board) B/L and Received for Shipment B/L

Shipped B/L is issued by the shipping company after the goods are actually shipped on board the designated vessel. Both the name of the vessel and the date of issue of the B/L are indicated on the shipped B/L. Since shipped bill of lading provides better guarantee for the consignee to receive the cargo at the destination, the importer normally requires the exporter to produce shipped B/L and most bill of lading forms are pre-printed as "Shipped Bill".

Received for shipment B/L arises where the word "shipped" does not appear on the bill of lading. It merely acknowledges that the goods have been received by the carrier for shipment. Therefore, the goods could be in the dock or warehouse.

2. Clean B/L and Unclean B/L

A clean B/L is a B/L that is free from any adverse remarks, made by the shipping company about the condition, packing, or quantity of the goods being shipped. Usually the words "apparent good order and condition", "clean on board" or the like are indicated on the B/L. A clean bill of lading provides proof that up until the time goods were transferred to the carrier, no damage has occurred. This assists in placing responsibility if in fact goods are eventually delivered in other than undamaged condition.

Unclean B/L also called foul B/L or claused B/L, is a B/L with adverse remarks or notations (called "clauses") by the carrier that the goods received for shipping (or their packing) look wet, damaged, or otherwise in doubtful condition, or not of correct quantity. Importers and their banks normally do not accept foul B/L for payment under a letter of credit.

3. Straight B/L, Blank B/L and Order B/L

Straight bill of lading has designated consignee. Under this bill, only the consignee at the destination is entitled to take delivery of the cargo. As it is not transferable, it is not commonly used in international trade and normally applies to high value shipments or goods for special purposes.

Blank B/L also called Open B/L or Bearer B/L, means that there is no definite consignee of the goods. Words like "To bearer" usually appear in the field of consignee. Anyone who holds the bill is entitled to the goods the bill represents. No endorsement is needed for the transfer of the blank bill. Due to the exceedingly high risk involved, this bill is rarely used.

Order B/L is widely used in international trade. It means that the goods are consigned or destined to the order of a named person. In the field of consignee, "To order", "To order of the shipper", or "To order of the consignee" is marked. This type of bill of lading is a negotiable instrument. That is, it may be used to transfer title to goods being shipped to another party. The transfer may occur at any time during the transit process simply by conveying the order bill to another party. Unless provided otherwise, a consignment that is "to order" means to order of the shipper.

Order B/L can be transferred only after endorsement is made. Endorsement here means a signature used to legally transfer the B/L. There are two types of endorsement: blank endorsement and special endorsement. The blank endorsement is an open endorsement that carries only the signature of the endorser and does not specify in whose favor it is made. In such instance, whoever bears the B/L after endorsement holds the title to the goods. Special endorsement names the endorser and requires its endorsement for further negotiation. If the B/L is made out "To order of the consignee", the consignee will endorse the bill to transfer it.

4. Direct B/L, Transshipment B/L and Through B/L

Direct B/L means the B/L that indicates the goods are shipped from the port of loading direct to the port of destination without involving transshipment.

Transshipment B/L means the B/L that indicates the goods need to be transshipped at an intermediate port as there is no direct service between the shipment port and the destination port.

Through B/L is usually issued for containerized door-to-door shipments that have to use different ships and/or different means of transportation (aircraft, rail, cars, ships, tucks, etc.) from origin to destination. Unlike in case of a multimodal bill of lading, the principal carrier or the freight-forwarder (who issued the through B/L) is liable under a contract of carriage only for its own phase of the journey, and acts as an agent for the carriers executing the other phases.

5. Liner B/L, Charter-party B/L and Container B/L

Liner B/L is issued by a liner company for shipment on scheduled port calls through scheduled routes.

Charter-party B/L is issued by the carrier (or its agent) based on the charter-party. This bill of lading is subject to the clauses of charter-party. That's why when a charter-party B/L is accepted by the bank or the buyer, the copy charter-party is required.

Container B/L is issued when the goods are conveyed by container.

6. Long form B/L and Short form B/L

Long form B/L is more detailed with the terms and conditions of carriage which are printed on the back of the page. The long form bill of lading is commonly used in international shipping.

Short form B/L (or blank back B/L) is an abbreviated type of document. The terms and conditions of carriage on the reverse (back) of the bill of lading are omitted; instead they are listed on a document other than the B/L. Unless otherwise stipulated in the letter of credit (L/C), a short form B/L saves the cost of printing (i.e., no printing on the back of the B/L) and if the terms and conditions of carriage change, there is no need to reprint the B/L form.

7. Miscellaneous B/L

On deck B/L: A B/L contains the notation that the goods have been loaded on the deck of the vessel. It applies to goods like livestock, plants, dangerous cargo, or awkwardly shaped goods that cannot fit into the ship's hold. On deck transit is more dangerous than if cargo is carried in the hold of a ship. Insurance and financing for such transit may be more difficult to obtain or may be more costly.

Stale B/L: A B/L presented to the consignee or buyer or its bank after the stipulated expiry date of presentation or after the goods are due at the port of destination are described as a "Stale B/L". It is important that the Bill of Lading is available at the port of destination before the goods arrive or, failing this, at the same time. Otherwise, the buyer cannot collect the goods. The late arrival of this important document may have undesirable consequences such as warehouse rent, etc., therefore should be avoided. Sometimes especially in the case of short sea voyages, it is necessary to add a clause of "Stale B/L is acceptable".

Ante-dated B/L: This is a B/L which is dated before the date on which it is issued. When the actual shipment date is later than that stipulated in the L/C, the carrier sometimes, at the shipper's request, issues a B/L with a date of signature that suits the requirement so as to avoid non-acceptance by the bank. Due to the risk of the goods being rejected by the buyer arising from the issuance of such a bill, it is advisable to avoid this malpractice even when it seems necessary in certain circumstances.

Advanced B/L is the B/L issued in advance when the expiry date of the L/C is due but the shipment has not yet been effected. The purpose of issuing such a bill is to negotiate payment with the bank in time within the validity of the L/C. The issuance of advanced B/L is also a malpractice and should be avoided.

All the above mentioned bills are not independent of each other. Some types may be combined into one like "Clean on board, to order, blank endorsed B/L". A receipt for shipment bill may also be a straight and clean bill. B/L are made out in sets, consisting of a number of originals (usually three) and a number of copies and marked "original" and "copy" respectively. Only the originals signed by the carrier enable the consignee to take delivery of the goods. The copies are just for reference.

Section Three Delivery Conditions

Delivery conditions include the time of delivery, and in several cases including the time of loading and unloading, and the charges resulting from loading and unloading operations, the port of shipment, the port of destination, partial shipments and transshipments, shipping documents, etc..

1. Time of Delivery

The time of delivery refers to the time limit during which the seller shall deliver the goods to the buyer at the agreed place by the agreed methods. There are the following ways to stipulate the time of delivery in the contract.

(1) Stipulate the define time of delivery, for example:

Shipment on or before July 16th, 2017.

(2) Stipulate a period of fixed time, the seller can arrange shipment during whichever date, such as:

Shipment during March 2017.

Shipment during January/February/March 2017.

Shipment by first available vessel.

Shipment by first opportunity.

Shipment subject to shipping space available.

July shipment—the exporter is required to make delivery to a designated ship during the month of July, that is, on any day from July 1 to July 31, and secure from the steamship company a B/L dated in July.

(3) Stipulate shipment within×××days after receipt of the letter of credit, for ex-

ample:

Shipment within 30 days after receipt of L/C.

Shipment within 3 months after receipt of L/C.

(4) Stipulate the goods shall be shipped in the near future, for example:

Immediate shipment.

Shipment as soon as possible.

Prompt shipment.

But there are not unanimous explanations about these terms in the international made. And thus, it is quite easy to result in disputes, so we should try to avoid using them.

2. Port of Shipment and Port of Destination

- The points that we should pay attention to when stipulating the port of shipment in an export contract.

(1) The port of shipment shall be close to the origin of the goods.

(2) We should take into consideration the loading and unloading, and specific transportation conditions and the standards of freight and various charges at home and abroad.

(3) Add the name of export country behind the name of port.

(4) In export trade, it is the usual practice to designate only one port of shipment in one transaction, but exceptionally, when large amounts of goods are involved and, in particular, the goods are stored at different places, two or more ports of shipments are also specified, such as "Shanghai and Tianjin", "Dalian/Guangzhou/Shanghai". Sometimes, as the port of shipment is not yet determined at the time the transaction is being concluded, a general clause like "China ports" may be used.

- The port of destination is usually proposed and determined by the buyer, which shall be convenient for reselling the goods and shall be the one at which the vessel may safely arrive and be always of load. When we determine the port of destination, we must pay attention to the following points:

(1) We should not accept the port in the country with which our government does not permit to do business.

(2) The stipulation on the port of destination shall be definite and specific. We

should not use ambiguous terms, such as "main ports in Europe" or "main ports in Asia".

(3) If we have to choose a port which has no direct liner to stop by or the trips are few, we should stipulate "transshipment to be permitted" in the contract.

(4) The port of destination shall be the one at which the vessel may safely arrive and be always afloat.

(5) As to the business with an inland country, we usually choose a port which is nearest to the country. We usually do not accept an inland city as the place of destination unless through combined transportation for which the combined transport operator will be responsible.

(6) Facilities in the port of loading or unloading are also very important and therefore reasonable attention should be given to issues such as loading and unloading facilities, freightage and additional freightage, etc.. The ports of shipment should be, in principle, ports that are close to the source of goods, while port of destination should be ports that are near the users.

(7) In case the middle man abroad has not found a proper buyer when the contract is concluded, in order to make it convenient for him to sell the cargo afloat, the "optional port" may be accepted upon request of the foreign party, the buyer is allowed to choose one from the several ports of destination provided.

(8) Pay attention to the names of foreign ports. Many ports have the same names. For example, there are as many as eight or nine ports called "Victoria" in this world. Please add the name of import country behind the name of port.

3. Partial Shipments

In case of an export business covering a large amount of goods, it is necessary to make shipments lots by several carriers sailing on different dates.

Reasons for partial shipment: It is done because of the limitation of shipping space available, poor unloading facilities at the port of destination, dull market season, or possible delay in the process of manufacturing of the goods, etc.

Notes:

(1) Generally speaking, partial shipments are favorable to the seller, which shall put the seller in a better position to the relevant contract. According to the relevant

stipulations of the UCP600 unless the credit stipulates otherwise, partial shipments are allowed. But contractual laws in some country stipulates that: Partial shipments and transshipment, if not stipulated in the contract, shall not be deemed to be allowed. It, therefore, should be clearly stipulated in the relevant contract.

(2) According to the relevant of the UCP600 (Uniform Customs and Practice for Documentary Credits), transport documents which appear on their face to indicate that shipment has been made on the same means of conveyance and for the same journey, provided they indicate the same destination, will not be regarded as covering partial shipments, even if the transport documents indicate different dates of issuance and/or different ports of shipments, places of taking in charge, or dispatch. If transshipment is necessary in case of no director suitable ship available for shipment, clause in these regard can be included in the contract.

(3) In case where such kind of clause as "partial shipments are allowed" is stipulated in the contract (such as, shipment during March and April in two equal monthly lots), then, the seller should strictly follow the stipulations of the contract. According to the relevant stipulations of the UCP600, if any installment is not shipped within the period allowed for that installment, the credit ease to be available for that and any subsequent installments, unless otherwise stipulated in the credit.

4. Transshipment

Transshipment in ocean shipping, is the movement of goods in transit from one carrier to another at the ports of transshipment before the goods reach the port of destination. Reasons for transshipment: Transshipment is necessary when ships sailing direct to the port of destination are not available, the port of destination does not tie along the sailing route of the liner, or the amount of cargo for a certain port of destination is so small that no ships would like to call at that port.

If transshipment is necessary in case of no director suitable ship available for shipment, clause in these regard can be included in the contract. According to the relevant stipulations of the UCP600, unless the credit stipulates, otherwise partial shipments and transshipment are allowed.

5. Shipping Advice

The usual practice of international trade under an FOB term is for the seller, if having got ready for shipment, to send a notice to the buyer before the agreed shipment date (usually 30-45 days before the shipment date) so that the buyer can arrange the relevant vessel for taking the delivery. The buyer, after receiving the relevant notice from the seller, should at the agreed time, notify the seller of the name of the vessel and the estimated arrival date of the vessel. And the seller, after the goods are placed on board the vessel, should at the agreed time, notify the buyer of the contract number, the name and weight of the goods, the invoice amount, the vessel's name and the date of shipment so that the buyer can make necessary arrangements for purchasing the relevant insurance and taking delivery of the goods. As following document is a shipping advice:

NANJING FORGIGN TRADE IMP. AND EXP. CORP.

SHIPPING ADVICE

FAX	56489542	**INVOICE NO.**	JS09256
TEL	56489545	**L/C NO.**	H2108
		S/C NO.	ST355

MESSRS:
EAST AGENT COMPANY
126 ROOM STREET, ANTERWEIP, BELGIUM

DEAR SIRS:

WE HEREBY INFORM YOU THAT THE GOODS UNDER THE ABOVE MENTIONED CREDIT HAVE BEEN SHIPPED. THE DETAILS OF THE SHIPMENT ARE STATED BELOW.

SHIPPING MARKS:	**COMMODITY :**	LADIES LYCRA LONG PANT
CBD	**TOTAL G.W.:**	2000KGS
LONDON	**OCEAN VESSEL:**	DAFENG E002
NOS1-200	**DATE OF DEPARTURE:**	OCT 20, 2009
	B/L NO.:	HJSHB142323
	PORT OF LOADING:	NANJING
	DESTINATION:	LONDON

Fig. 5-2 Shipping Advice

Part B Key Terms

Containerization 集装箱化

Full Container Load (FCL) 整箱货

Less than Container Load (LCL) 拼箱货

Container Yard (CY) 集装箱堆场

Container Freight Station (CFS) 集装箱货运站

Marine transportation 海洋运输

Liner terms 班轮条件

Charter transportation 租船运输

Clean B/L 清洁提单

Order B/L 指示提单

Stale B/L 过期提单

Freight ton(F/T) 运费吨

Time of shipment 装运期

Time of delivery 交货期

Optional port 选择港

Partial shipment 分批装运

Transshipment 转运

Lay time 装卸时间

Demurrage 滞期费

Dispatch 速遣费

Part C Exercises

Ⅰ. Review and Discussion Questions

1. What are the major types of transportation in international cargo transport?
2. What are the characteristic of liner transport?
3. What are the differences between voyage charter and time charter?
4. What are the main functions of B/L?
5. What should be considered when choosing port of shipment and port of desti-

nation?

6. Why can the advice of shipment coordinate the responsibilities of the exporter and the porter?

7. What are the main responsibilities of multimodal transport operator?

8. What main points are included in the clause of shipment?

Ⅱ. Calculation

There is one consignment of 10 cartons of leather shoes. Measurement of each carton is 50cm×50cm×50cm, and gross weight of each is 15kg. Freight basis is W/M and the quotation is USD100 per F/T. How much is the total freight?

Ⅲ. Case & Study

In 2008, a Human Provincial Foreign Trade Corporation and an American Greens Corp. signed an export contract of "Xi Mas" lights goods. During May and June, with the letter of credit settlement, the company exported two shipments. The settlement was done smoothly after the bank negotiation. In October, they successively exported 7 consignments, taking into account the previous settlement was in good condition, they chose D/P as collection method for settlement, totaling about USD 270 000. Although the collecting bank repeatedly urged the foreign businessman, the American buyer did not pay to redeem bills. In March, 2009, the company learnt that the goods had been picked up by the client with a copy of the bill of lading, then they demanded the bank to return the documents. In April, the company got the original bill of lading and with it to negotiate with the shipping company American Brothers Ltd., but the company was rejected on the grounds that the bill of lading was a straight bill of lading, in accordance with local practice, the consignee may pick up the goods without the original bill of lading. At this point, the company suffered huge economic losses by losing both the goods and payment.

Questions:

1. What is straight bill of lading?

2. What can be learnt from this case?

第五章

国际货物运输

在国际贸易中，卖方交付货物与买方支付货款是对等条件。买卖合同签订后，按照合同规定的时间、地点和方式将货物运至买方指定的承运工具上，是卖方所承担的基本义务。

在英美法中，根据历年的例子，英美法国家把品质条款、数量条款、交货期作为合同的要件条款。如果违反了要件条款，后果则十分严重。装运期和交货期是两个不同的概念，但是在 FOB、CFR、CIF 条件下，卖方以交单代替了交货，也就是说，只要把货交到装运港的船上或运输工具上，卖方的交货义务就算完成。承运人在运输单据上所注明的日期即作为交货日期，货物的装运地点即作为交货地点。也就是说，在 CIF、FOB、CFR 象征性交货的贸易术语下，"装运"就意味着交货，成为同一个概念，交货期等于装运期。

第一节　运输方式

运输一般都可以通过陆运、空运和水运完成。陆运可以使用火车、卡车、拖拉机等工具运输货物；空运可以使用飞机或直升机运输货物。类似地，水上可以使用轮船和汽船等来运输货物。这些是人们所熟知的运输方式。货物也可以通过多式联运，即各种不同的运输方式的组合进行运输。

1. 海洋运输

这里的海洋运输，是指货物借助船舶通过海洋，利用水运进行移动的方式。

海洋运输在国际贸易发展中发挥了重要作用。几个世纪以来,船舶一直是国家间商业及沟通的主要方式。今天,四分之三的国家间贸易通过水运完成。水运长久以来被认为是大批量货物运输的最经济的方式。

海洋运输有许多优势:对于庞大且笨重的货物,这是相对经济的运输方式。就事故发生率而言,这又是一种安全的运输方式。由于航线是自然形成的,因此,维护与建设成本很低。但是,与陆上运输或航空运输相比,海洋运输速度慢,易受恶劣天气影响,也不够准时。

根据货物量的大小,有多种方式供托运人(卖方或买方)选择。如果货物量不足以装满船舶的全部舱位,托运人一般会找一个班轮舱位。如果货物量足以装满船舶的全部舱位,托运人就会租用整船。因此,我们来讨论两种基本的国际海洋运输服务方式:班轮运输和租船运输。

班轮运输

班轮运输又称定期程租船,简称班轮,指船舶按照预定的航行时间表,在固定的航线和港口往返航行,从事客货运输业务并按事先公布的费率收取运费。班轮运输适合批量小、次数多的商品。国际贸易中大部分的货物还是采用班轮运输。班轮运输的特点有"四固定",即固定的航线、固定的停靠港、固定的船期和固定的运费率。责任:货物由班轮公司负责配载和装卸,装卸费已包含在运费内,班轮公司和托运人双方不计装卸费、滞期费和速遣费。班轮公司和货主双方的权利、义务和责任豁免均以班轮公司签发的提单条款为依据。对某些运量大、货价低的货物,如粮食、豆类、矿石、煤炭,由船货双方协商定价。

- 班轮运费

运费是指因运输货物而付给承运人的报酬。付给班轮运输费用与付给不定期船的费用是不一样的。

$$班轮运费 = Fb + \sum S$$

式中,Fb——基本运费;

S——附加运费。

计重标准如下:

(1)按货物毛重计收,即以重量吨为计算单位计收运费,在运价表内用"W"表示。笨重的货物一般都采用这种方法。此外,国际上现在还有用长吨(英制)和短吨(美制),一重量吨为一公吨(1 000 千克)或一长吨(1 016 千克)或一短吨(907.18 千克)。

(2)按货物体积或尺码吨计收,在运价表内用"M"表示,一尺码吨为 1 立方米或40立方英尺。通常轻型货物用这种方法。

(3)按商品的价格计收,如按FOB价的一定百分比计收,称从价运费,用"A.V."或"Ad-Val"表示。此项计算标准适用于贵重或高价商品,如金、银、宝石和贵重的古董画作等,百分比一般为1%~4%。

(4)按货物的毛重或体积,由船公司选择其中收费高的一种计收运费,在运价中用"W/M"表示。

(5)选择货物的毛重、体积或价值三者中较高的一种计收运费,在运价中用"W/M or A.V."表示。在此方式中,由承运人从三者中选择较高的那一种计收运费。

(6)按货物的毛重或体积,再加上货物价值的一定百分比,在运价中用"W/M plus A.V."表示。

(7)按货物的件数计收。如卡车按每辆(Per Unit)、活牲畜按每头(Per Head)计收。

(8)按船主与托运人之间临时签订的协议计收运费。

- 基于不同的起草人,班轮运费可以分为以下四种类型:

(1)航运公司运价表。

(2)班轮公司运价表。

(3)货方运价表。

(4)双方运价表。

- 主要特殊附加费如下:

(1)超重附加费;

(2)超长附加费;

(3)直航附加费;

(4)转船附加费;

(5)港口拥挤费;

(6)港口附加费;

(7)燃料附加费;

(8)选港费;

(9)变更港口附加费;

(10)绕航附加费。

除了上述提到的附加费外,还有冷冻附加费、清洗罐附加费、币值调整附加费、熏舱附加费等。

● 班轮运费的计算方法

首先,翻译出托运货物的英文名称,在"货物分级表"中查出该商品所属的等级和计算标准。

其次,根据等级和目的港航线,查出基本运费率和附加费率或附加费额。

最后,商品的基本运费率加各种附加费,即为该商品每一运费吨的单位运价。用公式表示为:

每一运费吨的运费=基本费率+附加费率

商品运费总额=(货物的运费吨×每运费吨的运费)

=运费吨×基本运费×(1+附加费率)

租船运输

租船运输又称不定期租船运输,指包租整船或部分舱位进行运输。与班轮运输相反,"四不固定",即没有固定的航线、没有固定的停靠港、没有固定的船期和没有固定的运费。租船运输又分为定程租船、定期租船和光船租船三种类型。与出口企业关系较为密切的是定程租船运输。这里着重讲述定程租船运输。

(1)定程租船

定程租船又称为不定期船、航次租船。定程租船按其租赁方式的不同,可分为单程租船、来回航次租船、连续航次租船。由船舶所有人负责提供船舶在指定港口之间进行一个航次或数个航次承运指定货物的租船运输。特点是:运输价值较低的粮食、煤炭、木材、矿石等大宗货物为主。

定程租船的计算方法有两种:按运费率计算,按货物的单位重量或体积计费;或者是包干运费,按整船定一个总值。

定程租船的装卸费,由租方和船方共同协商后,在合同中做出规定,可由船方负担,也可由货方负担,规定的方法有以下五种:

● 班轮条件

船方负担装卸费。

● 船方不管装,不管卸

船方不负担装卸费。

● 船方管卸,不管装

船方不负担装船费。

● 船方管装,不管卸

船方不负担卸货费。

● FIOST

船方不管装、不管卸、不管理舱、不管平舱。

在定程租船的运输方式中,货物在装卸港口装卸时间的长短直接关系到船舶的使用周期和船方的利益。租方在和船方签订租船合同时,要就船舶在装卸港的时间作出具体的规定。如租船人未能在约定的装卸时间内将货物装完或卸完,而延长了船舶在港停留的时间,从而延长了航次时间,这对船舶所有人来说,既可能增加船舶在港口停泊的时间而增加了港口费用的开支,又因航次时间延长而降低了船舶的周转率。装卸时间的规定直接关系到船方和租方的切身利益。

(2)定期租船

定期租船又称期限租船,是以期限为基础的租船方式,即由船舶所有人将船舶出租给租船人使用一定的期限,在此期限内由租船人自行调度和经营管理。租用时间可以是一年或数年。

在租船期间,货船的经营、管理和使用权都归承租人。同时,由于装卸货物、平舱理舱等引起的燃油费、港口费、装卸费等也由承租人负担。船东要负责支付船员的工资,并保证在租用期间货船适合海洋运输及相关费用和货船的保险费。

(3)光船租船

光船租船,也是期租的一种。所不同的是:在定期租船方式下,船主不仅提供货船,还有船员;而在光船租船方式下,船主不提供船员,光一条船交给租方使用,由租方自行配备船员,支付船员的工资和费用,负责船舶的经营管理和航行各项事宜(如船舶的维护、修理以及机器的正常运转等)。

2. 铁路运输

铁路运输具有货运量大、速度快、安全可靠、运输成本低、运输准确和受气候影响较小等特点。铁路运输有以下三种类型:

(1)内地铁路运输;

(2)国家之间的铁路运输;

(3)国际铁路货物联运。

根据“国际铁路联盟”、“国际铁路货物联运协定”和“国际铁路货物运送公约”的规定,只要承运人在起运地签发铁路运输提单,出口货物就可以直接运往目的地。

铁路运输单据主要有铁路货运提单和其复印件。铁路货运提单实质上是约束收货人、托运人和承运人三者的一种运输合同。它随货物一起从出发地运至目的地,然后由收货人付款索单。托运人也可通过银行交换铁路货运提单的复印件。

3. 航空运输

航空运输的优点是航行速度快、交货迅速、货损率低以及节省包装、储存等费用,货物可以运往世界各地而不受地面条件的限制;缺点是运量小、运价高,易受恶劣气候的影响。因此,它适用于一些时间性强、量少而急需、重量轻而贵重的货物运输。航空运输可分为以下四种:班机运输、包机运输、集中托运、急件运送。

空运提单,也称为航空托运单,是用来证明货物已由承运人通过航空方式交给收货人。空运提单有以下特性:

(1)空运提单是托运人/发货人与承运人/航空公司之间签订的货物运输协定。

(2)空运提单是航空公司开给托运人的托运货物的收据。

(3)空运提单通常都是按国际标准用英语和启运地的语言印制,这样方便途中经由不同国家中两至三条航线转到目的地。一般来说,空运提单可以有12份以便交给不同的有关当事人,如托运人、收货人、承运人、第二承运人(如果有的话)、第三承运人(如果有的话)、目的地机场、起飞机场以及其他用途(如果有的话)。每份空运提单有三份正本。

第一份由托运人签署交给承运人或其代理人保存,作为运输契约凭证。

第二份由承运人与托运人共同签署,连同货物备交收货人,作为核收货物的依据。

第三份由承运人签署,于收到货物后,交付托运人,作为收到货物的运输契约证明。

4. 集装箱运输

随着国际贸易的不断扩大,使用集装箱运输越来越普遍。这种成组运输因其装载量大,往往又能使船舶、火车、汽车、飞机等各种运输工具衔接在一起,从而降低近一半的成本而成为一种新型的现代化运输方式。集装箱按照标准的大小尺寸用金属制作,大多数从10到40英尺不等。国际标准化组织(ISO)对集装箱的规格从 1A 到 3A 共分成 3 个系列 13 种标准规格。其中应用最多的是 1A 型(8 英尺×8 英尺×40 英尺)、1C 型(8 英尺×8 英尺×20 英尺)和 1AA 型(8 英尺×8.6 英尺×40 英尺)。

集装箱运输分为整箱货(FCL)和拼箱货(LCL)两种。对于托运数量达到整箱要求的整箱货,可以由发货人在自己的工厂或仓库自行装箱,也可以由承运人代为装箱后直接运往设在进口码头的集装箱堆场(CY)。对于托运数量达不到一个集装箱容积或负荷量要求的拼箱货,则一般由发货人将货物交承运人码头的集装箱货运站(CFS)或内陆集装箱货运站(Inland Container Depot),由承运人根据货物的性质、目的地、重量等,将多个货主的货物拼装成箱,并运交集装箱堆场。

5. 国际多式联运

国际多式联运是在集装箱运输的基础上产生和发展起来的一种综合性的连贯运输方式。它一般是以集装箱为媒介,把海、陆、空多种传统的单一运输方式有机地结合起来,组成一种国家间的连贯运输。

它通常包括:

(1)火车—飞机(或者货车—飞机,船—飞机)的联合运输方式。出口货物先由铁路或卡车或船运往香港,然后在香港将货物装上飞机。

(2)火车—船的联合运输方式。中国内陆省份的出口货物先通过铁路运往香港,然后在香港转船运往国外港口。

(3)集装箱运输方式。

6. 大陆桥运输

大陆桥运输是指使用横贯大陆上的铁路或公路运输系统作为中间桥梁,是海—陆—海的连贯运输。大陆桥运输一般以集装箱为媒介,是国际多式联运的一种形式,它具有集装箱运输的优点。目前世界上主要的大陆桥有:美洲大陆桥、西伯利亚大陆桥、新欧亚大陆桥。

7. 邮包运输

邮包运输是托运人在托运地邮局办理邮件托运手续后,由邮局负责将邮件传递到目的地,收货人直接在目的地邮局提取邮件的一种运输方式。邮包分为普通邮包和航空邮包两种。

这种运输方式的特点是手续简便,费用不太高,具有国际性和“门到门”的运输性质。根据各国邮政的规定,国际邮包运输限定每件长度不能超过1米,重量不能超过20千克,所以邮包运输只适用于量轻体小的商品,如精密仪器、机器零件、金银首饰、药品以及各种样品和零星物品等。

8. 管道运输

管道运输是利用管道输送如原油和气体等物品的一种运输方式。这种管道运输线路长,一般埋于海底。油价的不断上涨,使得管道运输越来越受青睐。此外,对于运输易燃物品而言,管道运输安全、可靠。

第二节　运输单据

在国际贸易中,单证的要求是非常高的,从某种程度上来说国际贸易是一种单证的交易,叫做“象征性交易”,因为运输单据代表着对货物的所有权。比如,在信用证条件下,买方只有在获取运输单证后才能提货,而卖方也只有在交出运输单证后才能得到货款。要使用什么样的单据,以及如何仔细、准确地完成这些单证非常值得我们注意。一般来说,每一笔销售合同都要规定各种所需的单据。如果忽略这些单证将会产生严重的后果,这在国际贸易中并不罕见。因此,对进出口双方来说,遵守这些规定是很必要的。商业发票、提单、保险单、装箱单、重量单等通常会被称为运输单证。此外,运输单据还包括买方所要求的以及与对进口货物征收关税有关的单证,如形式发票、领事发票、产地证、价值证书和检验证书等。在国际贸易中,商业发票、提单和保险单是最主要的单证。在每一笔进出口货物交易中,它们都是必不可少的。本节将主要介绍提单。

提单是指由海运承运人向已与其订立了运输合同的托运人所签发的运输单据。海运提单在国际贸易中发挥了关键的作用。

提单有三个作用:提单是货物收据、运输合同的证明以及货物所有权凭证。

(1)货物收据

提单是签收货物的收据。提单描述已装船货物的情况,写明货物数量及状况。提单通常由托运人提前填好。在货物装船之后,承运人要负责检查货物,检查所装货物是否与提单所列一致。但是,承运人只负责检查外表是否一致——即标签相符,包装没有损坏。如果一切正常,合适的承运人代理就在提单上签字，并将提单退还给托运人。

(2)运输合同的证明

提单是托运人和承运人之间的运输合同的证明。提单一旦被转让给善意的第三方，便是运输合同条款的确凿证据。

(3)货物所有权凭证

通过正当转让，善意取得提单的指定收货人或提单持有人，具有货物所有权，并通过交付提单，提取货物。承运人有义务凭正本提单交货。承运人如果在提单未出示的情况下交货，须对提单持有人承担合同责任或民事侵权责任。

由于持有提单即视为持有货物，买方只要通过对提单背书，便可将海运中的货物出售给第三方。第三方成为提单持有人后，即可在货到之后要求交货。而且，提单作为物权凭证，具有提供安全性的重要作用。比如，在信用证业务中正是提单的这种物权凭证功能，使其成为海上贸易中非常重要的单据。

但并非所有提单都可以转让。如果要被赋予转让功能，提单需要做成指示提单，也就是说，承运人要将货物运到指定的收货人或其指定的人，或受让人。必须要注意的一点是，做成指定收货人的提单，叫做记名提单，不可转让。

提单有不同的种类。下列是最常见的。图 5-1 是一个联合运输的提单。

<table>
<tr><td colspan="2">Shipper
B/L NO. SHANGHAI CHEMICALS IMPORT AND EXPORT CORPORATION
16 JIANGYAN ROAD, SHANGHAI</td><td rowspan="3">B/L NO.
PACIFIC INTERNATION LINES (PTE) LTD
(Incorporated in Singapore)
COMBINED TRANSPORT BILL OF LADING
Received in apparent good order and condition except as otherwise noted the total number of container or other packages or units enumerated below for transportation from the place of receipt to the place of delivery subject to the terms hereof. One of the signed Bills of Lading must be surrendered duly endorsed in exchange for the Goods or delivery order. On presentation of this document (duly) Endorsed to the Carrier by or on behalf of the Holder, the rights and liabilities arising in accordance with the terms hereof shall (without prejudice to any rule of common law or statute rendering them binding on the Merchant) become binding in all respects between the Carrier and the Holder as though the contract evidenced hereby had been made between them.
SEE TERMS ON ORIGINAL B/L</td></tr>
<tr><td colspan="2">Consignee
TO ORDER OF COMMERCIAL BANK OF ETHIOPIA</td></tr>
<tr><td colspan="2">Notify Party
MAGIC INTERNATIONAL PLC
DEBRE ZEIT ROAD,
ADDIS ABABA ETHIOPIA</td></tr>
<tr><td>Vessel and Voyage Number
GUANG HANG V.312</td><td>Port of Loading
SHANGHAI</td><td>Port of Discharge
ASSAB</td></tr>
<tr><td>Place of Receipt</td><td>Place of Delivery</td><td>Number of Original Bs/L
THREE</td></tr>
</table>

<table>
<tr><th colspan="5">PARTICULARS AS DECLARED BY SHIPPER - CARRIER NOT RESPONSIBLE</th></tr>
<tr><td>Container Nos/Seal Nos.
Marks and/Numbers</td><td colspan="2">No. of Container/Packages/Description of Goods</td><td>Gross Weight
(Kilos)</td><td>Measurement
(cu-metres)</td></tr>
<tr><td>MAGIC INT'L PLC
P.O.BOX 147140
ADDIS ABABA
ETHIOPIA
VIA ASSAB</td><td>75PACKAGES</td><td>TRANSMISSION BELT

ON BOARD
AT SHANGHAI
ON GUANGHANG V.312
MARCH 19.2009</td><td>8820KGS</td><td>20CBM</td></tr>
<tr><td colspan="3" rowspan="4">FREIGHT & CHARGES
FREIGHT PREPAID
FREIGHT CHARGE:USD6574.00</td><td colspan="2">Number of Containers/Packages (in words)
SEVENTY FIVE PACKAGES ONLY</td></tr>
<tr><td colspan="2">Shipped on Board Date:
2009-3-19</td></tr>
<tr><td colspan="2">Place and Date of Issue:
SHANGHAI, MARCH 19, 2009</td></tr>
<tr><td colspan="2">In Witness Whereof this number of Original Bills of Lading stated above all of the tenor and date one of which being accomplished the others to stand void.

for PACIFIC INTERNATIONAL LINES (PTE) LTD as Carrier</td></tr>
</table>

图 5-1 联合运输的提单

1. 已装船提单和备运提单

已装船提单是指在货物实际装上指定的船舶之后,由船公司签发的提单。已装船提单中要显示船名和提单签发日期。由于已装船提单更能保证收货人在目的地收到货物,进口方一般会要求出口方提供已装船提单。大部分提单上都预先印好“已装船提单”字样。

没有显示“已装船”字样的提单,为备运提单。备运提单只是确认承运人收到待装运货物。所以,货物有可能还在码头或仓库里。

2. 清洁提单和不清洁提单

清洁提单是由船公司签发的,对已装船货物的状况、包装或数量没有任何不良批注的提单。一般来说,会在提单上注明“状况明显良好”、“已装船清洁”等诸如此类的标注。清洁提单证明货物直到转给承运人时,都未发生任何损毁。如果货物最终送达时实际上有损毁,这些标注有助于明确责任。

不清洁提单也叫不正常提单或者附条款的提单，是承运人签发的，上载所收到的货物（或其包装）看上去受潮、受损或有可疑情况，或数量不对等不良批注或标注（称作“条款”）的提单。信用证支付方式下，进口方和银行通常不接受不正常提单。

3. 记名提单、空白提单及指示提单

记名提单有指定收货人。该提单下，只有目的地的收货人有权提取货物。由于该提单是不可转让的，国际贸易中一般不使用，通常只用于高价值货物或特定目的的货物。

空白提单，也称敞开提单或持票人提单，是指无明确收货人的提单。“提单收货人”一栏通常有“交持有人”字样。持有单据的人，即对提单所代表的货物拥有所有权。空白提单转让不需要做任何背书。由于风险超高，所以此种提单不太使用。

指示提单广泛运用于国际贸易之中，是指货物运送至指定人所指示的人。在收货人栏，要标记“凭指示”，“凭托运人指示”或“凭收货人指示”。这种提单是一种可转让的工具，即该提单可用于向另一方转让所运货物的所有权。这种转让可以发生在运输过程中的任何时间内，只要将指示提单交给另一方。除非另有规定，托运货物凭指示，意思是凭托运人的指示。

指示提单要经背书后方可转让。背书在这里是指在提单上签名，合法转让提单。背书有两种：空白背书和记名背书。空白背书是指只有背书人签名，并未指定背书给谁，或谁是被背书人。在此种情况下，任何经背书后持有提单者都拥有货物所有权。记名背书写明被背书人，再次转让，还需要背书。如果提单做成“凭收货人指示”，则收货人背书转让提单。

4. 直运提单、转运提单及联运提单

直运提单是指写明所装货物直接从装运港运至卸货港，没有转船的提单。

转运提单是指写明货物需要在某个中途港转运的提单，这是因为装运港与目的港之间没有直运服务。

联运提单，通常是为必须使用不同船和/或不同运输方式（飞机、铁路、小车、船舶、卡车等），从启运地到目的地进行集装箱门到门运输所签发的提单。与多式联运提单不同，联运提单的主承运人或运输商（签发联运提单的人），仅对其所承担的那段航程负责，其也是下几段航程承运人的代理。

5. 班轮提单、租船提单和集装箱提单

班轮提单,是班轮公司签发的提单,用于在固定航线上停靠固定停泊港的货物运输。

租船提单,是承运人(或其代理)基于租船合同所签发的提单。这种提单以租船合同条款为准。这就是为什么银行或买方接受租船提单时,要求交一份租船合同副本的原因。

集装箱提单,是在货物采用集装箱运输时所签发的提单。

6. 全式提单和简式提单

全式提单,是指提单背面写有详细的运输条款的提单。国际货物运输中常使用全式提单。

简式提单(又称背面空白提单),是一种简化单据,提单背面没有详细的运输条款。这些条款列在单据上,而不是列在提单上。除非信用证另有规定,可以接受简式提单。简式提单可以节约印刷费用(比如提单背面不印任何文字)。如果运输条款改变,则没有必要重印提单。

7. 其他各种提单

舱面提单:该提单上注明货物已经装在船舶甲板上。该提单适用牲畜、植物、危险品或形状不规则、不能放入船舱的货物的运输。舱面运输比货物装入船舱内运输危险性更大。这种运输的保险或融资,可能难以取得,或者成本较高。

过期提单:在规定的交单日期之后,或者在货物到达目的港之后,才向收货人、买方或买方银行交付的提单,称为过期提单。提单在货物到达目的港之前到达,或与货物同时到达,非常重要;否则,买方可能无法提货。重要单据的延迟到达,可能会造成不希望看到的结果,比如,仓储费等。因此,应该尽量避免提单过期。有时,特别是在短途海运中,应加上“过期提单可以接受”的条款。

倒签提单是指提单日期早于其签发日期的提单。在实际装船时间晚于信用证规定的时间时,承运人有时在托运人的要求下,按符合要求的日期签发提单,以避免银行拒收单据。由于签发这种提单会造成买方拒收货物的风险,因此,即便在某些看似有必要的情况下,也要避免这种不法行为。

预借提单是指信用证有效期已到,但货物尚未装运时提前签发的提单。签

发这种提单的目的是在信用证有效期内,能及时到银行议付款项。签发预借提单也是一种不合法的做法,应该避免。

上述所有提单彼此之间并不独立。几种提单可以组合成一种“已装船、凭指示的空白背书提单”。备运提单也可以是记名提单和清洁提单。提单制成成套的,包括许多份正本(通常是三份)和许多份副本,分别注有“正本”和“副本”字样。收货人只能凭承运人签名的正本提单提货,副本仅供参考。

第三节　装运条款

装运条款主要包括装运时间,在大多数情况下包括装卸时间、装卸费用、装运港和目的港、分批和转船以及货运单据的规定等内容。

1. 装运时间

装运时间(也称为装运期)是指货物装上指定的运输工具,并在规定的时间内卖方将货物交给买方。在进出口合同中对装运时间的规定方法主要有以下几种:

(1)明确规定具体时限。例如:

2017 年 7 月 16 日前装运(装运期不迟于 7 月 16 日)。

(2)规定了某一段装运时间,卖方可以选择其中任何一天装运,如:

2017 年 3 月份装运。

2017 年 1/2/3 月装运。

由第一艘货轮装运。

第一时间安排装运。

有舱位时安排装运。

7 月安排装运,可以在 7 月,即 7 月 1 日到 7 月 31 日中的任何一天,都可以安排装运。

(3)规定在收到信用证后××天内安排装运,比如说:

收到信用证后 30 天内安排装运。

收到信用证后 3 个月内安排装运。

(4)规定即将安排装运,如:

立即装运。

尽快装运。

即刻装运。

但这类术语在国际上并无统一的解释,极易引起争议和纠纷。因此,我们应该避免使用这类术语。

2. 装运港和目的港

● 在出口合同中规定装运港时要特别注意的问题:

(1)选择靠近商品原产地的装运港。

(2)要考虑国内外装运港口的装卸条件、具体的运输条件、收费标准等。

(3)在港口名称后面加上出口国的名称。

(4)在出口贸易中,习惯做法是只规定一个港口为装运港,并明确列出具体港口的名称。但如果该批货物太多,特别是分放在几个地方,这时候可以破例规定两个或三个装运港,如"装运港上海和天津","装运港大连、广州和上海"。有时在签订合同时,而装运港却还没有定下来,也可以规定为"在中国装运"。

● 目的港一般是由买方根据使用、转售的需要而提出,经卖方同意后确定的,目的港要方便货船抵达和停靠。合同中规定目的港的方法有以下几种:

(1)如果我国政府规定不能与某个国家做外贸业务,那就不能选择该国的港口为目的港。

(2)对于目的港的规定必须明确、具体,最好不用模棱两可的措辞,如"欧洲主要港口"、"亚洲主要港口"等。

(3)如果我国没有直达船或者直达船很少,就应该在合同中写明"允许转船"。

(4)所选择的目的港必须适合货船的停靠。

(5)如果与内陆国家的公司做业务,那么应该选择距离这个国家最近的港口。除非有联合直达运输服务,否则一般不选择内陆国家作为目的港。

(6)码头的装卸设备也很重要,因此,必须注意码头的装卸设备、货运条件等问题。一般来说,装运港应该靠近货源地,而目的港则要靠近买方。

(7)如果在签订合同时,国外的中间商未能找到合适的买家,为了便于该中间商销售货物,可以根据外国客户的要求,接受买方的"选择港口"条件,但必须是合同中指定的那几个港口。

(8)应注意国外目的港的重名问题。世界上重名港很多,比如说名叫维多利亚的港口就有八九个之多。请在港口名称后面加上进口国的名称。

3. 分批装运

所谓分批装运，是指一笔成交的货物分若干批次于不同航次装运。

分批装运的原因：由于舱位不够或装卸港条件以及市场销售的影响和限制，或工厂生产加工延误等原因而需分批装运。

注意事项：

(1)一般来说，分批装运对卖方有利，卖方可以争取主动。按《跟单信用证统一惯例》(UCP600)的有关规定，除非信用证有相反的规定，可允许分批装运。但按有些国外合同法，如果没有在合同中规定分批装运，那么将视为不可以分批装运。因此，一般应对此条款明确规定。

(2)按《跟单信用证统一惯例》(UCP600)的有关规定，如果运输单据表面注明货物是使用同一运输工具并经过同一路线运输的，而且运输单据注明的目的地相同，那么即使每套运输单据注明的装运日期不同和/或装货港、接受监管地、发运地不同，也不作为分批装运。如果没有合适的船舶可以装运，则转运是必要的，这些方面的条款可以包括在合同中。

(3)但如果在合同中规定了分批装运条款(例如，3 月和 4 月分两批每月平均装运)，那么，卖方应严格按合同规定执行。按《跟单信用证统一惯例》(UCP600)的有关规定，除非另有规定，否则其中任何一批未按规定装运，则本批及以后各批均告失效。

4. 转运

所谓转运，是指货物通过中途港重新装卸和转运。转运的原因：由于没有直达船，或者货船航行的线路不经过所要到达的目的港，或者装运的货物太少而没有货船愿意驶往该目的港等原因而需转船。

有直达船或无合适的船舶运输而需要转运的，可以要求在合同中订立允许装船条款。按《跟单信用证统一惯例》(UCP600)的有关规定，除非信用证有相关的规定，可允许分批装运和转船。

5. 装运通知

按国际贸易的一般做法，在 FOB 条件下，卖方应在约定装船前(一般为30~45 天)向买方发出货物备妥通知，以便买方派船接货。买方在接到卖方发出的通知后，应按约定的时间，将船名、船舶到港日期等通知卖方。卖方在货物装船后应在约定时间将合同号、货物品名、重量、发票金额、船名及装船日期等内容告知买方,以便买方办理保险并做好接卸货物的准备。图 5-2 是一个装运通知的样本:

NANJING FORGIGN TRADE IMP. AND EXP. CORP.

SHIPPING ADVICE

FAX	56489542	**INVOICE NO.**	JS09256
TEL	56489545	**L/C NO.**	H2108
		S/C NO.	ST355

MESSRS:
EAST AGENT COMPANY
126 ROOM STREET, ANTERWEIP, BELGIUM

DEAR SIRS:

WE HEREBY INFORM YOU THAT THE GOODS UNDER THE ABOVE MENTIONED CREDIT HAVE BEEN SHIPPED. THE DETAILS OF THE SHIPMENT ARE STATED BELOW.

SHIPPING MARKS:		
CBD	**COMMODITY** :	LADIES LYCRA LONG PANT
LONDON	**TOTAL G.W.**:	2000KGS
NOS1-200	**OCEAN VESSEL**:	DAFENG E002
	DATE OF DEPARTURE:	OCT 20, 2009
	B/L NO.:	HJSHB142323
	PORT OF LOADING:	NANJING
	DESTINATION:	LONDON

图 5-2　装运通知

Chapter 6

International Cargo Transportation Insurance

Part A Text

In international buying and selling of goods, there are a number of risks, which, if they occur, will involve traders in financial losses. For instance cargoes in transit may be damaged due to breakage of packing, clash or fire etc.. These hazards, and many others, may be insured against. Every year, a certain amount of cargo was destroyed or damaged by perils of the sea in transit, but whichever particular cargo it would be it can not be anticipated. All cargo owners take the risk of loss through the perils. However, foreign traders can insure themselves against many of these risks. Based on the principle that the fortunate helps the unfortunate, the industry of insurance has been developed to overcome these financial losses. Insurance is a process for spreading risk, so that the burden of any loss is borne not by the unfortunate individual directly affected but by the total body of person under consideration. In return for a payment known as a premium paid by the insured, an insurance company will agree to compensate the insured person in the event of losses during the period of insurance.

The history of insurance goes back as far as the twelfth century, when marine insurance was known to exist in North Italy. In the fourteenth century, Italian merchants came to Britain and brought their system of insurance to safeguard ships and cargo with them. In those days, of course, there were no insurance companies; merchants would group together and write their names under a promise to pay for ships or cargoes lost in storms or taken by pirates, and this is how the term "underwriters" came into existence. If the ship was lost, the financial loss was spread and no single merchant risked all his money.

In China, the People's Insurance Company of China (PICC), established in 1949, is the sole stated-owned insurance organization which underwriters almost all kinds of insurance and has agents in almost all main ports and regions over the world. Since the establishment of the PICC, it has become the practice of Chinese foreign trade corporations to have their imports insured with the PICC. Insurance on China's exports may also be covered here if the foreign importers consider it appropriate.

Before examining the content of insurance, it is appropriate first of all to consider three concepts: risks, losses and expenses.

Risks: Marine Risks in connection with cargoes in transit can be classified into two categories: Marine Risks and Extraneous Risks. (1) Marine Risks are caused by Natural Calamity and Accidents. (2) Extraneous Risks consist of General Extraneous Risks and Special Extraneous Risk.

Disasters such as tsunami, earthquake or volcanic eruption, lightning and heavy weather etc. fall into the category of Natural Calamity; while fire, explosion, sunk, grounding, stranding, collision, missing, etc. belonging to Accidents. It should be noted that Marine Risks do not include all the risks at sea. For instance, fresh and/or water damage are/is not included in the Marine Risks.

Extraneous Risks are risks that are beyond the coverage of the Marine Risks mainly including General Extraneous Risks and Special Extraneous Risks.

General Extraneous Risks include: the pilferage, contamination, breakage, sweating and/or heating, taint of odor, rusting, fresh and/or rain water damage, shortage in weight, clashing etc..

Special Extraneous Risks: war, warlike operations, hostile acts, armed conflicts or piracy capture, seizure, arrest, restraint or detainment etc..

It is very important to have a clear understanding of the above mentioned concepts, since some of the risks are not covered by the relevant insurance. For instance, partial losses or damages caused by Natural Calamity are not covered by F. P. A.; while Special Extraneous Risks are not in the coverage of All Risks.

At present, according to the different transportation methods, there are ocean marine transportation insurance, overland transportation insurance, air transportation insurance and parcel post transportation insurance in our country. Among all these, ocean marine transportation insurance is mostly and widely used in international trade practical business. The ocean marine transportation insurance is also the first used insurance and so has the longest history among the all. The overland transportation insurance and air transportation insurance have been developed on the basis of ocean marine transportation insurance. Even though they have different obligations, their basic principles and guarantees provided by the insurance companies are nearly the same. In this unit we are going to deal with ocean marine transportation insurance.

Section One Risks, Losses and Expenses

According to the loss or damage caused by risks included in different coverage and the expenses involved, the insurance company is responsible for indemnifying the insured goods. Obviously, risk, loss and coverage are closely related to each other. In order to have a clear understanding of the contents of insurance, these three terms should be clarified.

1. Risks

While the cargo traveling to another country, it is likely to encounter various perils which may cause the goods to suffer loss of one kind or another. Marine risks in connection with cargo in transit can be classified into two types: perils of the sea and extraneous risks. Perils of the sea are caused by natural calamities and fortuitous accidents; the latter, by various extraneous reasons, including general extraneous risks and special extraneous risks.

- Perils of the sea: natural calamities and fortuitous accidents.
- Extraneous risks: general extraneous risks and special extraneous risks.

(1) Perils of the Sea

Perils of the sea are those caused by natural calamities and fortuitous.

Natural calamities—Disasters such as vile weather, thunder and lighting, tsunami, earthquake, floods, etc..

Fortuitous accidents—Accidents such as ship stranded, striking upon the rocks, ship sinking, ship collision, colliding with icebergs or other objects, fire, explosion, ship missing, etc..

(2) Extraneous Risks

Extraneous risks are risks caused by extraneous reasons, consisting of general extraneous risks and special extraneous risks.

General extraneous risks include: theft or pilferage, rain, shortage, contamination, leakage, breakage, train of odor, dampness, heating, rusting hooking, etc..

Special extraneous risks include: war risks, strikes, non-delivery of cargo, refusal to receive cargo, etc..

2. Losses

Marine losses are the damages or losses of the insured goods incurred by perils of the sea. Losses sustained by the insured because of the risks listed above come from not only the loss of the goods or the damage done to the goods, but also from the expenses the insured sustained in rescuing the goods in danger. According to the extent of damage, losses in marine insurance fall into two types: total loss and partial loss. The former may be subdivided into actual total loss and constructive total loss; the latter, general average and particular average. The losses and damages done to the goods can fall into:

- Total loss: actual total loss and constructive total loss.
- Partial loss: general average and particular average.

(1) Total loss

Total loss refers to the loss of the entire shipment caused by the occurrence of one of the perils of the sea, fire, or some other reasons.

①Actual total loss

The actual total loss occurs where the insured goods have been totally lost or damage, or found to be totally valueless on arrival.

②Constructive total loss

Constructive total loss is found in the case where an actual total loss appears to be unavoidable or the cost to be incurred in recovering or reconditioning the goods together with the forwarding cost to the destination named in the policy would exceed their value on arrival.

(2) Partial loss

Partial loss refers to the loss of part of a consignment. According to different causes, partial loss can be either general average and particular average.

①General average

In the insurance business the term "average" simply means "loss" in most cases. It all goes back to the situation where a ship is in danger, and somebody's cargo has to be abandoned. Whose should it be? The captain has make a decision, and one of the shippers will suffer. To cover this situation the concept of general average was introduced. It means that whichever shipper loses all or part of his cargo, all the others will club together to recompense him for his loss. All policies the insured take out automatically cover them against it.

②Particular average

A particular average means that a particular consignment is suffered by one whose goods are partly lost or damaged. When there is a particular average loss, other interests in the voyage (such as the carrier and other cargo owners whose goods were not damage) do not contribute to the partial recovery of the one suffering the loss. An example of a particular average occurs when a storm or fire damages part of the shipper's cargo and no one else's cargo has to be sacrificed to save the voyage. The cargo owner whose goods were damaged looks to his insurance company for payment, provided, of course, his policy covers the specific type of loss suffered.

Since most of losses encountered by shippers are partial, that is, of the particular average nature, it is important to know exactly what provisions for such partial losses are in the insurance policy.

3. Expenses

Losses sustained by the insured because of the risks come from not only the loss of the goods or the damage done to the goods, but also from the expenses the insured sustained in rescuing the goods in danger. Transportation insurance not only insures the losses caused by risks but also the losses of expenses. The main expenses include:

(1) Sue and Labor Expense

These expenses are the expenses arising from measures properly taken by the insured, the employee and the assignee, etc. for minimizing or avoiding losses caused by the risks covered in the insurance policy. The insurer is held responsible to compensate for such expenses.

(2) Salvage Charges

Salvage charges are expenses resulting from measures properly taken by a third party other than the insured, the employee and the assignee, etc..

Section Two Marine Insurance Cover of CIC

According to *People's Insurance Company of China Ocean Marine Cargo Clauses*, the insurance is mainly classified into two groups: Basic Insurance Coverage and Additional Insurance Coverage. The applicant can purchase Basic Insurance Coverage individually. However, before purchasing an Additional Insurance Coverage, he has to purchase a Basic Insurance Coverage. Basic Insurance Coverage is further classified into the following three conditions: Free from Particular Average (F.P.A.), With Particular Average (W.P.A.) and All risks. The F.P.A. covers mainly Total Loss and General Average, while the W.P.A. covers Particular Average in addition. The all risks cover, in addition to the scope of W.P.A., such as Extraneous Risks, Shortage Risk, Inter-mixture and Contamination Risk, Leakage Risk, Clash and Breakage Risk, Taint of Odor Risk, Sweating and Heating Risk, Hook Damage Risk, Rust Risk, Breakage of Pacing Risk, etc.. In case of F.P.A. or W.P.A., one or several kinds of these Extraneous Risks may be covered in addition.

1. Basic Insurance Coverage

(1) Free from Particular Average

Free from particular average, basically, is a limited form of cargo insurance cover in as much as that no partial loss or damage is recoverable from the insurers unless that actual vessel or craft is stranded, sunk or burnt. Under the latter circumstances, the F.P.A. cargo policy holder can recover any losses of the insured merchandise which was on the vessel at the time as would obtain under the more extensive W.P.A. policy. The F. P. A. policy provides coverage for total losses and general average emerging from actual"marine perils".

According to PICC's Ocean Marine Cargo Clauses revised in January 1,1981, F.P.A. insurance covers:

①Total or Constructive Total Loss of the whole consignment hereby insured caused in the course of transit by natural calamities—heavy weather, lightning, tsunami, earthquake and flood. In case a constructive total loss is claimed for, the insured shall abandon to the company the damage goods and all his rights and title pertaining thereto. The goods on each lighter to or from the seagoing vessel shall be deemed a separate risk. "Constructive Total Loss" refers to the loss where an actual total loss appears to be unavailable or the cost to be incurred in recovering or reconditioning the goods together with the forwarding costs to the destination named in the policy would exceed their value on arrival.

②Total or partial loss caused by accidents—the carrying conveyance being grounded stranded, sunk or in collision with floating ice or other objects as fire or explosion.

③Partial loss of the insured goods attributable to heavy weather, lightning and/ or tsunami, where the conveyance has been grounded, stranded, sunk or burnt, irrespective of whether the event or events took place before or after such accident.

④Partial or total loss consequent on falling of entire package or packages into sea during loading, transshipment or discharge.

⑤Reasonable cost incurred by the insured in salvaging the goods or averting or minimizing a loss recoverable under the policy, provided that cost shall not exceed the sum insured of the consignment so save.

⑥Losses attributable to discharge of the insured goods at a port of distress following a sea peril as well as special charges arising from loading, warehousing and forwarding of the goods at an intermediate port of call or refuge.

⑦Sacrifice and contribution to general average and salvage charges.

⑧Such proportion of losses sustained by the shipowners as is to be reimbursed by the Cargo Owner under the Contract of Affreightment "Both to Blame Collision" clause.

(2) With Average/With Particular Average (W.A./W.P.A.)

This insurance covers wider than F.P.A.. Aside from the risks covered under F.P.A.conditions as above, this insurance also covers partial losses of the insured goods caused by heavy weather, lightning, tsunami, earthquake and/or food.

(3) All Risks

The cover of all risks is the most comprehensive of the three. Aside from the risks covered under F.P.A. and W.P.A. conditions as above, this insurance also covers all risks of loss of or damage to insured goods whether partial or total, arising from external causes in the course of transit. It should be noted that "All Risks" does not, as its name suggests, really cover all risks. The "All Risks" clause excludes coverage against damage caused by war, strikes, riots, etc.. These perils can be covered by a separate clause. And it covers only physical loss or damage from external causes.

(4) The free obligation of the above three basic coverages

The three coverages i.e.F.P.A.and W.P.A. and all risks do not cover:

①Loss or damage cased by the international act or fault of the insured.

②Loss or damage falling under the liability of the consignor.

③Loss or damage arising from the inferior quality or shortage of the insured goods prior to the attachment of this insurance.

④Loss or damage arising from normal loss, inherent vice or nature of the insured goods, loss of market and/or delay in transit and any expenses arising therefrom.

⑤Risks and liability covered and excluded by the ocean marine cargo was risks clauses and strike, riot and civil commotion clauses of this company.

(5) Insurance Duration

We take the practice stipulated by the international insurance market called Warehouse to Warehouse Clause to decide the insurance duration.

W/W indicates that the insurance company undertakes an insurance liability over the insured cargo from the warehouse or the place of storage of the shipper named in the policy until the cargo has arrived at the warehouse or the place of storage of the receiver named in the policy. The insurance liability terminates once the cargo arrives at the warehouse of the receiver.

If the insured cargo unloaded from the ship but does not arrive at the warehouse of the receiver immediately:

①The insurance shall be limited to sixty days after completion of discharge of the insured goods at the final port of discharge before they reach the above mentioned warehouse of storage.

②The cargo shall be transshipped from the destination not indicated in the policy. Then the insurance shall terminate when transshipment begins.

In the international insurance business, the insurance company does not hold W-W liabilities in the insurance contract. As the sole characteristics of the insurance, the ownership of the cargo is constantly changing, which requires that the buyer shall hold insurance benefit to the insurance subject when asking for claims. At this time, the right of the recourse is transferred to the buyer. Under the FOB, CFR, FCA and CPT contracts, the seller delivers the cargo at the port of shipment. Thus, their insurance liability is from ship to warehouse.

2. Additional Risks

Additional risks include general additional risks and special additional risks. Additional risks cover losses caused by Extraneous Risks and Extraneous Risks include General Extraneous Risks and Special Extraneous Risks, so Additional Risks are divided into General Additional Risks and Special Additional Risks.

General Additional Risks shall go with F.P.A. and W.P.A. according to the characteristics of the cargo. If General Additional Risks is insured, it is All Risks insured. Therefore, General Additional Risks are in the coverage of All Risks. There is no need to apply for General Additional Risks if All Risks are obtained.

- General additional risks:

(1) Theft, Pilferage and Non-delivery;

(2) Fresh water rain damage (F.W.R.);

(3) Risk of shortage;

(4) Risk of Inter-mixture & Contamination;

(5) Risk of leakage;

(6) Risk of clash & Breakage;

(7) Risk of odor;

(8) Damage caused by heating & sweating;

(9) Hook damage;

(10) Loss or damage caused by breakage of packing;

(11) Risks of rust.

Rust should be in transit. Compensation is not suitable for rust in packing.

All these additional risks should go with three basic types of risks as one type or several types of risks added.

All risks cover all these eleven general additional risks; therefore, it is not necessary to insure general additional risks if all risks are obtained (excluding special additional risks).

- Special additional risks

Special additional risks are not in the coverage of all risks. There are 8 types of special additional risks, among which war risk and strikes risk are the main ones.

- War risk

War risk shall go with one of the three types of basic insurance coverage.

War risk is one of the main types of special additional risks. Though it cannot be solely insured, it is more independent than other additional risks. It includes insurance coverage, exclusions, and commencement and termination.

(1) Insurance coverage

①Losses caused by war, war-like events, armed conflicts or piratical behaviors;

②Damage resulted from arrest, detain, inhibition or seizure caused by the above mentioned reasons;

③Losses caused by regular arms such as torpedo and tombs;

④General average or expenses caused by coverage under this clause.

(2) Exclusions

It does not cover loss, damage, or expenses arising from any hostile use of atomic or nuclear weapons of war.

Exceptions are losses or damage caused by atomic bomb, hydrogen bomb, detention and seizure by the administrative authority and military groups.

Coverage of the commencement and termination: Warehouse to warehouse clauses are not suitable for war risk, war risk is only applicable for the peril on the water and the peril of the transportation. Once the cargo unloads from the ship, the responsibility is terminated.

(3) Commencement and Termination of War Risk

It is based on "ocean" clauses and limited to ocean risks, which is totally different from warehouse to warehouse clauses. That is to say, the insurer's coverage begins when the cargo is loaded at the port of shipment dominated by the insurance policy and ends when the cargo is unloaded at the port of destination. If the cargo fails to be unloaded at the port of destination, then the war coverage automatically ends by 15 days after the cargo arrives at the port of destination if transshipment happens, whether or not the cargo is unloaded locally, the insurance coverage ends by 15 days after the cargo arrives at the port of destination and once the cargo is loaded on another ship, the insurance coverage continues to be valid.

In conclusion, commencement and termination of war risk is from the port of shipment to the port of destination, which does not conform to warehouse to warehouse clauses.

- Strikes Risk

It covers loss of or damage to the cargo insured directly caused by acts of strikers and locked-out workmen. But it does not cover loss of or damage to the cargo caused by lack of labor force or failure to apply the workforce. For instance, cargo suffers losses without fuel added or due to the malfunction of the air-conditioner.

According to the international insurance practice, the insurance shall not be charged with any other expense as long as the insurance has already covered war risk and generally war risk is covered together with strikes risk.

- Insurance under Other Transportation Methods

In international trade, in addition that the goods shipped by sea must be insured, the goods transported by land, air and parcel post should also be insured. Therefore, the insurance company may have different clauses and terms to meet the need of different transportation.

Section Three Institute Cargo Clauses

Insurance business originating from United Kingdom enormously affects the whole world. The Institute Cargo Clauses (I.C.C.) were initially published by the Institute of London Underwriters in 1912 and were revised in 1981 and the newest clauses came into effect on Jan.1, 1982. Currently, almost 2/3 of the countries follow Institute Cargo Clauses in the insurance business, which has a great effect in the world. We shall accept Institute Cargo Clauses if foreign clients demand.

1. Different Kinds of ICC Clauses

It is mainly composed of the following 6 clauses:

(1) Institute Cargo Clauses A(ICC(A));

(2) Institute Cargo Clauses B(ICC(B));

(3) Institute Cargo Clauses C(ICC(C));

(4) Institute War Clauses(Cargo);

(5) Institute Strikes Clauses(Cargo);

(6) Malicious Damage Clauses.

The first 5 kinds can be independently covered without being attached to any other particular coverage. Meanwhile, ICC (A) clauses include malicious damage clauses, but malicious damage clauses should be attached to ICC(B) or ICC(C).

2. Characteristics of ICC Clauses

(1) It cancels regulations divided by total loss or partial loss;

(2) Franchise ratio is not calculated when compensations are made;

(3) Insurance policy under ICC clauses is blank with clear and definite notes and without insurance conditions and remarks;

(4) Insurable interest clauses, successive freight clauses, value added clauses, default clauses, laws and practice are newly added to ICC clauses.

3. Coverage of Marine Cargo Insurance of ICC

ICC(A)

It is similar to that of all risks under China Marine Cargo Insurance Clauses.

- Insurance Coverage

It adopts the method of "all risks except for exclusions", that is to say, except for exclusions; the insurer is responsible for the rest risks. In comparison, ICC(B) and ICC(C) cover named perils.

- Exclusions

(1) General Exclusions: willful misconduct of the assured; ordinary leakage, ordinary loss in weight or volume, ordinary wear and tear; unsuitable packing; inherent vice; delay; insolvency or financial default of the owners, managers, characters or operators of the vessel; any weapon or device employing atomic or nuclear fission and/or fusion.

(2) Exclusions of Unseaworthiness and Unfitness: unseaworthiness and unfitness of vessel for the safe carriage of the subject-matter insured, where the assured are privy to such unseaworthiness or unfitness, at the time the subject-matter insured is loaded; unfitness of container or conveyance for the safe carriage of the subject-matter insured.

(3) Exclusions of War: war, civil war, revolution, rebellion, insurrection, civil strife, or any hostile act by or against a belligerent power; capture, seizure, arrest, restraint or detainment, and the consequence thereof or any attempt thereat; derelict mines, torpedoes, bombs or other derelict weapons of war.

(4) Exclusions of Strikes: strikers, locked-out workmen, or persons taking part in labor disturbances, riots or civil commotions; strikes, lock-outs, labor disturbances, riots or civil commotions; any act of terrorism being an act of any person acting on behalf of, or in connection with, any organization; any person acting from a political, ideological or religious motive.

ICC(B)

It is similar to W.P.A. Clauses.

- Insurance Coverage

In short, it covers named perils, namely, it specifies insurable risks one by one for the insurant's choice and is convenient for settlement of compensation. The indemnity is determined by degree of loss, but not types of risks. There is no indication for franchise ratio.

- Specific Coverage

(1) Losses or damages caused by fire, explosion, vessels or craft being stranded, grounded, sunk, capsized, overturning, derailment of land conveyance, collision, contact of vessel craft or conveyance with any external object other than water, discharge of cargo at a port of distress, earthquake, volcanic eruption or lightning.

(2) General average sacrifice, jettison or washing overboard, entry of sea, lake or

river water into vessel, craft hold, conveyance, container, lift van or place of storage; total loss of any package lost overboard or dropped whist loading on to, or unloading from, vessel or craft.

- Exclusions

In addition to the exclusions of ICC(A), it shall not cover deliberate damage to or deliberate destruction of the subject-matter insured or any part thereof by the wrongful act of any person or persons only excludes loss, damage or expenses attributable to willful misconduct of the assured.

ICC(C)

It is similar to F.P.A. clauses.

- Insurance Coverage

It only covers losses caused by important events and is not liable for unimportant accidents and natural calamities. In detail, it does not cover jettison or washing overboard, entry of sea, lake or river water into vessel, craft hold and total loss of any package lost overboard or dropped whist loading on to, or unloading from vessel or craft.

- Exclusions

The exclusions of ICC(C) are the same as that of ICC(B). The coverage of ICC (A) and ICC(B) are wider than that of W.P.A. and F.P.A. under China Marine Cargo Insurance Clauses. ICC (A) adds regulations on compensations for the third party's intentional and paretic damages to the cargo. Moreover, it covers entry of sea, lake or river water into vessel, craft hold, which is not indicated in China Marine Cargo Insurance Clauses.

Section Four　Insurance Practice

In the cargo transportation insurance practice, the insured will undergo different steps after fixing the risks to be covered in the completion of the insurance contract. These steps include: to calculate the insurance amount; to apply for marine insurance and determine insurance premium; to sign an insurance document and to lodge a insurance claim.

According to the export contract or the letter of credit, after preparing the goods and confirming shipping tools and shipping dates, the seller shall apply for insurance and fill in an insurance policy which indicates name of the insurant, name and quantity of the cargo insured, packing methods, shipping marks, port of shipment and destination, name of vessel and voyage number, insurance amount, risks covered insurance date and place for settlement.

1. Several Ways of Calculating the Insurance Premium are Listed as Follows:

(1) Amount Insured

It is the maximal indemnity paid by the insurer, which is the basis of checking the insurance premium.

Customarily, accounting to the invoice amount plus 10% insured bonus:

Amount Insured = CIF×(1+10%)

(2) Premium Expenses

It is the consideration paid by the insurer to the insurant, laying the pre-conditions for the insurer to undertake the insurance liability.

(3) Premium Rate

Insurance premium is determined by the amount insured and the premium rate. The premium rate is determined by risks covered and loss rate. The premium rate is based on the risk of insurance, the risk level, and the rate of loss. The insurance premium is calculated as:

Insurance premium = Insurance Amount×Premium Rate

= [CIF×(1+10%)]×Premium Rate

E.g. some 10 000 pieces of cargo exported to the USA by USD 10/pc CIF New York are to be covered against All Risks and War Risk and the premium rates are respectively 0.6% and 0.4%. Try to calculate the insurance premium

Then Amount Insured = CIF×(1+10%)

Insurance Premium = Insurance Amount×Premium Rate

= [CIF×(1+10%)]×Premium Rate

= [10×10 000×(1+10%)]×(0.6%+0.4%)

= 110 000×1%

$= 1\ 100$ USD

Import insurance includes open cover and open policy. Under FOB, CFR, CPT and FCA import trade terms, insurance is covered by the importer. We usually adopt simplified measures, that is, our exporter signs various kinds of open insurance contracts with insurance companies. As to open insurance contracts, exporter does not need to sign insurance policies one by one, but to handover shipping notice from the seller to the insurer, thus finishing import insurance procedures.

2. Insurance Documents

An insurance document is the evidence of the insurance contract entered into by the insurer and the applicant or the insurant. It serves as a document defining the obligations of the insurer and the insurant. It is also the document according to which the insurant lodges a claim and the insurer settles a claim when the loss or damage which is answerable under the terms of the coverage occurs. Under CIF and CIP contracts, the seller must provide the buyer with insurance documents. And insurance documents are negotiable by endorsement.

Under CIF and CIP terms, the insurant is the seller or the exporter, which is also called beneficiary in letter of credit and the principal in collection.

According to UCP600 section 28 item e: "the date of the insurance document must be not later than the date of shipment, unless it appears from the insurance document that the cover is effective from a date not later than the date of shipment."

- Types of insurance documents

(1) Insurance Policy

Insurance policy is the most commonly used document that contains all the details concerning the name of the insured. The name of the insured goods, the quantity, the weight, the transportation mark, the means of transport, the number of the voyage, the location of the insurance, the insurance currency and the premium amount, whether the premium has been paid, and the insurance is used. In addition to the date, the insurer's scope of responsibility and the detailed terms of the insurer's and the insured's respective rights and obligations are also printed on the back. The document as following is a marine cargo insurance policy:

中保财产保险有限公司

The People's Insurance (Property) Company of China, Ltd.

发票号码　　INV52148　　　　保险单号次

Invoice No.　　　　　　　　　Policy No.

海洋货物运输保险单

MARINE CARGO TRANSPORTATION INSURANCE POLICY

被保险人：
Insured：　NANJING FORGIGN TRADE IMP. AND EXP. CORP.

中保财产保险有限公司(以下简称本公司)根据被保险人的要求,及其所缴付约定的保险费,按照本保险单承担险别和背面所载条款与下列特别条款承保下列货物运输保险,特签发本保险单。

This policy of Insurance witnesses that the People's Insurance (Property) Company of China, Ltd. (hereinafter called "The Company"), at the request of the Insured and in consideration of the agreed premium paid by the Insured, undertakes to insure the undermentioned goods in transportation subject to conditions of the Policy as per the Clauses printed overleaf and other special clauses attached hereon.

保险货物项目 Descriptions of Goods	包装数量 Packing	单位 Unit Quantity	保险金额 Amount Insured
LADIES LYCRA LONG PANT	200CTNS	2 400PCS	USD52 800.00

承保险别
Conditions
COVERING RISKS AS PER "INSTITUTE CARGO CLAUSES(A)",
AND: INSTITUTE WAR CLAUSES(CARGO)".

货物标记
Marks of Goods
CBD
LONDON
NOS1-200

总保险金额：

Total Amount Insured: U.S.DOLLARS FIFTY TWO THOUSAND EIGHT HUNDRED ONLY

保费　　　　　　　运输工具　　　　　　　开航日期

Premium As arranged　Per conveyance S.S DAFENG　Slg. on or abt OCT. 20, 2009

起运港　　　　　　目的港

Form　NANJING　　To　LONDON

所保货物,如发生本保险单项下可能引起索赔的损失或损坏,应立即通知本公司下述代理人查勘。如有索赔,应向本公司提交保险单正本(本保险单共有　份正本)及有关文件。如一份正本已用于索赔,其余正本则自动失效。

In the event of loss or damage which may result in acclaim under this policy, immediate notice must be given to the Company's Agent as mentioned here under. Claims, if any, one of the original policy which has been issued in original (s) together with the relevant documents shall be surrendered to the Company. If one of the original policy has been accomplished, the others to be void.

赔款偿付地点

Claim payable at　LONDON

日期　　　　　　　　　　　　　　　　　　　在
Date　OCT. 20,2009　　　　　　　　　　　　at　NANJING

地址:
Address: 318 ANSHI ROAD NANJING,CHINA

Fig. 6-1　Marine Cargo Insurance Policy

(2) Insurance certificate

It is the simplified form of the insurance policy certifying that insurance has been affected and that a policy has been issued. It does not list all the details at the back but it is of the same legal validity as an insurance policy.

(3) Endorsement

After issuing the insurance policy, insurance company modifies or complements its contents as required by the insurant, and then this modified or complemented insurance policy is called endorsement.

Once the insurance policy is modified, the insurance company is liable for it. Endorsement is attached to the insurance policy, added stamps on it as one indivisible part which is of the same equal validity.

(4) Insurance Declaration

Under FOB, CFR, FCA, and CPT terms, the insurance is covered by the buyer on its own expense. The buyer signs the contract with the foreign insurer and the seller directly dispatches the insurance declaration to the insurer dominated by the buyer after shipping the cargo.

The duplicate of the insurance declaration of the seller is one of negotiable documents to the seller. In fact, this practice is after-shipment service supplied by the seller to the buyer.

3. Claim Procedure

In the event of loss or damage for which the insurer may be liable, and for the purpose of averting or minimizing a loss and to ensure that all rights against carriers or other third parties are properly preserved and exercised, the insured or their agents are required:

(1) Apply for survey: In the event of any damage to the goods, the insured shall immediately apply for survey to the surveyor stipulated in the policy.

(2) Claim for damages on the carrier and/or other parties concerned. If the carrier or the other relevant authorities (Customs and Port Authorities etc.) are responsible for such damages, the insured shall lodge a claim with them in writing and, if necessary, obtain their confirmation of an extension of the time limit of validity of such claims. In addition, the insured shall obtain from the carrier or other relevant authorities certificate of loss or damage.

(3) Take proper measures. The insured shall also, take proper measures immediately in salvaging the goods or preventing or minimizing a loss or damage thereto. The measures so taken by the insured shall not be considered respectively, as a waiver of abandonment here-under, or as an acceptance thereof.

(4) Prepare documents for claim. To enable claims to be dealt with promptly, the insured or their agents should submit all available supporting documents without delay, including when applicable: ① Original policy or certificate of insurance; ②Original or copy shipping invoices, together with shipping specification and/or weight notes; ③Original bill of lading and/or other contract of carriage; ④Survey report or other documentary evidence to show the extent of the loss or damage; ⑤Landing account and weight notes at final destination.

Part B Key Terms

Broker 保险经纪人

Perils of the sea 海上风险

Extraneous risks 外来风险

Natural calamities 自然灾害

Fortuitous accidents 意外事故

General extraneous risks 一般外来风险

Special extraneous risks 特殊外来风险

Total loss 全部损失

Actual total loss 实际全损

Constructive total loss 推定全损

Partial loss 部分损失

General average loss 共同海损

Particular average loss　单独海损
Salvage charges　救助费用
Sue and labor expenses　施救费用
Free of particular average　平安险
With average　水渍险
All risks　一切险
Additional risks　附加险
General additional risks　一般附加险
Theft, pilferage and non-delivery　偷窃、提货不着险
Fresh water rain damage　淡水雨淋险
Risk of shortage　短量险
Risk of inter-mixture and contamination　混杂、玷污险
Risk of leakage　渗漏险
Risk of clash & breakage　破损、破碎险
Risk of odor　串味险
Risk of sweating & heating damage　受潮受损险
Risk of hook damage　钩损险
Risk of packing breakage　包装破裂险
Risk of rusk　锈损险
Special additional risks　特殊附加险
Risk of failure to deliver　交货不着险
Risk of import duties　进口关税险
Deck risk　舱面险
Rejection risk　拒收险
Aflatoxin risk　黄曲霉素险
Fire risk extension clause—for storage of cargo at destination HongKong, including Kowloon, or Macao　货物出口到香港(包括九龙)或澳门存仓火险责任扩展条款
Strikes risk　罢工险
War risk　战争险
Insurance policy　保险单
Insurance certificate　保险凭证

Open policy 预约保单

Insurance endorsement 保险批单

Part C Exercises

Ⅰ. Answer the following questions

1. What is insurance?
2. What parties are involved in insurance?
3. What risks are covered by marine insurance?
4. How is insurance claim lodged?
5. What documents are needed in filing a claim?

Ⅱ. Give the definition to the following terms

1. Free from Particular Average
2. With Average
3. All Risks
4. Theft, pilferage and non-delivery
5. Partial loss
6. General average
7. Salvage charge
8. Sue and labor expenses

Ⅲ. Case & Study

Is the loss particular average or general average?

On October 20th 2008, Company A from our country signed a CFR contract with Company B from a certain country to buy 52 500 metric tons of fertilizer from Company B. The letter of credit issued by Company A specifies that the date of shipment is from January 1st, 2009 to January 10th. But due to the fact that the "Shun Feng" cargo ship, which was hired by Company B to make the shipment, encountered a hurricane when it was on its way to a foreign harbor, the shipment was not made until January 20th, 2009. It must be noted that after the carrier got the letter of guarantee from Company B, it signed the bill of lading, which was in accordance with the letter of credit. In addition, Company A took the W.P.A. insurance for the cargo.

The "Shun Feng" cargo ship departed from the port of shipment on January

30th,2009 and was on fire when it was crossing over the Panama Canal,resulting in the wet destruction of part of the fertilizer. Then,some part amount of the fertilizer was destroyed during the fire-fighting.As the result of the delay at the port of shipment,the cargo ship arrived at the destination at a time when the price of the fertilizer was falling,forcing Company A to sell the remaining fertilizer at such a low price level that it suffered a great loss.

Questions:

Based on the above case,please answer the following questions:

(1) What kind of loss does the loss of the fertilizer burned on the way belong to and who should the loss? Why?

(2) What kind of loss does the loss of the fertilizer of wet destruction on the way belong to and who should bear the loss? Why?

(3) Whether can Company A recover the loss from the carrier due to the falling price of the fertilizer? Why?

第六章

国际运输货物保险

国际贸易货物的买卖存在着各种各样的风险,这些风险的发生将会给有关的商人们带来经济损失。比如,货物在运输途中由于包装破损、碰损或火灾等原因而损坏等。这些风险以及其他一些风险都可以通过保险来加以防范。虽然,每年都有一定数目的货物在运输途中不可避免地要遭受到海上风险而被摧毁或受损,但是灾难会降临到哪一批货上事先是不可预知的。所有的货主都要冒货物灭失的风险。然而,从事国际贸易的商人可以通过保险来防止很多危险。根据“幸运的帮助不幸的”这个原则,保险业发展起来,用于弥补这些经济上的损失。保险的目的是将风险分摊,这样风险发生时,就可以由所有的相关人员分摊而不是由直接遭遇方单独承担。当保险人交付保险费后,如在保险期内发生损失,保险公司将同意向保险人赔付该损失。

保险的历史可以追溯到12世纪,据说当时在意大利的北方,已经存在着海运保险。在14世纪,意大利商人来到了英国,随之也带来了保护他们的船只和货物的保险制度。在那个时代,当然还没有保险公司,商人们总是聚集在一起,共同保证偿付在风暴中遭受损失的或被海盗抢劫的船只或货物,并在保证书下面签字画押。这就是“underwriters”(字面的意思是“在下面签署的人”,但是,实际的意思是“保险商”或“保险公司”)一词的来源出处。如果船只沉没,经济损失由大家分摊,而不是由哪一个商人单独出资承担所有的风险。

中国人民保险公司(PICC)成立于1949年,是中国唯一一家国有保险机构。它可以承担几乎所有险别的保险,在全世界主要港口和地区都有代理。自从中国人民保险公司成立以来,进口货物在该公司投保已经成为我国外贸公司的习惯做法。中国的出口货物,在外方买家认为适宜的情况下,也可在人保公司投保。

在了解保险的内容之前应首先了解三个概念:海洋货物运输的风险、损失和费用。

海洋货物运输的风险主要分为海上风险和外来风险两大类:(1)海上风险由自然灾害和意外事故引起;(2)外来风险包括一般外来风险和特殊外来风险。

自然灾害主要包括海啸、地震或火山爆发、雷电和恶劣气候等。意外事故包括火灾、爆炸、沉没、搁浅、触礁、碰撞和失踪等。值得注意的是,海上风险并不是指海上发生的一切风险,比如,淡水雨淋就不属于海上风险。

外来风险是指海上风险以外的其他外来风险,主要包括一般外来风险和特殊外来风险。

一般外来风险包括偷窃、玷污、渗漏、破碎、受热受潮、串味、生锈、淡水雨淋、短少和提货不着、短量、碰损等。

特殊外来风险包括战争、类似战争的行为、敌对行为、武装冲突或海盗行为,以及由此引起的捕获、拘留、逮捕、管制或扣押等。

分清楚上述这些概念很重要,因为保险承保范围并不是包括所有风险的。比如,平安险对自然灾害引起的部分损失就不赔偿;而一切险则对特殊外来风险引起的损失不赔偿。

目前,我国办理的进出口货物运输保险业务,按照运输方式的不同,主要分为海洋运输保险、陆上运输货物保险、航空运输货物保险和邮包运输保险等,其中业务量最大、涉及面最广的是海洋运输货物保险。海洋运输保险也是起源最早、历史最悠久的一种保险。陆上、航空等货物运输保险都是在海洋运输货物保险的基础上发展起来的。尽管各种不同货物运输保险的具体责任有所不同,但它们的基本原则、保险公司保障的范围等基本一致。在这一章中,我们将重点讨论海上运输保险。

第一节 风险、损失和费用

保险公司按照不同险别包括的风险所造成的损失和发生的费用承担赔偿责任。所以在保险业务中,风险、损失和费用三者有着密切的联系。为了准确地理解保险的内容,我们有必要澄清这三个概念。

1. 风险

在货物运到另一个国家的途中，它可能要遭遇到各种各样的风险，这些风险会引起货物受到这样或那样的损失。海洋货物运输的风险主要分为海上风险和外来风险两大类。海上风险是由海上发生的自然灾害和外来风险引起；外来风险是由各种外来原因引起的风险，它包括一般外来风险和特殊外来风险。

- 海上风险：自然灾害和意外事故。
- 外来风险：一般外来风险和特殊外来风险。

(1)海上风险

海上风险是由自然灾害和意外事故引起的风险。

自然灾害是指恶劣气候、雷电、海啸、地震、洪水等灾难。

意外事故是指船舶搁浅、触礁、沉没、船舶互撞、与流冰或其他物体相撞、起火、爆炸以及船只失踪等事故。

(2)外来风险

外来风险由各种外来原因所引起，包括一般外来风险和特殊外来风险。

一般外来风险包括偷窃、雨淋、短量、污染、渗漏、破损、串味、受潮、受热、锈损和钩损等。

特殊外来风险包括战争、罢工、交货不着、拒绝收货等风险。

2. 损失

海损一般是指海运保险货物在海洋运输中由于海上风险所造成的损坏和灭失。被保险货物遭遇保险责任范围内的事故，除了使货物本身受到损毁导致损失外，还会产生费用方面的损失。根据货物所遭受的损失可分为：

- 全部损失：实际全损和推定全损。
- 部分损失：共同海损和单独海损。

(1)全部损失

全部损失是指由于海难、火灾或其他原因引起的全部运输货物的全部损失。

①实际全损

实际全损是指该批被保险货物完全灭失或完全变质已失去原有的使用价值。

②推定全损

推定全损是指该批被保险货物受损后,实际全损已经不可避免,或者恢复受损货物并将其送到保险单所注明的目的地所需的费用将超过货物的价值。

(2)部分损失

部分损失是指货物损失的只是部分。根据损失产生的原因不同,部分损失可分为共同海损和单独海损。

①共同海损

在保险业中,“average”一般是“海损”的意思。这个词来源于船舶遇到海难时,有的货物必须抛弃入海。该抛弃谁的货物呢?船长必须做出决定,而总有一个发货人要受到损失,为了应付这种情况就提出了“共同海损”这一概念。意思是说不论哪个发货人损失了全部或部分货物,所有其他发货人将凑钱分摊他的损失。这就是共同海损,被保险人取得了保险单则自动为他们承保共同海损。

②单独海损

单独海损是指因货物丢失或损坏而蒙受的损失。在单独海损中,运输中的其他被保各方(如承运人和其他货物没有受到损失的货主)不必分摊受损一方的补偿费用。例如,暴风雨或火灾将发货人的货物部分损坏,其他货主没有必要去牺牲自己的货物来挽救整个货物运输。受损的货主可根据保险单规定的险别向保险公司要求赔偿。

由于发货人遇到的大部分损失都是部分损失,所以确切地了解保险单中有关部分损失的条款是非常重要的。

3. 费用

被保险货物遭遇保险责任范围内的事故,除了使货物本身受到损毁导致损失外,还会产生费用方面的损失。运输保险除保障损失外,还有保障费用的损失,这些费用主要有:

(1)施救费用

施救费用是指在保险范围内,由被保险人、雇用人员和受让人等为抢救保险货物,以防止损失扩大所采取措施而支出的合理费用。保险公司有责任赔偿此类费用。

(2)救助费用

救助费用是指在货物保险范围内,由被保险人、雇用人员和受让人以外的第三者采取救助行为而向其支付的报酬费用。

第二节　我国海运货物保险条款

根据《中国人民保险公司海洋运输货物保险条款》,保险可分为两大类:基本险和附加险。购买者可以单独购买基本险。然而,在购买附加险以前,他必须购买基本险。基本险可再分为平安险(F.P.A.)、水渍险(W.P.A.)和一切险。平安险主要包括全部损失和共同损失,而水渍险则再加上单独海损。一切险除水渍险的范围外,还包括诸如偷窃、提货不着险;短量险;混杂玷污险;渗漏险;碰撞、破碎险;串味险;受潮受热险;钩损险;锈损险;包装破损险等。投保平安险或水渍险可加保这些外来风险的一种或数种。

1. 基本险别

(1)平安险

从基本上讲,平安险是一种有限制的货物保险形式,因为承保人不会对部分损失或损坏进行赔偿,除非船舶的确遭受搁浅、沉没、失火等损失。在这种情况下,平安保险单持有人可得到船上被保险货物的损失赔偿,这与保险范围更广的水渍险一样。平安险提供由于实际海难所造成的全部损失和共同海损的保险。

根据 1981 年 1 月 1 日修订的《中国人民保险公司海洋运输货物保险条款》的规定,平安险负责赔偿:

①被保险货物在途中由于恶劣气候、雷电、海啸、地震、洪水等自然灾害造成整批货物的全部损失或推定全损。当被保险人要求赔付推定全损时,须将受损货物及其权利委付给保险公司。被保险货物用驳船运往或运离海轮的,每一驳船所装的货物可视作一整批。推定全损是指被保险货物的实际全损已经不可避免,或者恢复、修复受损货物以及运送货物到原定目的地的费用超过该货物的价值。

②由于遭受搁浅、触礁、沉没、互撞、与流冰或其他物体碰撞以及失火、爆炸意外事故造成货物的全部或部分损失。

③在运输工具已经发生搁浅、触礁、沉没、焚毁等意外事故的情况下,货物在此前后又在海上遭受恶劣气候、雷电、海啸等自然灾害所造成的部分损失。

④在装卸或转运时由于一件或数件、整件货物落海造成的全部或部分损

失。

⑤被保险人对遭受承保责任内危险的货物采取抢救、防止或减少货损的措施而支付的合理费用,但以不超过该批被救货物的保险金额为限。

⑥运输工具遭遇海难后,在避难港由于卸货所引起的损失,以及在中途港、避难港由于卸货、存仓以及运送货物所产生的特别费用。

⑦共同海损的牺牲、分摊和救助费用。

⑧运输契约订有“船舶互撞责任”条款,根据该条款规定,应由供货方偿还船方的损失。

(2)水渍险

水渍险的负责赔偿范围比平安险广。除了上述平安险的各项责任以外,水渍险还负责被保险货物在运输途中由于恶劣气候、雷电、海啸、地震、洪水等造成的部分损失。

(3)一切险

在三种基本险别中,一切险承保的范围最为广泛。除了包括上述平安险和水渍险的各项责任以外,该保险还负责被保险货物在运输途中由于外来因素所致的全部或部分损失。要注意的是,一切险并不是像其名称所说的那样,承包所有的风险。一切险条款排除对由于战争、罢工、动乱等因素造成的损失的赔偿。这些风险可由单独的条款来负责赔偿。并且,一切险只负责赔偿由于外来原因所造成的物理性灭失或损坏。

(4)基本险别的除外责任

上述三种险别对下列损失不负赔偿责任:

①被保险人的故意行为或过失所造成的损失。

②属于发货人所引起的损失。

③在保险开始前,被保险货物已存在的品质不良或数量短差所造成的损失。

④被保险货物的自然损耗、本质缺陷、特性以及市价跌落、运输延迟所引起的损失或费用。

⑤本公司海洋运输货物战争险条款和货物运输罢工险条款规定的责任范围和除外责任。

(5)保险期限(保险责任的起讫)

我国采用国际保险市场上有关保险责任起讫规定的惯例:仓至仓条款。

仓至仓条款是保险责任起讫的条款。它是指自被保险货物运离保险单所载明的启运地发货人的仓库时生效,包括正常的运输过程,直至该货物运交保险单所载明的目的地收货人的仓库时为止。当货物一进入收货人的仓库,保险责任即行终止。

若货物卸离海船后,没有马上进收货人仓库,则:

①保险公司的责任延续60天。如果在60天内某日进入仓库,保险责任也即行终止。

②如在上述60天内被保险货物需转运至非保险单所载明的目的地时,则以该项货物开始运转时终止。

在国际保险业务中,保险公司并不是对所有保险合同都承担仓至仓责任的。由于海上货物运输保险本身的特殊性质,货物所有权是在不断地转让之中,它仅要求在保险标的发生损失、买方索赔时必须具有保险利益。此时保险单的求偿权已转移给买方。具体到贸易术语,如:FOB、CFR、FCA、CPT术语订立的买卖合同,卖方在装运港船上交货。所以以上贸易术语,它们的保险责任起讫实际上是“船至仓”。

2. 附加险

附加险包括一般附加险和特殊附加险。

由于附加险承保的是外来风险造成的损失,而外来风险又有一般外来风险和特殊外来风险之分,所以附加险也可分为一般附加险和特殊附加险。

一般附加险不能作为一个单独的项目投保,而只能在投保平安险或水渍险的基础上,根据货物的特性和需要加保一种或若干种。如加保所有的一般附加险,这就叫投保一切险。可见,一般附加险被包括在一切险的承保范围内,故在投保一切险时,不存在再加保一般附加险的问题。

- 一般附加险:

(1)偷窃、提货不着险;

(2)淡水雨淋险;

(3)短量险;

(4)混杂、玷污险;

(5)渗漏险;

(6)碰撞、破碎险;

(7)串味险;

(8)受热、受潮险;

(9)钩损险;

(10)包装破裂险;

(11)锈损险。

锈损必须在运输过程中发生。对于包装时就已发生的锈损,不予赔偿。

这些附加险都不能单独投保,只能在投保三种基本险别的基础上加保一种或若干种附加险。

一切险已包含所有 11 种一般附加险,所以不需要再加保一般附加险(不包含特殊附加险)。

- 特殊附加险

特殊附加险不包括在一切险范围内,目前共有 8 种。战争险和罢工险为其中最主要的特殊附加险。

- 战争险

战争险不能单独投保,必须在投保一种基本险别的基础上加保。

战争险是特殊附加险的主要险别之一,它虽然不能独立投保,但对其他附加险而言又有很强的独立性,其内容包括责任范围、除外责任、责任起讫等。

(1)承保责任范围

①由于直接战争、类似战争行为、敌对行为、武装冲突或海盗行为等所造成的运输货物的损失;

②由于上述原因所引起的捕获、拘留、扣留、禁制、扣押等所造成的运输货物的损失;

③各种常规武器(水雷、炸弹等)所造成的运输货物的损失;

④由本险责任范围所引起的共同海损牺牲、分摊和救助费用。

(2)战争险的除外责任

由于敌对行为使用原子弹或热核制造的武器导致被保险货物的损失和费用不负责赔偿。

例外条款:原子弹、氢弹、执政当局、武装集团命令、扣押、拘留引起的损失。

战争险起讫范围:不采用“仓至仓条款”,仅限于水上危险或运输工具上的危险。一旦卸离,水上或运输工具上的危险即停止。

(3)战争险的责任起讫

战争险的责任起讫与基本险所采用的“仓至仓”条款不同,而是采用“水面”条款,以“水上危险”为限,是指保险人的承保责任自货物装上保险单所载明的启运港的海轮或驳船开始,到卸离保险单所载明的目的港的海轮或驳船为止。如果货物不卸离海轮或驳船,则从海轮到达目的港当日午夜起算满 15 日之后责任自行终止;如果中途转船,不论货物在当地卸货与否,保险责任以海轮到达该港可卸货地点的当日午夜起算满 15 天为止,等再装上续运海轮时,保险责任才继续有效。

总的来说,战争险的保险责任起讫,不适用于仓至仓条款,而是从装运港装上船,保险责任开始生效,到目的港卸离海轮终止。

- 罢工险

罢工险是指对罢工人员行为所造成的损失进行保险,但对由于罢工而造成的劳力不足或不能运用劳力而造成的货物受损,不赔,例:货物因无人加油或空调不工作造成的货物受损,不能赔偿。

根据国际保险业的惯例,承保这一险别时,只要投保人已投保战争险就不再另收保费,而且一般都是与战争险同时承保。

3. 其他运输方式下的货运保险

在国际贸易中,不仅海洋运输的货物需办理保险,陆上运输、航空运输、邮包运输的货物也都需要办理保险。因此,保险公司对用不同方式运输的货物都订有相应的专门条款。

第三节　伦敦保险协会海运货物保险条款

英国的保险业历史悠久发达,对世界各国影响很大,“英国伦敦保险协会”的《协会货物条款》最早制定于 1912 年,最近的一次修订完成于 1981 年,并于 1982 年 1 月 1 日起开始实行。目前,世界上有 2/3 的国家在海上保险业务中采用了《协会货物条款》,对世界保险业的发展产生了很大的影响。我国的保险公司承保的业务,如果外商要求按 I.C.C.条款投保,我方则可以接受。

1. 伦敦保险协会修订的海运货物保险条款种类

伦敦保险协会修订的海运货物保险条款种类主要有以下 6 种:

(1)协会货物条款(A)[ICC(A)];

(2)协会货物条款(B)[ICC(B)];

(3)协会货物条款(C)[ICC(C)];

(4)协会战争险条款;

(5)协会罢工险条款;

(6)恶意损害险条款。

前5种险别可以单独投保。另外,ICC(A)险中包括恶意损害险,但在投保ICC(B)险或ICC(C)险时,应另行投保恶意损害险。

2. 伦敦保险协会海运货物保险条款的特点

(1)ICC条款的各种险别取消了按全部损失与部分损失区分险别的规定;

(2)ICC条款的各种险别赔偿时不计免赔率;

(3)ICC条款规定的保单是一种空白格式的保险单,其内容简单、明确,不包括保险条件,也取消了附注;

(4)ICC条款新增加了可保利益条款、续运费条款、增值条款、放弃条款和法律与惯例条款5个条款。

3. 伦敦协会货物保险条款规定保险责任的方法

ICC(A)

ICC(A)相当于我国海洋货物运输保险条款的一切险。

- ICC(A)承保的责任范围

ICC(A)采取"一切风险除外责任的方法",即除"除外责任"项下所列的风险,保险人不予负责外,其他风险均予负责,而ICC(B)险、ICC(C)险为"列明风险"。

- ICC(A)的除外责任

(1)一般除外责任包括:由于被保险人故意的不法行为造成的损失或费用;自然渗漏、重量或容量的自然损耗或自然磨损:包装或准备不足或不当所造成的损失或费用;保险标的内在缺陷或特性所造成的损失或费用;直接由于延迟所引起的损失或费用;由于船舶所有人、经理人、租船人或经营破产或不履行债务造成的损失或费用;由于使用任何原子或热核武器所造成的损失或费用。

(2)不适航和不适货除外责任:不适航和不适货除外责任是指在装船时,被保险人或其受雇人已经知道船舶不适航,以及船舶、装运工具、集装箱等不适货,违法适航、违法适货的默示保证为被保险人或其受雇人所知道。

(3)战争除外责任:战争除外责任是指由于战争、内战、暴动、起义、敌对行为等造成的损失或费用;由于捕获、拘留、扣留等(海盗除外)所造成的损失或费用;由于水雷、鱼雷或其他废弃的战争武器等所造成的损失或费用。

(4)罢工除外责任:罢工除外责任是指由于罢工者、被迫停工工人等所造成的损失或费用;任何恐怖主义者或出于政治动机而行动的人所造成的损失或费用。

ICC(B)

ICC(B)相当于我国保险条款的水渍险。

- ICC(B)规定保险责任的方法

可以概括为四个字:"列明风险"。即将承保范围内的风险一一列举出来,便于投保人选择险别,又便于保险公司处理损害赔偿。一律按损失程度给予赔偿,不因险别不同而对部分损失赔偿。无免赔率的规定。

- ICC(B)具体承保的风险

(1)灭失或损害由于下列原因:火灾、爆炸;船舶或驳船触礁、搁浅、沉没或倾覆;陆上运输工具倾覆或出轨;船舶,驳船或运输工具同水以外的外界物体碰撞;在避难港卸货;地震、火山爆发、雷电。

(2)灭失或损害由于下列原因造成:共同海损牺牲;抛货;浪击落海;海水、湖水或河水进入船舶、驳船、运输工具、集装箱、大型海运箱或贮存处所;货物在装卸时落海或摔落造成整件全损。

- ICC(B)的除外责任

ICC(B)的除外责任包括ICC(A)的除外责任的内容,另外,加上对海盗造成的损失和对第三方的恶意损害,都是ICC(B)险的除外责任。也就是说,ICC(B)都不予赔偿。

ICC(C)

ICC(C)相当于我国海洋货物运输保险的平安险。

- ICC(C)规定保险责任的方法

ICC(C)只赔偿重大意外事故造成的损失,对非重大意外事故和自然灾害造成的损失都不赔偿,对浪击落海,海水、湖水或河水进入船舱和集装箱以及货物装卸时单件或数件落海都不予赔偿。

- ICC(C)的除外责任

ICC(C)的除外责任与ICC(B)相同。ICC(A)和ICC(B)比我国海洋货物运输的平安险和水渍险的范围要大。ICC(A)增加了对第三方恶意损害的赔偿和对海盗造成的损失进行赔偿。另外,对浪击落海,海水、湖水或河水进入船舱给予赔偿。这两个条款是我国海洋货物运输保险条款所没有的。

第四节 保险实务

在进出口货物运输保险业务中,被保险人在选择确定投保的险别后通常涉及的工作有:确定保险金额、办理投保并交付保险费、领取保险单证以及在货物受损时办理保险索赔等。

外贸企业在装船前根据出口合同或信用证的规定,在备妥货物,确定运输工具和装运日期后即可申请投保,填写投保单,列明被保险人名称、保险标的物名称、数量、包装方式、运输标志、起止地点、船名、航次、保险金额、投保日期、赔款地点等。

1. 保险费的计算方法有以下几种

(1)保险金额(投保金额)

投保金额是保险公司可以赔偿的最高金额,也是核算保险费的基础。

习惯上,按发票金额加一成(即10%)投保加成:

$$保险金额=CIF(总值)\times(1+10\%)$$

(2)保险费

保险费是投保人给保险人的对价,是保险人承担保险责任的前提条件。

(3)保费率

保费率是计收保险费的依据。保险人交纳保险费的多少主要取决于保险金额和保费率,保费率是根据保险险别、风险大小、损失率高低制定的。保险费的计算公式为:

$$保险费=保险金额\times保费率=\{CIF\times[1+10\%(投保加成率)]\}\times保费率$$

例如:某商品出口美国,共10 000件,每件10美元,CIF纽约。投保一切险加战争险,保费率分别为0.6%和0.4%。试计算保险费。

答:保险金额=[CIF×(1+10%)]

保险费=保险金额×保费率

=[CIF×(1+10%)]×保费率

=[10×10 000×(1+10%)]×(0.6%+0.4%)

= 110 000×1% = 1 100(美元)

进口货物运输保险分为进口预约保险合同(open cover)和预约保单(open

policy)。凡按 FOB、CFR、CPT、FCA 签订的进口合同,由进口方投保。我国外贸企业为了简化手续,大多采用预约保险的做法,也就是由我方外贸企业与保险公司签订各种不同运输方式的进口预约保险合同。按照预约保险合同的规定,外贸企业无须逐笔填写投保单,只须将国外卖方出口商的装运通知送交保险公司,即为办妥了进口保险手续。

2. 保险单据

保险单据是保险公司在接受投保后签发的承保凭证,是保险人和被保险人之间订立的保险合同。在被保险货物受到保险合同责任范围的损失时,它是被保险人索赔和保险人理赔的主要依据。在 CIF、CIP 合同中,保险单据是卖方必须向买方提供的主要单据之一。保险单是可以背书转让的。

在 CIF 或 CIP 价格条件下,被保险人即为卖方(出口商),信用证方式下指的是受益人(卖方),托收方式下为委托人(卖方)。

UCP600 第二十八条 e 款规定:“保险单据日期不得晚于发运日期,除非保险单据表明保险责任不迟于发运日生效。”

- 保险单据的种类

(1)保险单

保险单俗称大保单,是一种正规的保险合同。保险单除载明被保险人名称,被保险货物名称、数量、重量、运输标志、运输工具、航次、起讫地点、承保险别、保险币别和保险金额、保费是否已付、赔偿地点、出具保单日期外,在背面还印有保险人的责任范围以及保险人与被保险人各自的权利、义务等内容的详细条款。图 6-1 是一份出口保险单样本:

中保财产保险有限公司

The People's Insurance (Property) Company of China, Ltd.

发票号码
Invoice No. INV52148

保险单号次
Policy No.

海洋货物运输保险单

MARINE CARGO TRANSPORTATION INSURANCE POLICY

被保险人:
Insured: NANJING FORGIGN TRADE IMP. AND EXP. CORP.

中保财产保险有限公司(以下简称本公司)根据被保险人的要求,及其所缴付约定的保险费,按照本保险单承担险别和背面所载条款与下列特别条款承保下列货物运输保险,特签发本保险单。

This policy of Insurance witnesses that the People's Insurance (Property) Company of China, Ltd. (hereinafter called "The Company"), at the request of the Insured and in consideration of the agreed premium paid by the Insured, undertakes to insure the undermentioned goods in transportation subject to conditions of the Policy as per the Clauses printed overleaf and other special clauses attached hereon.

保险货物项目 Descriptions of Goods	包装数量 Packing	单位 Unit Quantity	保险金额 Amount Insured
LADIES LYCRA LONG PANT	200CTNS	2 400PCS	USD52 800.00

承保险别

Conditions

COVERING RISKS AS PER "INSTITUTE CARGO CLAUSES(A)", AND :INSTITUTE WAR CLAUSES(CARGO)".

货物标记

Marks of Goods

CBD

LONDON

NOS1-200

总保险金额:

Total Amount Insured: U.S.DOLLARS FIFTY TWO THOUSAND EIGHT HUNDRED ONLY

保费

Premium As arranged

运输工具

Per conveyance S.S DAFENG

开航日期

Slg. on or abt OCT. 20,2009

起运港

Form NANJING

目的港

To LONDON

所保货物,如发生本保险单项下可能引起索赔的损失或损坏,应立即通知本公司下述代理人查勘。如有索赔,应向本公司提交保险单正本(本保险单共有 份正本)及有关文件。如一份正本已用于索赔,其余正本则自动失效。

In the event of loss or damage which may result in acclaim under this policy, immediate notice must be given to the Company's Agent as mentioned here under. Claims, if any, one of the original policy which has been issued in original (s) together with the relevant documents shall be surrendered to the Company. If one of the original policy has been accomplished, the others to be void.

赔款偿付地点

Claim payable at LONDON

日期

Date OCT 20,2009

在

at NANJING

地址:

Address: 318 ANSHI ROAD NANJING, CHINA

图 6-1 出口保险单样本

(2)保险凭证

保险凭证俗称小保单,是一种简化的保险凭证,除正面内容与大保单相同外,背面未印有详细条款。在法律上,与保险单具有同等的效力。

(3)批单

保险单出具后,如需要补充或变更,保险公司可应投保人的请求修改保险内容的凭证,该凭证称为批单。

保险单一经修改,保险公司就要对批单的内容负责。批单被贴在保险单上加盖骑缝章,作为保险单不可分割的一部分,法律上具有同等效力。

(4)保险通知书

在FOB、CFR、FCA、CPT条款下,出口交易中由买方自费办理投保,买方与国外保险公司订有预保合同,卖方装船以后直接向进口商指定的保险公司发出保险通知,自动承保。

保险通知副本作为卖方向买方议付的单据之一,此项业务实际上是卖方向买方提供的装运后服务。

3. 索赔程序

在发生保险人应承担的灭失或损失的情况下,为了避免损失发生或使损失最小,以及保证承运人或其他第三方的所有权利得到适当保护或行使,被保险人或其代理应该:

(1)申请检验。在货物发生任何损坏的情况下,被保险人应该立即向保险单上写明的检验员申请检验。

(2)向承运人和/或其他相关方索赔。如果承运人或其他相关机构(海关和港口机构)对损失负责任,那么,被保险人应书面向他们提出索赔,并且如果有必要,应取得延长索赔期限的许可。此外,被保险人应从承运人或其他相关机构处获取灭失或损坏的证明材料。

(3)采取适当的措施。被保险人还应该立即采取措施,救助货物或避免或减少货物灭失或损坏。所采取的措施不应视作放弃委付或接受委付。

(4)取得索赔文件。为了使索赔得到及时处理,被保险人及其代理应毫不延迟地递交支撑文件,如果适用的话,文件包括:①保险单或保险证明正本;②运输发票正本或副本,连同运输详情和/或重量单;③正本提单和/或其他运输合同;④检验报告或其他文件证明,表明灭失或损坏程度;⑤目的地登录记录和重量单。

Chapter 7

International Payment

Part A Text

In international trade, the most frequently used means of payment include currencies and bills. As both a kind of security and credit instrument, bills are often used as a substitute for cash for international payment and in circulation. The most commonly used bills in international payments and settlements are bill of exchange (draft), promissory note and cheque (check).

There are three most commonly used payment methods in international trade: remittance, collection and Letter of Credit (L/C). According to the flow direction of money and the transfer direction of instruments, payment methods can be divided into favorable exchange and adverse exchange. Favorable exchange means that both of the two directions are the same, which is adapted in remittance and L/C. Adverse exchange means that the two directions are opposite, which is adapted in collection.

Section One Bill of Exchange /Draft

1. Definition

Bills of exchange are widely used in international settlement. According to *Nego-*

tiable Instruments Law of the People's Republic of China, A draft is a bill signed by the drawer, requiring the entrusted payer to make unconditional payment in a fixed amount at the sight of the bill or at a fixed date to the payee or the holder. A bill of exchange, namely a draft or a bill, is formally defined in *Bill of Exchange Act established in 1882 in Britain* as "an unconditional order in writing, addressed by one person (drawer) to another (drawee), signed by the person giving it, requiring the person to whom it is addressed to pay on demand, or at a fixed or determinable future time, a sum certain in money, to or to the order of, a specified person (payee), or to bearer". In short, a bill of exchange is a writing order from drawer for drawee to pay unconditionally.

2. Parties to a Bill of Exchange

There are three immediate parties to a bill of exchange: the drawer, the drawee and the payee.

The Drawer is the party who writes an order and gives directions to another person to pay a specific sum of money. He is usually the exporter or his bank in international trade.

The Drawee, namely the Payer, is the party to whom the order is addressed and who is to honor a bill at the order of the drawer. He is usually the importer or his bank in international trade. In addition, the drawee will become both the accepter and the principal debtor of the draft when he accepts a time bill.

The Payee is the party who receives the payment and who is the creditor of a bill. The drawer and payee is often the same person. Furthermore, the original payee will become an endorser and an endorsee will become the current payee when a bill of exchange is endorsed.

3. Essentials to a Bill of Exchange

In comply with *Negotiable Instruments Law of the People's Republic of China*, a bill of exchange must fulfill the following requisites to be regarded as valid:

(1) The words of "Bill of Exchange". The purpose of indicating these words on a bill is to make the bill recognizable and to distinguish it from other credit instruments such as promissory notes or cheques.

(2) An unconditional order in writing. It is a one-off payment without proviso.

(3) A certain sum. The sum of money is indicated accurately in both Arabic numbers and words in a definite kind of currency, not allowed to be described with ambiguous words and approximate sum.

(4) The name of payer. The payer, namely the drawee, is usually the importer or his bank.

(5) The name of payee. The payee is usually the exporter or his bank.

(6) The issuance date. The issuance date must be written on the draft so as to confirm the qualification of the drawer and calculate the payment date.

(7) The signature of drawer. The signature can be sign or seal or sign and seal. If the signature is fake or not authorized, the draft is invalid.

A specimen of bill of exchange is showed as follows:

BILL OF EXCHANGE

Dawn under WESTPAC BANKING CORPORATION ADELAIDE, AUSTRALIA

Irrevocable L/C No. AD25009/504919

Date MAY.23, 2009 Payable with interest @ ×××% per annum

No. 9005 Exchange for USD32 095.00 Nanjing, China AUG.15, 2009

At 30 DAYS AFTER BILL OF LADING DATE sight of this first of Exchange (Second of Exchange being unpaid)

pay to the order of BANK OF CHINA, JIANGSU BRANCH

the sum of U.S.DOLLARS THIRTY TWO THOUSAND AND NINETY FIVE ONLY.

To: WESTPAC BANKING CORPORATION ADELAIDE, AUSTRALIA

For and on behalf of

JIANGSU TOP IMPORT & EXPORT TRADING CO., LTD.

Fig. 7-1 Bill of Exchange Specimen

4. Types of Draft

According to different classification criteria, bills of exchange are usually divided into following types:

(1) Commercial draft vs. Banker's draft

According to different drawers, there are commercial draft and banker's draft.

Commercial draft is a draft drawn by a trader on another trader or a banker. The drawer is a firm or an individual, while the drawee (the payer) is a firm, an individual, or a bank. It is often used in foreign trade finance. Usually, a commercial draft is presented to the importer or the payment bank (L/C opening bank) through the bank in the exporter's place or the correspondent bank of it in the importer's place.

Banker's draft is a draft drawn by a bank on another bank or on its head/branch office. Usually, a banker's draft is sent to payee by remitter, with which the payee can exchange the money from the payer (another bank).

(2) Clean bill vs. Documentary bill

According to whether or not commercial documents are attached, there are clean bill and documentary bill.

A clean bill is one that has no relevant commercial documents attached and is normally used alone in international settlement. Clean bill is generally used in international trade to collect payment in small and sundry charges, such as commission, interest, sample fee and cash in advance etc.. A banker's draft is usually a clean bill.

A documentary bill is one that should be accompanied by relevant commercial documents to complete an export transaction. Commercial documents can be invoice, bill of lading, insurance policy and certificate of origin etc. This kind of bill is guaranteed by exporter's credit as well as the goods. A commercial draft is usually a documentary bill.

(3) Sight bill / Demand bill vs. Time bill / Usance bill

According to different payment time, there are sight bill and time bill.

Sight bill, namely demand bill, is supposed to be paid when it is first seen by the drawee. It can be expressed as payable at sight / on demand / on presentation.

Time bill, namely usance bill, requires acceptance before payment. It is a bill payable at a fixed or determinable future time. It will be further classified into different types, such as:

①At ×× days after sight, such as "30 days sight" or "60 days sight";

②At ×× days after date, such as "90 days after sight";

③At ×× days after date of Bill of Lading, such as "45 days after date of Bill of Lading";

④Fixed date, such as "On April 30th, 2018".

(4) Commercial Acceptance Bill vs. Banker's Acceptance Bill

According to different acceptors, there are commercial acceptance bill and banker's acceptance bill.

A commercial acceptance bill is a time bill that is accepted and will be paid by a commercial firm or a person.

A banker's acceptance bill is a time bill that is accepted and will be paid by a bank.

5. Acts Relating to a Bill of Exchange

(1) Issuance

To issue a draft comprises two acts to be performed by the drawer. One is to draw a draft and sign it; the other is to deliver it to the payee. The issuance is regarded to be fulfilled only after the bill is sent to the drawee. When issuing a bill, the drawer must draw it in its complete written form, containing all the essentials stipulated.

There three kinds of ways to fill up the payee:

①Restrictive order: Writing the words on the draft as "pay ×× only", or "pay ××, not negotiable". This type of draft is not transferable, and only the payee is qualified to accept the payment.

②Demonstrative order: Writing the words on the draft as "pay to ×× or to order", or "pay to the order of ××". This kind of bill is transferable to others with endorsement.

③Payable to bearer: Writing the words on the draft as "pay to bearer". It is transferable without endorsement.

(2) Presentation

Presentation is to be made by the holder to drawee for payment if it is a sight bill or for acceptance and payment if it is a time bill.

Presentation for payment means that the draft holder presents the draft to the payer asking for the sight payment.

Presentation for acceptance means that the draft holder presents the draft to the payer and asks for the acceptance at sight of the draft and payment on the maturity time.

(3) Acceptance

It is a promise made by the payer that it will make payment against a time draft. A valid acceptance requires two acts. One is for the drawee to write the word "Accepted" on the face of the bill remarking the acceptance date and sign below. The other one is for the drawee to return the accepted bill to the payee.

The principal debtor of a bill changes from the drawer to the acceptor after the acceptance. When it comes to endorsement, all the subsequent endorsees can recourse towards to the drawer before the acceptance.

(4) Payment

Payment is an act that the payer pays the sum of money to the bearer of the bill. Payment of a sight bill is made when the bill is presented to the drawee and payment of a time bill is made at maturity. After payment, all debts of a bill terminates.

(5) Endorsement

Endorsement is a legal procedure of the transfer of rights on bill of exchange. It means that the bearer records endorsement sentences on the back of a bill and signs, and then delivers the bill to the endorsee. Endorsement comprises two acts: one is to sign on the back of a draft; the other is to deliver it to the endorsee. By endorsement, the rights on the bill transfer from endorser to the endorsee, namely transferee. A bill can be transferred ceaselessly by endorsements.

There are three main kinds of endorsement: restrictive endorsement, demonstrative endorsement and blank endorsement. To the transferee, all the endorsers before him and the drawer are his prior parties. To the transferor, all the transferees after him are his subsequent parties. Prior parties have the responsibility to pay the bill to subsequent parties. There are three types of endorsements according to different endorsees. Bills of exchange are negotiable and transferable except for restrictive order.

①Restrictive endorsement is one that limits the bill for further negotiation, such as "pay ×× only" or "pay ×× non-transfer". Once the bill is restricted endorsed, it can't be transferred any more.

②Demonstrative endorsement bears the signature of the endorser and at the same time spells out the name of the endorsee. It specifies an endorsee to whom or to whose order the draft is to be paid, such as "pay to ×× or order" or "pay to the order of ××".

③Blank endorsement only bears the signature of the endorser and no endorsee is specified. It is also referred to as general endorsement.

Furthermore, a bearer of a time bill can get the money before the payer pays by discounting. In detail, a bank or a discount company reduces certain discount interest from the face value of an acceptance time bill and pays the rest amount of money to the bearer before the maturity date.

(6) Dishonor

Dishonor is a failure or a refusal to make acceptance or payment of a bill of exchange when presented to the drawee. Dishonor also happens when the payer return the bill, keeps away from the bill, dies or is bankrupted.

The draft holder has the right of recourse in case that the draft is not accepted when it is presented within a reasonable time or it is not paid on the maturity date. The bill holder has the right to claim for the payment against his prior parties.

(7) Recourse

The right of recourse means that the holder of bills of exchange has the right to claim compensation from the drawer and the endorsers in the event that the bill has been dishonored. The protest is an official document made by the local notary public, bank, chamber of commerce or court testifying that the draft has been dishonored. It is the legal proof with which the holder can exercise his right of the recourse against the prior parties.

It is to be worthy of attention that the drawer of a bill can add the words of "Without Recourse" when he draws or endorses a bill in order to avoid the responsibility of recourse. This kind of bill is untransferable in market.

Section Two Promissory Note

1. Definition

According to *Negotiable Instruments Law of the People's Republic of China*, a promissory note is the note issued by the drawer, promising to make unconditionally a definite sum of money to the payee or the note holder at sight of the note. According to *Bills of Exchange Act*, "A promissory note is an unconditional promise in writing made by one person (the maker) to another (the payee) and signed by the maker engaging to pay on demand or at a fixed or determinable future time a sum certain in money to or to the order of a specified person or bearer." In short, promissory note is a bill on which the drawer promises an unconditional payment to the payee.

2. Parties to a Promissory Note

There are two immediate parties to a promissory note: the Drawer and the Payee. The payer of a promissory note is the drawer himself. Acceptance is not applicable to a time promissory.

3. Essentials to a Promissory Note

There are different stipulations on the content of a promissory note in laws of different countries. It is stipulated in *Negotiable Instruments Law of the People's Republic of China* that the key elements in the promissory note are as follows: the word of "promissory note"; unconditional payment promise; a sum certain in money; the name of payee; the issuance date; the signature of drawer.

4. Types of Promissory Note

Promissory notes are usually divided into bank promissory note and commercial promissory note.

A commercial promissory note is also called a general promissory note, drawn by commercial firms or individuals. General promissory notes are divided into sight promissory notes and time promissory notes.

A bank promissory note is issued and signed by banks. Bank promissory notes are sight. Since a bank promissory note is based on bank credit, it is widely used in international payment settlement.

It is stipulated in *Negotiable Instruments Law of the People's Republic of China* that the promissory note is named as the bank promissory note, issued and sighed by the central bank of China or other financial institutions. Therefore, there are only bank promissory notes in China but no commercial promissory notes.

5. A Comparison between a Promissory Note and a Bill of Exchange

As international payment instruments, both bills of exchange and promissory notes are bills. But there are some differences between them as follows:

A promissory note is a promise made by the drawer to make payment to the note holder. However, a bill of exchange is an order to pay.

There are only two parties in a promissory note, including drawer and payee. But three parties in a B/E, namely drawer, drawee and payee.

The drawer of a promissory note is the payer. Acceptance is not applicable to a time promissory while acceptance is generally required for a time bill.

The drawer is the principal debtor of a promissory note in every situation. However, the drawer of a bill will change from the principal debtor to the second after the bill is accepted by the payer for the acceptor becomes the principal one.

A promissory note is a solo note when issued; whereas a B/E is usually in a duplicate set when issued.

Section Three Cheque/Check

1. Definition

In *Negotiable Instruments Law of the People's Republic of China*, a check means a bill issued and signed by the drawer, appointing the bank or other financial institutes to make payment of a sum certain in money unconditionally to the payee or the check holder. It is stipulated in Bill of Exchange Act that, "a check is an unconditional order drawn on a banker by the drawer, requiring the banker to pay on demand a sum certain in money to or to the order of a specified person or bearer."

2. Parties to a Cheque

There are three immediate parties to a cheque: the drawer, the drawee and the payee.

The Drawer is the person who writes the cheque. He should first be the banker's customer who maintains an account with the banker. Secondly, when he draws a cheque, it is his responsibility to make sure that there is enough balance in his account to cover the cheque amount. Otherwise, the cheque will be bounced.

The Drawee is the banker on whom the cheque is drawn and to whom the order to pay is given. He is the banker with which the drawer maintains an account.

The Payee is the person to whom a cheque is paid.

The drawer writes a sum certain in money on the cheque and draws on a banker requiring the banker to pay the sum to the specified person or to the bearer. The drawer shall be committed to the obligation for the cheque and on the law. The obligation of the cheque means that the drawer shall take the responsibility of making payment to the payee; the legal obligation refers to that the drawer shall keep an account in the paying bank with the deposit not lower than the sum on the cheque. If the deposit is insufficient, the cheque will be dishonored when the bearer presents it to paying bank for the payment. In this case, a cheque is called a bad cheque and the drawer shall be held for the legal responsibility.

3. Essentials to a Cheque

The key elements in a check according to *Negotiable Instruments Law of the People's Republic of China* are as follows: the word of "check" or "cheque"; unconditional payment promise; a sum certain in money; the name of payee; the issuance date; the signature of the drawer. A check without any of these stipulated elements is regarded as invalid.

4. Types of Cheque

There is no time cheque but only demand cheque.

According to *Negotiable Instruments Law of the People's Republic of China*, cheques are classified into cash cheques and transfer cheques. In other countries, cheques are divided into crossed cheques and uncrossed cheques.

A crossed cheque is crossed with two parallel lines on the up-left of the cheque, and the payee cannot cash the cheque but receive the payment through the bank transfer. Payee of the uncrossed cheque can both cash the money and make transfer.

Section Four Remittance

1. Definition and Parties

Remittance refers to a payment method that the payer makes payment to the payee through a bank or other institutions. For the remittance in the international trade, the buyer makes payment to the seller by bank according to the condition and the payment time stipulated in the contract.

There are four immediate parties in remittance: the remitter, the beneficiary or the payee, the remitting bank and the paying bank.

The Remitter is the party who makes payment by remittance. Usually the importer or the buyer is the remitter.

The Beneficiary or the Payee is the party who receives payment. Usually the seller is the payee or the beneficiary.

The Remitting Bank is the bank which issues a remittance instruction at the request of the buyer. Usually, the remitting bank is the bank in the importer's country.

The Paying Bank is the bank that transfers the money to the account of the seller following the instruction of the remitting bank. The paying bank is usually the bank in the exporter's country.

An application form of remittance is demanded when a remitter request a remittance, which is a contract that concluded between the buyer and the remitting bank.

Besides, the paying bank is the agency bank of the remitting bank and it is committed to the obligation of making payment.

2. Types of Remittance

There are three main types of remittance: M/T, T/T and D/D.

(1) Mail Transfer, M/T

Mail Transfer refers to remittance that the remitting bank sends a remittance instruction letter by mail to the paying bank at the request of the payer, authorizing the paying bank to make payment of a sum of money to the payee.

Advantage: Low cost;

Disadvantage: Long time for receiving the payment.

(2) Telegraphic Transfer, T/T

Telegraphic Transfer refers to remittance that the remitting bank sends the remittance instruction to the paying bank by telex, tele-transmission or SWIFT at the request of the payer.

Advantage: Speedy, beneficial to the seller's capital turnover as it can receive the payment in a short time;

Disadvantage: High cost.

The T/T procedure is shown as follows:

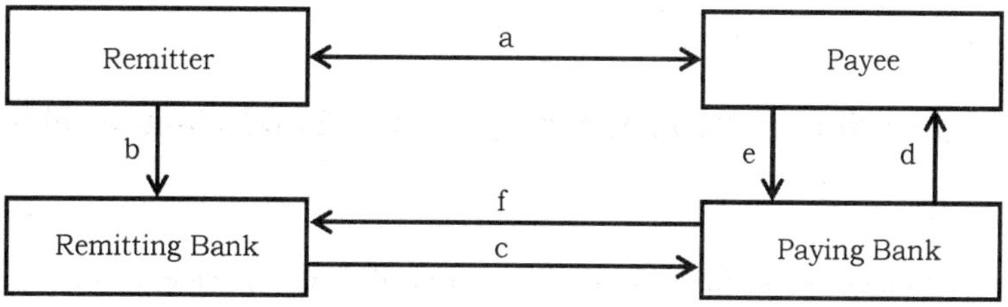

Fig. 7-2 T/T Procedure

a. The buyer (the remitter) and the seller (the payee) sign the sales contract stipulating payment by T/T.

b. The remitter gives his signed written application to his bank (the remitting bank), instructing it to transfer the funds through T/T. The remitter needs to have sufficient funds in his account in the bank. Meanwhile, banking commissions and charges should be paid to the bank for his service.

c. The remitting bank will debit the remitter's a/c with the amount to be reknitted together with its commission and cable charges (if any) and then issue and send the payment instruction by cable/telex/SWIFT to the paying bank.

d. When the overseas branch or correspondent bank receives the remittance instruction, it becomes the paying bank and then notifies the payee. The paying bank checks the identity of the payee before payment.

e. The payee issues a receipt as a certificate of receiving payment.

f. After payment, the paying bank sends the debit advice to the remitting bank to claim reimbursement.

(3) Remittance by Banker's Demand Draft, D/D

Demand draft refers to remittance that the remitting bank draws a banker's sight draft on its branch bank or agency bank on behalf of the payer after the payer pays some charges for the draft, and sends the draft to the payee; the payee gets the payment from the paying bank with the draft.

There are some differences between D/D and the other two. First of all, the paying bank doesn't need to inform the payee get the money, instead, the bearer of the bill comes to the bank by himself. Secondly, this kind of bill can be endorsed and transferred while the rights of receivable of the other two cannot. Therefore, D/D is relatively more flexible and convenient.

3. Application of Remittance in International Commercial Settlement

The remittance is usually applied in cash on delivery, payment in advance, payment of deposit, installments and payment of commission etc.

(1) Cash on Delivery, COD

The buyer will make payment on receipt of the documents or goods from the seller. Actually, it is a kind of credit offered by the seller to the buyer as well as a kind of credit sale. For the seller, the risk is the greatest. It totally depends on the credit of the buyer whether the seller will be paid after the delivery of the goods.

(2) Payment in Advance

The buyer will make payment prior to the seller's delivery of the goods. In this way, the buyer offers credit to the seller thus the buyer takes some risks? It is sometimes called Cash with Order (CWO). The buyer will make payment to the seller by T/T or M/T in a few days after the conclusion of the contract.

4. Characteristics of Remittance

Remittance belongs to commercial credit. Although the banks are intermediary in remittance, they provide no guaranty of settlement to both buyer and seller.

To the seller of cash on delivery and the buyer of payment in advance, whether the seller will be paid or the buyer will receive his goods depends on the other side's credit. There will be one side who takes huge risks.

The capital obligation, always belongs to one side of the contract, is extremely unbalanced during the entire transaction.

Section Five Collection

1. Definition

The definition from International Chamber of Commerce (ICC) URC522: Collections means the handling by banks, on instructions received, of documents (financial documents and/or commercial documents), in order to: a. obtain acceptance and/or, as the case may be, payment, or b. deliver commercial documents against acceptance and/or, as the case may be, against payment, or c. deliver documents on other terms and conditions. In short, collection, namely bank collection, is an arrangement whereby the seller draws a draft on the buyer and authorizes its bank to collect.

Financial documents means bills of exchange, promissory notes, cheques, payment receipts or other similar instruments used for obtaining the payment of money. Commercial documents means invoices, shipping documents, documents of title or other similar documents, or any other documents not being financial documents.

2. Parties to a Collection

There are several parties to a collection as follows:

The Principal is usually the seller.

The Remitting Bank is the bank in the exporter's country is authorized by the principal to effect the collection on behalf of the principal.

The Collecting Bank is the bank in the importer's country who receives the authorization from the remitting bank to collect the funds from the payer. It's usually the overseas branch or the agency bank of the remitting bank. The collecting bank can either act as the presenting bank or entrust the bank with the account of the payer to make the presentation.

The Presenting Bank is the bank who presents the shipping documents with the draft to the payer.

The Payer, namely the buyer, is the drawee. The payer is the person who presents the document according to the collection instruction. If a bill of exchange is adopted, the payer is the drawee of the bill, usually the importer.

3. Types of Collection

The collection is classified into two kinds which are clean collection and documentary collection. Clean collection means the collection of financial documents with no commercial documents accompanied. Documentary collection means collection of financial documents accompanied with commercial documents or collection of commercial documents not accompanied with financial documents. Documentary collection is widely used in international trade.

The documentary collection is divided into Documents against Payment (D/P) and Documents against Acceptance (D/A).

(1) Documents against Payment, D/P

D/P refers to collection that the seller delivers the documents after receiving the payment from the buyer (importer). The buyer can't get the documents until he makes the payment to the seller.

The documents are vital for a documentary collection, for the delivery of documents means the transfer of the ownership of cargo. The collecting bank in the importer's country will make presentation to the importer with the bill and the documents it received from the remitting bank, but will not release the documents to the importer until the importer makes payment to the collecting bank.

According to different time of payment, D/P can be divided into D/P at sight and D/P after sight.

①D/P at sight

Under D/P at sight, after the shipment, the seller draws a sight draft and makes presentation of it with the full set of commercial documents to buyer through the banks, and the buyer makes the payment at sight of the bill; the bank releases the documents to the buyer after receiving the full payment from the buyer.

Collection procedure under D/P at sight is shown as follows:

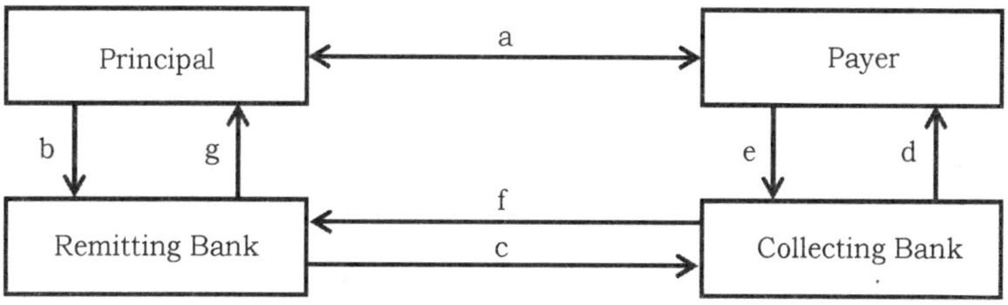

Fig. 7-3 Collection Procedure under D/P At Sight

a. The buyer and the seller conclude the sales of contract stipulating payment by D/P at sight.

b. After the shipment and the shipping documents are obtained, the exporter draws a sight draft and fills the application form for collection, indicating clearly that documents will be released under D/P at sight. The exporter submits them with shipping documents to his banker (remitting bank) for collection.

c. The remitting bank sends the full set of collecting documents to the collecting bank, entrusting them to collect the payment.

d. The collecting bank makes presentation for payment to the buyer.

e. The importer makes payment and gets the documents.

f. The collecting bank informs the remitting bank and makes transfer of the payment to the remitting bank.

g. The remitting bank credits the payment to the account of the exporter.

②D/P after sight

Under D/P after sight, after the shipment, the seller draws a time draft and makes presentation of it with the full set of commercial documents to buyer through the banks, and the buyer accepts the bill after confirming it and makes the payment on the mature date; then the bank releases the documents to the buyer.

To sum up, only after payment has been made can the buyer obtain the shipping documents, and take delivery of or resell the goods, whether it is D/P at sight or D/P after sight. Therefore, D/P represents less risk for the seller compared to using remittance.

(2) Documents against Acceptance, D/A

D/A refers to collection that the seller delivers the document after the buyer's acceptance on the draft. After the shipment, the seller draws an usance bill and makes presentation to the buyer through banks with the full set of documents; the collecting bank releases the documents to the buyer after the acceptance of the buyer. The buyer will fulfill the payment when the bill falls due. D/A means the buyer obtains the ownership of cargo before making payment and thus the seller is at a great risk. The seller will suffer losses in goods and money once the buyer fails to pay at maturity. Therefore, the international trade companies in our country are very cautious to the payment under D/A.

4. Characteristics of Collection

Collection is a kind of commercial credit which is favorable to the buyer. The payment by collection has no complicated procedures as the L/C, with no requirement of bank deposit, with lower bank service charges, and doesn't occupy capital. The remitting banks and collecting banks are not committed to the obligation of payment, and thus it completely depends on the buyer's credit whether the seller can receive the payment or not. The seller may not be paid if the buyer goes bankruptcy, loses the ability of discharging debt or refuses to pay in purpose. Although D/P is to deliver the documents after receiving the payment, the buyer may refuse to make payment and give up the documents when the market is shrinking. In this case, the seller will bear the losses in money and goods as well. The banks are not committed to the obligation to keep or take deliver the goods, and the seller has to pay for the settlement charges of delivery, customs clearance, warehouse storage, insurance, resale, auction or shipping back, etc. For the payment under D/A, the risk of the seller is larger.

Section Six Letter of Credit (L/C)

Letter of Credit (L/C) is a main payment instrument used in international trade. Under the circumstances that the seller and the buyer are not familiar with each other and lack of mutual trust, L/C is a good solution which replaces commercial credit with bank credit by getting a bank involved in the payment obligation. The payment promise to the seller from a bank before the delivery of goods greatly assists the transactions, further boosting the development of international trade. Except for sellers, L/C payment is favorable to the buyers, too. In a L/C transaction, the buyer can restrict the seller with the clauses of L/C to the fulfillment of the contract by ensuring the quality, quantity and delivery time of the goods. The seller won't be paid if he breaches the contract. Therefore, Letter of Credit has become a safe and speedy payment instrument in international trade.

1. Definition

According to *Uniform Customs and Practice for Documentary Credits, 2007 Revision, ICC Publication No. 600 (UCP600)*, a letter of credit means any arrangement, however named or described, that is irrevocable and thereby constitutes a definite undertaking of the issuing bank to honor a complying presentation.

"To honor" means to pay at sight if the credit is available by sight payment; to incur a deferred payment undertaking and pay at maturity if the credit is available by deferred payment; to accept a bill of exchange drawn by the beneficiary and pay at maturity if the credit is available by acceptance.

In short, a letter of credit is a conditional document undertaking of payment by a bank. In details, it is a kind of warrant issued by a bank at the request of the buyer and addressed to the exporter that promises to pay in a certain amount and under a certain condition. "A certain amount and a certain condition" means that the payment made by the issuing bank is under the condition of the seller's presentation of the documents complying with the L/C clauses.

2. Parties to a Letter of Credit

There are many parties to a letter of credit as follows.

The Applicant or Opener is the party which applies to the bank for the opening of a L/C, namely the importer.

The Issuing or Opening Bank is the bank which issues a credit to the seller. Usually, the issuing bank is located in the country of the importer.

The Advising or Notifying Bank is the bank nominated by the issuing bank and transfers a credit to the bank of the exporter's country. Usually, it is the branch bank or the correspondent bank of the issuing bank and is located in the country of the exporter.

The Beneficiary is the party entitled to use the credit and be reimbursed. Usually, it is the exporter or the actual supplier.

The Negotiating Bank is the bank willing to purchase or discount bill and/or the documents presented by the beneficiary under a L/C. It may be a bank designated by the issuing bank or another bank which is able to negotiate under the credit. The negotiating bank has the right of resource to the beneficiary.

Negotiation means that, after confirming the documents in compliance with the L/C, the negotiating bank discounts the bill and buyers the shipping documents according to the L/C clauses, and then pay the reimbursement sum to the beneficiary in advance, which is the balance that deducting the interests accrued from the negotiation date to the estimated payment date. Negotiation is actually a financing way for the beneficiary; after negotiation the bank becomes the holder of the bill with recourse.

The Paying or Drawee Bank is the bank which is specified in a L/C, which is usually the issuing bank or a branch bank/ correspondent bank of the issuing bank. Due to the transfer of money, the issuing bank may nominate another bank as the paying bank. The paying bank has the equal status of the issuing bank. Once the paying bank makes the payment, it has no recourse to the beneficiary.

The Confirming Bank is the bank which adds the confirmation to a L/C at the request of the issuing bank. The confirming bank is responsible for the L/C separately concerning the commitment of making payment or negotiation. The confirming bank has the same obligation and status of the issuing bank. It can be acted by Advising/ Notifying Bank or other kinds of banks.

The Reimbursing Bank is the bank which is specified in a L/C to make reimbursement on behalf of the issuing bank or the paying bank. The bank is not committed to examine the documents but makes payment with the authorization of the issuing bank, and the payment is final. The reimbursing bank is requested to fulfill the payment resulting from the capital movement or that the capital of the issuing bank abundantly deposited in the reimbursing bank.

3. Procedures of L/C payment

(1) Application

In international trade, the applicant of a L/C is usually the importer. After the conclusion of the sales contract, the buyer (L/C applicant) applies to the opening bank for the credit. The applicant fills out the application form based on the sales contract. The buyer shall pay for the credit according to the clauses of sales contract without changing the terms and conditions and obligations in the contract. Once the credit is opened, the beneficiary shall fulfill the obligation of the documents presentation according to the L/C terms, upon which the opening bank makes payment.

For the application of the credit, the applicant shall pay a certain margin to the issuing bank, as well as the opening charges and correspondence charges.

(2) Issuance

The issuing bank issues the credit at the request of the applicant. The clauses of the credit shall be in compliance with the contents of the application form. The issuing bank then undertakes the payment responsibility to the beneficiary once the credit is issued.

(3) Advice

After receiving the credit from the opening bank, the advising bank notifies the credit beneficiary contact required by the opening bank. The advising bank shall deliver credit to the beneficiary promptly after verifying the test key and the signature of the credit.

(4) Verification and Modification

The beneficiary shall verify the credit after receiving it, confirming that the contents are in compliance with those of the sales contract. In case of any discrepancies, unacceptable credit clauses or soft clauses, the beneficiary shall notify the buyer to amend the credit. A credit can neither be amended nor cancelled without the agreement of the issuing bank, the confirming bank, if any, and the beneficiary.

(5) Presentation and Negotiation

The beneficiary may prepare the goods and arrange for the shipment according to the clauses in the credit after receiving and confirming of it or receiving the amendment notification.

The beneficiary may go to a local bank for negotiation when obtains the full set of documents after the shipment. The local bank advances funds to the beneficiary after deducting the bank interest which is calculated from the advance date to the reimbursement date, offering a financing to the beneficiary, and gaining interests and serve charges.

(6) Honor and Payment

The opening bank shall notify the applicant to make payment for the documents after transferring the funds to the negotiating bank. The applicant shall go to the opening bank and check the shipment documents on receipt of the notification from the opening bank. After verifying the documents, the applicant settles all payment including the charges involved and gets the document. The deposit, if any, will be deducted from the payment; the collateral, if any, shall be returned to the applicant after paying. Thereby, the relationship between the applicant and the opening bank due to the credit terminates.

The procedure of a documentary sight L/C payment is shown as follows:

a. Sales contract is established between the exporter and the importer, agreeing to settle the payment by documentary sight L/C.

b. The importer (the applicant) fills an application form and requests his banker (the issuing bank) to issue a credit.

c. The issuing bank issues a credit in favor of the exporter (the beneficiary) and delivers it to the advising bank.

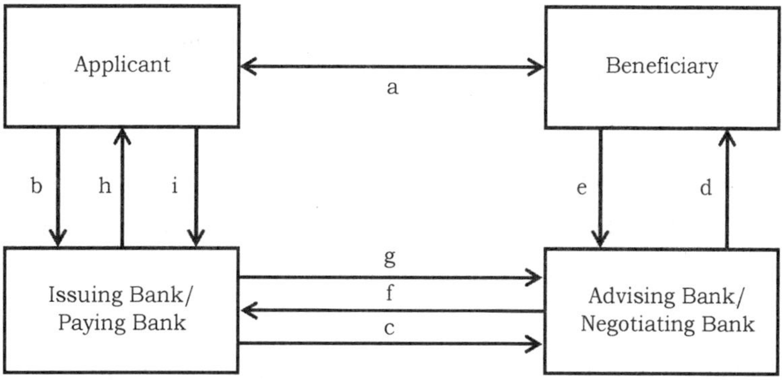

Fig. 7-4 Procedure of a Documentary Sight L/C Payment

d. The advising bank examines the credit and transfers it to the seller.

e. The seller presents the documents for negotiation after shipment.

f. The negotiating bank delivers the documents to the issuing bank for reimbursement.

g. The opening bank makes payment to the negotiating bank after verifying the documents.

h. The opening bank notifies the buyer.

i. The buyer pays for documents.

4. Contents of a L/C

The contents of a L/C mainly consist of the requests on documents based on the contract clauses and the payment guaranty of the bank.

(1) General information of L/C

The general information of a credit is mainly as follows: whether the credit is confirmable or not, and transferable or not; the conception of revocable credit has been deleted from *UCP600*, and all credits are irrevocable; credit number; sum, currency, and spelling in words and figures; expiry date and place; whether there is an overseas expiry date.

(2) Information required on the draft

Under a letter of credit, the information about the drawer, drawee, payee, sum, and other main terms must be specified on the draft.

(3) Description of the goods

The details including the name, types, specification, quantity, packing, price of the goods must be stated in a credit, as well as the contract which the credit is subject to.

(4) Shipment clauses

In a credit, the details of loading port (place), destination port (place), time of shipment and partial shipment/transshipment or not, etc. must be specified.

(5) Documents

In a credit, the documents required shall be specified as follows:

①Documents about the goods

There are invoice, packing list, certificate of origin, inspection certificate, etc..

②Shipping documents

The most important one is the ocean bill of lading, which is the warrant of cargo ownership.

③Insurance policies

In *UCP600*, it is stipulated as follows: "An insurance document, such as insurance policy, an insurance certificate or a declaration under an open cover must appear to be issued and signed by an insurance company, an underwriter or their agents or their proxies. When the insurance document indicates that it has been issued in more than one original, all originals must be presented. Cover notes will not be accepted. An insurance policy is acceptable in lieu of an insurance certificate or a declaration under an open cover. The date of the insurance document must be no later than the date of shipment, unless it appears from the issuance document that the cover is effective from a date not later the date of shipment. The insurance document must indicate the amount of insurance coverage and be in the same currency as the credit. If there is no indication in the credit of the insurance coverage required, the amount of insurance coverage must be as least 110% of the CIF or CIP value of the goods."

(6) Special clause

Special clause includes the special instruction, special requirement for the negotiation, payment route, confirmation information of bank.

Bank's promise of payment: For example, "we hereby agree with the drawers, endorsers and bona fide holders of drafts drawn under and in compliance with the terms of this credit that such drafts will be duly honored on due presentation to the drawee if negotiated on or before expiry date and paid on maturity."

"The advising bank is requested to notify the beneficiary without adding their confirmation."

(7) A declaration to subject to *UCP600*

For example, "this credit is subject to *Uniform Customs and Practice for Documentary Credit 2007 Revision by ICC (International Chamber of Commerce) and Publication No. 600.*"

Two L/C specimens are showed as follows:

2009MAY24 02:16:37			LOGICAL TERMINAL	PAL5
MT S700			ISSUE OF A DOCUMENTARY CREDIT	PAGE 00001
			FUNC	MSC700
			UMR	1080003
MSGACK DWS765I AUTHENTICATION SUCCESSFUL WITH PRIMARY KEY				
BASIC HEADER			F 01 BKCHCNBJA872 5619 928007	
APPLICATION HEADER			0 700 1159 090523 WPACAU2SAXXX 3458 193456 090524 0216 N * WESTPAC BANKING CORPORATION * ADELAIDE, AUSTRALIA	
USER HEADER			BANK. PRIORITY 113: MSG USER REF. 108:	
SEQUENCE OF TOTAL	*	27	1/1	
FORM OF DOC. CREDIT	*	40 A	NON-TRANSFERABLE	
APPLICABLE RULES		40E	UCP LATEST VERSION	
DOC. CREDIT NUMBER	*	20	AD25009/504919	
DATE OF ISSUE		31 C	090523	
EXPIRY	*	31 D	DATE 090905 PLACE CHINA	
APPLICANT	*	50	TONY COLYER PTY.LTD. 50 CHAPEL STREET NORWOOD SA 5067 AUSTRALIA	
BENEFICIARY	*	59	DESUN TRADING CO., LTD. HUARONG MANSION RM2901 NO. 85 GUANJIAQIAO, NANJING 210005, CHINA TEL: 0086-25-4715004 FAX: 0086-25-4711363	
AMOUNT	*	32 B	CURRENCY USD AMOUNT 32095.00	
MAX. CREDIT AMOUNT		39 B	MAXIMUM	
AVAILABLE WITH/BY	*	41 D	BANK OF CHINA JIANGSU BRANCH BY NEGOTIATION	
DRAFTS AT ...		42 C	SIGHT	
DRAWEE		42 A	WESTPAC BANKING CORPORATION	

			ADELAIDE, AUSTRALIA
PARTIAL SHIPMENTS		43 P	ALLOWED
TRANSSHIPMENT		43 T	ALLOWED
PORT OF LOADING		44 E	 TIANJIN
PORT OF DISCHARGE		44 F	 ADELAIDE
GOODS DESCRIPT.		45 A	 WHITE AND DYED TOWELS CONTRACT 01KHAU08-INDENT 5980 CONTRACT 01KHAU09-INDENT 5962 CFR ADELAIDE
DOCS REQUIRED		46 A	 DOCUMENTS REQUIRED: + COMMERCIAL INVOICE IN 2 FOLD. + FULL SET CLEAN "ON BOARD" OR "SHIPPED" NEGOTIABLE MARINE BILLS OF LADING TO ORDER/BLANK ENDORSED MARKED FREIGHT PREPAID. + INSURANCE BUYERS CARE.
DD. CONDITIONS		47 A	 ADDITIONAL CONDITION: GOODS ARE TO BE SHIPPED AS FULL 20 FOOT CONTAINER FCL.
CHARGES		71 B	ALL BANK CHARGES OUTSIDE AUSTRALIA ARE FOR A/C BEN
PRESENTATION PERIOD		48	DOCUMENTS TO BE PRESENTED WITHIN 15 DAYS AFTER THE DATE OF ISSUANCE OF THE TRANSPORT DOCUMENT(S) BUT WITHIN THE VALIDITY OF THE CREDIT.
CONFIRMAT INSTR	*	49	WITHOUT
REIMBURS. BANK		53 A	WPACAU2SADE * WESTPAC BANKING CORPORATION * ADELAIDE, AUSTRALIA IN REIMBURSEMENT, NEGOTIATING BANK TO FORWARD DRAFT TO BANK NA AS DRAWEE. PLEASE FORWARD FIRST SET OF DOCUMENTS BY COURIER, AND SECONDS. BY ORDINARY AIRMAIL TO: ADELAIDE I.B.C 1ST FLOOR 2-8 KING WILLIAM STREET ADELAIDE SA 5000. THE NUMBER AND DATED OF THE CREDIT AND THE NAME OF OUR BANK MUS BE QUOTED ON ALL DRAFTS REQUIRED.
TRAILER		72	ORDER IS 〈AUT:〉〈ENC:〉〈CHK:〉〈TNG:〉〈PDE:〉 MAC: 3A630ED9 CHK: CF7F79B1EDF1 DLM:

Fig. 7-5 L/C Specimen 1

Issue of a Documentary Credit

Opening Bank		BKCHCNBJA08E SESSION:000 ISN:000000 BANK OF CHINA LIAONING NO. 5 ZHONGSHAN SQUARE ZHONGSHAN DISTRICT DALIAN CHINA
Destination Bank		KOEXKRSEXXX MESSAGE TYPE:700 KOREA EXCHANGE BANK SEOUL 178.2 KA, ULCHI RO, CHUNG-KO
Type of Documentary Credit	40A	IRREVOCABLE
Letter of Credit Number	20	LC84E0081/99
Date of Issue	31G	150916
Date and Place of Expiry	31D	151015 KOREA
Applicant Bank	51D	BANK OF CHINA LIAONING BRANCH
Applicant	50	DALIAN WEIDA TRADING CO., LTD.
Beneficiary	59	SANGYONG CORPORATION CPO BOX 110 SEOUL KOREA
Currency Code, Amount	32B	USD 1,146,725.04
Available with...by...	41D	ANY BANK BY NEGOTIATION
Drafts at	42C	45 DAYS AFTER SIGHT
Drawee	42D	BANK OF CHINA LIAONING BRANCH
Partial Shipments	43P	NOT ALLOWED
Transshipment	43T	NOT ALLOWED
Shipping on Board/Dispatch/Packing in Charge at/ from	44A	RUSSIAN SEA
Transportation to	44B	DALIAN PORT, P.R.CHINA
Latest Date of Shipment	44C	150913

Description of Goods or Services: 45A

FROZEN YELLOWFIN SOLE WHOLE ROUND (WITH WHITE BELLY) USD770/MT CFR DALIAN QUANTITY: 200MT

ALASKA PLAICE (WITH YELLOW BELLY) USD600/MT CFR DALIAN QUANTITY: 300MT

Documents Required: 46A

1. SIGNED COMMERCIAL INVOICE IN 5 COPIES.
2. FULL SET OF CLEAN ON BOARD OCEAN BILLS OF LADING MADE OUT TO ORDER AND BLANK ENDORSED, MARKED "FREIGHT PREPAID" NOTIFYING LIAONING OCEAN FISHING CO., LTD. TEL: (86) 411-3680288 LIAONING OCEAN FISHING CO., LTD. TEL: (86) 411-3680288
3. PACKING LIST/WEIGHT MEMO IN 4 COPIES INDICATING QUANTITY/GROSS AND NET WEIGHTS OF EACH PACKAGE AND PACKING CONDITIONSAS CALLED FOR BY THE L/C.
4. CERTIFICATE OF QUALITY IN 3 COPIES ISSUED BY PUBLIC RECOGNIZED SURVEYOR.
5. BENEFICIARY'S CERTIFIED COPY OF FAX DISPATCHED TO THE ACCOUNTEE WITH 3 DAYS AFTER SHIPMENT ADVISING NAME OF VESSEL, DATE, QUANTITY, WEIGHT, VALUE OF SHIPMENT, L/C NUMBER AND CONTRACT NUMBER.
6. CERTIFICATE OF ORIGIN IN 3 COPIES ISSUED BY AUTHORIZED INSTITUTION.
7. CERTIFICATE OF HEALTH IN 3 COPIES ISSUED BY AUTHORIZED INSTITUTION.

ADDITIONAL INSTRUCTIONS: 47A

1. CHARTER PARTY B/L AND THIRD PARTY DOCUMENTS ARE ACCEPTABLE.
2. SHIPMENT PRIOR TO L/C ISSUING DATE IS ACCEPTABLE.
3. BOTH QUANTITY AND AMOUNT 10 PERCENT MORE OR LESS ARE ALLOWED.

Charges	71B	ALL BANKING CHARGES OUTSIDE THE OPENNING BANK ARE FOR BENEFICIARY'S ACCOUNT.
Period for Presentation	48	DOCUMENTSMUST BE PRESENTED WITHIN 15 DAYS AFTER THE DATE OF ISSUANCE OF THE TRANSPORT DOCUMENTS BUT WITHIN THE VALIDITY OF THE CREDIT.
Confirmation	49	WITHOUT
Instructions to the Paying/Accepting/Negotiating Bank: 78 1. ALL DOCUMENTS TO BE FORWARDED IN ONE COVER, UNLESS OTHERWISE STATED ABOVE. 2. DISCREPANT DOCUMENT FEE OF USD 50.00 OR EQUAL CURRENCY WILL BE DEDUCTED FROM DRAWING IF DOCUMENTS WITH DISCREPANCIES ARE ACCEPTED.		
		KOEXKRSEXXX MESSAGE TYPE: 700
Advising Through Bank	57A	KOREA EXCHANGE BANK SEOUL 178.2 KA, ULCHI RO, CHUNG-KO

Fig. 7-6　L/C Specimen 2

5. Ways of Opening a L/C

The ways of opening a L/C mainly include open by airmail and open by cable.

(1) Open by Airmail

By this way, the issuing bank types the credit on a preprinted form with details transmitted from the application form and then sends it to the advising bank by registered airmail service. Open by airmail is rarely used nowadays.

(2) Open by cable

By this way, the issuing bank transmits the full credit through cable, telex, fax or SWIFT to the advising bank. Currently, SWIFT is the main way to transmit L/C in international trade.

"SWIFT" is the abbreviation of *Society for Worldwide Interbank Financial Telecommunication*. It is a non-profitable membership-based international interbank cooperation organization which was established in May of 1973 in Belgium. Every member bank of the association has its own code, namely SWIFT code (namely BIC), ensuring a speedy and accurate payment transfer to the payee's account. Most of China's banks are the members of the association. For a credit of SWIFT, the credit must be issued according to the regulations in the SWIFT manual, adopting the tag stipulated in the SWIFT manual. According to *UCP600*, the undertaking clauses of banks can be omitted in the credit but not the obligations of banks.

Before the SWIFT L/C, the credits are mainly issued by cable or telex. The criterions, clauses and forms differ in different countries and the languages are verbose.

Since the SWIFT L/C is adopted, credits are issued in standard fixed and unified form, with speedy transmission and low cost. Therefore, SWIFT L/C has been widely used in northern Europe, America and Asian countries.

6. Types of L/C

According to various natures, due times and usage modes, there are many types of L/C as follows:

(1) Documentary L/C vs. Clean L/C

Documentary L/C is a credit that the opening bank makes payment against a documentary draft or only the documents. Documentary credit is widely used in international trade.

Clean L/C is referred to a credit that requires the issuing bank to make payment by the presentation of a clean draft or non-shipping documents. Payment in advance usually adopts clean credit.

(2) Irrevocable L/C

An irrevocable credit means that the issuing bank is irrevocably bound to honor since the credit is issued. In another word, an issuing bank can't amend or revoke a credit without the approval of the parties involved; an issuing bank must effect payment so long as the beneficiary makes a presentation of flawless documents.

Before the publication of *UCP600*, credits are classified into being revocable and irrevocable. Since *UCP600* came into effect on 1st July, 2007, the conception of revocable credit is deleted, that is to say, "a credit is irrevocable even if there is no indication to that effect."

(3) Sight L/C vs. Usance L/C

①Sight L/C

Under sight L/C, namely "L/C by sight draft", the issuing bank or paying bank effects payment immediately upon the presentation of the documentary draft and shipping documents complying with the letter of credit by the beneficiary. Payment in this way is speedy and safe, and favorable to capital turnover.

In a sight credit, T/T Reimbursement Clause is also added sometimes, which means that the issuing bank allows the negotiating bank to notify the issuing bank or the nominated paying bank by cable or fax that the documents presented are complied with the credit clauses, and the issuing bank is responsible for effecting payment to the negotiating bank by T/T after receiving above-mentioned notification.

②Usance L/C

An usance L/C, namely "L/C by time draft", is a letter of credit under which the payment is made by the issuing bank or paying bank within the stipulated time of a draft after receiving the documents. There are three mainly types of usance credits as follows:

- Acceptance L/C

It is a credit accepted by a bank. A nominated bank will make acceptance after receiving the time draft and shipping documents that presented by the beneficiary, and then it will make payment on the maturity date.

For the draft under this credit, the bank undertakes the rights and obligations subject to the credit to the exporter before the acceptance, and undertakes liability for payment to the bill drawer, holder, or endorser after the acceptance. This kind of credit is also referred to as bank acceptance L/C.

- Deferred Payment L/C

It is stipulated in credit by the issuing bank that the payment is to be made within several days after shipment or receipt of documents. Under the kind of credit, the exporter is not required to issue a draft, thus the exporter can't discount the draft to get money in advance, but only pays for the goods or borrow money from bank. In export business, the price of goods under this credit will be a little higher than the bank acceptance L/C in order to balance the difference between the interest rate and discount rate. For a transaction in large amount, it is better to combine this kind of credit payment with the export loan of government.

- Usance L/C Payable at Sight

It is also named as "buyer's usance L/C". In this kind of credit, an usance draft is drawn by the beneficiary, and will be discounted by the paying bank with all interests paid by the importer. This kind of credit appears to be an usance credit, but actually the exporter can receive the payment in full amount at sight. Therefore, it is called usance L/C payable at sight.

(4) Restricted Negotiation Credit vs. Freely Negotiable Credit

A restricted negotiation credit, namely nominated negotiation credit, is a credit can only be negotiated by a pointed bank. A sentence such as "Negotiation under this credit is restricted to ×× Bank" is usually written on this kind of credit.

A freely negotiable credit, namely open invitation negotiable credit, is a credit can be negotiated by any bank in any city or country. A sentence such as "Available With Any Bank" is usually seen on this kind of credit.

(5) Confirmed vs. Unconfirmed L/C

Credits can be divided into confirmed L/C and unconfirmed L/C according to whether there is another bank adding its confirmation.

①Confirmed L/C

A confirmed L/C is a credit issued by the issuing bank, and guaranteed by another bank to fulfill the payment for the presentation of corresponding documents. The bank which adds its confirmation to the credit is called Confirming Bank.

As an independent principal, a confirming bank is responsible independently for the beneficiary, undertaking the primary obligation to pay to the beneficiary. In another word, the same as the issuing bank, a confirming bank undertakes the primary liability for payment. A confirmed credit is a credit with double guaranty, which is most favorable to the exporter. A confirming bank is usually the advising bank, or the other bank in the exporter's country or the third country bank. The confirmation is effected through adding confirmation clauses to the credit by the confirming bank.

②Unconfirmed L/C

An unconfirmed L/C means that the credit issued by the issuing bank is not confirmed by any bank. An unconfirmed credit is usually issued when the issuing bank is with a good reputation or the credit amount is small.

(6) Transferable L/C

According to whether the beneficiary can transfer a credit, there are transferable L/C and nontransferable L/C.

Transferable L/C is a credit under which the beneficiary ("first beneficiary") may request the advising bank or negotiating bank to transfer the full or partial credit rights to another person named transferee or second beneficiary. After transferring, it is the second beneficiary who draws the draft, presents the shipping documents and receives the payment, but it is still the first beneficiary who bears the responsibility of the seller stipulated in the sales contract.

In *UCP600*, it's stipulated that "transferrable credit means a credit that specifically states it is transferable". A transferable credit may be made available in whole or in part to another beneficiary ("second beneficiary") at the request of the beneficiary ("first beneficiary").

(7) Revolving L/C

A revolving credit is established for a certain sum and quantity of goods with a provision that the credit can be repeatedly used until the stipulated frequency or total amount.

There are revolving credits by time and by amount. A revolving credit by time means that the beneficiary can draw money repeatedly in a certain period. A revolving credit by amount means that the total amount will automatically recover for negotiation and payment again after the negotiation until the present total amount is used up.

(8) Reciprocal L/C

Reciprocal L/C refers to that two parties open letters of credit in favor of each other. The drawer and the beneficiary of one credit are normally the drawee and the payer of another one; the opening bank of one credit is the advising bank of another one. The amount of the two credits is the same or almost the same. The two credits can be opened to each other at the same time or one after another. Reciprocal L/C is usually used in barter trade and feeding processing trade. Both parties of trade can restrict each other by being mutually involved and conditioned.

(9) Back to Back L/C

Back to back L/C means that the beneficiary requires the advising bank of the original credit or other bank to issue a new credit with similar contents on the basis of the original one. The beneficiary of back to back L/C can be foreign or domestic. This kind of credit is normally opened for the resale of goods by middleman to make profit, or in case that direct trade business is not allowed in two countries and a third party is needed to link up the transaction. In this case, the trade is on the basis of two sales contracts signed by exporter, middleman and importer. The first credit, also named the original credit, is opened based on the contract signed by middleman and exporter. The second one, namely subsidiary credit or back to back credit, is opened based on the contract signed by middleman and exporter. The beneficiary of the original credit is the applicant of the subsidiary credit. The original credit is still valid after the subsidiary credit is issued. The contents of a back to back credit are usually as same as the contents of the original credit except for the applicant, opening bank, beneficiary, sum, price, shipment time, and valid time. The price of the original credit is higher than that of a back to back credit, while the difference of these two is the profit or commission of the middleman.

(10) Standby L/C

Standby L/C is also called Commercial Paper L/C or Guarantee L/C, which is a guaranty issued by the opening bank on behalf of the applicant declaring that the bank will undertake certain obligations. In details, the issuing bank guarantees that when the applicant fails to fulfill its obligation that has to be done, the beneficiary can make a bill of exchange to the issuing bank according to the stipulations of the standby credit (or not), and present to the opening bank the statements or evidence papers that testify the applicant's failure to perform his obligations, to effect the payment. The standby credit belongs to the bank credit, and the issuing bank undertakes the primary responsibility for payment.

7. Characteristics of L/C

The characteristics of letter of credit payment method are mainly reflected in the following three aspects:

(1) Opening bank undertaking the primary responsibility of payment

It is a kind of absolute and primary responsibility. In another word, after opening a credit, the opening bank has to fulfill the payment according to L/C terms whenever the buyer is bankrupt, with solvency, dead or not. Without the consent of the beneficiary, a credit can't be revoked or revised.

(2) L/C is a self-sufficient instrument

A letter of credit is another contract, which is issued based on the sales of contract, but independent from the sales contract and the application form. A letter of credit is actually a contract between the issuing bank and the beneficiary. The rights and obligations of the parties involved are subject to the credit, not bound by the sales contract. Therefore, a payment or acceptance promise made by a bank is not bound by the restriction of the claims or defenses between the applicant and the issuing bank or the beneficiary based on the existing relationships.

(3) L/C is a transaction of documents

Under a letter of credit, a bank makes payment against documents. A bank makes payment depending on the documentary compliance with the shipping documents and the credit, which is not concerned with the goods, the sales contract and the truth or falsity of the documents.

With the principle of strict compliance, the documents must comply with the credit as well as each other. The paying bank must make payment as long as the documents are correct even though the actual shipment has something wrong. The paying bank can refuse payment if the documents are wrong even though the shipment is right. In case that the goods are faked or the seller acts dishonestly, the way to make refusal of the payment is to find out the documentary discrepancies.

Section Seven Usage of Different Payment Methods

In the practice of international trade, in order to conclude the deal, both parties may adopt two or more payment methods combined together if they fail to reach agreement on a certain payment method. The frequently used combination of payment methods are listed as follows:

1. Combination of L/C and Remittance

It means that the payment is partially made by L/C and the balance is paid by remittance. For example, for the transaction of ores, both parties may agree that certain percent of the invoice amount is paid by L/C with presentation of the shipping documents, and the balance is paid by remittance according to commodity inspection result and the actual quality or weight after the arrival of the goods.

2. Combination of L/C and Collection

Payment effected in this way will partly be made by L/C and partly by collection. This will require the buyer to open a L/C for a certain percentage of the whole payment of the goods, and the balance is to be collected. It is usually operated in the way as follows: Two bills of exchange are issued according to the credit, the payment by credit is made with the clean draft and the payment by collection is made by sig or time D/P with the presentation of the full set of documents. For safety, clause such as "the documents delivered upon the full payment" must be stated in the letter of credit.

3. Combination of Remittance, Collection and L/C

For the transactions of whole set equipment, large mechanical products and vehicles, due to the large contract sum and long production cycle of the products, the payment is usually made by installment according to the project schedule and delivery schedule. Under this circumstance, the combination of remittance, collection and L/C is adapted.

Part B Key Terms

Draft/ bill of exchange 汇票
Presentation 提示
Endorse 背书
Honor 承付
Accept 承兑
Dishonor 拒付
Discount 贴现
Right of recourse 追索权
Promissory note 本票
Remittance 汇付
Collection 托收
Applicant 开证申请人
Opening bank 开证行
Advising bank 通知行
Negotiating bank 议付行
Beneficiary 受益人
Cash on delivery 货到付款

Payment in advance　预付货款
T/T　电汇
M/T　信汇
D/D　票汇
D/P　付款交单
D/A　承兑交单
SWIFT
UCP600

Part C　Exercises

Ⅰ. Reflection questions

(1) What are the difference between the commercial bill and the banker's bill?

(2) What is the endorsement of the bill of exchange? How many types are there for the endorsement?

(3) What is the property of the collection? How to use it in international trade?

(4) What are the main contents included in a letter of credit?

(5) What are the differences between a standby credit and a documentary credit?

Ⅱ. Calculation

Suppose the exporter drew a documentary draft on April 20th, 2017, and the bank at the country of the importer made the presentation to the importer on the same day when the draft was received on April 27th, 2017, then under circumstances of D/P at sight, D/P at 30 days and D/A at 30 days, give the presentation and acceptance date of the draft, the date of payment, and the date of the documents releasing in the table below.

Circumstances/Date	Presentation	Acceptance	Payment	Documents Releasing
D/P at sight				
D/P at 30 days				
D/A at 30 days				

Ⅲ. Case & Study

A Chinese exporter reached a contract with a French buyer about some commodities in a large quantity in terms of CIF and irrevocable sight L/C payment, stipulating the shipment shall be effected in September in the contract, but no specific L/C issuing date mentioned therein. Later, the French buyer delayed the issuance of L/C because of the decrease of market price of the commodity. To avoid the delay of the shipment, the exporter had urged the buyer to issue L/C for many times since the middle of August, the buyer finally issued the L/C up to 9th September. However, it is too late for the exporter to arrange for the shipment as scheduled, who therefore required the buyer to extend the shipment time and the L/C negotiation expiry date for one more month. The French buyer refused the requirement, and cancelled the contract unilaterally excusing that the exporter failed to effect shipment on time. The exporter did nothing but accepted it. Please make analysis and comment about it: Had the exporter settled the matter in a proper way? What lessons shall we learn from it?

第七章

国际货款的收付

在国际贸易中，主要的支付工具是现金和票据。国际货款的收付，采用现金结算的较少，大多使用非现金结算。票据作为一种信用工具和有价证券，可以代替现金在市场上进行支付和流通。在进出口贸易中，最常使用的票据主要有三种：汇票、本票和支票。

在国际贸易中经常使用的支付方式主要有三种：汇付、托收和信用证。按资金的流向与支付方式的传递方向，支付方式可以分为顺汇和逆汇两种。顺汇是指资金的流动方向与支付工具的传递方向相同，汇付和信用证采用的是顺汇方法；逆汇是指资金的流动方向与支付工具的传递方向相反，托收采用的是逆汇方法。

第一节　汇　票

1. 定义

汇票是国际货款结算中使用最为广泛的一种票据。根据《中华人民共和国票据法》（简称“我国《票据法》”）的规定，汇票是出票人签发的，委托付款人在见票时或者在指定日期应无条件支付确定的金额给收款人或持票人的票据。根据各国广泛引用和参照的《英国票据法》的规定，“汇票是由一人签发给另一个人的无条件书面命令，要求受票人见票时或于未来某一规定的或可以确定的时间，将一定金额的款项支付给某一特定的人或其指定的人或持票人”。简言之，汇票是出票人要求受票人无条件付款的书面命令。

2. 汇票当事人

一般来说，汇票涉及三方面的基本当事人，即出票人、受票人和收款人。

出票人是签发汇票要求另一人支付一定金额的人。在进出口贸易中，汇票的出票人通常是出口方或出口地银行。

受票人，又称付款人，是接受汇票并将付款的人。在进出口贸易中，汇票的受票人通常是进口方或进口地银行。当受票人承兑一张远期汇票时，他就成为汇票的承兑人和主债务人。

收款人是收取票款的人，也是汇票的债权人。在进出口贸易中，汇票的出票人和收款人通常是同一人。若汇票进行背书转让，汇票的原收款人成为汇票的背书人，汇票的被背书人成为汇票的收款人。

3. 汇票要项

各国票据法对汇票内容的规定有所不同，根据我国《票据法》的明确规定，汇票必须记载下列事项：

(1)表明“汇票”字样。这样做是为了方便使用者辨认汇票，并将汇票和其他的票据支付工具(如本票、支票)区别开来。

(2)无条件的支付命令。汇票的支付不附带条件，且为一次性的支付。

(3)确定的金额。汇票上的金额是以一定的货币表示的确切数目，不能用大约或模棱两可的描述，并且要用文字大写、数字小写分别列明。

(4)付款人名称。付款人，即受票人，通常为进口方或其指定的银行。

(5)收款人名称。收款人通常为出口方或其指定的银行。

(6)出票日期。汇票上必须记载出票日期，用来确定出票人在签发汇票时是否有行为能力，并以此计算付款日。

(7)出票人签章。签章可以是签名、盖章或签名加盖章。若仿造签章，或为未经授权的签章，汇票被视为无效。

图 7-1 为汇票样本。

BILL OF EXCHANGE

Dawn under WESTPAC BANKING CORPORATION ADELAIDE, AUSTRALIA
Irrevocable L/C No. AD25009/504919
Date MAY.23, 2009 Payable with interest @ ×××% per annum
No. 9005 Exchange for USD32 095.00 Nanjing, China AUG.15, 2009

At 30 DAYS AFTER BILL OF LADING DATE sight of this first of Exchange (Second of Exchange being unpaid)
pay to the order of BANK OF CHINA, JIANGSU BRANCH
the sum of U.S.DOLLARS THIRTY TWO THOUSAND AND NINETY FIVE ONLY.

To: WESTPAC BANKING CORPORATION ADELAIDE, AUSTRALIA

For and on behalf of
JIANGSU TOP IMPORT & EXPORT TRADING CO., LTD.

图 7-1 汇票样本

4. 汇票的种类

根据不同的分类标准,汇票通常有以下几种类型:

(1)商业汇票和银行汇票

按出票人不同,汇票可分为商业汇票和银行汇票。

商业汇票是指由企业或个人签发的汇票,其出票人可以是企业和个人,而受票人可以是企业、个人,也可以是银行。商业汇票一般用于外贸金融。商业汇票通常由一国的卖方(即出口方)向另一国的买方(即进口方)或其付款银行开出,票款通常经由出口地银行或该银行在进口地的代理行向进口人或其委托的银行(如信用证开证行)进行收取。

银行汇票是指由银行签发的汇票,其受票人也是银行。银行汇票通常交由汇款人寄给受款人或亲自交给受款人,凭以向付款人(为另一家银行)兑取票款。

(2)光票和跟单汇票

按流通转让时有无随附商业单据,汇票可分为光票和跟单汇票。

光票，是指不附带商业单据的汇票。光票在国际贸易中通常用于收取小额费用或杂费，如佣金、利息、样品费及预付货款等。银行汇票多为光票。

跟单汇票，是指随附商业单据的汇票。随附单据可能是发票、提单、保险单、产地证明等。这种汇票既有人的信用担保，又有物的担保。商业汇票多为跟单汇票。

(3)即期汇票和远期汇票

按付款时间不同，汇票可分为即期汇票和远期汇票。

即期汇票，是指付款人在见票后立即付款的汇票，又称"见票即付"汇票。

远期汇票，是指付款人先承兑后付款的汇票，即付款人在出票一定期限后或在特定日期付款的汇票。对远期汇票付款日期的描述有多种类型，如：

①见票后若干天付款，如"见票后 30 天或 60 天付款"；

②出票后若干天付款，如"出票后 90 天付款"；

③提单签发日后若干天付款，如"提单签发日后 45 天付款"；

④指定日期付款，如"于 2018 年 4 月 30 日付款"。

(4)商业承兑汇票和银行承兑汇票

按承兑人不同，汇票可分为商业承兑汇票和银行承兑汇票。

商业承兑汇票是指以企业或个人为付款人和承兑人的远期汇票。

银行承兑汇票是指以银行为付款人和承兑人的远期汇票。

5. 汇票行为

(1)出票

出票，即汇票的签发。完整的出票行为包括两个动作。第一，制作书面汇票；出票人在汇票上填写付款人、付款金额、付款日期和地点、受款人等项目，并由出票人签字。第二，出票人将汇票交给受票人；只有经过汇票的交付才算完成出票行为。

在制作和填写汇票时，受款人的抬头通常有以下三种类型：

①限制性抬头。如在汇票上注明"仅付××"、"付××，不准流通"。限制性抬头的汇票不能流通转让，仅限指定的受款人收取票款。

②指示性抬头。如在汇票上注明"付××或其指定的人"。除指定受款人可以收取票款外，记名抬头的汇票也可以经过受款人自己背书，再转让给第三者。

③持票人或来人抬头。此种汇票无须背书，仅凭交付汇票即可转让。

(2)提示

提示,又称见票,是指收款人或持票人将汇票提交付款人要求付款或承兑的行为。由此,提示又可分为付款提示和承兑提示。

付款提示是指持票人向付款人出示汇票要求付款的行为。

承兑提示是指持票人向付款人出示远期汇票要求付款人办理承兑手续、承诺到期付款的行为。

(3)承兑

承兑是指远期汇票付款人对远期汇票表示承担到期付款责任的行为。完整的承兑行为包括两个动作。第一,付款人在汇票上写明“承兑”字样,注明承兑日期,并签字。第二,付款人把汇票交还持票人,才算完成承兑行为。付款人对汇票做出承兑,即为承兑人。

汇票在付款人承兑前,主债务人是出票人;在付款人承兑后,主债务人是付款人,出票人成为第二债务人。因为出票人可转让其汇票,在付款人承兑前,所有后手都可以向出票人追索。

(4)付款

付款是指付款人向持票人按汇票金额支付票款的行为。对即期汇票,在持票人提示汇票后,付款人即应付款;对远期汇票,付款人经过承兑后,在汇票到期日付款。付款后,汇票的一切债务即告终止。

(5)背书

背书是转让汇票权利的一种法定手续,指持票人在汇票背面记载背书文句、签名,并把汇票交付给被背书人的行为。完整的背书行为包括两个方面:一是持票人在汇票背面背书;二是将汇票交付给被背书人。只有通过交付,才算完成背书。通过背书,汇票的权利由背书人转给被背书人,即受让人,被背书人获得票据所有权。汇票可以经过背书不断转让下去。

汇票背书有三种方式:限制性背书、指示性背书和空白背书。对于受让人来说,所有在他以前的背书人以及原出票人都是他的“前手”;对于出让人来说,所有在他让与以后的受让人都是他的后手。前手对后手负有担保汇票必然会被偿付的责任。除限制性抬头的汇票外,汇票也可以在金融市场上流通转让。

①限制性背书。背书人在背书中加注“限制汇票继续流通”的文字,例如“仅付××”或“付××不准转让”。汇票经限制性背书后,就不能再流通转让。

②指示性背书。背书人在汇票背面先作被背书人的记载,再签字,例如“付给××或其指定人”。此种汇票可经被背书人自己背书,再转让给第三者。

③空白背书。背书人在汇票背面签字,但不记载被背书人的名字,也被称

为“不记名背书”。

此外，在国际市场上，一张远期汇票的持有人如想在付款人付款前取得票款，可以将汇票进行贴现。贴现是指远期汇票承兑后，尚未到期，由银行或贴现公司从票面金额中扣减按一定贴现率计算的贴现利息后，将余款付给持票人的行为。

(6)拒付

拒付，也称退票，指持票人提示汇票要求付款或承兑时，遭到拒绝付款，或遭到拒绝承兑。此外，付款人拒不见票、死亡或宣告破产，以致付款事实上已不可能时，也称拒付。

如汇票在合理时间内提示遭到拒付，持票人有权向其“前手”追索票款。持票人可以不按照汇票债务人的先后顺序，对其中任何一人、数人或全体行使追索权。

(7)追索

追索权，是指汇票遭到拒付时，持票人对其前手(如背书人、出票人)有请求其偿还汇票金额及费用的权利。在行使追索权时，持票人必须提供拒付证书。拒付证书是由付款地的法定公证人，如法院、银行、商会等，出具的证明拒付事实的文件，它是持票人凭以向其背书人、出票人以及汇票的其他债务人进行追索的法律依据。

值得注意的是，汇票的出票人或背书人为了避免承担被追索的责任，可在出票时或背书时加注“不受追索”的字样。凡加注“不受追索”字样的汇票，在市场上难以流通。

第二节　本　票

1. 定义

根据我国《票据法》规定，本票是由出票人签发的，承诺自己在见票时无条件支付确定的金额给收款人或者持票人的票据。根据《英国票据法》的定义，“本票是一个人向另一个人签发的，保证即期或定期或在可能确定的将来时间，对某人或其他持票人支付一定金额的无条件承诺”。简言之，本票是出票人对收款人承诺无条件支付一定金额的票据。

2. 本票当事人

本票的基本当事人只有两个:出票人和收款人。本票的出票人即付款人本人,远期本票无须办理承兑手续。

3. 本票要项

各国票据法对本票内容的规定各不相同。我国《票据法》规定,本票必须记载下列事项:表明“本票”字样;无条件的支付承诺;确定的金额;收款人名称;出票日期;出票人签字。本票上未记载以上规定事项之一的,本票无效。

4. 本票种类

本票通常可以分为商业本票和银行本票两种类型。

商业本票,也称为一般本票,是由工商企业或个人签发的本票,有即期本票和远期本票两种。

银行本票,是由银行签发的本票,只有即期。在国际贸易中使用的本票,大多是银行本票。由于银行本票建立在银行信用的基础上,因此,它在国际货款结算中被广泛使用。

我国《票据法》规定,本票即为银行本票,由中国人民银行或其他金融机构签发。因此,在我国只有银行本票,没有商业本票。

5. 本票与汇票的区别

作为国际支付工具,本票和汇票都属于票据的范畴,但两者又有所不同,其主要区别有:

本票是出票人承诺自己向持票人付款,而汇票是一个人向另一个人发出的支付命令。

本票的票面有两个当事人,即出票人和收款人;而汇票则有三个当事人,即出票人、受票人和收款人。

本票的出票人即是付款人,远期本票无须办理承兑;而远期汇票则要办理承兑手续。

本票在任何情况下,出票人都是绝对的主债务人,一旦拒付,持票人可以立即要求法院裁定,命令出票人付款;而汇票的出票人在承兑前是主债务人,在承兑后,承兑人是主债务人,出票人则处于从债务人的地位。

本票只能开出一张，而汇票可开出两张。

第三节　支　票

1. 定义

根据我国《票据法》的规定，支票是出票人签发的，委托办理支票存款业务的银行或者其他机构在见票时无条件支付确定金额给收款人或持票人的票据。根据《英国票据法》的定义，“支票是以银行为付款人的即期汇票，即存款人对银行无条件支付一定金额的委托或命令”。

2. 支票当事人

支票的基本当事人和汇票一样，共有三个：出票人、付款人和收款人。

出票人就是签发支票的人，他在银行已经开设存款账户并且订有支票协议，且在签发支票时，必须保证其在该银行账户的余额可以覆盖签发的支票金额，以委托该银行付款。

付款人是出票人的开户银行，即支票的付款银行，接受出票人的付款指令。

收款人是接受支票款项的人。

出票人在签发支票后，应负票据上的责任和法律上的责任。前者是指出票人对受款人担保支票的付款；后者是指出票人签发支票时，应在付款的银行存有不低于票面金额的存款。如存款不足，支票持有人在向付款银行提示支票要求付款时，就会遭到拒付。这种支票叫做空头支票。开出空头支票的出票人要负法律上的责任。

3. 支票要项

我国《票据法》规定，支票必须记载下列事项：表明“支付”字样；无条件的支付委托；确定的金额；付款人名称；出票日期；出票人签字。支票上未记载以上规定事项之一的，支票无效。

4. 支票种类

支票只有即期，没有远期。

我国《票据法》规定,支票可分为现金支票和转账支票;在其他国家,支票又可分为划线支票和未划线支票。

划线支票是指在支票正面划两道平行线的支票。划线支票不同于一般支票。一般支票可委托银行收款入账,也可由持票人自行提取现款。而划线支票只能委托银行代收票款入账。

第四节 汇 付

1. 汇付的含义

汇付,又称汇款,是指付款人主动通过银行或其他途径将款项汇交收款人的一种结算方式。国际货款的收付如采用汇付,一般是由买方按合同约定条件(如收到单据或货物)和时间,将货款通过银行,汇交给卖方。

在汇付业务中,通常涉及四个基本当事人:汇款人、受款人、汇出行和汇入行。

汇款人,即汇出款项的人,在进出口交易中,汇款人通常是进口人。

收款人,即收取款项的人,在进出口交易中,收款人通常是出口人。

汇出行,即受汇款人的委托汇出款项的银行,通常是在进口地的银行。

汇入行,即受汇出行委托解付汇款的银行,故又称解付行,在对外贸易中,通常是在出口地的银行。

汇款人在委托汇出行办理汇款时,要出具汇款申请书。汇款申请书是汇款人与汇出行之间的一种契约。此外,汇出行与汇入行之间事先订有代理合同,汇入行对汇出行承担解付汇款的义务。

2. 汇付的种类

汇付方式主要包括信汇、电汇和票汇三种。

(1)信汇

信汇是指汇出行应汇款人的申请,将信汇委托书邮寄给汇入行,授权解付一定金额给收款人的一种汇款方式。

优点:费用低廉。

缺点:收款人收取汇款时间长。

(2)电汇

电汇是指汇出行应汇款人的申请,拍发加押电报、电传或 SWIFT 给在另一个国家的分行或代理行(即汇入行),指示解付一定金额给收款人的一种汇款方式。

优点:速度快,收款人能尽快收到货款,有利于卖方资金周转。

缺点:费用较高。

电汇业务流程如下所示:

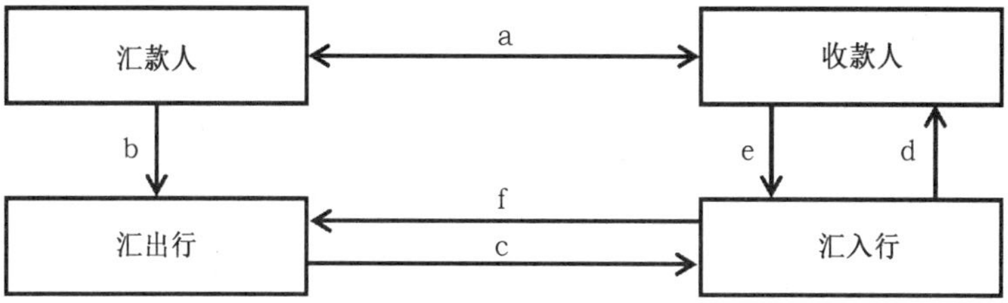

图 7-2　电汇业务

a. 交易双方签订进出口合同,约定采用电汇方式结算货款或其他款项。

b. 汇款人填写汇款申请书,明确采用电汇方式,连同货款及手续费等交汇出行。

c. 汇出行用电报或电传或 SWIFT 等对汇入行作出解付指示。

d. 汇入行核对汇出行的指示无误后,通知收款人。汇入行核对收款人的身份,对收款人解付款项。

e. 收款人出具收款收据。

f. 汇入行将付讫通知、收款收据等寄汇出行要求偿付。

(3)票汇

票汇是指汇出行应汇款人的申请,在汇款人向汇出行交款并支付一定费用的条件下,代替汇款人开立以其分行或代理行为解付行、支付一定金额给收款人的银行即期汇票,寄交收款人,由收款人凭以向汇入行取款的汇款方式。

票汇与电汇、信汇的不同在于,汇票的汇入行无须通知收款人取款,而由持票人登门取款。这种汇票除有限制转让和流通的规定外,经收款人背书,可以转让流通,而电汇、信汇的收款人则不能将收款权转让。因此,票汇具有较大的灵活性,使用也较方便。

3. 汇付方式在国际贸易中的使用

在国际贸易中,汇付方式通常用于货到付款、赊销、预付货款、随订单付现、支付定金、分期付款以及支付佣金等费用。

(1)货到付款

货到付款是指进口方在收到出口方的单据或货物后,再进行付款的方法,实际上是卖方向买方提供的一种信用,也是一种赊销。对卖方来说,风险最大,卖方交货以后,能否得到偿付,全凭买方个人信用。

(2)预付货款

预付货款是指进口商先将货款汇付给出口商,出口商收到货物再发货的方法。这种方式下买方向卖方提供了信用,买方存在一定的风险。这种做法有时叫做随订单付现。在合同签订后若干天,买方即将货款电汇或信汇给卖方。

4. 汇付的特点

汇付的性质是商业信用。汇付虽然是以银行为媒介进行国际结算的,但银行在此过程中仅承担收付委托款项的责任,不承担买卖双方在履行合同中的义务。

对于货到付款的卖方和预付货款的买方来说,能否按时收款或收货,完全取决于对方的信用。因此,买卖双方必定有一方要承担较大的风险。

整个交易过程中需要的资金,或者由卖方,或者由买方承担,资金负担极为不平衡。

第五节　托　收

1. 托收的含义

托收是委托收款的简称。国际商会《托收统一规则》(URC522)对托收作了如下定义:托收是指由接到托收指示的银行根据所收到的指示处理金融单据和/或商业单据,以便取得付款或承兑,或凭付款或承兑交出商业单据,或凭其他条款或条件交出单据。简言之,托收,又叫银行托收,是指债权人(卖方)出具汇票,委托银行向债务人(买方)收取货款的一种支付方式。

金融单据又指资金单据，是指汇票、本票、支票、付款收据或其他类似于用于取得付款的凭证。商业单据是指发票、运输单据、物权单据或其他类似单据，或除金融单据以外的其他单据。

2. 托收的当事人

托收方式涉及的当事人主要有：

委托人，即委托银行向国外付款人代收货款的人，通常为出口人。

托收行，是指接受委托人的委托办理托收业务的出口地银行。

代收行，是指接受托收行的委托向付款人收取货款的进口地银行，它通常是托收行的国外分行或代理行。代收行可以自己兼任提示行，也可以委托与付款人有账户往来关系的银行作提示行。

提示行，是指向付款人做出提示汇票和单据的银行。

付款人，是根据托收指示，向其提示单据的人。若使用汇票，即为汇票的受票人，通常为进口人。

3. 托收的种类

根据委托人签发的汇票是否附有单据，托收可分为光票托收和跟单托收。光票托收是指金融单据的托收，不附有商业单据。跟单托收是指附有商业单据的托收。在国际贸易中，货款的收取大多采用跟单托收。

在跟单托收的情况下，按照货物和货款的支付是否同时进行，即向进口人交单条件的不同，又分为付款交单和承兑交单两种。

(1)付款交单

付款交单，是指出口人的交单是以进口人的付款为条件，即出口人发货后，取得装运单据，委托银行办理托收，并指示银行只有在进口人付清货款后，才能把商业单据交给进口人。

跟单托收中的单据很重要。在象征性交货的国际贸易中，货物的买卖实际上是一种单据的买卖，代表货物所有权的单据不能轻易脱手。国外代收行将托收行寄来的汇票和单据向进口人提示后，进口人必须先向代收行付款，付款后，代收行才可将单据交付进口人。

在付款交单情况下，如按付款时间的不同，又可细分为即期付款交单和远期付款交单。

①即期付款交单

在即期付款交单方式下,卖方装运货物后开具即期汇票,随附商业单据,通过银行向买方提示,买方见票后立即付款,买方付清货款后向银行领取全套商业单据。

即期付款交单的托收业务流程如图 7-3 所示:

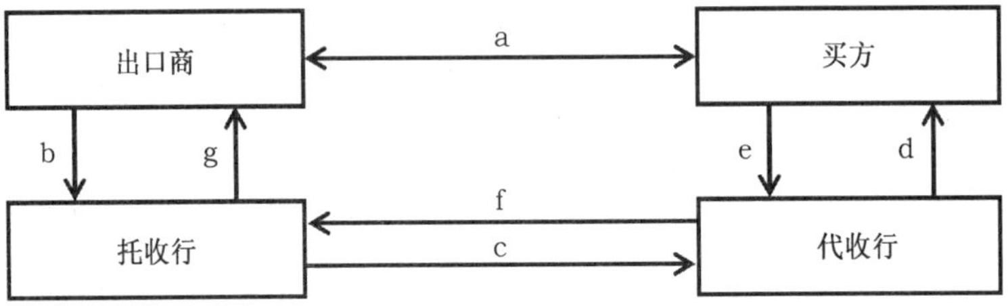

图 7-3 即期付款交单的托收业务流程

a. 买卖双方签订进出口合同,约定采用即期付款交单方式结算货款。

b. 出口商发货后,填写托收申请书,声明"付款交单",开立即期汇票,连同全套货运单据交付托收行委托其代收货款。

c. 托收行将全套托收单据寄交进口地银行(代收行)委托代收货款。

d. 代收行向买方做付款提示。

e. 进口商付清货款,赎取全套单据。

f. 代收行电告托收行,款已收妥转账。

g. 托收行向出口商支付货款。

②远期付款交单

在远期付款交单方式下,卖方装运货物后开出远期汇票,随附商业单据,通过银行向买方提示,买方审核无误后即在汇票上进行承兑,于汇票到期日付清货款后再向银行领取全套商业单据。

上述两种做法说明,不论是即期付款交单还是远期付款交单,都是买方必须在付清货款之后才能取得代表货物所有权的单据,才能提货或转售货物。所以,与汇付相比,托收的风险对卖方来说略小。

(2)承兑交单

承兑交单,是指出口人的交单以进口人在汇票上承兑为条件,即出口人在装运货物后开出远期汇票,随附全套单据,通过银行向进口人提示,进口人承兑汇票后,代收行即将全套单据交给进口人,在汇票到期时,进口人再来履行付款义务。承兑交单实际上是买方先取得货物所有权,以后再来付款,所以对卖方来说风险非常大。一旦买方到期不付款,卖方就会遭到货款两空的损失。所以,对采用承兑交单这种方法,必须从严掌控。

4. 托收方式的特点

托收的性质是商业信用,对买方有利,它不需要像信用证那样办理繁琐的手续,不需银行押金,减少费用支出,不占压资金。托收虽然通过银行办理,但银行只是代收代付,并不承担付款的责任,卖方能否收到货款完全依赖买方的个人信用,所以托收对卖方仍然存在较大的风险。如买方破产或丧失清偿债务的能力或有意赖账,出口人则有可能收不回或延迟收回货款。虽然付款交单是以买方首先付款为条件,但在市场处于下跌状态时,信誉不好的买方可能溜之大吉,既不赎单,也不付款,那么卖方同样要遭受货款两空的损失。在这种情况下,银行没有义务代为保管或提取货物,出口人还要承担在进口地办理提货、缴纳进口关税、存仓、保险、转售以至于货物被低价拍卖或运回国内的损失。在承兑交单的情况下,卖方的损失会更大,风险也更大。

第六节　信用证

信用证是我国外贸进出口结算的一种主要方式,它以银行信用取代商业信用,以银行的付款责任取代买方的付款责任,在买卖双方缺乏信任、互不熟悉的情况下,信用证的付款方式很好地解决了支付中的难题,卖方在交货以前就能得到银行付款的承诺,使交易得以顺利进行,有利于国际贸易的快速发展。在信用证交易中,买方也有得天独厚的好处,它可以利用信用证条款约束卖方履行合同,保证所购买货物的品质、数量、交货期符合合同的规定,卖方如果违约将得不到偿付。因此,信用证已经成为国家贸易中获取货款的一种较为安全和迅速的支付方式。

1. 信用证的含义

根据国际商会《跟单信用证统一惯例(UCP600)》(2007 年修订版)的定义,信用证意指一项不可撤销的安排,不论其如何命名或描述,该项安排构成开证行对相符交单予以承付的确定承诺。

"承付"是指:如果信用证为即期付款信用证,则即期付款;如果信用证为延期付款信用证,则承诺延期付款并在承诺到期日付款;如果信用证为承兑信用证,则承兑受益人开出的汇票并在汇票到期日付款。

简言之,信用证是一种银行开立的有条件的承诺付款的书面文件。具体地说,就是银行(即开证行)应进口人的请求和指示,向出口人开立一定金额的在一定条件下保证付款的凭证。所谓"一定金额,一定条件",是指开证行的付款是以卖方提交符合信用证的单据为条件。

2. 信用证涉及的当事人

信用证支付方式所涉及的当事人较多,通常有以下几个:

开证申请人,指要求开立信用证的人。在实际业务中,申请人通常为进口商。开证行也可以自身名义开证。

开证行,指应开证申请人的要求或代表自己开出信用证的银行。在实际业务中,开证行一般为进口地的银行。

通知行,指应开证行要求向受益人通知信用证的银行。通知行通常是出口地银行,而且一般是开证行的代理行。

受益人,指信用证上所指定的有权使用该证并得到偿付的人。在实际业务中,受益人通常是出口商或实际供货人。

议付行,指愿意买入或贴现受益人按信用证规定提交的汇票及/或单据的银行。议付行可以是指定的银行,也可以是非指定的银行,由信用证的条款来规定。议付行对受益人有追索权。

议付又称押汇、买单,是指议付行在审单无误的情况下,按信用证的条款贴现受益人的汇票,买入信用证项下的货运单据,从票面金额中扣除从议付日到估计收到票款之日的利息,将余款先行支付给受益人。议付实际上是银行向受益人先行垫付资金,银行在议付之后就成为汇票的正当持票人,具有追索权。

付款行,指信用证上指定的付款银行,一般是开证行,也可以是开证行以外的分支行或代理行。由于资金调拨的原因,开证行可以指定另一家银行为付款银行。付款行与开证行具有同等的法律地位,其付款都是终局性的。付款行一经付款,对受益人不得追索。

保兑行,指根据开证行的请求在信用证上加具保证的银行。保兑行在信用证上加具保兑后,即对信用证独立负责,承担必须对相符交单承付或议付的责任。保兑行具有与开证行相同的责任和地位。保兑行可以由通知行兼任,也可由其他银行加具保兑。

偿付行,又称清算行,指信用证指定的代开证行向议付行、承兑行或付款行清偿垫款的银行。偿付行不负责审单,只根据开证行的授权付款,付款也是终局性的。偿付行的出现,往往是由于开证行的资金调度或集中在该银行的缘故,要求该银行代为偿付信用证规定的款项。

3. 信用证支付的一般程序

(1)申请开立信用证

在国际贸易的货物买卖中,开证人一般为进口人。买卖合同订立后,买方(开证申请人)向开证行申请开立信用证。开证人申请开证时,应填写开证申请书。开证申请书的内容实际上完全反映了买卖合同的内容,虽然银行开立信用证是根据买方的开证申请书,但信用证开立的基础条件却是买卖合同,买方申请开立信用证必须完全遵循买卖合同的条款和义务,不得利用开证的机会,擅自改变合同的条款。信用证一旦开立,受益人就必须按照信用证的条款履行交单义务,这也是开证行履行付款的依据。

开证人申请开立信用证,应向开证行交付一定比率的押金。开证人还应按规定向开证行支付开证手续费和邮电费。

(2)开证行开立信用证

开证行根据开证人的申请向受益人开立信用证。所开信用证的条款必须与开证申请书所列一致。开证行开立信用证后,对受益人承担付款责任。

(3)通知行通知信用证

通知行收到开证行开来的信用证后,通知行通知开证行要求的收件人立即将信用证的密押和签字印鉴进行核对,在核对无误后,立即交信用证的受益人。

(4)审证与修改信用证

受益人接到信用证后应首先审核信用证,检查买方开证时是否与买卖合同相符。如发现不符或某些条款不能接受或有软条款,应立即通知买方修改信用证。未经开证行、保兑行(如有的话)及受益人同意,信用证既不得修改,也不得撤销。

(5)交单议付

受益人收到信用证,经审查无误,或收到修改通知书认可后,即可根据信用证规定的条款进行备货和安排出运。

受益人在装船后取得全套单据,可以据以向所在地银行进行押汇,也称为议付,即由当地银行将出运货物的货款扣除预计收到货款的这段时间的利息后先行给付受益人,以给受益人资金融通,银行从中赚取利息和手续费。

(6)开证申请人付款赎单

开证行将全部票款拨还议付银行后,应立即通知开证人付款赎单。开证人接到开证行的通知后,也应立即到开证行核验单据,认为无误后,将全部票款及有关费用一并向开证行付清并赎取单据。如申请开证时曾交付押金,付款时可扣除押金;如申请开证时曾递交抵押品,则在付清票款和费用后,抵押品由开证行发还。此时,开证人与开证行之间由于开立信用证所构成的权利义务关系即告终结。

即期跟单信用证结算的一般业务流程如图 7-4 所示:

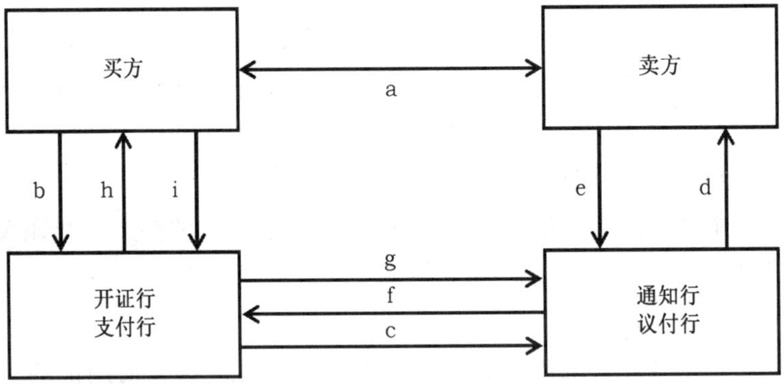

图 7-4　即期跟单信用证结算的一般业务流程

a. 交易双方签订进出口合同,约定采用即期跟单信用证方式结算货款;

b. 进口商填写开证行申请书,向开证行申请开证;

c. 开证行开出以出口商为收益人的信用证,并向通知行寄交信用证;

d. 通知行审验信用证的真伪后向卖方转递;

e. 卖方装船后向议付行交单议付;

f. 议付行将全套单据寄交开证行并向其索偿垫付款项;

g. 开证行核对单据无误后,向议付行付款;

h. 开证行向买方提示;

i. 买方付款赎单。

4. 信用证的主要内容

信用证的内容主要就是买卖合同条款的单据要求加银行的付款保证。

(1)对信用证本身的说明

主要包括:信用证是否可保兑、是否可转让,UCP600 取消了可撤销信用证的概念,所有信用证都是不可撤销的;编号;金额、货币、单词、数字拼写;有效期及到期地点;是否有境外有效期。

(2)对汇票的说明

在信用证项下,如使用汇票,要明确汇票的出票人、受票人、收款人、汇票金额、主要条款等内容。

(3)对货物的说明

在信用证中要注明货物的名称、品种、规格、数量、包装、价格,并注明根据某某买卖合同。

(4)对装运的说明

在信用证中应列明装运港(地)、目的港(地)、装运期限以及可否分批、转运等项内容。

(5)对单据的说明

在信用证中应列明所需的各种货运单据,主要有以下几种:

①货物单据

包括发票、装箱单(包装清单)、产地证、商检证明书等。

②运输单据

其中最重要的是海运提单,它是货物所有权的凭证。

③保险单据

UCP600 规定:“保险单据,例如保险单或预约保险项下的保险证明书或者说明书,必须看似由保险公司或承保人或其代理人出具并签署。如果保险单据表明其以多份正本出具,所有正本均需提交。暂保单不被接受。可以接受保险单代替预约保险项下的保险证明书或声明书。保险单据日期不得晚于发运日期,除非保险单据表明保险责任不迟于发运日生效。保险单据必须表明投保金额并以与信用证相同的货币表示。如果信用证对投保金额未做规定,投保金额须至少为货物的 CIF 或 CIP 价格的 110%。”

(6)特殊条款

银行对议付或付款路线或是否保兑,做出特别指示,或有特别要求。

银行保证付款的承诺:例如,“我们兹向根据本证开出并符合本证条款的汇票的出票人、背书人和正当持票人承诺,只要你们在本证的有效期内向付款行提示或议付(远期汇票在汇票的到期日向付款行提示),将立即得到付款。”

“请通知行通知受益人本证未加以保兑。”

(7)声明本证遵循 UCP600

例如:“本证遵循国际商会 2007 年修订本第 600 号出版物规定的《跟单信用证统一惯例》。”

两个信用证样本如下所示:

2009,MAY 24 02:16:37			LOGICAL TERMINAL PAL5
MT S700			ISSUE OF A DOCUMENTARY CREDIT PAGE 00001
			FUNC MSC700
			UMR 1080003
MSGACK DWS765I AUTHENTICATION SUCCESSFUL WITH PRIMARY KEY			
BASIC HEADER			F 01 BKCHCNBJA872 5619 928007
APPLICATION HEADER			0 700 1159 090523 WPACAU2SAXXX 3458 193456 090524 0216 N * WESTPAC BANKING CORPORATION * ADELAIDE,AUSTRALIA
USER HEADER			BANK. PRIORITY 113: MSG USER REF. 108:
SEQUENCE OF TOTAL	*	27	1/1
FORM OF DOC. CREDIT	*	40 A	NON-TRANSFERABLE
APPLICABLE RULES		40E	UCP LATEST VERSION
DOC. CREDIT NUMBER	*	20	AD25009/504919
DATE OF ISSUE		31 C	090523
EXPIRY	*	31 D	DATE 090905 PLACE CHINA
APPLICANT	*	50	TONY COLYER PTY.LTD. 50 CHAPEL STREET NORWOOD SA 5067 AUSTRALIA
BENEFICIARY	*	59	DESUN TRADING CO.,LTD. HUARONG MANSION RM2901 NO. 85 GUANJIAQIAO, NANJING 210005,CHINA TEL:0086-25-4715004 FAX:0086-25-4711363
AMOUNT	*	32 B	CURRENCY USD AMOUNT 32095.00
MAX. CREDIT AMOUNT		39 B	MAXIMUM
AVAILABLE WITH/BY	*	41 D	BANK OF CHINA JIANGSU BRANCH BY NEGOTIATION
DRAFTS AT ...		42 C	SIGHT
DRAWEE		42 A	WESTPAC BANKING CORPORATION ADELAIDE,AUSTRALIA
PARTIAL SHIPMENTS		43 P	ALLOWED
TRANSSHIPMENT		43 T	ALLOWED
PORT OF LOADING		44 E	

		TIANJIN
PORT OF DISCHARGE	44 F	
		ADELAIDE
GOODS DESCRIPT	45 A	
		WHITE AND DYED TOWELS
		CONTRACT 01KHAU08-INDENT 5980
		CONTRACT 01KHAU09-INDENT 5962
		CFR ADELAIDE
DOCS REQUIRED	46 A	
		DOCUMENTS REQUIRED:
		+ COMMERCIAL INVOICE IN 2 FOLD.
		+ FULL SET CLEAN “ON BOARD” OR “SHIPPED” NEGOTIABLE MARINE BILLS OF LADING TO ORDER/BLANK ENDORSED MARKED FREIGHT PREPAID.
		+ INSURANCE BUYERS CARE.
DD. CONDITIONS	47 A	
		ADDITIONAL CONDITION:
		GOODS ARE TO BE SHIPPED AS FULL 20 FOOT CONTAINER FCL.
CHARGES	71 B	ALL BANK CHARGES OUTSIDE AUSTRALIA
		ARE FOR A/C BEN
PRESENTATION PERIOD	48	DOCUMENTS TO BE PRESENTED WITHIN 15 DAYS AFTER THE DATE OF ISSUANCE OF THE TRANSPORT DOCUMENT(S) BUT WITHIN THE VALIDITY OF THE CREDIT.
CONFIRMAT INSTR	* 49	WITHOUT
REIMBURS BANK	53 A	WPACAU2SADE
		* WESTPAC BANKING CORPORATION
		* ADELAIDE, AUSTRALIA
		IN REIMBURSEMENT, NEGOTIATING BANK TO FORWARD
		DRAFT TO BANK NA AS DRAWEE.
		PLEASE FORWARD FIRST SET OF DOCUMENTS BY COURIER, AND SECONDS.
		BY ORDINARY AIRMAIL TO: ADELAIDE I.B.C 1ST FLOOR 2-8 KING
		WILLIAM STREET ADELAIDE SA 5000.
		THE NUMBER AND DATED OF THE CREDIT AND THE NAME OF OUR BANK MUS
		BE QUOTED ON ALL DRAFTS REQUIRED.
TRAILER	72	ORDER IS 〈AUT:〉〈ENC:〉〈CHK:〉〈TNG:〉〈PDE:〉
		MAC: 3A630ED9
		CHK: CF7F79B1EDF1
		DLM:

图 7-5　信用证样本 1

Issue of a Documentary Credit

Opening Bank		BKCHCNBJA08E SESSION:000 ISN:000000 BANK OF CHINA LIAONING NO. 5 ZHONGSHAN SQUARE ZHONGSHAN DISTRICT DALIAN CHINA
Destination Bank		KOEXKRSEXXX MESSAGE TYPE:700 KOREA EXCHANGE BANK SEOUL 178.2 KA,ULCHI RO,CHUNG-KO
Type of Documentary Credit	40A	IRREVOCABLE
Letter of Credit Number	20	LC84E0081/99
Date of Issue	31G	150916
Date and Place of Expiry	31D	151015 KOREA
Applicant Bank	51D	BANK OF CHINA LIAONING BRANCH
Applicant	50	DALIAN WEIDA TRADING CO.,LTD.
Beneficiary	59	SANGYONG CORPORATION CPO BOX 110 SEOUL KOREA
Currency Code,Amount	32B	USD 1,146,725.04
Available with...by...	41D	ANY BANK BY NEGOTIATION
Drafts at	42C	45 DAYS AFTER SIGHT
Drawee	42D	BANK OF CHINA LIAONING BRANCH
Partial Shipments	43P	NOT ALLOWED
Transshipment	43T	NOT ALLOWED
Shipping on Board/Dispatch/Packing in Charge at/ from	44A	RUSSIAN SEA
Transportation to	44B	DALIAN PORT,P.R.CHINA
Latest Date of Shipment	44C	150913

Description of Goods or Services:45A

FROZEN YELLOWFIN SOLE WHOLE ROUND (WITH WHITE BELLY) USD770/MT CFR DALIAN QUANTITY: 200MT

ALASKA PLAICE (WITH YELLOW BELLY) USD600/MT CFR DALIAN QUANTITY: 300MT

Documents Required: 46A

1. SIGNED COMMERCIAL INVOICE IN 5 COPIES.
2. FULL SET OF CLEAN ON BOARD OCEAN BILLS OF LADING MADE OUT TO ORDER AND BLANK ENDORSED, MARKED "FREIGHT PREPAID" NOTIFYING LIAONING OCEAN FISHING CO., LTD. TEL:(86) 411-3680288 LIAONING OCEAN FISHING CO., LTD. TEL:(86)411-3680288
3. PACKING LIST/WEIGHT MEMO IN 4 COPIES INDICATING QUANTITY/GROSS AND NET WEIGHTS OF EACH PACKAGE AND PACKING CONDITIONSAS CALLED FOR BY THE L/C.
4. CERTIFICATE OF QUALITY IN 3 COPIES ISSUED BY PUBLIC RECOGNIZED SURVEYOR.
5. BENEFICIARY'S CERTIFIED COPY OF FAX DISPATCHED TO THE ACCOUNTEE WITH 3 DAYS AFTER SHIPMENT ADVISING NAME OF VESSEL, DATE, QUANTITY, WEIGHT, VALUE OF SHIPMENT, L/C NUMBER AND CONTRACT NUMBER.
6. CERTIFICATE OF ORIGIN IN 3 COPIES ISSUED BY AUTHORIZED INSTITUTION.
7. CERTIFICATE OF HEALTH IN 3 COPIES ISSUED BY AUTHORIZED INSTITUTION.

ADDITIONAL INSTRUCTIONS: 47A

1. CHARTER PARTY B/L AND THIRD PARTY DOCUMENTS ARE ACCEPTABLE.
2. SHIPMENT PRIOR TO L/C ISSUING DATE IS ACCEPTABLE.
3. BOTH QUANTITY AND AMOUNT 10 PERCENT MORE OR LESS ARE ALLOWED.

Charges	71B	ALL BANKING CHARGES OUTSIDE THE OPENNING BANK ARE FOR BENEFICIARY'S ACCOUNT.
Period for Presentation	48	DOCUMENTSMUST BE PRESENTED WITHIN 15 DAYS AFTER THE DATE OF ISSUANCE OF THE TRANSPORT DOCUMENTS BUT WITHIN THE VALIDITY OF THE CREDIT.
Confirmation	49	WITHOUT
Instructions to the Paying/Accepting/Negotiating Bank: 78 1. ALL DOCUMENTS TO BE FORWARDED IN ONE COVER, UNLESS OTHERWISE STATED ABOVE. 2. DISCREPANT DOCUMENT FEE OF USD 50.00 OR EQUAL CURRENCY WILL BE DEDUCTED FROM DRAWING IF DOCUMENTS WITH DISCREPANCIES ARE ACCEPTED.		
		KOEXKRSEXXX MESSAGE TYPE: 700
Advising Through Bank	57A	KOREA EXCHANGE BANK SEOUL 178.2 KA, ULCHI RO, CHUNG-KO

图 7-6　信用证样本 2

5. 信用证开立的方式

信用证开立的方式主要有信开本和电开本两种。

(1)信开本

信开本是指开证行采用印就的信函格式的信用证,开证后以空邮寄送通知行。这种方式现已很少使用。

(2)电开本

电开本是指开证行使用电报、电传、传真、SWIFT 等各种电讯方法,将信用证条款传达给通知行。目前,在国际贸易中以 SWIFT 传递信用证是一种主要形式。

SWIFT(Society for Worldwide Interbank Financial Telecommunications)是环球银行金融电讯协会的简称。该组织是一个国际银行同业间非营利性的国际合作组织,于 1973 年在比利时成立,采用会员制,凡该协会的成员银行都有自己的代码,即 SWIFT Code(又称 BIC),能保证汇款快速、准确地到达收款人账户。我国的主要银行大多是该协会会员。采用 SWIFT 信用证,必须遵守 SWIFT 使用手册的规定,使用 SWIFT 手册规定的代号(tag)。信用证必须按国际商会制定的 UCP600 的规定,在信用证中可以省去银行的承诺条款,但不能免去银行所应承担的义务。

过去进行全电本开证时,都采用电报或电传开证,各国银行标准不一,条款格式也各不相同,而且文字繁琐;采用 SWIFT 开证后,使信用证具有标准化、固定化,统一格式的特性,而且传递速度快,成本低,现在已被西北欧、美洲、亚洲等国家银行广泛使用。

6. 信用证的种类

信用证根据其性质、期限、使用方式等特点,可以从不同的角度分为以下几种:

(1)跟单信用证和光票信用证

跟单信用证是指开证行凭跟单汇票或仅凭装运单据付款的信用证。国际贸易中使用的信用证,绝大部分是跟单信用证。

光票信用证是指开证行凭光票付款的信用证。有的信用证要求汇票附有非货运单据,也属光票信用证。在采用信用证方式预付货款时,通常是使用光票信用证。

(2)不可撤销信用证

不可撤销信用证,是指开证行自开立信用证之时起即不可撤销地承担付款责任。也就是说,未经信用证的有关当事人同意,开证行不得片面修改和撤销信用证,只要受益人提交了符合信用证的单据,开证行必须履行付款义务。

在 UCP600 之前,信用证还区分为可撤销信用证和不可撤销信用证。在 UCP600 于 2007 年 7 月 1 日生效之后,已经没有了可撤销信用证的概念:“凡是信用证都是不可撤销的,即使未如此表明。”

(3)即期信用证和远期信用证

①即期信用证

即期信用证,即“即期汇票信用证”,是指开证行或付款行收到符合 L/C 条款的即期汇票和/或装运单据后,立即履行付款义务的信用证。采用这种方式收汇,迅速、安全,有利于资金周转。

在即期信用证中,有时还加列电汇索偿条款,指开证行允许议付行电报或电传通知开证行或指定付款行,说明各种单据与信用证要求相符,开证行接到电报或电传通知后,有义务立即用电汇将货款拨交议付行。

②远期信用证

远期信用证,即“远期汇票信用证”,是指开证行或付款行收到信用证的单据时,在远期汇票规定期限内履约付款义务的信用证。远期信用证主要有 3 种:

- 承兑信用证

承兑信用证,是指由某一银行承兑的信用证,即当受益人向指定银行开具远期汇票并提示时,指定行即行承兑,并于汇票到期日履行付款。

这种信用证项下的汇票,在承兑前,银行对出口商的权利义务以信用证为准;承兑后,银行作为汇票承兑人对出票人、持票人、背书人承担付款责任。这种信用证也称为银行承兑信用证。

● 延期付款信用证

延期付款信用证,是指开证行在信用证中规定,货物装船后若干天付款,或开证行收到单据后若干天付款的信用证。这种信用证不要求出口商开立汇票,所以出口商不能利用其贴现市场资金,只能用资金垫付或向银行借款。在出口业务中,使用这种信用证的货价应比银行承兑信用证高些,以便拉平利息率与贴现率之间的差额。成交金额较大时,要与政府的出口信贷结合起来使用。

● 假远期信用证

假远期信用证,也称"买方远期信用证",它规定受益人开立远期汇票,由付款行负责贴现,并规定一切利息由进口人承担。这种信用证表面上看是远期信用证,但从上述条款规定来看,出口人可以即期收到十足的货款,因此被称为"假远期信用证"。

(4)限制议付信用证和自由议付信用证

信用证中指定特定银行为议付行的,称为限制议付信用证,或称指定议付信用证。信用证上一般注明"本证限××银行议付"。

可由任何银行议付的信用证,称为自由议付信用证,或称公开议付信用证。信用证上通常载有自由议付的文句,如"允许任何银行议付"。

(5)保兑信用证和不保兑信用证

信用证按是否有另一家银行加保兑,可以分为保兑信用证和不保兑信用证。

①保兑信用证

保兑信用证,是指开证行开出的信用证由另一家银行保证对符合信用证条款规定的单据履行付款义务。对信用证加保兑的银行,叫做保兑行。

保兑行以独立的"本人"身份对受益人独立负责,并对受益人负首先付款责任。也就是说,保兑行同开证行一样,承担第一性的付款责任。这是一种双重保证的信用证,对出口商最为有利。保兑行通常可以由通知行来承担,也可以是出口地的其他银行或第三国银行。保兑手续一般是由保兑行在信用证上加列保兑文句。

②不保兑信用证

不保兑信用证,是指开证银行开出的信用证没有经过另一家银行保兑。当开证银行资信较好或成交金额不大时,一般都使用这种不保兑的信用证。

(6)可转让信用证

根据受益人对信用证的权利可否转让,信用证分为可转让信用证和不可转让信用证。

可转让信用证,是指信用证的受益人(第一受益人)可以要求通知行或议付行将信用证的全部或部分转让给第二受益人使用的信用证。信用证转让之后,第二受益人开立汇票,提示单据并取得货款,但仍由第一受益人承担贸易合同中的责任。

根据 UCP600 的规定,唯有开证行在信用证中明确注明“可转让”,信用证方可转让。可转让信用证只能转让一次,即只能由第一受益人转让给第二受益人,第二受益人不得要求将信用证转让给其后的第三受益人。

(7)循环信用证

循环信用证,是指信用证被全部或部分使用后,其金额又恢复到原金额,可再次使用,直到达到规定的次数或规定的总金额为止。

循环信用证又分为按时间循环的信用证和按金额循环的信用证。按时间循环的信用证是受益人在一定的时间内可多次支取信用证规定的金额;按金额循环的信用证是信用证金额议付后,仍恢复到原金额可再次使用,直到用完规定的总额为止。

(8)对开信用证

对开信用证,是指两张信用证的开证申请人互以对方为受益人而开立的信用证。对开信用证的特点是第一张信用证的受益人(出口人)和开证申请人(进口人)就是第二张信用证的申请人和受益人,第一张信用证的通知行通常就是第二张信用证的开证行。两张信用证的金额相等或大体相等,两证可同时互开,也可先后开立。对开信用证多用于易货贸易或进料加工贸易方式。采用这种互相联系、互为条件的开证办法,交易双方彼此得以约束。

(9)背对背信用证

背对背信用证,又称“转开信用证”,是指受益人要求原证的通知行或其他银行以原证为基础,另开一张内容相似的新信用证。背对背信用证的受益人可以是国外的,也可以是国内的。背对背信用证的开立通常是当中间商转售他人货物、从中图利,或两国不能直接办理进出口贸易时,通过第三者以此种方法来促进贸易。这种贸易由三方即出口商、中间商、进口商签订两份买卖合同,按照中间商与进口商签订的第一份合同开出的信用证称为原信用证;按照中间商与出口商签订的第二份合同开出的第二张信用证称为背对背信用证，也称从属信用证。原信用证的受益人就是背对背信用证的开证申请人。新证开出后，原证仍然有效。背对背信用证的内容除开证人、受益人、金额、单价、装运期限、有效期限可有变动外，其他条款一般与原证相同。原信用证价格高于背对背信用证的价格，差额就是中间商赚取的利润或佣金。

(10)备用信用证

备用信用证，又称“商业票据信用证”、“担保信用证”或“保证信用证”，是指开证行根据开证申请人的请求对受益人开立的承诺承担某项义务时，受益人只要凭备用信用证的规定向开证行开具汇票(或不开汇票)，并提交开证申请人未履行义务的声明或证明文件，即可取得开证行的偿付。备用信用证属于银行信用，开证银行承担的是第一位的责任。

7. 信用证支付方式的特点

信用证支付方式的特点，主要表现在下列三个方面：

(1)开证行承担第一付款人的责任

这种责任是一种绝对的、第一位的责任。也就是说，开证行在开出信用证后，只要卖方提交了符合信用证规定的单据，无论买方是否破产、是否有清偿能力、是否死亡都与卖方无关，开证行必须按照信用证的承诺对卖方付款，未经受益人同意，银行不得撤销或者更改信用证。

(2)信用证是一种自足文件

信用证是基于买卖合同为基础开立的，但是信用证一旦开立就独立于买卖合同和开证申请书，成为与买卖合同无关的另一个契约。信用证实际上是开证行与受益人之间的一个合同。信用证的各方当事人的权利、义务都以信用证为准，不受买卖合同的约束。因此，一家银行做出付款、承兑的承诺，不受申请人与开证行或与受益人之间在已有关系上产生索偿或抗辩的制约。

(3)信用证业务是一种单据的买卖

在信用证项下，银行实行的是凭单付款的原则，银行付款的依据仅仅是单据和信用证的规定表面相符，银行与货物无关，与买卖合同无关，与单据的真假无关。

在信用证条件下实行严格相符的原则，不仅要做到单证一致，还要做到单单一致。在信用证项下，只要交单正确，即使货物有假，银行也必须付款。如果单据有错误，即使货物正确，银行也可以拒付。如果发现货物有假或者卖方存在欺诈行为，买方如果想让银行拒付，唯一的办法就是寻找单据的不符点。

第七节　不同支付方式的应用

在实践中，有时为了促成交易，在双方未能就某一种支付方式达成协议时，也可以采用两种或多种方式结合使用的方式，常见的有以下几种：

1. 信用证与汇付相结合

这种方式是指部分货款用信用证支付，余数用汇付方式结算。例如，对于矿砂等初级产品的交易，双方约定，信用证规定凭装运单据先付发票金额的若干成，余数待货到目的地后，根据检验的结果，按实际品质或重量计算出确切的金额，另用汇付方式付出。

2. 信用证与托收相结合

这种方式是指部分货款用信用证支付，余数用托收方式结算。一般做法是，信用证规定出口人开立两张汇票，属于信用证部分的货款凭光票付款，而全套单据附在托收部分汇票项下，按即期或远期付款交单方式托收，但信用证上必须订明“在发票金额全部付清后才可交单”的条款，以确保安全。

3. 汇付、托收、信用证三者相结合

在成套设备、大型机械产品和交通工具的交易中，因为成交金额较大，产品生产周期较长，一般采取按工程进度和交货进度分若干期付清货款，即分期付款和延期付款的方法，采用汇付、托收和信用证相结合的方式。

Chapter 8

Commodity Inspection and Claim

Part A Text

Section One Inspection of Commodity

Commodity inspection has become an indispensable part in international trade. In the international trade, most of the sellers and buyers are far away from each other. They can't make delivery face to face, which is quite different from the domestic trade, thus the damage due to long distance transportation is unavoidable. In order to verify the reasons for the damages, and clarify the respective responsibilities of the parties involved, an usual practice is that a qualified third party who has conflict of interest with the concerning parties is authorized to inspect the quality, quantity, weight, packing of goods, etc., and issues the relevant certificate as the evidence for the delivery of goods, the settlement of payment and claims. Related legal provisions and inspection clauses (inspection time and place; inspection authority; inspection certificate; inspection methods, contents and standards; re-inspection) will be introduced as follows.

1. Related Legal Provisions

(1) According to *Sales of Goods Act, 1893 (Revised in 1979)*

The buyer who has not made inspection on the goods can't be assumed to be acceptable to the goods, therefore he is not deprived of the right of refusing the goods until he is grated reasonable opportunity to inspect.

(2) According to *United Nations Convention on Contracts for the International Sale of Goods*

The buyer shall implement the inspection or have others to do it in the shortest practical time. The inspection can be put off to the time when the goods arrive at the destination in case of the involvement of the transportation.

There is a common principle in the above-mentioned law and convention: The buyer shall be granted the inspection right before accepting the goods unless there is another agreement between the buyer and the seller.

(3) Import and Export Inspection in China

①*Law of the People's Republic of China on Import and Export Commodity Inspection*

The law has stipulated the work of the commodity inspection authorities of China and the range of the legal inspection. The commodity inspection is the inspection and supervision on the production and the sales of the import and export commodities.

②The Inspection Range of the Inspection Authority in China

The governmental inspection authorities are committed to implementing the compulsory inspection on important import and export commodities relating to national economy and people's livelihood in accordance with relevant laws and regulations. The commodities, which are not inspected or failed to pass the inspection, are not released by the customs.

It is not all commodities that are compulsory to be inspected. The specific regulations on the commodities which are compulsory to the inspection are as follows:

- The commodities which are listed in *Catalogue of Entry-Exit Goods* that shall be inspected and quarantined by CIQ;
- The export food shall be inspected for their sanitary purpose;
- The appraisal for function and operation of the packing container for the ex-

port dangerous goods;

- The cargoworthiness inspection of the means of transportation such as container and cabin of export perishable and frozen food;
- The inspection of import and export commodities which are required by relevant international treaties;
- The inspection of import and export commodities which are required by other laws or administrative regulations and rules.

2. Inspection Clauses

The inspection clauses contain: inspection time and place; inspection authority; inspection certificate; inspection methods, contents and standards; re-inspection.

(1) Inspection Clauses in the Contract

The inspection clauses in a sales contract are usually as follows: "It is mutually agreed that the Inspection Certificate of quality and quantity (weight) issued by the China Import and Export Commodity Inspection Bureau at the port of shipment shall be part of the documents to be presented for negotiation under the relevant L/C. The buyers shall have the right to re-inspect the quality and quantity (weight) of the cargo. The re-inspection fee shall be borne by the buyers. If the quality and/or quantity (weight) be found not in conformity with that of the contract, the buyers are entitled to lodge with the sellers a claim. The claim, if any, shall be lodged within ×× days after arrival of the cargo at the port of destination."

In addition, for an import transaction, the import contract is important especially for the buyer. With implementing the principle of equality and mutual benefit, the buyer must be familiar with and understand relevant international practice, operate the business in flexible ways and avoid economic losses.

(2) Inspection Time and Place

The inspection time and place refer to when and where the inspection is implemented to the goods. The inspection right means that the buyer or the seller has the right to exercise inspection on the goods, with the inspection result as the evidence for the delivery and the acceptance of the goods. The confirmation of the inspection time and place means to confirm which party exerts the inspection right, in another way, to confirm which party's inspection certificate is taken as the final inspection result.

There are normally four ways to regulate the inspection time and place:

①Inspection in Export Country

There are two ways including the inspection as at manufacturing place (factory) and at the loading port.

For the inspection at the loading port, which is also called "shipping quality, shipping weight", the inspection authority specified in the sales contracts makes the inspection and appraisal on the cargo's quality and weight (quantity), and the inspection certificate issued by the authority is taken as the final evidence. The seller is not responsible for the changes of the cargo after the delivery. Therefore, the clause is a great disadvantage to the buyer as it denies the re-inspection right of the buyer.

②Inspection in Import Country

It is also divided into the inspection at the destination port and the inspection in the buyer's business location or the final user's location.

The inspection at the destination port or discharging port is also called "landed quality, landed weight", meaning that the cargo is inspected by the inspection authority specified in the contract within the specified time on the spot after the cargo arriving in the destination port or place, and the inspection certificate issued by the authority is taken as the final evidence of the cargo delivered by the seller. In the way, the buyer has the right to claim for the compensation with the inspection result made at the destination port or place in case that the quality, weight (quantity) is not in conformity with the contract.

The clause is disadvantageous to the seller. Under the trade term of CIF (CIP, CFR, CRT), the seller is responsible for carrying the goods to the destination, but according to "International rules for the interpretation of trade terms of 2010", the obligation of the seller has been completed after the goods are loaded on the ship (delivered to the carrier) in the export country, the risk has been transferred to the buyer when the goods are on the board. The regulation of the inspection time and place means that the conditions of the goods are subject to the final inspection result in the destination, actually transferring the risks of the cargo losses that have occurred during the transportation to the seller. During the transportation, the goods have been out of supervision of the seller, but under the control of the carrier, thus it is quite unfair to the seller with the inspection clause against the regulation of the seller's obligation in the above-mentioned trade terms.

③Inspection in Export Country and Re-inspection in Import Country

The inspection certificate issued by the export country's inspection authority is taken as one of the negotiation documents for payment, but not as the final inspection proof. After the arrival of the cargo, the inspection certificate issued by the import country's inspection authority is taken as the final inspection result to confirm that the quantity and the quality of the goods are right and as the proof for the buyer's claims.

It is fair and reasonable to the buyer and the seller to regulate the inspection time and place in this way, thus it is the way most commonly used in international trade, complying with the international practice.

④Weight Inspection in Export Country and Quality Inspection in Import Country

It is also called "shipping weight, landed quality", meaning that for the inspection of goods in large amount, in order to conciliate the conflict of the buyer and the seller on the inspection, the inspection on the weight and the quality are respectively carried out. In another way, the inspection certificate of weight issued by the inspection authority at the loading port or place is taken as the final proof for the weight of the delivered goods, and the quality inspection certificate issued by the inspection authority at the destination port is taken as the final proof of the commodity quality.

(3) Inspection Authority

The inspection organizations are divided into following three types, which are governmental inspection authority, government related inspection authority, non-governmental inspection authority.

According to the regulation of *Law of the People's Republic of China on Import and Export Commodity Inspection* ("*Law of Inspection*" for short), *General Administration of Quality Supervision, Inspection and Quarantine of the People's Republic of China* is in charge of the inspection of the import and export commodities throughout the whole country, the local *Entry-Exit Inspection and Quarantine Bureaus* are in charge of the local inspection of the import and export commodities.

(4) Inspection Certificate

An inspection certificate is a testifying document in written form issued and signed by the inspection authority after the inspection and appraisal of the imported and exported commodities.

In practical business, there are several common types of inspection certificates as follows: inspection certificate of quality、inspection certificate of quantity、inspection certificate of weight、inspection certificate of value、inspection certificate of origin、sanitary inspection certificate、veterinary inspection certificate、disinfection inspection certificate and inspection certificate on damage cargo etc..

Functions of inspection certificate:

①To certify whether the quality, quantity, packing and the sanity condition of the goods delivered by the seller comply with the requirements stipulated in the contract;

②For customs to release the goods;

③For sellers to settle the payment;

④As the evidence of making claims and settlement.

(5) Inspection Basis and Methods

①Inspection Basis

The inspection bases of commodities include the reference sample, standard sample contract, letter of credit, and standards, etc..

The inspection standards are the measures and rules adopted for the inspection entity and inspection process, which are the criterion to appraise and identify whether the commodities comply with the relevant regulations and requirement.

According to *Law of Inspection* in China, all the import and export commodities listed in the catalogue must be inspected according to the governmental technical regulation; for the commodities which are not required by the governmental technical regulations, the inspection can be made in reference to the related standards of foreign countries that stipulated by national commodity inspection authority.

②Inspection Methods

The inspection result of the same commodity varies by different methods. Therefore, it is better to specify the method to inspect the goods in contrast in order to avoid any dispute.

In import and export, the inspection is made according to the following standards:

- According to the requirement in the import contract about the quality, specification, packing, and sampling inspection;

- According to the packaging standard of the manufacturing country, the import country, or the usual standard adopted internationally in case that the standard is not specified in the contract;
- The laws and rules of the state and the international practice are prior to the contract clauses;
- For some international standards such as ISO9000 or the standard of International Wool Secretariat, it is decided by both the seller and the buyer to adopt them or not.

(6) Re-inspection

The re-inspection right of buyer is not compulsory, and is not the basic condition for the acceptance of goods, only depending on the buyer's selection. The buyer must finish the re-inspection within a reasonable time if the re-inspection is needed. The reasonable time is regulated in the contract. The time for re-inspection shall be specified in the contract according to various characteristics of the cargo.

Section Two Disputes and Claims

Disputes arise in international trade for many reasons. After the disputes, usually a claim will be made by injured party against the other. For the claims concerning the international cargo trade, there are three kinds of claims, namely, the transaction of cargo claim, the transportation claim and the insurance claim. In this section, the first type, namely, the transaction of cargo claim will be discussed.

1. Dispute and Claim

Breach of contract means the refusal or failure by a party to fulfill his obligations in the contract. Breach of contract gives rise to dispute, which probably leads to claim, arbitration and legal action.

There are many reasons for disputes in international trade, but the main reasons are the following three:

(1) Breach of Contract by the Seller

A seller may breach a contract if he fails to make delivery within the delivery time stipulated in the contract, fail to deliver the goods, fail to deliver the goods that are in conformity with the contract or the L/C in respect of quality, specification, quantity and packing, etc., or fails to offer the full set of shipping documents.

(2) Breach of the Contract by the Buyer

A buyer may breach a contract if he fails to open the L/C on time, fails to open the L/C under a L/C payment, fails to make payment and honor the shipping documents according to the clause in the contract, or fails to accept the goods without sufficient reasons.

(3) Contract without Specific Clauses

One party or both parties may breach a contract resulting in disputes if both parties have misunderstanding or difficult explanation for the clauses in the contract due to some unclear clauses.

From the nature of the breach of contract, there are two kinds of reasons leading to the dispute; one kind of dispute is caused by the intentional act; the other kind of dispute is because of the negligence, fault or the unfamiliarity. In addition, the indifference on the contractual obligations also results in the breach of contract and the disputes.

2. Claim

Claim means that in international trade, one party breaks the contract and causes losses to the other party directly or indirectly, the party suffering the losses may ask for compensation for the losses. In some contract, the two parties often stipulate clauses on settlement of claim as well as claim causes.

(1) Claim Clause in Contract

There are two kinds of claim clauses in contracts: One is the clause of dispute and claim clause, the other is the penalty clause. Generally speaking, there is only dispute and claim clause in most sales contracts, but in the contracts of the goods in large amount or large mechanical equipment, there are dispute and claim clause and penalty clause.

(2) Dispute and Claim Clause

The clause stipulates that one party is entitled to lodge claim against the other party who breaches a contract. Moreover, it includes the proofs and effective period, the ways of compensation for the loss, and the compensation sum, etc..

The proofs for lodging a claim contain necessary evidence and certification organization. Proofs for claims include legal proofs and fact proofs. The former refers to the trade contract and the related national laws and regulations while the latter refers to the facts and the written evidence of the breach to verify the truth of the breach.

The effective period means the period in which the claimant can make a claim against delinquent party. The delinquent party can refuse a claim after the effective period. Therefore, the effective period for a claim shall be stipulated reasonably according to different commodities; the warranty period shall be added in the contract for the commodity with quality warranty. The warranty period can be one year or more. In conclusion, in order to avoid extra obligation undertaken by the seller, the stipulated claim period shall not be too long expect for some special commodities such as mechanical equipment; and to assure the time for buyers to file a claim, the stipulated claim period shall not be too short either.

The ways of settling claims and the compensation sum will be stipulated in the contract in general. It is difficult to expect the exact compensation sum and the losses caused prior to the breach of contract, thus there is no specific stipulation about the compensation sum.

The clause of dispute and claim is a restriction for the seller to fulfill the contract as well as for the buyer. No matter which party breaches the contract, the other party suffering the losses has the right to make a claim for compensation.

(3) Penalty Clause

The clause is applicable to the situations including the delayed delivery of goods by the seller or the buyer, the deferred issuance of L/C, the delayed payment, etc.. One party shall make payment in a certain sum of money to the other party in loss as the compensation when the party fails to fulfill the contract. The penalty is also called as the fine for the breach of contract. The sum of penalty depends on the breach time with a maximum amount.

There are two ways to calculate the due time of the penalty: One is to calculate from the end of delivery time in the contract or the end of the L/C issuance time. The other is to stimulate one period extended after the termination time period. The penalty is exempt within the grace period, and the penalty sum will be calculated from the end of the grace period. The seller shall not be exempt from the obligation to fulfill the contract after paying the penalty.

Generally, only the clause of dispute and claim will be stipulated in the contract for import and export. But for the contracts of the goods in large amount with delivery in installments or mechanical equipment, the penalty clause will be added to the contract.

Part B Key Terms

Inspection authority 检验机构
Inspection certificate 检验证书
Inspection methods 检验方法
Re-inspection 复检
Breach of contract 违约
Dispute 争议
Claim 索赔
Penalty clause 罚金条款

Part C Exercises

Ⅰ. Reflection questions

(1) What is legal inspection? Which commodities belong to the range of the legal inspection?

(2) How is it stipulated about the time and the place in international trade?

(3) What are included in the import and export commodity inspection items? What are the bases for the import and export commodity inspections?

(4) What kinds of import and export commodities need to be inspected?

(5) What is penalty item? What are its functions?

Ⅱ. Case & Study

An American company purchased Christmas trees from a trader abroad for the Christmas market. The contract stipulated that the seller shall ship the goods by the end of November. But the seller effected shipment in December 20th. Consequently, the goods missed the selling season and hardly sold out. Therefore, the American company refused the goods, and required to cancel the contract. In this case, does the buyer have the right to refuse the cargo and cancel the contract?

第八章

商品检验和索赔

第一节　商品检验

商品检验在国际贸易中是不可缺少的环节。国际贸易的买卖双方大多远隔重洋，与国内买卖不同的是，他们不能当面交接货物。商品在长途运输中，发生残损也难免。为了便于查明事故起因，分清各方当事人的责任，在长期的贸易实践中形成一种习惯做法，即由一有资格的、与有关当事人无任何利害关系的第三者对商品的质量、数量、重量、包装等方面进行检验并出具证书，作为交接货物、结算货款、处理索赔、理赔的依据。有关国际贸易商品检验的相关法律、贸易合同中检验条款的内容（检验时间、地点；检验机构；检验证书；检验方法、内容、依据；商品复验）介绍如下：

1. 相关法律规定

（1）英国《1893年货物买卖法》（1979年修订本）的规定

凡是事先未经过检验的货物，都不能认为是买方已经接受了货物，因而他没有丧失拒收货物的权利，直至有合理的机会检验货物为止。

（2）《联合国国际货物销售合同公约》的规定

买方必须在按实际情况可行的最短时间内检验货物或由他人检验货物。如果合同涉及运输，检验可推迟到货物到达目的地后进行。

上述有关法律和公约都体现了一个共同的原则：除非买卖双方另有约定，

买方在接受货物之前应享有对货物进行检验的权利。

(3)我国进出口商品实施检验的规定

①《中华人民共和国进出口商品检验法》(以下简称《商检法》)

我国《商检法》规定了我国商检机构的任务和法定检验的实施范围。商品检验体现为国家对进出口商品的生产、销售和进口商品按规定实施检验和监管。

②我国商检机构实施法定检验的范围

国家检验机构根据有关的法律、法规,对关系到国计民生的重要进出口商品实施强制性检验。未经检验或检验不合格的商品,海关不予放行。

并不是所有的商品都必须进行法定检验。国家对必须进行法定检验的商品做了明确的规定,主要有以下几种:

- 列入《出入境检验检疫机构实施检验检疫的进出境商品目录》的商品;
- 对出口食品的卫生检验;
- 对出口危险货物包装容器的性能鉴定和使用鉴定;
- 对装运出口易腐烂变质食品、冷冻品的船舱、集装箱等运输工具的适载检验;
- 对有关国际条约规定须经商检机构检验的进出口商品的检验;
- 对其他法律、行政法规规定必须经商检机构检验的进出口商品的检验。

2. 检验条款的主要内容

检验条款主要包括:检验时间、地点;检验机构;检验证书;检验方法、内容、依据;商品复验。

(1)合同中的检验条款

在买卖合同中,检验条款通常是这样规定的:“双方同意装运港中国进出口商品检验局签发的品质的数(重)量检验证书作为信用项下议付单据的一部分。买方有权对货物的品质、数(重)量进行复验。复验费由买方负担。如发现品质和/或数(重)量与合同不符,买方有权向卖方索赔。索赔期限为货到目的港××天内。”

另外,在进口贸易中,作为买方,进口合同要特别慎重,既要贯彻平等互利的原则,又要熟悉和了解有关的国际惯例,采取灵活做法,在经济上避免遭到损失。

(2)检验的时间和地点

检验的时间和地点是指在何时、何地行使对货物的检验权。所谓检验权，是指买方或卖方有权对所交易的货物进行检验，其检验结果即作为交付与接收货物的依据。确定检验的时间和地点，实际上就是确定买卖双方中的哪一方行使对货物的检验权，也就是确定检验结果以哪一方提供的检验证书为准。

关于检验的时间和地点的规定有以下 4 种方法：

①在出口国检验

这种方法又分为在产地(工厂)和装运港检验两种。

在装运港检验，也称为“离岸品质，离岸重量”，是指货物在装运港或装运地交货前，由买卖合同中规定的检验机构对货物的品质、重量(数量)等项内容进行检验鉴定，并以该机构出具的检验证书作为最后依据。卖方对交货后货物所发生的变化不承担责任。因此，这种规定办法从根本上否定了买方的复验权，对买方极为不利。

②在进口国检验

这种方法又分为在目的港检验和买方营业处或最终用户所在地检验。

在目的港/地卸货后检验，也称为“到岸品质，到岸重量”，是指货物运达目的港或目的地时，由合同规定的检验机构在规定的时间内，就地对商品进行检验，并以该机构出具的检验证书作为卖方所交货物品质、重量(数量)的最后依据。采用这种方法时，买方有权根据货物运抵目的港或目的地时的检验结果，对属于卖方责任的品质、重量(数量)不符合，向卖方索赔。

这种规定方法对卖方不利。因为在使用 CIF(CIP、CFR、CRT)术语的情况下，虽然卖方要负责把货运到目的地，但按照《2010 年国际贸易术语解释通则》的解释，卖方的交货义务实际上是在出口国装运港装上船(或交承运人)时即完成，风险在装运港越过船舷时转移至买方。这种检验时间、地点的规定方法以最后到目的港的检验为准，实际上要把运输中产生的货损、货差的风险由卖方承担。在运输途中，货物已经脱离了卖方的监管，是在承运人的监控之下，这对卖方极不公平，违反了上述贸易术语有关卖方义务的规定。

③出口国检验，进口国复验

以出口国检验机构出具的检验证书，作为卖方向银行议付货款的单据之一，不作为最后的依据。货到目的港后，以进口国检验机构出具的检验证书，作为卖方交货品质数量合格与否的最后依据，也是买方索赔的依据。

这种检验时间、地点的规定方法对买卖双方公平、合理，因而它是国际贸易中目前最常用的一种规定方法，符合国际惯例。

④出口国检验重量,进口国检验品质

也称为“离岸重量,到岸品质”,是指在大宗商品交易的检验中,为了调和买卖双方在商品检验问题上存在的矛盾,常将商品的重量和品质检验分开进行,即以装运港或装运地验货后检验机构出具的重量检验证书,作为卖方所交货物重量的最后依据;以目的港或目的地检验机构出具的品质检验证书,作为商品品质的最后依据。

(3)检验机构

检验机构的类型大体可归纳为官方检验机构、半官方检验机构和非官方检验机构三种。

根据我国《商检法》的规定,国家质检总局主管全国进出口商品检验工作,国家质检总局设在各地的出入境检验检疫局管理其所辖地区内的进出口商品检验工作。进出口商品的检验工作由地方出入境检验检疫机构和经国家质检总局认可的检验机构负责。

(4)检验证书

检验证书是检验机构对进出口商品进行检验、鉴定后签发的书面证明文件。

在实际业务中,主要有以下几种常见的检验证书:品质检验证书、数量检验证书、重量检验证书、价值检验证书、产地检验证书、卫生检验证书、兽医检验证书、消毒检验证书和验残检验证书等。

检验证书的作用:

- 是证明卖方所交货物的品质、数量、包装以及卫生条件等方面是否符合合同规定的依据;
- 是海关验关放行的依据;
- 是卖方办理货物结算的依据;
- 是办理索赔和理赔的依据。

(5)检验依据和检验方法

①检验依据

商品的检验依据主要有成交样品、标样合同、信用证、标准等。

检验标准是指检验机构从事检验工作在实体和程序方面所遵循的尺度和准则,是评定检验对象是否符合规定要求的准则。

根据我国《商检法》的规定,凡列入目录的进出口商品,按照国家技术规范的强制性要求进行检验,没有国家技术规范非强制性要求的,可以参照国家商检部门制定的国外有关标准进行检验。

②检验方法

同一商品用不同的方法进行检验可以得出完全不同的结果。所以,最好在合同中明确规定用哪种方法进行检验,以免事后发生纠纷。

在进出口业务中,一般按以下检验标准进行:

- 按进口合同中对品质、规格、包装、抽样检验的规定办理。
- 包装未规定标准的一般按生产国标准、进口国标准,或按国际上已用标准。无国际标准的,按进口国标准。
- 有国家法规、国际惯例的,按法规、惯例优先于合同进行。
- 是否采用某些国际标准,由买卖双方自愿决定,如ISO9000、国际羊毛局标准等。

(6)复验

买方对到货的复验权不具有强制性,也不是接受货物的前提条件,由买方自己决定。若进行复印,买方则必须在合理的时间内完成。合理的时间期限由买卖双方在合同中规定。要在合同中规定复验时间的长短,并根据货物性质的不同来规定具体的时间。

第二节　争议与索赔

国际贸易中,常常由于这样或那样的原因而引起争议。在争议发生后,在合同中受损害的一方往往要向另一方提出索赔。涉及国际货物买卖的索赔,一般有三种情况,包括货物买卖索赔、运输索赔和保险索赔。本节讲述的主要是货物买卖的索赔。

1. 违约和争议

违约是指合同的一方拒绝或未能完成合同中所规定的义务。违约引起争议,争议很可能引起诉讼、仲裁或法律行为。

在国际贸易中,导致争议产生的原因很多,一般可归纳为以下三种情况:

(1)卖方违约

例如,不按合同的交货期交货,或不交货,或所交货物的品质、规格、数量、包装等与合同(或信用证)规定不符,或所提供的货运单据种类不齐、份数不足等。

(2)买方违约

例如,在按信用证支付方式条件下不按期开证或不开证,或不按合同规定付款赎单,或无理拒收货物等。

(3)合同规定不明确

例如,因合同条款规定不明确,致使双方理解或解释不统一,造成一方违约而引起纠纷;或在履约中,双方均有违约行为。

从违约的性质看,争议产生的原因,一是当事人方的故意行为导致违约而引起争议;二是由于当事人一方的疏忽、过失或业务生疏导致违约而引起争议。此外,对合同义务的重视不足,往往也是导致违约、发生纠纷的原因之一。

2. 索赔

索赔,是指争议发生后,遭受损害的一方向违约方提出赔偿的要求。买卖双方通常都会在合同中写明索赔的办法以及有关索赔的条款。

(1)合同中的索赔条款

进出口合同中的索赔条款有两种规定方式:一种是异议和索赔条款,另一种是罚金条款。一般在买卖合同中,多数只订立异议和索赔条款,只有在买卖大宗商品和机械设备一类商品的合同中,除订明异议与索赔条款外,再另订罚金条款。

(2)异议与索赔条款

异议与索赔条款的内容,除规定一方违反合同,另一方有权索赔外,还包括索赔的依据、索赔期限、索赔损失的办法和赔付金额等内容。

索赔依据主要规定索赔必需的证据和出证机构。索赔依据包括法律依据和事实依据两个方面。前者是指贸易合同和有关的国家法律规定;后者则指违约的事实真相及其书面证明,以证实违约的真实性。

索赔期限是指索赔方向违约方提赔的有效期限。逾期提赔,违约方可不予受理。因此,关于索赔期限的规定必须根据不同种类的商品,做出合理安排,对有质量保证期限的商品合同应加订保证期。保证期可规定一年或一年以上。总之,除一些性能特殊的产品(如机械设备)外,索赔期限一般不宜过长,以免使卖方承担多重责任;也不宜规定得太短,以免使买方无法行使索赔权,要根据商品性质及检验所需时间多少等因素而定。

处理索赔的办法和索赔金额通常在合同中只做一般规定。因为违约的情况比较复杂,究竟在哪些业务环节上违约和违约的程度如何等,订约时难以预计,因此对于违约的索赔金额也难以预知,所以在合同中不做具体规定。

异议和索赔条款不仅是约束卖方履行合同义务的条款,同时也对买方起约束作用。不论何方违约,受害方都有权向违约方提出索赔。

(3)罚金条款

此条款一般适用于卖方延期交货或买方延期接运货物、拖延开立信用证、拖欠货款等场合。当一方履行合同时,应向对方支付一定数额的约定金额,以补偿对方的损失。罚金亦称“违约金”或“罚则”。罚金的数额大小以违约时间的长短为转移,并规定出最高限额。

违约金的起算日期有两种:一种是合同规定的交货期或开证期终止后立即起算;另一种是规定优惠期,即在合同规定的有关期限终止后再宽限一段时间,在优惠期内免于罚款,待优惠期届满后起算罚金。卖方支付罚金后并不能解除继续履行合同的义务。

在一般情况下,我国的进出口合同中只订立“异议与索赔条款”,而只有对于连续分批交货的大宗货物买卖合同和机械设备一类商品的合同,才同时订立“罚金条款”。

Chapter 9

Force Majeure and Arbitration

Part A Text

Section One Force Majeure

In international trade, both buyers and sellers have the obligation to fulfil the contract. Any party that fails to perform its obligations shall bear legal liability. However, some unpredictable and uncontrolled events caused by nature or social forces may take place occasionally after the conclusion of the contract. These events will make one party unable to fulfill the contract on time. At this point, how should both parties safeguard their own rights and interest ?

Suppose a British importer signed a contract with a Chinese exporter for 1 500 metric tons of wheat at £ 348 per metric ton CIF London. The stipulated time of delivery was in May. Unfortunately, a drought in China reduced the wheat harvest by 30% , leaving Chinese exporters unable to complete their contracts on time. In this case, is it feasible for Chinese exporters to extend the contract until next year?

1. The Meaning of Force Majeure

Force majeure, also known as the Act of God, is an unpredictable, inevitable, uncontrolled event that is caused by natural or social forces such as rainstorm, tsunami and fire after the conclusion of the contract, not due to the negligence of the parties involved, leading to the failure or the delay of fulfillment of the contract. At this time, the party that fails or delays to fulfill the contract due to such event can be free from liabilities or be given an option of postponing the performance of the contract. The other party is not entitled to claim the loss. In other words, force majeure refers to that party under a foreign trade contract could be exempted from failing to perform its obligations totally or partially due to the occurrence of uncontrollable events. In this case, since it is absolutely impossible for them to predict, avoid or overcome these events at the time of the conclusion of the contract, it is not responsible for non-fulfillment of this obligations and the other party is not entitled to lodge a claim for the loss. So, it can be found that the force majeure clause is essentially an exemption clause.

Please note that not any unexpected event that leads to the failure of the fulfillment of contract can be regarded as force majeure event. Usually, there are two types of force majeure events: events caused by natural factors such as earthquakes, floods, storms, tsunamis, fires, snowstorms, etc. and other social factors, such as wars, strikes, and government bans on imports and exports of certain goods.

In international trade, the interpretation of the term "force majeure" varies from country to country, but it is considered that the composition of the force majeure event requires the following four conditions:

(1) The event must occur after the signing of the contract.

(2) The occurrence of an event is caused by natural or social causes, rather than by intentional or negligent actions of one party.

(3) The occurrence of the event is not foreseeable by the parties when signing the contract.

(4) The occurrence and impact of the event is that the parties cannot control and avoid, the market risk, commodity price fluctuation, exchange rate fluctuation cannot be regarded as force majeure.

2. Notification and Proof of Force Majeure

When the force majeure event affects the performance of the contract, the parties need to achieve the following two points:

First, the party which fails to perform the obligations under the contract must promptly notify the other party of the incident so that the other party can take remedial measures on time. Otherwise, the parties shall be liable for losses or extended losses. The party receiving the notice shall reply to the other party as requested.

Secondly, when the parties request disclaimer, they shall submit to the other party a certificate issued by the issuing authority within a reasonable period of time. In our country, the proof material is usually issued by the China council for the promotion of international trade or its branch at the port. If the parties fail to provide the relevant supporting documents, or if the documents are not in conformity with the facts, the parties shall not be wholly or partially exempt from liability.

3. Legal consequences of force majeure

There are two ways of settlement of force majeure event: postponement of the contract and termination of the contract. The adoption of the settlement ways is according to the effect of force majeure event.

If the effect of a force majeure event is temporary or will be eliminated for a short time, the contract may be suspended. After the impact of the event is eliminated, the contract should resume. For example, if a shipment is delayed because of rainstorm, the contract will be suspended. When the rainstorm is over, the contract should continue and the seller has to go on shipping the goods. If the damage of the force majeure event is long-term and makes it impossible to fulfill the contract, then the contract should be terminated. For example, if the goods were destroyed by the floods, then the contract cannot but terminated.

4. Force Majeure Clause in the Contract

Different countries have different interpretations of "force majeure", so there are differences in the method of establishing force majeure clauses in the contract. In order to clearly define the term of force majeure in a particular contract, the expression of force majeure clauses in foreign trade contracts usually has the following three types:

(1) Brief stipulation

Under brief stipulation, the contract does not definitely stipulate the scope of force majeure cases, just generalize it. For example:

If the shipment of the contract goods is prevented or delayed in whole or in part due to force majeure, the seller shall not be liable for non-shipment or late shipment of the goods of this contract. However, the seller shall notify the buyer by cable or telex and furnish the latter within 15 days by registered airmail with a certificate issued by the China Council for the Promotion of International Trade attesting such event or events.

In the above provisions, the specific contents and scope of the force majeure event in this clause are not mentioned and enumerated. This kind of stipulation is too vague to be evidence of a dispute settlement. The parties often misinterpret or maliciously exploit it.

(2) Concrete stipulation

Under concrete stipulation, the force majeure event shall be listed. If any event not specified in the contract in the future, it shall not be invoked as a force majeure event. Such as:

If the shipment of the contract goods is prevented or delayed in whole or in part by reason of war, earthquake, flood, fire, storm, heavy snow, the seller shall not be liable for non-shipment of the goods of this contract. However, the seller shall notify the buyer by cable or telex and furnish the latter within 15 days by registered airmail with a certificate issued by the China Council for the Promotion of International Trade attesting such event or events.

In the above stipulation, the scope of the force majeure event is specified, but it is difficult to list all the force majeure events that may occur in the sales contract. The parties cannot invoke the force majeure clause to safeguard their own interests if the occurrence of the accident is not specified in the terms.

(3) Synthesized stipulation

Sometimes, the force majeure clause can be stipulated by the combination of the two ways mentioned above. That means besides the various force majeure events listed in common, both parties would also add words "other causes of force majeure" to the trade contract. For example:

The seller shall not be held responsible for failure or delay to perform all or any part of this contract due to war, earthquake, flood, fire, storm, heavy snow or other cause of force majeure. However, the seller shall advise the buyer immediately of such occurence, and within 15 days thereafter, shall send by registered airmail to the buyer for their acceptance a certificate issued by the competent government authorities of the place where the accident occurs as evidence therefore, under such circumstance, the seller however, is still under the obligation to take all necessary measure to hasten the delivery of the goods. In case the accident lasts for more than 3 weeks, the buyer shall have the right to cancel the contract.

The synthesized stipulation is specific and flexible, which can make up the deficiency of the two methods mentioned above. In case that some unexpected accidents that are not listed in the clauses, the parties may find out reasonable solutions through friendly negotiations. Thus, this way of stipulation is widely adopted in international trade practice. The following is another example:

In the event of prohibition of export, refusal to issue export license, war, blockade, mobilization or any other actions of government authorities, riots, civil commotions, strikes, lockout, shortage or control of power supply, plague or other epidemics, fire, flood, tidal waves, typhoon, earthquake, explosion, or any other causes beyond the control of seller or force majeure, seller shall not be liable for any delay in shipment or nondelivery, or destruction or deterioration, of all or any part of the merchandise, or for any default in performance of this contract arising there form, and buyer is bound to accept delay in shipment or delivery within the reasonable time of the termination of the aforesaid causes or to accept cancellation of all or any part of this contract as the case may be. In any of such cases, seller shall not be responsible for any loss or damage.

Section Two Arbitration

In international trade, if there is a trade dispute between buyers and sellers, various methods can be used to settle disputes, such as negotiation, mediation, arbitration or litigation. Among them, negotiation is the most friendly method, which can not undermine the good atmosphere of both parties, and minimize the impact on future business dealings. In some cases, the parties cannot solve the problem through consultation, and then they will be settled through a third party mediation. The third party mediator only facilitates the negotiation between the two parties and does not make any evaluation or decision on the dispute. Therefore, the impact on the relationship between the two parties is small. If mediation still fails to resolve the dispute, it will need to be arbitrated. Unlike mediation, arbitration is often used in international trade because it is more flexible, faster, and less costly than public litigation.

1. Definition of Arbitration

Arbitration refers to trade both parties sign a written agreement, before or after the dispute be submitted voluntarily to both sides to agree to a third party arbitration ruling a way of solving trade disputes. The third party's decision is final, and once the decision is made, it will be legally effective without having to be filed or saved by the court. Neither party shall lodge a complaint with the court or any institution.

Generally, the arbitral tribunal dealing with trade disputes consists of three arbitrators. First, the plaintiff and the defendant shall elect one arbitrator, and then the two arbitrators shall jointly elect a third arbitrator to complete the arbitration. If the parties agree to submit the dispute to arbitration, the court cannot comment on the arbitrator's ruling. Of course, if there is an agreement between the parties not to settle the dispute through arbitration, or if the arbitrator is too arbitrary and biased in the arbitration, such arbitration will not be valid.

2. Characteristics of Arbitration

(1) Voluntary

The most prominent feature of arbitration is voluntary. All the arbitration are based on the voluntary of two parties. That is, matters such as whether to adopt arbitration to settle the dispute, the consist of the arbitration tribunal and the way of arbitration are decided through the friendly negotiation of both parties. So, arbitration is the best way to reflect the parties wishes.

(2) Flexible

Differ from litigation, arbitration is based on the voluntary and its procedures are decided by the parties, so arbitration is more flexible and elastic.

(3) Time-saving

Disputes can be settled swiftly through arbitration since its award is final and effective once the arbitration tribunal was made.

(4) Economical

The economical efficiency of arbitration may display in two aspects. Firstly, the cost of arbitration is relative low because of its time-saving advantage. Secondly, there are several judicial levels in litigation, but usually one in arbitration, thus the expense made by arbitration is lower. Thirdly, fierce confrontation between parties tend to be avoided in the arbitration which is based on the voluntary and confidential. Besides, business secrets will not be disclosed and the effect on between both parties is little.

3. Forms and Functions of Arbitration Agreement

An arbitration agreement is a kind of agreement in writing, which are signed before or after a dispute between both parties arise, agreeing that the dispute should be resolved by arbitration. It is a necessary document for the application for arbitration. Any party of a dispute who asks for arbitrating a dispute should mention the arbitration agreement. Without it, the arbitration would be groundless.

(1) Forms of Arbitration Agreement

According to the time of conclusion, there are mainly two forms of arbitration agreement. One is the arbitration clause in the contract concluded before the occurrence of dispute, agreeing to settle the dispute occurred in the future through arbitration. Such agreement is generally included in the relevant sales contract as one clause of the contract. The other is the agreement for arbitration concluded after the dispute, agreeing to settle the dispute through arbitration. Although above two forms of arbitration agreement are concluded in different time, the function and effectiveness is the same.

(2) Functions of Arbitration Agreement

a. The both parties involved are bound to the arbitration agreement. When a dispute arises, it shall be settled through arbitration, instead of resorting to litigation.

b. An arbitration agreement can exclude the jurisdiction of court effectively. If one party breaches the arbitration agreement and has resorts to the court at its own will, the other party may require the court to refuse the case according to the arbitral tribunal for judgment.

c. The arbitration tribunal or arbitrator is granted the jurisdiction of the case concerning the dispute.

The core of the above functions is the second item, namely the exclusion of the court's jurisdiction of the case. Therefore, the both parties should stipulate arbitration clause in the contract before the dispute arise if they are not willing to submit the dispute to court, in case of they resort to the court for the settlement of disputes.

4. Arbitration Clause

Arbitration Clause refers to the statement in a contract which indicated that both parties agree to arbitration in case of a dispute. Generally speaking, an arbitration clause in any import or export contract should specifically stipulate the place of arbitration, the body of arbitration, the applicable arbitration rules and the arbitral award.

(1) Place of arbitration

The arbitration place, which will determine which arbitration rules and relevant law are applicable. It is a key element in an arbitration clause. The arbitration place can be anywhere in the seller's country, the buyer's country or a third country. Different countries apply different laws, so the interpretations about the rights and obligations of the parties concerned may be different. In that case, the concerned parties always try to choose a place they trust and know the local laws quite well.

In an import or export trade contract, arbitration place can be generally determined by three ways. First of all, the parties involved would choose their countries as arbitration place. For example, Chinese traders will hope any disputes arising shall be referred to China International Economic and Trade Arbitration Commission for arbitration. But things are not always as one wishes, both parties can agree to adopt the arbitration rules of the defendant. This is the second method, and commonly used in international trade practice. The third way is to submit disputes to a third country agreed between them. In general, the arbitration place finally determined in arbitration clause depends on the factors such as bargaining position of involved parties, details of contract and so on.

(2) Arbitration Institution

The name of a certain organization of arbitration by which arbitration is to be held is usually included in an arbitration clause. Arbitration body in international trade can be either a permanent arbitration organization for arbitration stipulated in the arbitration clause or an interim arbitration tribunal which is formed of arbitrators appointed by the two parties. At present, most of the countries and international organizations in the world have their permanent arbitration organization specialized in the settlement of commercial disputes, such as the Arbitration Court of International Chamber of Commerce, the London Court of Arbitration, American Arbitration Association. In China, China International Economic and Trade Arbitration Commission (CIETAC) and Maritime Arbitration Commission are the permanent arbitration organizations. Interim arbitration tribunal is consist of the arbitrators agreed by the parties and it shall be automatically dismissed after the dispute is settled. So, the two parties should explicitly stated, in the contract, the name of arbitrators, number of arbitrators and manner of arbitration, etc. As the permanent staff of the permanent arbitration organization could provide normal service, its operation is more smoothly and management is better than the interim arbitration tribunal.

(3) Applicable Arbitration Rules

In international trade contract, the applicable arbitration rules may not always go with arbitration place. According to the usual international practice, arbitrators apply the arbitration rules in arbitration place in principle. While, in some cases, some countries' law permit parties in accordance with the contract signed before to apply arbitration rules of the arbitration organization in other country (region). In China, the applicable arbitration rule is *the Chinese International Economic and Trade Arbitration Commission Rules.*

(4) Arbitration Procedures

Arbitration should be conducted by certain procedures. Almost every permanent organization of arbitration has its own procedures of arbitration. The procedures will stipulate how arbitration is to apply, how arbitrators are to be appointed, how the case will be heard and which party to bear the cost of the arbitration, etc.. It can be divided into several steps as shown in Fig. 9-1:

(5) Arbitration Award

An arbitration award is a determination on the merits by an arbitration tribunal in an arbitration. Once the award of arbitration is made, it is usually final. In order to

Fig. 9-1 Procedures of Arbitration

avoid ambiguities, the arbitration clauses in contracts often have such words like "the arbitration award is final and shall have binding force upon the two parties". If an arbitration clause does not conclude that the arbitral award is final, CIETAC will not accept the case.

(6) Arbitration fees

Generally, the arbitration clause shall provide that the arbitration fees shall be borne by the losing party.

5. Examples of Arbitration Clauses in Contract

The followings are some examples of arbitration clauses in the contract of import and export business:

(1) All disputes arising out of the performance of, or relating to this contract, shall be settled amicably through friendly negotiation. In case no settlement can be reached through negotiation, the case shall then be submitted to the China International Economic and Trade Arbitration Commission, Beijing, China, for arbitration in accordance with its Rules of Arbitration. The arbitral award is final and biding upon both parties.

(2) All disputes arising out of the performance of, or relating to this contract, shall be settled amicably through friendly negotiation. In case no settlement can be reached through negotiation, the case shall then be submitted for arbitration. The location of arbitration shall be in the country of the domicile of the defendant. If in China, the arbitration shall be conducted by the China International Economic and Trade Arbitration Commission, Beijing, in accordance with its Rules of Arbitration. If in ××, the arbitration shall be conducted by ×× in accordance with its rules of arbitration. The arbitral award is final and binding upon both parties.

(3) All disputes arising out of the performance of, or relating to this contract,

shall be settled amicably through friendly negotiation. In case no settlement can be reached through negotiation, the case shall then be submitted to ×× for arbitration, in accordance with its rules of arbitration. The arbitral award is final and binding upon both parties.

(4) All disputes to be settled by arbitration, in London, in the manner provided for by the Rules of the General Produce Brokers' Association of London, and the decision of the Arbitration shall be final and binding on both parties.

(5) Any disputes or whatever nature arising out of or in any way relating to the contract or to its fulfillment may be referred to arbitration. Such arbitration shall take place in Washington City, USA. Each party to the dispute shall appoint one arbitrator and the arbitrators thus appointed shall name a referee before entering upon the reference. In case either party fails to make his appointment within thirty days after being called to do so by the other party, the arbitrator appointed by such other party shall act as sole arbitrator in the reference as though appointed by the consent of both parties, and the arbitration shall be held and shall proceed accordingly. All other rules shall be in accordance with those of American Arbitration Association.

Part B Key Terms

Breach of contract 违约
Dispute 纠纷
Litigation 诉讼
Parties to a contract 合同当事人
Arbitration 仲裁
Arbitration clause 仲裁条款
Arbitration agreement 仲裁协议
Penalty clause 惩罚条款
Force majeure 不可抗力
Arbitral award 仲裁裁决
Arbitral tribunal 仲裁庭

Part C Exercises

Ⅰ. True or False

(1) Settlement of disputes through negotiation is, therefore, even more expensive and complicated than going to the court. (   )

(2) In international trade, the arbitration clause in sales contract should vaguely stipulated the place of arbitration, the organization of arbitration, the applicable arbitration rules and the arbitral award. (   )

(3) Force Majeure actually means that the frustration of the contract by the party in question results from natural or social forces which include flood, earthquake, typhoon, fire, war and government decrees of prohibition out of the control of mankind. (   )

(4) One of the best way to avoid performing contractual obligations in international trade is to declare a force majeure event. (   )

(5) Once a force majeure event happens, the party who fails to perform its obligations must inform the other party of the event. (   )

(6) The party who incurs a force majeure event may delay the performance of the contract if this party is able to continue the contract. (   )

(7) When setting disputes, the conciliator may force the parties in disputes to act his advice. (   )

(8) Usually the parties who require arbitration in settlement of claims may not appeal to the court. (   )

(9) The conclusion of the award shall be declared to the parties at the opening session of the hearings. (   )

(10) Penalty clause is fixed when the seller fails to make timely delivery: the buyer fails to issue the relevant letter of credit or the buyer fails to take delivery on time, and the penalty ceilings are also included in the contract. (   )

Ⅱ. Reflection questions

(1) What is force majeure?

(2) What are the characteristics of force majeure?

(3) What are the application scope of force majeure?

(4) How do we make a regulation of force majeure in a sales contract?

(5) What are the forms of arbitration agreement?

(6) What are the functions of arbitration agreement?

Ⅲ. Case & Study

1. On February 13th, 2008, Company A signed a contract with Company B in Hong Kong, which was about processing and compensation trade for the cellulose acetate board. The main substance of the contract was that Company A processed the materials on the use of the equipment provided by both Company B and Hong Kong two finance institutions. Per metric ton cellulose acetate board charged USD 1 600 as processing fee, and the Hong Kong Company B was responsible for the provision of cellulose acetate board to Company A, read: providing not less than 80 M/T cellulose acetate board in 2008; not less than 150 M/T in 2009; not less than 200 M/T in 2010; and not less than 200 M/T in later annual.

The processing fee was used by Company A to the principal and interests of the equipment. But in actual performance, Company B only provided 34 M/T cellulose acetate board on December 30th, 2008; 17 M/T on September 17th, 2009; 1.1 T/M on February 16th, 2010; totally 52.1 M/T. In May, 2010, both sides signed a supplementary agreement, stipulating the obligations and the quantities of Company B for the provision of cellulose acetate board again. It was the supplementary agreement not being perform at last so that the equipments brought in by Company A could not be used well. Company A only could repay a small part of the principle and the interests.

Company A requested for arbitration, asking Company B to claim compensation for the economic losses including the equipment loans. Company B defended that: the reason for Company B's failure to well perform the contract was the significant changes in the international market; the price of raw materials was rocking up, supply in shortage. That caused the raw material unobtainable. After the company's manufacturing such raw materials shutdown, they were more unobtainable. This was a force majeure; Company B should not hold the responsibility.

Questions:

In this case, please try to analyse whether Company B (Hong Kong Company) should hold the responsibility.

2. Chinese Company A has concluded an export contract with foreign Company B. The arbitration clause in the contract stipulates that the place of arbitration is Beijing. Soon after the signing the contract, quality dispute about delivery goods occurred between the two parties. Foreign Company B are reluctant to go to Beijing to arbitrate the dispute and filed a lawsuit with a local court. Then the local court serve a summons to Company A.

Question: Please analyze what shall the Company A do?

3. A French buyer visited a Chinese trading company to buy some goods in the morning. When the Chinese seller offered the price, he did not say anything. But in the afternoon, the French buyer visited again and accepted the morning's offer. At this moment, Chinese company found the price of this goods on the international market was rising.

Question: How could the Chinese trading company deal with? Why?

第九章

不可抗力和仲裁

第一节 不可抗力

在国际贸易中，买卖双方都具有履行合同的义务。不履行义务的任何一方都将承担法律责任。然而，有时会出现当事人因某一不可预测、不可控事件的发生，而无法按时履行合同的情况。此时，当事人该如何保护自身的权益呢？

假设一位英国进口商与中国出口商签订了一份1 500公吨小麦的合同，每公吨伦敦到岸价为348英镑。规定的交货时间是五月。不幸的是，中国发生旱灾，当年的小麦收成减少30%，导致中国出口商无法按时完成合约。在此情况下，中国出口商提议将合同延长到明年可行吗？

1. 不可抗力的含义

不可抗力又称人力不可抗拒，是指在签订买卖合同后，并非因当事人的过错或疏忽，而是由于自然原因或社会原因引发的诸如暴风雨、海啸、火灾等当事人无法预测、避免和控制，并导致合同不能履行或不能按时履行的意外事件。此时，遭受不可抗力事件的一方可免除不履行或延期履行合同的责任，而另一方不得要求赔偿损失。换句话说，不可抗力是指对外贸易合同中的一方因发生不可控制的事件而完全或部分地免除履行义务的行为。在这种情况下，当事人绝对不可能预测、避免或克服它们，因此未履行义务的一方无需对此负责，另一方无权就损失提出索赔。由此看出，不可抗力条款实质上是一项免责条款。

需要注意的是,并不是任何一件导致合同无法履行的意外事件都可作为不可抗力事件。通常,不可抗力事件分为两类:一类是由于自然因素引起的事件,如地震、洪水、暴风雨、海啸、火灾、雪灾等;另一类是由于社会因素引起的事件,如战争、罢工、政府禁止进出口某些货物等。

国际贸易中,各国对"不可抗力"这个术语的解释虽有不同,但都认为不可抗力事件的构成需要具备以下四个条件:

(1)事件必须发生于签订合同之后。

(2)事件的发生是由于自然或社会原因导致,而非是因一方当事人的故意或疏忽造成的。

(3)事件的发生是双方当事人在签订合同时无法预见的。

(4)事件的发生及产生的影响是当事人无法控制、避免的,市场风险、商品价格波动、汇率变动等不能被视为不可抗力。

2. 不可抗力的通知和证明

在不可抗力事件影响合同履行时,当事人要取得免责权就必须做到以下两点:

第一,无法按合同约定履行义务的一方,必须及时将事件情况通知对方,以便对方能够及时采取补救措施;否则,当事人仍应对造成的损失负责。接到对方通知的一方应当按要求答复对方。

第二,当事人在要求免责时,应在合理期限内向对方提交由出证机构出具的证明材料。在我国,证明材料通常由中国国际贸易促进委员会或其设在口岸的分会出具。如果当事人未能提供相关的证明文件,或证明文件与事实不符,则当事人不能全部或部分免责。

3. 不可抗力的法律后果

不可抗力事件发生后,合同的处理方式一般分为暂缓执行和终止执行两种。何时采取暂缓执行,何时采取终止执行,则应根据不可抗力事件的影响程度而定。

若不可抗力事件对合同履行的影响是暂时的,短时间内会消除,则合同暂缓执行。待不可抗力事件结束后,恢复合同的执行。如因暴风雨导致货物不能准时发出,合同可暂缓执行。待暴风雨过后,应该按合同继续发货。若不可抗力事件对合同履行的影响是长期的,甚至使合同履行成为不可能,则可解除合同。如货物因洪水而被冲毁,那么合同就不得不终止了。

4. 合同中的不可抗力条款

因各国对“不可抗力”的解释不同,所以合同中订立不可抗力条款的方法也存在差异。为了明确地界定不可抗力这个术语在某一特定合同中的所指范围,外贸合同中不可抗力条款的表达通常有以下三种:

(1)概括式

在合同中,对不可抗力事件仅做笼统的概述,不具体订明哪些现象属于不可抗力范围。例如:

若由于不可抗力的原因,致使卖方不能全部或部分装运或延迟装运合同,卖方对于这种不能装运或延迟装运本合同货物不负有责任。但卖方须用电报或电传通知买方,并须在 15 天内以航空挂号信向买方提交由中国国际贸易促进委员会出具的证明此类事故的证明书。

在上述规定中,未提及并列举该条款中不可抗力事件的具体内容和范围。这种规定过于含糊,很难作为纠纷解决的证据。当事人往往误解或恶意利用它。

(2)具体式

在合同中,把不可抗力事件一一列出来,若今后发生合同中未说明的事件,均不可作为不可抗力事件加以援引。例如:

若由于战争、地震、洪水、火灾、台风、雪灾的原因,致使卖方不能全部或部分装运或延迟装运合同货物,卖方对于这种不能装运或延迟装运本合同货物不负有责任。但卖方须用电报或电传通知买方,并须在 15 天内以航空挂号信件向买方提交由中国国际贸易促进委员会出具的证明此类事件的证书。

在上述规定中,详细说明了不可抗力事件的范围,但很难列出销售合同中可能发生的一切不可抗力事件。一旦发生的事故在条款中未被明确指出,当事人就无法援引不可抗力条款来维护自身的利益。

(3)综合式

在贸易合同中规定不可抗力事件时,可将概括式和具体式结合起来,在列明常发生的不可抗力事件的同时,也写明“以及双方同意的其他不可抗力事件”的句子。例如:

由于战争、地震、洪水、火灾、台风、雪灾或其他不可抗力的原因,致使卖方不能全部或部分装运或延迟装运合同货物,卖方可不负责任。但卖方应立即将事件通知买方,并于事件发生后15天内将事件发生地政府主管当局出具的事件证明书用航空挂号信件邮寄买方为证,并获得买方认可。在上述情况下,卖方仍有责任采取一切必要措施从速交货。如果事件持续超过3个星期,买方有权撤销合同。

此种规定方法,弥补了前两种规定方法的不足,既具体、明确,又保有一定的灵活性。如发生其他的条款中未列明的不可抗力事件,双方可通过协商合理解决。在国际贸易中,常采用这种综合式的订立办法。以下是另一例子:

在下列情况下,诸如:出口限制、拒绝签发出口许可证、战争、封锁、国家动员或其他的政府强制性措施、暴乱、内战、罢工、停业、动力供应不足或限制、瘟疫及其他传染病、火灾、水灾、海啸、台风、地震、爆炸或其他卖方不可控制的不可抗力原因而引起的装船延期或未能装船,货物全部或部分损坏或变质及其他由事故引起的任何违约行为,卖方不负任何责任。另一方面,买方必须同意推迟装船或交货,如果符合事实,则还需同意全部或部分取消订货。上述事件任何一种发生后,卖方不对任何损失或破损负担责任。

第二节　仲　裁

在国际贸易中,买卖双方若发生贸易纠纷,可采用多种办法来解决争议,例如:协商、调解、仲裁或公诉。其中,协商是最友好的一种方法,不易破坏买卖双方的良好氛围,最小程度地减少对将来生意往来的影响。有些情况下,双方当事人无法经协商解决问题,此时就会通过第三方调解解决。第三方调解员只是促成双方协商解决问题,不对争议做任何评价或裁决,因此对双方关系的影响较小。若调解仍无法解决纠纷,这时就需要通过仲裁这一途径。与调解不同,仲裁对争议作出裁决,比公诉灵活,处置迅速,费用较低,因此,在国际贸易中常常被使用。

1. 仲裁的定义

仲裁是指贸易双方在发生争议之前或之后签订书面协议,自愿将争议提交至双方都同意的第三方仲裁机构裁决的一种解决贸易纠纷的方式。第三方的裁决是最终的,一旦决定,即具有法律效用,无需提交法院登记或保存。任何一方都不得向法院或任何机构起诉。

通常,处理贸易纠纷的仲裁庭由三位仲裁成员组成。先由原告和被告各推选一位仲裁员,再由这两位仲裁员共同选出第三位仲裁员,共同来完成仲裁工作。如果双方当事人同意将争议提交仲裁,那么法院就无法对仲裁员的裁定做出评论。当然,如果双方有协议规定不通过仲裁解决争议,或仲裁员在仲裁时过于武断、带有偏见,那么这种仲裁将不再有效。

2. 仲裁的特点

(1)自愿性

当事人的自愿性是仲裁最突出的特点。仲裁以双方当事人的自愿为前提,即当事人之间的纠纷是否提交仲裁,仲裁庭如何组成,以及仲裁的审理方式等都是在当事人自愿的基础上,由双方当事人协商确定的。

(2)灵活性

由于仲裁充分体现当事人的意思自治,仲裁中的诸多具体程序都是由当事人协商确定与选择的,因此,与诉讼相比,仲裁程序更加灵活,更具有弹性。

(3)快捷性

仲裁实行一裁终局制,仲裁裁决一经仲裁庭作出即发生法律效力,这使得当事人之间的纠纷能够迅速得以解决。

(4)经济性

仲裁的经济性主要表现在以下方面:第一,时间上的快捷性使得仲裁所需费用相对减少;第二,仲裁无需多审级收费,使得仲裁费往往低于诉讼费;第三,仲裁的自愿性、保密性使当事人之间通常没有激烈的对抗,且商业秘密不必公之于世,对当事人之间今后的商业关系影响较小。

3. 仲裁协议的形式和作用

仲裁协议是双方当事人在争议发生之前或之后,自愿将争议提交仲裁机构审理的书面协议,是仲裁案件受理的依据。发生争议的双方中任何一方申请仲裁时必须提出双方当事人订立的仲裁协议,否则,仲裁就没有根据。

(1)仲裁协议的形式

仲裁协议按订立协议的时间,可分为两种形式:一种是仲裁条款,订立于争议发生前,以合同条款的形式表明双方当事人在将来发生争议时愿意通过仲裁机构解决的书面协议。这类协议通常作为合同中的一项条款列入相关的销售合同中。另一种是仲裁协议,在争议发生后,双方共同签署把争议提交仲裁机构解决的书面协议。虽然,以上两种形式的协议在订立时间上有所不同,但其作用和效力是相同的。

(2)仲裁的作用

a. 约束双方当事人只能以仲裁方式解决争议,不得向法院起诉。

b. 排除法院对有关案件的管辖权。如果一方违背仲裁协议,自行向法院起诉,另一方可根据仲裁协议要求法院不予受理,并将争议案件退交仲裁庭裁断。

c. 仲裁庭或仲裁员被授予对争议案件的管辖权。

上述作用的中心是第二条,即排除法院对争议案件的管辖权。因此,双方当事人不愿将争议提交法院审理时,就应在争议发生前在合同中规定仲裁条款,以免将来发生争议后,由于达不成仲裁协议而不得不诉诸法院。

4. 仲裁条款

仲裁条款又称仲裁协议,是双方当事人在合同中说明愿意将其争议提交第三者进行裁决的声明。任何进出口合同的仲裁条款一般包括仲裁地点、仲裁机构、适用的仲裁规则、仲裁程序、仲裁的裁决和仲裁费用。

(1)仲裁地点

仲裁地点是仲裁条款中的一项重要内容,关系到仲裁所适用的原则和相关法律。仲裁地点可以在卖方所在国、买方所在国或第三方国家。不同仲裁地点,适用的法律可能不同,对双方当事人的权利和义务解释可能存在差异。交易双方在订立仲裁地点时一般会先选择自己对当地法律和仲裁程序比较熟悉的地方仲裁。

进出口贸易合同中,仲裁地点的规定一般有三种方法:第一种,力争在本国仲裁,例如,中国商人会希望将争议提交至中国国际经贸仲裁委员会或海事仲裁委员会仲裁;第二种,双方当事人可以规定在被告所在国仲裁,这也是国际上常用的一种方法;第三种,选择在双方认同的第三国仲裁。仲裁条款中最终确定的仲裁地点,将取决于当事人的谈判地位、合同的具体情况等因素。

(2)仲裁机构

在仲裁条款中通常注明将要进行仲裁的机构名称。在国际贸易中,仲裁机构可以是当事人在仲裁协议中规定的常设机构,也可以是由双方当事人指定组成的临时仲裁庭。目前,国际上许多国家和国际组织都设有专门从事外贸纠纷的常设仲裁机构。例如,国际商会仲裁庭院、伦敦仲裁院、美国仲裁协会、中国国际经济贸易仲裁委员会和海事仲裁委员会就是我国的常设仲裁机构。临时仲裁庭因是由当事人双方共同指定的临时机构,案件处理完毕即自动解散,故双方当事人在仲裁条款中应就双方指定的仲裁员、人数及办法等作出明确规定。因为常设仲裁机构的工作人员能够提供正常的服务,因此它具有操作便利、管理良好的优点。

(3)仲裁规则的适用

在外贸合同中,所采用的仲裁规则与仲裁地并非绝对一致。按照国际仲裁惯例,原则上采用仲裁所在地的规则,但有些国家(地区)的法律允许双方当事人依据在合同中约定的仲裁地以外其他国家(地区)的仲裁规则进行仲裁。在我国,适用的仲裁规则是指《中国国际经济贸易仲裁委员会仲裁规则》。

(4)仲裁程序

仲裁都要遵循一定的程序。几乎所有的常设仲裁机构都有它们自己的程序。这些程序将规定如何提出仲裁申请,如何指定仲裁员,如何审理案件以及由哪一方来承担仲裁费用等。仲裁的程序可分为以下几个步骤:

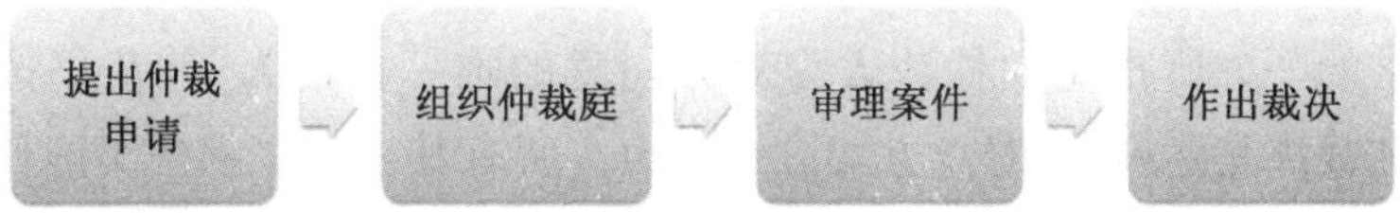

图 9-1　仲裁程序

(5)仲裁的裁决

仲裁裁决是仲裁庭根据事实和证据,对当事人提交的请求事项做出支持、驳回或部分驳回的书面决定。一旦作出仲裁,它一般是终局的。因此,在合同仲裁条款中通常有这样一句话"仲裁裁决是终局的,对双方都具有约束力",以免引起歧义。如果仲裁条款未说明仲裁裁决是终局的,中国国际经济贸易仲裁委员会将不予受理。

(6)仲裁费用

通常,仲裁条款规定仲裁费用由败诉方承担。

5. 合同中的仲裁条款实例

以下是进出口合同中仲裁条款的一些实例:

(1)凡因执行本合同所发生的或与本合同有关的一切争议,双方应通过友好协商解决。如果协商不能解决,应提交北京中国国际经济贸易仲裁委员会,根据该会仲裁规则进行仲裁。仲裁裁决是终局的,对双方均有约束力。

(2)凡因执行本合同所发生的或与本合同有关的一切争议,双方应通过友好协商解决。如果协商不能解决,应提交仲裁。仲裁在被诉方所在国进行。如果在中国,由中国国际经济贸易仲裁委员会根据其仲裁规则进行仲裁。如果在××国,则由××(对方所在国仲裁机构名称)根据其仲裁规则进行仲裁。仲裁裁决是终局的,对双方均有约束力。

(3)凡因执行本合同所发生的或与本合同有关的一切争议,双方应通过友好协商解决。如果协商不能解决,应提交××(某第三国某地及某仲裁机构的名称)根据其仲裁规则进行仲裁。仲裁裁决是终局的,对双方均有约束力。

(4)所有需要在伦敦通过仲裁解决的争议都应该按照伦敦生产经纪人总协会的规定进行裁决。仲裁人的裁决是终局的,对双方均有约束力。

(5)凡有关本合同的执行所发生的任何争议,可提交仲裁解决,仲裁在美国华盛顿市进行。争议双方各指定一名仲裁人,被指定的仲裁人在仲裁前指定一名公证人。如果一方没按另一方的要求在接到通知后 30 天内指定仲裁人,则提出要求的一方所指定的仲裁人为双方同意的唯一仲裁人,仲裁仍按规定进行。仲裁裁决是终局的,对双方均有约束力。所有其他程序都按美国仲裁协会的规则进行。

Chapter 10

Business Negotiation

Part A Text

Section One General Introduction of Business Negotiation

In international trade, the essence of the transaction is to conclude the relevant international trade contract with the foreign businessman and perform the process of the contract. A satisfactory contract cannot be concluded without careful negotiation between exporters and importers. Only if both parties have no objection to the terms of the negotiation, the business can be made and the sales contract can be signed. It can be said that the transaction negotiation is the basis of the contract and the most important link in the international trade business.

Business negotiation refers to the process of negotiation between the parties through correspondence or negotiation in order to conclude the transaction. Trade negotiations can be conducted through letters, telegraph, telex and e-mail, or through face-to-face meetings such as trade fairs and fairs. At present, the use of letters to establish business contacts is more extensive. The contents of the trade negotiation include: commodity name, quality, packaging, price, shipping, payment method, insurance, commodity inspection, claim, arbitration, force majeure, etc..

Regardless of the form and content of the negotiations, generally speaking, the negotiation of a transaction goes through five stages: enquiry, offer, counter-offer, acceptance and signing contract. Not every transaction goes through these five stages, but the offer and acceptance are two essential parts of every transaction. In some countries, the law stipulates that the offer and acceptance are two necessary conditions, and if the two are not one, they cannot sign the contract.

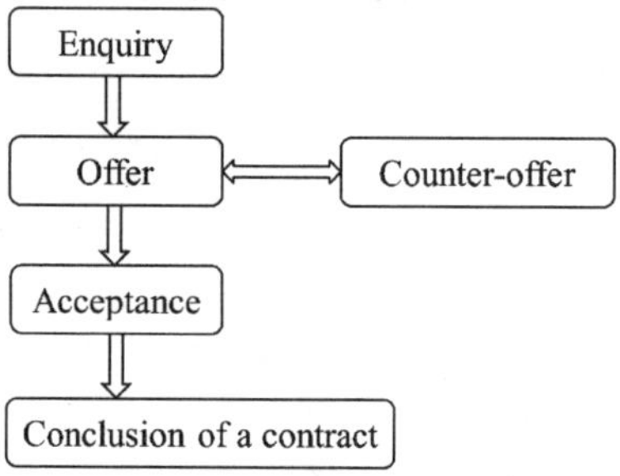

Fig. 10-1 Procedures of Business Negotiation

Section Two Enquiry

When a businessman wants to import some goods, he may enquire from the exporter about the quotation, trade terms of the goods he wishes to buy, or simply by asking for some general information about the goods. After receiving the enquiry, the exporter will reply to the enquiry. In that way, the negotiations can begin.

1. Definition of Enquiry

Enquiry also refers to the process whereby one party intends to purchase or sell a commodity, and ask the other party to buy or sell the goods. Generally speaking, enquiries are made by the buyers for information on prices, catalogues, samples and terms of trade. In some cases, the seller may make an offer to express his desire to sell a particular commodity to the buyer. It is important to note that enquiries are belong to the tentative business contact, has no legal binding force to both the seller and the buyer, enquiry of people don't need to undertake the obligation to must buy and sell the goods, and been enquiries can also don't answer. However, in order to lay the foundation for future business transactions, the buyers and sellers will immediately respond to the enquiry in accordance with business practices.

There are two types of enquiries, both verbal and written. If it is an enquiry in writing, there are often faxes, e-mails, letters and enquiries. An enquiry can be sent to multiple clients simultaneously. In this way, a party who send enquiries could receive the reply of the conditions of sale, choose the most beautiful quotation through sorting and comparison, and then to offer the most optimal one party consultation, conclude the transaction.

2. Types of enquiry

According to the content and purpose of the enquiry, enquiries can be divided into general enquiries and specific enquiries. If the importer only wants to know the general situation of the products or commodities that the exporter can provide, please send him the catalogue, price list and sample, which are the general enquiries. If the importer intends to purchase a particular commodity, the exporter shall be asked to make an offer for the goods, which are the specific enquiries.

The following are two enquiries sent to the supplier. The first one is a general enquiry, and the last one is a specific enquiry.

To whom it may concern,

Thank you very much for your letter of December 12th from which we now know that you are exporting electrical appliances. We want to enquiry about your products and their packing in details as soon as possible for our reference. We would also like to have your price list.

We would really appreciate if you quote us your most favorable terms.

Yours faithfully,

To whom it may concern,

Thank you for your fax of August 8, 2017 from which we learned that you are an exporter of pharmaceuticals.

Please quote the lowest prices on CIF Rotterdam for the following:

(1)2 MT Vitamin E 50%

(2)4 MT Vitamin B complex

Packing: 25KGS/BAG

Terms of payment: By Irrevocable L/C at sight

Time of Shipment: September 20th, 2017

Your prompt reply will be appreciated.

Yours faithfully,

3. How to Enquire Effectively

Most enquiries are very simple, and even many companies use the printed enquiry form directly. But if you want to get an ideal price from an enquiry, it is necessary to have some tips on how to write an enquiry. An initial enquiry, which is the first letter to a supplier who has not previously traded, should include:

(1) Explain how you get information from the other person. Your sources of information may be embassies, Chambers of commerce, trade fairs, exhibitions, Internet, newspapers and magazines.

(2) Self introduction. Brief introduction of the basic situation of the company, such as the nature of the enterprise, scope of business, performance of previous years, credit information, etc..

(3) Specify what you want the supplier to send you. For example: catalogue, price list, discount, payment method, delivery date and sample.

(4) Write the closing sentence of your enquiry and lay the foundation for your future business relationship.

4. Samples of Enquiry

Sample 1

> To whom it may concern,
>
> We learned from our Commercial Counselor's Embassy in Paris that you are the most well-know producer of a variety of hand-made gloves . We are one of the leading enterprise specialized in the the import of gloves here. We have our branches in many countries in Europe, and are in close relations with many retailers here.
>
> We are very interested in your company's products. Could you please send us your catalogue and price list together with samples of the different qualities of material used.
>
> Looking forward to receiving your immediately reply.
>
> Yours faithfully,

Sample 2

> To whom it may concern,
>
> We learned from the Internet that your company is a manufacturer and exporter of bamboo toys. We have been engaged in the import of bamboo toys for many years and are very interested in your products.
>
> Could you please provide us with a set of catalogue and price list for bamboo toys for us to choose? Please quote us your price at 2% CIF San Francisco. If your prices are reasonable and acceptable, we will place large orders regularly.
>
> Your prompt reply to this enquiry will be appreciate.
>
> Yours faithfully,

5. How to Reply Enquiries Effectively

The purpose of replying an enquiry letter is meeting the customer's requirements. As for the writing style, its content and expression should be fairly brief and plain, and does not need to be more than polite and direct. Normally, a replying letter will involve the following aspects:

(1) Thank the writer of the letter for enquiry.

(2) Supply all the required information and materials for reference, and inform the customer that catalogues, samples and other enclosures are enclosed by separate post.

(3) Provide additional information which is help for enlarging the sales amount but not requested by the customer.

(4) Assure the customer of good quality and services, then encourage he or she to place orders promptly.

Reply letter to an enquiry-sample 1

> To whom it may concern,
>
> Thank you for your enquiry of November 12, and appreciate your interest in our products.
>
> We are enclosing our illustrated catalogue and price list you ask for. Also by separate post, we are sending you some samples for you to examine and are confident that you will agree that our products are both excellent in quality and reasonable in price.
>
> We would like to draw your attention that our products are short in supply. Please order as soon as possible so that we can arrange the shipment.
>
> Yours faithfully,

Reply letter to an enquiry-sample 2

> To whom it may concern,
>
> We are very pleased to receive your enquiry of October 12 and are glad to inform you that all the items listed in your enquiry are on stock. Catalogue and export prices are enclosed, and samples of the products you are interested have been arranged to be sent to you.
>
> As you may be well aware, we are a trading company involved in exporting business throughout the world. Our company has been in this line for many years and enjoys high international prestige, so we can better serve our customers.
>
> If you wish to place an order, please let us know. We are happy to discuss discount with you. We can arrange shipment within three weeks after receiving your firm order.
>
> We think our products will be just what you are looking for, and hope to hear from you.
>
> Yours faithfully,

Section Three Offer

Making an offer is a most important step in business negotiation because agreement is the foundation of a contract. The parties reach an agreement by an offer made on one side which is accepted on the other. An offer is a promise conditioned on acceptance.

1. Definition of Offer

An offer refers to the terms and conditions of the transaction in which the other party proposes to purchase or sell a certain commodity, and proposes the proposal to sign the contract on such terms. The offer is usually made by letter, fax or quotation. The person who makes the offer is called the offeror, and the person who accepts the offer is called the offeree.

The offer may be made by the seller or by the buyer. In the actual business, more for the seller to put forward, called the sales offer. Once the seller receives the overseas enquiry, quotation must immediately to foreign customers, and explain the trade terms and conditions asked by foreign clients. But sometimes, the seller's goods are very popular or the seller does not understand the market, and cannot be sure whether the buyer has the intention to purchase, they usually ask the buyer to quote first. This offer, made by the buyer, is called a delivery.

There are different provisions for the specific content of the offer. Generally, offer to the main contract conditions, such as brand name, quality, quantity, packing, price, payment, delivery time and so on all have clear rules, so that once the offeree can accept to sign a binding upon both buyers and sellers of the contract.

2. Necessary conditions for a valid offer

As to in which conditions an offer can be made, there are clear stipulations in *the United Nations Convention on Contracts for the International Sale of Goods* article 14 (1), A proposal for concluding a contract addressed to one or more specific persons constitutes an offer if it is sufficiently definite and indicates the intention of the offeror to be found in case of acceptance. A proposal is sufficiently definite if it indicates the goods and expressly or implicitly fixes or makes provision for determining the quantity and the price. Article 14 (2), A proposal other than one addressed to one or more specific persons is to be considered merely as an invitation to make offers, unless the contrary is clearly indicated by the person making the proposal.

According to the provisions of *the United Nations convention on the international sale of goods*, an effective offer shall have the following four conditions:

(1) The offer must be sent to a particular receiver.

(2) The contents of the offer must be clear and complete.

(3) The offeror must indicate that he is bound by the offer within the validity of the offer.

(4) The offer must be served within the validity period.

3. Forms of offer

Offers can be divided as firm offers and non-firm offers. A firm offer refers to a kind of offer in which the offeror lists all the trade terms clearly and expresses his intention to make a contract. Once a firm offer is accepted by the offeree within its valid period, it cannot be revoked or amended. At this time, contract is concluded and the transaction is ended. A firm offer will lapse if it is not accepted within its validity. The lapsed offer no longer has any influence on the offeror. At this moment, even if the offeree expresses his acceptance, the offer is entitled to refuse it.

In contrast to a firm offer, a non-firm offer is a kind of offer without constraints. It has no clear and complete state about trade terms and no terms of validity. Moreover, the offeror makes the offer with reservation: the offer is subject to his final confirmation. So a non-firm offer usually includes such wording "this offer is subject to our final confirmation" or "the prices are subject to change without notice". In general, most offers are non-firm offers.

Through comparison, it can be found that non-firm offer is more flexible and the decision of conclude a trade contract can be made according to the market situation. However, offerees often regard it as ordinary business dealings and pay little attention to it. Therefore, firm offer can get more attention from offeree and promote the reach of a deal.

An example of firm offer letter:

> To whom it may concern,
>
> We acknowledge receipt of your letter of 20th this month, asking us to offer you a firm offer for peanuts CFR Amsterdam. We wrote back this morning, offering you 400 metric tons Shandong groundnuts, hand-packed, shelled and ungraded at RMB 1 500 per metric ton, CFR Amsterdam or any other European Main Port for shipment during July/August, 2017. This offer is firm, subject to your reply reaching us within one week.
>
> We wish to point out that this is the lowest price so we can't consider any counter-offer to you.
>
> Yours faithfully,

An example of non-firm offer letter:

> To whom it may concern,
>
> Thank you for your letter of July 10, 2017. We are glad to make you an offer. The offer is as follows:
>
> Goods name: embroidered satin miniskirt.
>
> Quantity: 10 000 dozen
>
> Price: $50 per dozen CFR New York.
>
> Packing: clear plastic bags.
>
> Shipment date: August 2017.
>
> Payment: irrevocable letter of credit payable by draft at sight.
>
> The offer is subject to our confirmation. If you accept it, please let us know as soon as possible.
>
> Yours faithfully,

4. Validity and Withdrawal of an Offer

The validity of the offer is a restriction on both parties of the transaction, which is the time limit for the acceptor to accept the offer, and the time limit for the offeree. Upon expiration of the validity period, the acceptance of the offeree shall be null and void, and the distributor shall not be obligated to enter into a contract in accordance with the terms of the offer. Therefore, the validity of the offer is a limitation for both parties and a guarantee for both parties. All the offer has validity, some offer a clear stipulation on the validity period, also some do not make clear stipulation.

There are two commonly used methods for the validity of the offer:

A. The deadline for acceptance, for example, is to return to this place on May 3, 2018. In the actual business, there is time difference between different countries, so it should be clearly stipulated in the offer when the time is taken. Usually, the offer period shall be subject to the time of the originator's location.

B. Stipulate a period of acceptance, for example: 5 days for the offer. In accordance with *the United Nations Convention on Contracts for the International Sale of Goods*, it shall be valid to begin the calculation of the letter or the offeror received from the offeror. If the last day of validity is a holiday or a non-working day of the recipient, the period of validity will be postponed accordingly. By contrast, the validity period of this method is easy to be controversial at the beginning and end time, and less in practice.

The withdrawal of the offer refers to the cancellation by the offeror before it has been delivered to the recipient before it has entered into force. In accordance with *the United Nations Convention on Contracts for the International Sale of Goods* article 15 (1), An offer becomes effective when it reaches the offeree. Article 15 (2), An offer, even if it is irrevocable, may be withdrawn if the withdrawal reaches the offeree before or at the same time as the offer.

5. The Revocation and Invalidation of an Offer

The revocation of the offer refers to the act by which the offer has been served and the offeror has taken action to remove the effect of the offer. The difference between it and the withdrawal is that the former cancels the legally effective offer, which has taken effect. *The United Nations Convention on Contracts for the International Sale of Goods* stipulates that, prior to the conclusion of the contract, the offeror shall send the notice to the recipient, and the offer shall be revoked. However, in the following two cases, the offer shall not be revoked: A. The expiry date of the offer is clearly specified in the offer or otherwise indicated that the offer is irrevocable; B. The recipient has reason to believe that the offer is irrevocable and has acted in the confidence of the distributor.

The failure of the offer indicates that the distributor is no longer bound by the offer and that the recipient also loses the right to accept the offer. *The United Nations Convention on Contracts for the International Sale of Goods* states in Article 17: An offer, even if it is irrevocable, is terminated when a rejection reaches the offeror.

The following situations will cause the failure of the offer:

(1) The recipient refuses or counter-offers.

(2) The offer has been overdue.

(3) The offeror shall withdraw or cancel the offer according to law.

(4) The occurrence of unexpected events such as force majeure.

For example, A Chinese importer received an offer from an American trader on Jul. 15th, 2017, "100 Raincoats USDOLLARS 16.5/piece CFR CHINA PORT AUGUST SHIPMENT SIGH L/C SUBJECT TO YOU REPLY REACHING US BY JUL. 20th". The Chinese importer replied on Jul. 16th stating "We can accept the offer if the unite price is USD15.0 CFR China port." The American trader replied: "The market is firm, the price cannot be reduced, please reply as soon as possible." At last, the Chinese importer replied immediately: "We accept your firm offer of 15th." In this case, American trader made an offer of Jul.15th, the Chinese importer made a counter-offer on Jul.16th, so the offer of Jul.15th is not established and invalid.

Section Four Counter-offer

Upon receipt of the offer, the recipient may conclude a transaction with the other party and enter into a contract. However, if the receiver is not satisfied with a certain item or a certain amount of item in the offer, he may directly decline the offer or make a counter-offer.

A counter-offer is the act of adding, restricting or altering a proposal to a person who does not agree to the terms of the trade. In fact, counter-offer is a process by which a receiver makes a counter-offer to the offeror. When the offeree put forward new terms of price, payment, quality, specification or quantity, the original offer is invalid and a new offer forms. At this point, the original originator becomes the receiver, and the original receiver becomes the originator. If, after the offeree because the international market price or exchange rate changes to his, and expressed a willingness to accept the offer, the offer shall have the right to decide to accept it or not, even as also in the period of validity of the original offer.

After receiving the counter-offer, the distributor may not be satisfied with the trading conditions of the counter-offer, and propose new conditions for the counter-offer, which is "counter-counter-offer". In the real business, this process would go on for many rounds until the negotiation ends and the contract is concluded.

Here are two examples of counter-offer letters:

Sample 1

To whom it may concern,

We are in receipt of both your offer of May 15th and the samples of Melon Seeds, thank you. While appreciating the good quality of yours Melon Seeds, we find your price is above the market level. We have also to point out that the products of the same quality in our market are 15% to 20% lower than your price.

In that case, we have to ask you to consider if you can make reduction on your price, say 10%. As our order would be worth around USD 100 000, it's worthwhile to make a concession.

Looking forward to your early reply.

Yours faithfully,

Sample 2

To whom it may concern,

We thank you for your letter of July 15th, offering us $55 per kilogram of walnut meat.

We regret to inform you that your price is a little high for the market we want to supply. Besides, there are many Korean manufacturers of walnut meat in our market. All these products are 5% lower than yours.

It is only in view of the long-term business relationship that we have given the above counter-offer. The market is declining and we hope you will take a positive attitude and reply to our counter-offer at an early date.

Yours faithfully,

Section Five Acceptance and Signing Contract

1. Acceptance

Acceptance means that the offeree agree with trade terms of the offer unconditionally and express his intention to conclude the contract.

As for acceptance, *the United Nations Convention on Contracts for the International Sale of Goods* stipulates article 18: (1) A statement made by or other conduct of the offeree indicating assent to an offer is an acceptance. Silence or inactivity does not in itself amount to acceptance. (2) An acceptance of an offer becomes effective at the moment the indication of assent reaches the offeror. An acceptance is not effective if the indication of assent does not reach the offeror within the time he has fixed or, if no time is fixed, within a reasonable time, due account being taken of the circumstances of the transaction, including the rapidity of the means of communication employed by the offeror. An oral offer must be accepted immediately unless the circumstances indicate otherwise. (3) However, if, by virtue of the offer or as a result of practices which the parties have established between themselves or of usage, the offeree may indicate assent by performing an act, such as one relating to the dispatch of the goods or payment of the price, without notice to the offeror, the acceptance is effective at the moment the act is performed, provided that the act is performed within the period of time laid down in the preceding paragraph.

Conditions that constitute an effective acceptance:

(1) Acceptance must be made by a specific offeree.

(2) Acceptance must be consistent with the content of the offer.

(3) Acceptance must be made within the validity period.

(4) Acceptance must be clearly expressed in a certain way.

But sometimes accept is conditional, the convention also gives stipulations article 19 for it: (1) A reply to an offer which purports to be an acceptance but contains additions, limitations or other modifications is a rejections of the offer and constitutes a counter-offer. (2) However, a reply to an offer which purports to be an acceptance but contains additional or different terms which do not materially alter the terms of the offer constitutes an acceptance, unless the offeror, without undue delay, objects orally to the discrepancy or dispatches a notice to that effect. If he does not so object, the terms of the contract are the terms of the offer with the modifications contained in the acceptance. (3) Additional or different terms relating, among other things, to the price, payment, quality and quantity of the goods, place and time of delivery, extent of one party's liability to the other or the settlement of disputes are considered to alter the terms of the offer materially.

There are different methods of time determination between different legal systems in the world. The Anglo-American legal system provides that the notification shall take effect immediately upon delivery of the post or e-mail within the validity period of the offer. If the letter is delayed or lost in the mail, it will not affect the validity of the contract. The civil law system stipulates that the receiving letter shall be effective in the effective period. If the letter is delayed or lost on the way, it is deemed invalid.

In *the United Nations Convention on Contracts for the International Sale of Goods*, an acceptance can be withdrawal as long as the notice of withdrawal reaches the offeror before he receives the notice of acceptance. Besides, an acceptance cannot be withdrawal in the Common Law, because the acceptance has become effective as soon as it is dispatched.

Here are two examples of accepting letters:

Sample 1

To whom it may concern,

We acknowledge receipt of your fax of 12 February and confirm the sale of the 50 long tons of rosin to you on the terms agreed upon by both parties.

We are enclosing a copy of our sales confirmation no. cf123 in duplicate, one of which is to be returned to us for the purpose of filing.

Yours faithfully,

Sample 2

To whom it may concern,

We are glad to know from your letter of July 10th that you have accepted our offer dated on July 4th.

In reply, we confirm having sold to you 15 000 metric tons of small red beans on the following terms and conditions:

Price: at US $400 per metric ton CFR Seattle.

Packing: in gunny bags of about 50 kilograms net each.

Shipment: to be effected from Shanghai to Seattle during December 2017.

Payment: by an irrevocable L/C in our favor, payable by draft at sight.

We are pleased to have transacted this first business with you and look forward to the further expansion of trade to our mutual benefit.

Yours faithfully,

2. Signing Contract

A contract is an agreement between two or more parties that is enforceable in a court of law. In international trade, a sales contract comes into existence through a chain of correspondence between the exporter and importer. The importer may come in with an initial inquiry requesting a price quotation for a certain type and quantity of merchandise. The seller, in turn, responds with the desired information. Usually, this response can already be interpreted as an offer that is binding on the exporter, provided the importer accepts it within a reasonable period of time. At this very moment, the transaction is completed and a contractual relationship between the seller and buyer is concluded. But, according to international trade practice, the seller and buyer still have to sign a written sales contract or sales confirmation, binding on them all, to further define their rights and obligations respectively.

In international trade, export and import contracts vary in both names and forms. The names that often appear are contract, confirmation, agreement and memorandum.

A contract or confirmation can be drawn up either by the seller or the buyer. Respectively, they are called a sales contract/confirmation or a purchase contract / confirmation. Whatever they are named, they are equally binding on the parties. The sales or purchase contract is more formal than that of the latter. The former usually consists of commodities, specifications, quantity, packing, marking, price, shipment, port of shipment and port of destination, and payment as well as those clauses concerning insurance, commodity inspection, claims, arbitration and force majeure, etc.; while the latter only includes several main items only. What's more, the former is appropriate to transaction of large amount and huge quantity because of its detailed clauses which can prevent the occurrence of disputes. If the amount is not large or the business is done by means of agency arrangement or exclusive sales agreement, the sales or the purchase confirmation is often used.

Many firms have printed order and offer forms which, when accepted, become contracts. This greatly simplifies buying and selling procedures in that details that are the same for most contracts of a particular firm need not be specifically typed each time. Major provisions are included in the printed part of the form. Variable provision can be typed in as required. However, it should be noted that the forms preprinted by one of the parties are only acceptable when this is traditional in the industry, the amounts involved are small, there is high degree of trust between the buyer and the seller, or when enough previous business has been done between the buyer and the seller to make repeated orders a routine.

Part B Key Terms

Enquiry 询盘
Offer 发盘
Counter offer 还盘
Acceptance 接受
Firm offer 实盘
Offeree 受盘人
Offeror 发盘人
Quotation 报价
Bid 递盘
Discount 折扣
Brochure 小册子

Agent 代理商

Part C Exercises

Ⅰ. True or False

(1) According to the GISG, once the offeror stipulates the validity on the offer, the offeror can still cancel the offer. (   )

(2) Offer and acceptance are two indispensable links for reaching an agreement and concluding a contract. (   )

(3) During the negotiation, the offer is made by seller and acceptance is made by buyer. (   )

(4) Enquiry, offer and acceptance are indispensable part of a negotiation. (   )

(5) An advertisement on paper is an effective offer. (   )

(6) If an offer remarks "irrevocable", it means the offeror has no right to withdraw the offer. (   )

(7) Same to the offer, acceptance also can be canceled. (   )

(8) An offer may not indicate the terms of payment. (   )

(9) The price-list and catalogue sent to some companies are also offers with binding effect. (   )

(10) According to *the United Nations Convention on Contracts for the International Sale of Goods*, an acceptance with non-material alteration or additions can still constitute a valid acceptance. (   )

Ⅱ. Reflection questions

(1) What are the steps in business negotiation? Which of them are the necessary steps?

(2) What are the differences between firm offer and non-firm offer?

(3) What are the necessary conditions for a valid offer?

(4) What are the conditions for a valid acceptance?

(5) Can the acceptance be withdrawn? Why?

Ⅲ. Compose a letter of enquiry with the following particulars

(1) You have the seller's name and address from Commercial Counsellor's

Office in London.

(2) You wish to buy textiles.

(3) State clearly price terms, payment terms, time of shipment, packing conditions, etc.

(4) Ask for illustrated catalogues.

Ⅳ. Please make your offer according to the following particulars

(1) You have got the enquiry of July 12th for Chinese Black Tea CFR Sydney.

(2) Quantity: 500 cases of Chinese Black Tea.

(3) Unit price: AUD 60 per case CFR Sydney.

(4) Payment: irrevocable L/C at sight.

(5) Shipment: September, 2017.

(6) In your letter, some comments on the goods can be illustrated.

Ⅴ. Write a counter-offer according to the following particulars

(1)告诉对方你已经收到其 2017 年 9 月 13 日关于中国绿茶的还盘信,感谢对方的还盘。

(2)明确表示很遗憾无法接受对方降价 10%的还盘,并说明按所报价格你们已经收到了大量的订单。

(3)强调你们的报价是适中、合理的,如果降价 10%,你们则将无利可图。

(4)建议对方重新考虑你们的报价并表示希望能在双方互利的情况下达成交易。

Ⅵ. Case & Study

1. On June 27th, 2017, at the request of a Duthch firm B, the Chinese company A made a firm offer of 200 metric tons of a product C514, on basis of CIF Rotterdam at RMB 1 950 per metric ton, immediate shipment. After receiving the offer, Firm B did not give any counter-offer. They requested company A to increase the quantities, reduce the price and extend the validity period again and again. The Chinese side, at last, increased the quantity to 300 metric tons, reduced the price to CIF Rotterdam at RMB 1 900 per metric ton. And the validity was extended twice to July 25th. The Dutch firm B accepted the offer on July 22nd by telegram, proposing "an irrevocable letter of credit, prompt shipment, shipment volume by calculation. In addition to the usual shipping documents, please provide documents as follows: the quarantine certificates, certificates of origin, weight memo, and certificate of proper and good bagging

for sea transport".

However, when receiving the telegram, the Chinese company A found the international market price of the subject product has been rocketing up. Then, the Chinese side refused to finalize the deal, and replied that: "As the world market changed, the goods had been sold out before receiving the telegram." But the Dutch firm B did not agree with the Chinese side's argument. They thought they accepted an offer within the validity period, and insisted on carrying out a contract according to the offer. Otherwise, the Chinese side must make up their losses of RMB 230 000, and accepted the arbitration award.

Question:

a. Was the offer made by Chinese Company A on June 27th a firm offer or a non-firm offer?

b. The Dutch firm B did not give any counter-offer. They requested for increasing the quantity, reducing the prices and extending the validity again and again. In such circumstances, the Chinese company A wired a reply, read "increase the quantity of the product C514 to 300 metric ton, RMB 1 900 per metric ton on CIF Rotterdam, extend the validity to July 25th". Was it a firm offer or a non-firm offer?

c. As to the message from the Dutch firm on July 22nd, shall we regard it as the expression of acceptance to show their intention to the proposal? Why?

d. When receiving the message from the Dutch firm on 22, the Chinese company cabled a reply to refuse to close the deal. Is it in conformity with the regulation and policy of international trade? Why?

e. How should this case be settled?

2. Business A in England makes an offer to businessman B in Germany on May 3rd for a certain of goods. B is in receipt of this offer the next day, and makes a complete answer to accept the offer in the morning of May 6th. After making the offer, A finds the commodity price upward, hence he cables business B to withdraw the offer in the afternoon of May 7th. It is in the morning of May 8th that A receives the acceptance from B.

Question:

a. According to the Britain Law, is it legal for businessman A to withdraw the offer?

b. If the case is applied to the CISG, will the contract relationship exist between both sides?

3. One day morning, a French businessman pays a visit to a Chinese trading company for purchasing certain goods. During negotiation, the Chinese trading company makes an oral offer, but the French businessman does not answer, and comes back again to express acceptance to the morning's offer in that day afternoon. At that time the Chinese company has also learned that there is an upward tendency in the international market for the goods.

Question: Then how will the Chinese company handle this situation?

第十章
交易的磋商

第一节　交易磋商的基本概念

在国际贸易中,交易的实质就是和外商签订有关的国际贸易合同,履行该项合同的过程。而一笔满意合同的签订离不开出口商和进口商之间缜密的交易磋商。只有双方对所磋商的条款都无异议,生意才能做成,销售合同才能签订。可以说,交易磋商是订立合同的基础,也是国际贸易业务中最重要的环节。

交易磋商是指交易双方通过函电或洽谈的方式,就买卖货物的交易条件进行协商,以求达成交易的过程。交易磋商可以通过信函、电报、电传和电子邮件等工具进行,也可通过参加交易会、博览会等面对面的形式进行。目前,用信函建立商业往来的方式运用得较为广泛。交易磋商的内容包括商品名称、品质、包装、价格、装运、支付方式、保险、商检、索赔、仲裁、不可抗力等各项交易条件。

不管磋商的形式和内容如何,一般来说,交易磋商要经过五个阶段:询盘、发盘、还盘、接受和签订合同。并不是每一笔交易都要经历这五个阶段,但发盘和接受是每笔交易必不可少的两个基本环节。有些国家的法律规定,发盘和接受是两个必要条件,若两者缺一就不能签订合同(见图 10-1)。

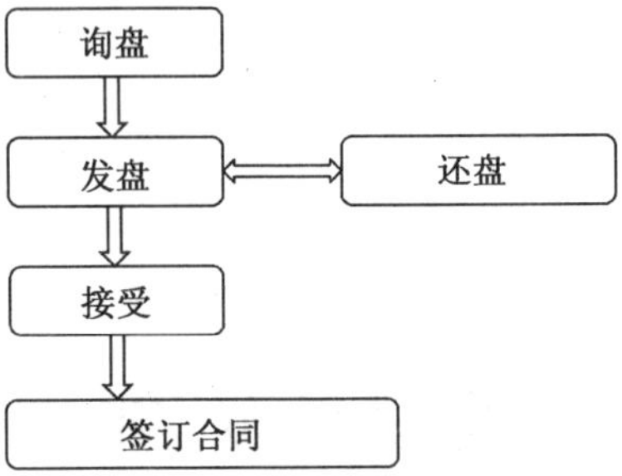

图 10-1　交易磋商的过程

第二节　询　盘

当一个商人想进口某种商品时,他就会向出口商询问他所想购买商品的报价和相关贸易条件,或仅仅是要求提供一些一般信息。出口商在接到这样的询问时将给出答复,这样,交易磋商就开始了。

1. 询盘的定义

询盘也称询价,是指交易的一方打算购买或出售某种商品,而向另一方询问买卖该项商品交易条件的过程。询盘一般由买方发出,询问有关商品价格、目录、样品及贸易条件等信息。有时,卖方也可主动发出询盘,向买方表达他想销售某种商品的意愿。需要注意的是,询盘属于试探性的业务联系,对于买卖双方都无法律约束力,询盘人无需承担必须买卖该商品的义务,而被询盘人也可以不作回答。但是,为了给今后的业务往来打下基础,买卖一方在收到询盘信后会按照商业惯例立即做出回复。

询盘有口头询盘和书面询盘两种类型。如果是书面形式的询盘,常常有传真、电子邮件、书信和询价单。一份询盘可同时发送给多个客户,这样,有利于发出询盘的一方把收到的回复中的销售条件进行整理、对比,选出最佳的报价,然后再与报价最优的一方进行磋商,达成交易。

2. 询盘信的分类

根据询盘的内容和目的,询盘信可分为一般询盘信和具体询盘信两类。若进口商只是为了了解出口商所能提供的产品或商品的大概情况，请出口商寄给他商品目录、价格单和样品，则属于一般询盘。若进口商打算购买某种商品，要求出口商为该商品报盘，则属于具体询盘。

下面两封是发给供货商的询盘信。前一封是一般询盘信，后一封是具体询盘信。

> 敬启者：
>
> 非常感谢你方12月12日的来信，我们得知贵公司出口电器产品。我方现对贵公司产品及包装进行询盘，请尽快提供详细信息，供我方参考。同时，请寄给我们有关贵方产品的价格单。
>
> 如果你方报最优惠条件，我们将不胜感激。
>
> 谨上

> 敬启者：
>
> 感谢贵方2017年8月8日发来的传真，从中得知贵公司是医药出口商。
>
> 请报下列产品的鹿特丹到岸最低价：
>
> (1)2公吨　50%维生素E
>
> (2)4公吨　复合维生素B
>
> 包装：25公斤/袋
>
> 支付方式：不可撤销即期信用证
>
> 装运时间：2017年9月20日
>
> 如能及时答复，不胜感激。
>
> 谨上

3. 怎样有效地询盘

大部分的询盘信都很简洁，甚至很多公司直接采用已印制好的询盘表。但若想通过询盘获得一个理想的价格，那么掌握一些写询盘信的技巧是有必要的。一份初始询盘，即第一封给以前没有贸易往来的供货商的询盘信，应包括：

(1)说明你是如何得到对方的信息的。你的信息来源渠道可能是大使馆、商会、交易会、展会，也可能是互联网、报刊等。

(2)自我介绍。简洁地介绍一下本公司的基本情况，如企业性质、经营范围、往年业绩、资信情况等。

(3)详细说明你要供货商寄给你的东西。例如:商品目录、价格单、折扣、付款方式、发货日期和样品等。

(4)写好询盘信的结尾句,为今后建立业务关系打下基础。

4. 询盘实例

实例 1

> 敬启者:
>
> 我们从驻巴黎的大使馆参赞处得知,贵公司是生产各种规格的手工手套的著名厂商。我方是本地最大的专营手套进口业务的企业之一。我们在欧洲很多国家都有分支机构,并与多数零售商保持密切联系。
>
> 我方对贵公司的产品很有兴趣。请您寄给我们有关的商品目录、价格单以及所用各种品质原料的样品。
>
> 期盼尽快回复。
>
> 谨上

实例 2

> 敬启者:
>
> 我们从互联网上了解到贵公司是竹制玩具的制造商和出口商。我方从事竹制玩具的进口业务已有多年,现对贵公司的产品很感兴趣。
>
> 能否请您给我们提供一整套竹制玩具的目录和价格单供我们选择?报价时,请按旧金山到岸价 2%佣金来报价。若贵方价格合理、可接受,我们会经常性地大量订购。
>
> 感谢你们对询价的答复。
>
> 谨上

5. 怎样有效地回复询盘

对于常规询盘的回复,重在满足询盘者的要求,回信的内容可以直截了当,语言需简朴、直接,没有必要过分的礼貌。通常,回复询盘的内容包括以下几方面:

(1)感谢询盘者的来信。

(2)为询盘者提供所要求的详细信息、资料,并说明商品目录、样品或其他附件已随函附上。

(3)提供一些询盘者未要求但对本公司扩大销售有利的相关信息,供询盘者参考。

(4)向顾客保证良好的商品及服务,鼓励顾客快速订购。

回复询盘信的实例 1

> 敬启者:
>
> 感谢你们 11 月 12 日的询盘,感谢你们对我公司产品的关注。
>
> 我们随函寄去你所要求的带图解的商品目录和价格单。与此同时,我们还另寄去了一些样品供你检验,相信当你检验后,你会认为我们的产品价廉物美。
>
> 我们提请你们注意,我们的产品供不应求。请你们尽快订货,以便我们安排装运。
>
> 谨上

回复询盘信的实例 2

> 敬启者:
>
> 我们非常高兴地收到你方 12 月 12 日的询盘,你们询盘信中所列举的所有商品我们都备有现货。商品目录和出口价格见附件,同时我们将随函寄出你们感兴趣的产品样品。
>
> 正如你所知,我们是一家在世界范围内经营出口的贸易公司。我们在这一行已经营多年,并拥有较高的国际声誉,因此我们能更好地服务公司客户。
>
> 如果你们想订货,请告知我们。我们很高兴与你们商讨折扣。在确定订货后,我们将在三周内安排发货。
>
> 我们认为我们的产品正是你们想要购买的,并期待你们的回信。
>
> 谨上

第三节　发　盘

发盘是交易磋商非常重要的一个步骤,因为双方意见一致是合同的基本要求。双方通过一方发盘、另一方接受达成协定。它是接受的承诺条件。

1. 发盘的定义

发盘是指交易的一方向另一方提出购买或出售某种商品的各项交易条件,并提议按此条件签订合同的建议。发盘一般以书信、传真或报价单形式进行。发出要约的人称为发盘人,接受发盘的人称为受盘人。

发盘既可以由卖方提出,也可以由买方提出。在实际业务中,多为卖方提出,称之为售货发盘。卖方一旦收到国外的询盘信,必须立即向外国客户报价,并就对方所询问的有关贸易条款和条件,根据可供出口商品的市场情况向对方说明清楚。但有时,卖方的货物非常畅销或卖方不了解市场,不能肯定买方是否有购买意向时,他们通常会要求买方先报价。这种由买方作出的发盘称为递盘。

各国法律在发盘的具体内容方面有不同的规定。一般,发盘应对合同的主要条件,如商品名称、品质、数量、包装、价格、支付方式、交货时间等都有明确的规定,以便受盘人一旦接受即可签订对买卖双方均有约束力的合同。

2. 发盘的构成条件

关于发盘的构成条件,《联合国国际货物销售合同公约》有明确的说明:第14条(1)款,向一个或一个以上特定的人提出的订立合同的建议,如果十分确定并且表明发价人在接受时承受约束,即构成发价。一个建议如果写明货物并且明示或暗示地规定数量和价格或规定如何确定数量和价格,即为十分确定;第14条(2)款,非向一个或一个以上特定的人提出的建议,仅应视为邀请做出发价,除非提出建议的人明确地表示相反的意向。

根据《联合国国际货物销售合同公约》的规定,一项有效的发盘应具备以下四个条件:

(1)发盘必须向特定的受盘人发出。

(2)发盘的内容必须十分明确、完整。

(3)发盘人必须表明在发盘有效期内受其约束。

(4)发盘必须在有效期内送达受盘人。

3. 发盘的类型

发盘一般可分为实盘和虚盘两类。当发盘人明确列明所有交易条款并表达愿意订立合同的意图时,该盘为实盘。在规定有效期内,实盘一旦被接受,报盘人就不能撤回、更改该盘。这时,就意味着交易结束,合同已达成。若超过有效期,受盘人仍未接受,则此发盘失效,对发盘人不再具有约束力。此时,即使是受盘人表示接受,发盘人也有权拒绝。

与实盘相反,虚盘是一种无约束力的报盘。虚盘对交易条件未做明确、完整的说明,对报盘的有效期也无规定,并且还附有保留条件:报盘要经最终的确认。因此,虚盘常常有这样的字句"以我方最后确定为有效"或"价格变化恕不通知"。多数情况下,报盘为虚盘。

两者相比,虚盘较为灵活,可根据市场情况做出成交决定。然而,受盘人往往把虚盘看作一般业务往来,不予重视。所以,实盘更能引起受盘人的重视,促进交易的达成。

实盘实例:

> 敬启者:
>
> 兹确认收到你方本月 20 日来信,要求我们报花生 CFR 阿姆斯特丹实盘。今晨我们回信手摘,带壳,不分等级的山东花生 400 公吨,CFR 阿姆斯特丹或其他欧洲主要口岸每公吨人民币1 500元,2017 年 7~8 月装运。此盘一周内复到有效。
>
> 我们愿指出,这是我方最低价格,故对你方的任何还盘均不能考虑。
>
> 谨上

虚盘实例:

> 敬启者:
>
> 感谢贵方2017年7月10日来函。我公司乐于向你方报盘。报盘如下:
>
> 货名:绣花缎超短裙
>
> 数量:10 000打
>
> 价格:每打50美元CFR纽约
>
> 包装:透明塑料袋
>
> 船期:2017年8月
>
> 支付方式:凭即期汇票支付的不可撤销的信用证付款。
>
> 本报盘以我方确认为准,如你方认可接受,请尽快函告我们。
>
> 谨上

4. 发盘的生效和撤回

发盘的有效期是对交易双方的一种限制,既是受盘人接受发盘的期限,又是发盘人受发盘约束的期限。一旦超过有效期,受盘人作出的接受无效,发盘人也不必承担按发盘条件订立合同的义务。因此,发盘的有效期是对双方的一种限制,也是对双方的一种保障。凡是发盘都有有效期,有的发盘对有效期做出明确规定,也有的不做明确规定。

发盘对有效期的规定有两种常用方法:

(1)规定最迟接受期限,例如:发盘限2018年5月3日复到此地。在实际业务中,不同国家之间有时差,因此发盘中应明确规定复到时间以何地的时间为准。通常,发盘有效期以发盘人所在地时间为准。

(2)规定一段接受时间,例如:发盘5天有效。根据《联合国国际货物销售合同公约》,有效期应从发盘人寄出信件或发盘人收到发盘开始计算。如果有效期的最后一天是节假日或受盘人的非工作日,则有效期相应地顺延。相较而言,通过这种方式规定的有效期,其开始与结束时间易产生争议,在实践中用得较少。

发盘的撤回是指一项发盘在尚未送达受盘人之前亦即尚未生效之前,由发盘人将其取消。根据《联合国国际货物销售合同公约》第15条(1)款规定:发价于送达被发价人时生效;第15条(2)款规定:一项发盘,即使是不可撤销的,得予撤回,如果撤回的通知于发盘送达受盘人之前或同时到达受盘人。

5. 发盘的撤销与失效

发盘的撤销是指一项发盘已送达受盘人，发盘人采取行动解除发盘效力的行为。它和发盘撤回的区别在于，前者取消的是法律上已生效的发盘，而后者取消的发盘还未生效。《联合国国际货物销售合同公约》规定，在未订立合同之前，发盘人将撤销通知送达受盘人，发盘得予撤销。但在以下两种情况下，发盘不得撤销：A. 发盘中明确规定了发盘的有效期或以其他方式表明发盘是不可撤销的；B. 受盘人有理由相信该项发盘是不可撤销的，并且已本着对该发盘的信赖行事。

发盘的失效表示发盘人不再受发盘的约束，受盘人也丧失了接受发盘的权利。《联合国国际货物销售合同公约》第 17 条规定：一项发盘，即使是不可撤销的，于拒绝通知送达发盘人时终止。

以下几种情况将造成发盘失效：

(1)受盘人拒绝或还盘；

(2)发盘的有效期届满；

(3)发盘人依法撤回或撤销发盘；

(4)不可抗力等意外事件的发生。

例如，中国进口商收到 2017 年 7 月 15 日美国贸易商报价，“100 件雨衣 CFR 中国港口的价格为每件 16.5 美元，8 月装运，此发盘以你方 7 月 20 日前复到为有效”。中国进口商 7 月 16 日回信道：“如果单价是 15.0 美元 CFR 中国港口，我们可以接受贵方发盘”。美国商人回答说：“市场坚挺，价格不能降低，请尽快回复。”最后，中国进口商立即回复：“我们接受你方 15 日的实盘”。在该案例中，因为中国进口商在 7 月 16 日对美国商人用 7 月 15 日的发盘进行还价，因此，7 月 15 日的发盘是不成立的、无效的。

第四节　还　盘

受盘人在收到发盘后，若认为交易条件可以接受，便可与对方达成交易，订立合同；但若受盘人对发盘中的某项或某几项条款表示不满意，便可直接拒绝报盘或进行还盘。

还盘是指受盘人不同意发盘中的交易条件而对其提出添加、限制或更改建议的行为。实际上,还盘是一个受盘者对发盘者进行反要约的过程。受盘人针对发盘中的货物价格、付款、质量、规格、交易数量等条款提出新的条件,均视为发盘条件的变更,形成了一个新的报盘,原报盘失效。此时,原来的发盘者成了受盘者,而原先的受盘者成了发盘者。假如之后,受盘人因为国际市场价格或外汇兑换率发生有利于他的变化,又表示愿意接受原报盘时,发盘人则有权决定接受与否,尽管此时还在原报盘的有效期内。

发盘人收到还盘后,对还盘的交易条件不满,还可提出新的条件,进行再还盘,这就是“反还盘”。在实际业务中,一项交易的达成往往需要经过多次的发盘和还盘,才能磋商成功,签订合同。

下面是两封还盘信的实例:

实例 1

敬启者:

你方 5 月 15 日报盘和瓜子的样品均已收悉,谢谢。我们尽管很欣赏产品的良好品质,但发现你们的价格高于市场水平。我们还要指出的是,在我方市场相同质量的产品的价格都比你方价格低 15%到 20%。

事情既然这样,我们不得不请你们考虑是否能减价,比方说 10%。由于我方订货价值将约值 10 万美元,你方定会认为是值得做出让步的。

盼早复。

谨上

实例 2

敬启者:

感谢你方 7 月 15 日函,给我方核桃仁 55 美元/千克的报价。

我们抱歉地奉告,贵方价格对我们所要供货的市场而言有些偏高。况且,在我方市场有很多韩国生产厂家提供的核桃仁,所有这些产品的价格都比你方低 5%。

只是鉴于双方长期的业务关系,我们才给予上述还盘。市价正在下跌,希望你方采取积极的态度加以考虑,并早日来函回复我方的还盘。

谨上

第五节　接受与签订合同

1. 接受

接受是指受盘人对接到发盘或还盘中的各项交易条件无条件同意，并愿意按这些交款与对方签订合同的一种肯定表示。

关于接受，《联合国国际货物销售合同公约》第 18 条规定：(1)被发价人声明或做出其他行为表示同意一项发价，即是接受。(2)接受发价于表示同意的通知送达发价人时生效。如果表示同意的通知在发价人所规定的时间内，如未规定时间，在一段合理的时间内，未曾送达发价人，接受就会无效，但需要适当地考虑到交易的情况，包括发价人所使用的通信方法的迅速程度。对口头发价必须立即接受，但情况有别者不在此限。(3)但是，如果根据该项发价或依照当事人之间确立的习惯做法或惯例，被发价人可以做出某种行为，例如，与发运货物或支付价款有关的行为，表示同意，而无需向发价人发出通知，则接受于该项行为做出时生效，但该项行为必须在上一款所规定的期间内作出。

构成有效接受的条件有：

(1)接受必须由特定的受盘人作出；

(2)接受必须与发盘的内容相符；

(3)接受必须在有效期内作出；

(4)接受必须以一定的方式明确表示出来。

但有时候接受是有条件的，《联合国国际货物销售合同公约》第 19 条对此规定如下：(1)对发价表示接受但载有添加、限制或其他更改的答复，即委婉拒绝该项发价，并构成还价。(2)但是，对发价表示接受但载有添加或不同条件的答复，如所载的添加或不同条件在实质上并不变更该项发价的条件，除发价人在不过分延迟的期间内以口头或书面通知反对其间的差异外，仍构成接受。如果发价人不做出这种反对，合同的条件就以该项发价的条件以及接受通知内所载的更改为准。(3)有关货物价格、付款、货物质量和数量、交付地点和时间、一方当事人对另一方当事人的赔偿责任范围或解决争端等的添加或不同条件，均视为实质上变更发价的条件。

对于接受的生效时间，国际上不同的法律体系间存在不同的判定方法。英美法系规定,接受通知在发盘有效期内一经投邮或电邮发出就立即生效。若函电在邮寄途中延误或遗失,也不影响合同成立。大陆法系则规定,接受的函电在有效期内送达发盘人才可算生效。若函电在途中延误或遗失,则视为无效。

根据《联合国国际货物销售合同公约》规定,接受在生效前是可撤回的,前提是撤回通知于接受通知送达发盘人之前或同时送达发盘人。另外,按照英美法系的规定,接受一经投邮,立即生效,合同成立,因此不存在接受的撤回问题。

下面是两封接受信函的实例:

实例 1

> 敬启者:
>
> 你方 2 月 12 日传真收悉,现按双方同意的条款,确认售予你方 50 长吨松香。
>
> 兹随函附寄第 CF123 号销货确认书一式两份,其中一份请签退我方,以便存档。
>
> 谨上

实例 2

> 敬启者:
>
> 我们很高兴地从你方 7 月 10 日的来信中得知,你方已接受我方 7 月 4 日的报盘。
>
> 为此,我方确认按下列条款出售给你方 15 000 公吨小红豆。
>
> 价格:每公吨成本加运费价到西雅图 400 美元。
>
> 包装:麻袋,每袋净重大约 50 公斤。
>
> 装运:2017 年 12 月船期,从上海到西雅图。
>
> 支付:以我方为受益人的不可撤销信用证,即期汇票支付。
>
> 非常高兴此次与你方达成第一笔交易,盼望以后能进一步发展双方互利的贸易。
>
> 谨上

2. 签订合同

合同是指两人或更多人之间有法律约束而相互履行义务的一种契约。在国际贸易中,凭进出口商之间来往的一系列信函就可以达成一项销售合同。进口商可以从索取一张某种类型和数量的商品报价单来开始进行最初的询价。作为回应,卖方通常提供买方所需的信息。如果买方愿意接受这些条件,那么在一定时间内,卖方的这些答复就能成为有约束力的报价。此时,磋商已完成,买卖双方达成了契约关系。然而,根据国际贸易惯例,买卖双方还要签订书面合同或销售确认书,以进一步明确双方的权利和义务。

在国际贸易中,进出口贸易书面合同的名称和形式,均无特定的限制。经常出现的名称有合同、确认书、协议书和备忘录。

合同和确认书可以由双方任何一方起草,分别称为销售合同/确认书、购货合同/确认书。不管它们有怎样的叫法,对双方都有约束力。销售或购货合同比销售或购货确认书正式,并且含有更多的细节。前者通常包含商品名称、规格、数量、包装、唛头、价格、装船、装运港、目的港、付款方法以及有关保险、商检、索赔和不可抗力等条款,而后者只包含主要的几项条款。再说,售货或购货合同对价值和数量较大的交易较为合适,因为合同制定了详细的条款,以免产生争议。如果数量不大或交易是通过代理或独销协议来进行的,人们则经常使用销售合同或购买确认书。

许多公司打印好订货单和报价单,一旦被接受,便可成为合同。在合同细节相似的情况下,某个公司的绝大多数合同不必每次都要特意打印,这样就极大地简化了买卖的程序。因为主要的条款已经打印在表格里面了,所以,只打印所要求的不同条款即可。然而,必须注意的是这种表示合同只有在其成为某一行业的惯例,合同涉及金额较小,买卖双方高度信任,且业务往来频繁,经常重复订货的情况下,才被接受。

Chapter 11

International Business Contract

Part A Text

Long time ago, people devised a means for bargaining for the conduct of others by exchanging promises. The exchange of promises came to be known as "agreements" and gradually became very important in the lives of the people and in the field of business. A promise or an agreement is reached as a result of the process of offer and acceptance. When an agreement is reached, a contract is formed, which creates legal obligations enforceable by law. Contracts can be long or short, formal or informal, simple or complicated, and verbal or written, of which the most popular is written contract for pre-printed contract.

The importance of a contract in an international business transaction cannot be underestimated. The international business made between the buyer and the seller are mainly the conclusion of the contract and the fulfillment of the contract. The international business contract is often the only document between the parties to which they may refer for clarification of mutual responsibilities, resolution of disputes, in the event of disagreement under the law frame and with binding force. And such a contract serves as a "living document" that may well survive the relationship it defines.

Section One Establishment of Contract

1. Definition of Contract

A contract is an agreement between two or more competent in which an offer is made and accepted, and each party benefits. It is an agreement which sets forth binding obligations of the relevant parties. The agreement can be formal, informal, written, oral or just plain understood. Some contracts are required to be in writing in order to be enforced. This term, in its more extensive sense, includes every description of agreement, or obligation, whereby one party becomes bound to another to pay a sum of money, or to do or omit to do a certain act. In its more confined sense, it is an agreement reached by two or more than two parties concerned, in order to establish, modify or terminate the civil right and obligation of the parties.

2. Time of Establishment of Contract

A contract becomes effective since it is established. However, the establishment of a contract is different from coming into effect of it. The establishment of a contract depends on the effectiveness of an acceptance, whereas a contract becoming effective means a contract with legal binding force. Usually, the moment of the establishment of as contract is also the time that the contract comes into effect, they are one the same time. However, sometimes a contract is established without coming into effect immediately, it will become effective when other condition are available.

In accordance with the *CISG*, a contract is concluded when the offeree accepts the offer and sends the acceptance to the offeror with the validity time of the offer. In the practice, the time of the date of confirming the contract from the other party.

3. Key Elements for An Effective Contract

According to the contract laws of countries, after the buyer and the seller have reached an agreement through offer and acceptance, and effective contract must be based on the following key elements:

(1)The parties concerned must be with the conduct capacity to sign a contract

The parties concerned of a contract shall be natural persons or juridical persons. For a natural person ,he shall be a mentally normal adult, a minor or a mentally ill person or the like shall be limited to conclude a contract; In case that the parties concerned are juridical persons, the laws of most countries take the opinion in common, that the contract must be signed by the authorized representative within the business scope of his. The contract out of the scope is not effective.

(2)A contract must be with Consideration or Cause

Consideration is a concept in the Common Law system, an important element for the establishment of a contract. It is also called as *Consideration* in the Common Law system and *Cause* in France Law. The so-called consideration refers to the price the party concerned has to pay for the benefit of the contract. "Some rights, benefits, profit of favor obtained by one party, or the restraint to perform a right, the suffer from a loss or the undertaking of an obligation."

Cause, refers to a direct objective pursued by the party concerned in the contract signed. In accordance with the rules of the Common Law system and the Continental Law system, a contract which is effective in law must be with Consideration or Cause.

(3)The objective of a contract must be legal

The goods involved in a contract shall be legal, which shall be allowed to be imported and exported by government. For the goods under the supervision and limitation of government, the concerning license or quota shall be obtain at first; a contract shall not be against, public order or public policy as well as custom and morality.

(4)A contract shall be in compliance with the stipulated form by law

The form of a contract is not limited in principle in *CISG*. Nevertheless, the member states in the *CISG* are permitted to make declaration for the reservation about it.

(5)The party concerned or a contract shall be in true willingness

In international business, the buyer and the seller reach an agreement in volunteer and true willingness, the contract involved in fraud, intimidation, or violence is invalid.

4. Significance of Signing A Contract

In business negotiation, a deal is concluded after an offer is accepted, then a contract relationship is established by the buyer and the seller. The correspondences between two parties in negotiation are taken as the written proof of the contract. Nevertheless, the buyer and the seller will sign a written contract to further make sure the right and obligation of both sides.

It is not necessary for an effective contract to sign a contract in written form. It is stated in the *CISG*, "a sales contract is not bound to be concluded or certified in written form, unlimited in the form. A sales contract may be certified in any ways including persons." However, in the international business practice, the parties concerned will usually sign a contract in written form after reaching an agreement through negotiation. There are the following three functions to sign a contract in written form:

(1) The evidence to prove a contract is established

According to the relevant law and rules, a contract must be certified with proof including witness testimony and material evidence. For a contract concluded by the negotiation with letter, e-mail or fax, it is no problem to provide the proof in writing. However, for a contract established through the oral negotiation, it is to prove it. Therefore, a contract established by an oral negotiation will probably not be protected by law due to the failure of being verified if the contract is not confirmed in written form, even the contract will be invalid. So, for an agreement reached through oral negotiation in particular, it is necessary to sign a contract in written form.

(2) The term with which a contract comes into effect

If one party claims that it is subject to the contract in written form, then the contract will not be established until a formal contract in written form is signed even though both parties concerned has reached an agreement on all trade terms during the negotiation. In this case, signing a contract in written form is the term for the contract coming into effect.

(3) The basis on which a contract is fulfilled

Whatever the deal is reached through oral negotiation or in written form, the trade terms agreed shall be combined clearly and completely and listed in a contract with a certain format. It is very important for both parties to further make clear of the rights and obligations of them, and with definite basis to fulfill the contract better.

Section Two Formation of Contract

1. Forms of Contract in Written Form

In international trade, export and import contracts vary in both names and forms. The names that often appear are contract, confirmation, agreement and memorandum. However, the contract and confirmation are most widely used.

A contract or confirmation can be drawn up either by the seller or the buyer. Respectively, they are called a sales contract/confirmation or a purchase contract/confirmation. Whatever they are named, they are equally binding on the parties. In addition, the legal effectiveness of the two forms of written contract is the same, but the format and contents are different. The sales or purchase contract is more formal than the sales or purchase confirmation. Next, the former contains more details than that in the latter. The former usually consists of commodities, specifications, quantity, packing, marking, price, shipment, port of shipment and port of destination, and payment as well as those clauses concerning insurance, commodity inspection, claims, arbitration and force majeure, etc.; while the latter only includes several main items. What's more, the former is appropriate to transactions of a large amount and huge quantity because of its detailed clauses which can prevent the occurrence of disputes. If the amount is not large or the business is done by means of agency arrangement or exclusive sale agreement, the sales or the purchase confirmation is often used.

2. General Content of Contract

A business contract is an agreement, enforceable by law. It may be formal or informal. The business contract which is generally adopted in international trade activities is the formal written one. Generally speaking, the business contract is usually made up of three parts: the contract heading, the main body and the witness clause.

(1) the Contract Heading

The contract heading is the first part of a contract. It usually includes the title and number of the contract, the names of the persons or corporations concede in the contract as parties, their principal places of business or residential address; the date and place of signing the contract.

Sometimes, the "Whereas" clause can also be seen in some contracts. *Recitals*, also know as "Whereas" clause, tell of a set of facts about the contract, such as the background, objective and so forth. They are agreements listed in series of paragraphs beginning with "Whereas" after the heading. Recitals serve as the basis on which the main body of a contract is interpreted. For a clear and brief idea of such compositions, presented here is the recitals taken from a Compensation Trade Contract.

Whereas Party B has machines and equipment, which are now used in Party B's manufacturing of steel wire rope, and is willing to sell to Party A the machines and equipment;

Whereas Party B agrees to buy the products, steel wire rope, made by Party A using the machines and equipment Party B supplies, in compensation of the price of the machines and equipment;

Whereas Party A agrees to purchase from Party B the machines and equipment;

Whereas Party A agrees to sell to Party B the products, the steel wire rope, in compensation of the price of Party B's machines and equipment.

(2) the Main Body

The main body is the most important part of a contract, which is usually made up of the following parts: name of commodities, quality, quantity, price, shipment, payment, inspection, claims, arbitration and force majeure.

①Price

When stating the contact price, sums of money are very likely to be expressed both in figures and in words. It is also vital to make clear the unit of currency concerned in the contract. A common pattern in legal and quasi-legal documents in the US is that the amount of money are capitalized when stated both in words and figures. For example, the amount of 56 053 800 US Dollars should be written in this way: USD56 053 800 (Say US Dollars Fifty Six Million Fifty Three Thousand Eight Hundred). The most common way of stating the name of commodity, quality, quantity, packing and price is as following:

(1) Name of Commodity and Specifications	(2) Quantity	(3) Unit	(4) Unit Price	(5) Amount
Total Value: USD56 053 800				

_% more or less of shipment is allowed

Total Value: Say US Dollars Fifty Six Million Fifty Three Thousand Eight Hundred

②Terms of Payment

It is very important to specify the terms of payment which may include currency of payment, method of payment, and means of payment. Payment may be made by remittance of money, by collection, or by letter of credit, which is the most widely accepted means of payment.

Remittance includes Mail Transfer (M/T), Telegraphic Transfer (T/T), and Demand Draft (D/D). When remittance is adopted in international trade, the buyer will on his own initial remit money to the seller through the bank according to the terms and time stipulated in the contract.

Collection is another mode of payment in international trade. In collection, payment is made through banks under the terms of Document against Payment (D/P), or Document against Acceptance (D/A). The seller issues a draft, to which the shipping document are attached, forward the draft to a bank in his place (i.e. the remitting bank), makes an application for collection and entrust the entrusting bank to collection price from the buyer through its correspondent bank (i. e. the collection bank).

A letter of credit (L/C) is a letter from a bank guaranteeing that a buyer's payment to a seller will be received on time and for the correct amount. It is a reliable and safe method of payment and facilitates trade with unknown buyers and gives protection to both sellers and buyers. And it's also the most essential method of collecting money in international business.

The following is typical clauses stating terms of payment in the three main way.

- Remittance: The buyers shall pay the total value to the sellers in advance by T/T not later than Mar. 4th.

- Collection: Upon first presentation the buyers shall pay against document draft drawn by the sellers at sight. The shipping documents are to be delivered against payment only.
- L/C: The Buyer shall, 10 days prior to the time of shipment /after this Contract comes into effect, open an irrevocable Letter of Credit in favor of the Seller. The Letter of Credit shall expire 15 days after the completion of loading of the shipment as stipulated.

③Shipment

Shipment clause is an integral and important part of a contract. Shipment means that the seller fulfills his obligation to load goods into the named carrier at given place/point and the time stipulated in the contract. The buyer usually insists on a specified deadline or time interval within which shipment must be made. To effect shipment before the deadline becomes especially important when dealing in seasonal goods, raw materials or semi-processed goods required for further manufacturing. After the date of shipment is fixed, the responsibility for effecting shipment must be stipulated in the contract, as this involves making various arrangements beforehand. Also, unforeseen events might bring about complications. CIF delivery stipulated that the seller undertakes the complete responsibility of effecting shipment within the time agree upon. FOB delivery entails the responsibility on the part of the buyer to book shipping space, or to charter a carrying vessel depending upon the size of the cargo. Sample is as follows:

The sellers shall within 2 days upon the completion of the loading of the goods, advise by fax to the buyers of the contract No., commodity, quantity, gross weight, invoiced value, and date of dispatch. In the event of the sellers' failure to effect loading when the vessel arrives duly at the loading port, all expenses including dead freight and/or demurrage charges thus shall be for the sellers' account.

④ Insurance

In international trade, there are a number of risks, which, if they occur, will involve trades in financial losses. For instance cargoes in transit may be damaged due to breakage of packing, clash or fire, etc.. These hazards, and many others, may be insured against. Every year, a certain amount of cargo was destroyed or damaged by perils of the sea in transit, but whichever particular cargo it would be it can not be anticipated. All cargo owners take the risk of loss through the perils. However, foreign traders can insure themselves against many of these risks. Insurance is a process for spreading risk, so that the burden of any loss is borne not by the unfortunate individual directly affected but by the total body of person under consideration. When the insurance clause is drafted, the clause should specify how to allocate the risk of loss, namely, it should make clear when and where the risk or loss of damage passes from the exporter to importer. The exporter then need not worry about loss and damage after risk has passed to the importer, and the importer need not worry about insurance covering damages that occur after the risk has passed onto him. Study the following sample:

The buying and selling of the Assembly Lines and the Color TV Sets shall be on FOB basis, thus the ocean marine cargo insurance on them shall be effected by Party A and Party B respectively. In the duration of this contract, Assembly Lines shall be insured by Party A. Should any loss or damage occur, Party A shall lodge claims against the insurer and pay a part of the indemnification received from the insurer to Party B, which shall be in proportion to the payment Party A has not made for the part of machinery involved in the loss or damage.

⑤ Inspection

Sometimes the buyers may desire to have the right to inspect the contract goods while being manufactured. More often the exporter is expected to submit a certificate of inspection or survey report before shipment. Therefore, the procedure and manner of inspection should be provided in the contract. Arrangement will be especially necessary to deal with the possibility that the manufacturer's inspection will yield different results from inspection upon receipt. Example is as follows:

The manufacturers shall, before delivery, make a precise and comprehensive inspection of the goods with regard to its quality, specifications, performance and quantity/weight, and issue inspection certificates certifying the technical data and conclusion of the inspection. After arrival of the goods at the port of destination, the buyer shall apply to China Commodity Inspection Bureau (CCIB) for a further inspection as to the specifications and quantity/weight of the goods. If damages of the goods are found, or the specifications and/or quantity are not in conformity with the stipulations in this contract, except when the responsibilities lies with insurance company or shipping company, the buyer shall, within 10 days after arrival of the goods at the port of destination, claim against the seller, or reject the goods according to the inspection certificate issued by CCIB. In case of damage of the goods incurred due to the design or manufacture defects and/or in case the quality and performance are not in conformity with the contract, the buyer shall, during the guarantee period, request CCIB to make a survey.

⑥ Claims

Mistakes do happen now and then. Customers sometimes receive goods of the wrong size or color. And they may receive damaged or defective merchandise. They may be billed at an incorrect price, or not be given promised discount. They may also receive their seasonal order too late to be useful, or not receive it at all. In these and many situations customers are titled to file a claim with the supplier. Claims means that in international trade, one party breaks the contract and causes losses to the other party directly or indirectly, the party suffering the losses may ask for compensation for the losses. In some contract, the two parties often stipulate clauses on settlement of claim as well as inspection and claim clauses. Study the following sample:

In case of quality discrepancy, claims should be filed by the buyer within 30 days after the arrival of the goods at port of destination, while for quantity discrepancy, claims should be filed by the buyer within 15 days after the arrival of the goods at port of destination. In all case, claims must be accompanied by survey reports of recognized public surveyors agreed to by the seller. If the goods have already been processed, the buyer shall thereupon lose the right to claim. Should the responsibility of the subject under claim be found to rest on the part of the seller, the seller should, within 20 days after receipt of the claim, send his reply to the buyer together with suggestion for settlement.

⑦ Arbitration

Arbitration is an important way to settle the disputes incurred in international trade. The arbitration refers to that the two parties, before or after the disputes arise, reach a written agreement that they will submit the disputes which cannot be settled through amicable negotiations to a third party for arbitration. Both parties shall settle the disputes complying with the result of arbitration as the arbitration result has legally binding force. Once the two disputing parties decide to solve problems by arbitration, they can't file a suit at the court. This is the main function of arbitration agreement, namely the exclusion of the court's jurisdiction of the case.

When set arbitration clauses there are four issues should be considered. Firstly, the place of arbitration. Since applicable laws concerning arbitration differ from country to country, and different applicable laws differ in their interpretations in respect of the rights and obligations of the parties concerned, therefore parties concerned are always making efforts to choose a arbitration place they trust and know quite well. Secondly, arbitration body. Disputes in international trade can be either referred to a permanent arbitration organization for arbitration as can be stipulated in the arbitration agreement by parties concerned or submitted for arbitration to an interim arbitration tribunal as formed by the arbitrators agreed by the two parties. At present, most of the countries and some of the international organizations in the world have their permanent arbitration organizations specialized in the settlement of commercial disputes. Thirdly, applicable arbitration rules. The country where the arbitration is going to be made and the relevant applicable arbitration rules should be made clear in the sales contract. Finally, the arbitral award. The arbitral award is usually final. But it is still important to stipulate in the contract that: the arbitration award is final and shall have binding force upon the two parties. Following is the example of arbitration clause:

All disputes in connection with this contract shall be settled friendly through negotiations. In case no settlement can be reached, the case may then be submitted for arbitration to China International Economic and Trade Arbitration Commission in accordance with the Arbitration Rules of Procedures promulgated by the said Arbitration Commission. The Arbitration shall take place in Shijiazhuang and the decision of the Arbitration Commission shall be final and binding upon both parties, and neither party shall seek recourse to a law court or other authorities to appeal for revision of the decision. Arbitration fee shall be borne by the losing party.

⑧ Force Majeure

Force Majeure, also called *Act of God*, refers to an event that can neither be anticipated nor be preventable, avoidable and controllable after the conclusion of the contract, not resulted from the fault or neglect of the parties involved, leading to the failure or the delay of the fulfillment of contract; the party who fails or delays to fulfill the contract due to such event can be free from the liabilities, or to be given an option of terminating the contract or postponing the performance of the contract. So the

Force Majeure clause actually is an escape clause in a contract, a legal principle as well. The scope of Force Majeure events includes natural disasters such as flood, fire, ice damage, storm, heavy snow, earthquake, etc.. It also includes some social disasters such as war, strike, the governmental ban, etc..

With a view to avoiding the unnecessary disputes due to a Force Majeure event, and preventing the arbitrary explanation of the Force Majeure event, unreasonable requirement proposed, or unreasonable refusal of the reasonable requirement proposed by the other party, it is very necessary to make a Force Majeure clause in a sales contract, specifying the nature, scope, principle, and settlement of the Force Majeure clearly so as to the execution of the contract. Following is the example of Force Majeure:

Either party shall not be held responsible for failure or delay to perform all or any part of contract due to flood, fire, earthquake, draught, war or any other events which could not be predicted at the time of conclusion of this contract, and could not be controlled, avoided or overcome by the relative party. However, the party affected by the event of Force Majeure shall inform the other party of its occurrence in writing as soon as possible and thereafter sends a certificate of the event issued by the relevant authorities to the other party within 15 days of its occurrence. If the event of Force Majeure lasts over 120 days, both parties shall have the right to terminate the contract.

(3) the Witness Clause (the ending part)

The witness clauses is the final part of a contract, which consists of the effective date, the language in which the contract is written and their validity, the signature of the parties concerned and attestation, the copies of the contract, etc.. We can see the example as follows:

The present contract is made in Chinese/English with equal validity, but the discords on the contract are to be explained with English version. And this contract shall be signed by authorized representatives of both parties, which shall come into force from the signing date. Finally it is made in 2(two) original copies, one copy to be held by each party in witness thereof.

THE BUYER	THE SELLER
(signature)	(signature)

Specimen 11-1 **Sales Contract**

Contract No.: HNJK13107
Date: 2013-12-12

CONTRACT

The Buyer: QingDao Glory Unit Trade CO., LTD.
Address: 88#, AnShan Road, SiFang Distract, QingDao, ShanDong, China.
Tel: 0532-88009672

The Seller: SenSo International Limited
Address: Laubacher Strabe 44, 14197 Berlin, Germany
Tel: +49 753188 -3688

The Buyers agree to buy and the Sellers agree to sell the following goods on terms and the conditions as set forth below:

1. Descriptions of Commodity

Commodity	Specification	Quantity	Unit Price
PCR	345×250×270 (L×W×H)	3 sets	USD 1 619
Total Value: USD 4 857			

10% more or less of shipment is allowed.

Total Value: Say US Dollars Four Thousand Eight Hundred Fifty Seven

2. Packing: To be packed in standard export packing that suitable to long distance sea/air transport, and being in accordance with inspection requirements for import packing material issued by China CIQ.

3. Shipping Marks: The Sellers shall mark on each package with fadeless paint the package number, gross weight, net weight, measurement and the wordings: "KEEP AWAY FROM MOISTURE", "HANDLE WITH CARE", "THIS SIDE UP", etc..

4. Time of Shipment: Within 60 days after receipt of T/T.

5. Port of Loading: Munich airport of Germany.

6. Port of Destination: Qingdao Liuting International Airport.

7. Payment: 100% value to be paid by T/T.

8. Insurance: To be covered by the Buyer for 110% of the invoice value against ALL risks and WAR risks.

9. Documents: The seller shall present the following documents required to the bank for negotiation.

(1) Airway bills marked "Freight to Collect" consigned to and notifying the buyer.

(2) Manually signed Invoice in three original and three copies, indicating Contract No..

(3) Packing list in three original copies.

(4) Certificate of Quality and Quantity in two original issued by the Manufacturer.

(5) Certificate of Origin in one original issued by the Manufacturer.

(6) Shipping advice in one original copy.

(7) Declaration of no-wood packing material or declaration of wood packing material indicated IPPC mark.

10. Shipping Advice: The Seller shall, within 48 hours after the shipment is effected, advise the Buyer by fax of the contract number, name of commodity, quantity, gross weight, invoiced value, car number and contact person.

11. Guarantee of Quality: The Seller shall guarantee that the Commodity hereof is made of the best materials with first class workmanship, brand new, unused, and corresponds to all respects with the quality, specifications and performance stipulated in this Contract.

12. Inspection and Claims: Within 90 days after the arrival of the goods at destination, should the quality, specifications, or quantity be found not in conformity with the stipulations of the Contract except those claims for which the insurance company or the owners of the vessel/airline company are liable, the Buyer shall, on the strength of the Inspection Certificate issued by the Inspection Bureau, notify the Seller promptly in writing of any claim for damages or for compensation, and all inspection charges shall be borne by the Buyer.

13. Force Majeure: The Sellers shall not be held responsible for any delay in delivery or non-delivery of the goods due to Force Majeure. However, the Sellers shall advise the Buyers immediately of such occurrence and within fourteen days thereafter, shall send by airmail to the Buyers for their acceptance a certificate issued by the competent government authorities of the place where the accident occurs as evidence thereof. Under such circumstances, the Sellers, however, are still under the obligation to take all necessary measures to hasten the delivery of the goods.

14. Late Delivery and Penalty: In case of delayed delivery ,except for force majeure cases, the Sellers shall pay to the Buyers for every week of delay a penalty amounting to 0.5% of the value of the goods whose delivery has been delayed .Any fractional part of a week is to be considered a full week. The total amount of penalty shall not, however, exceed 10% of the total value of the goods involved in late delivery and is to be deducted from the amount due to the Sellers by the paying bank at the time of negotiation, or by the Buyers direct at the time of payment.

15. Arbitration: All disputes in connection with this contract or execution thereof shall be settled through friendly negotiations. Should no settlement be reached, such dispute or claim may then be submitted to China International Economic & Trade Arbitration Commission (CIETAC) in accordance with the rules of procedures of the said Arbitration Committee. The Arbitration shall take place in Beijing. The decision of the Arbitration Committee shall be final and binding upon both Parties; neither Party shall seek recourse to a law court nor other authorities to appeal for revision of the decision. The arbitration fee shall be borne by the losing Party. The Arbitration may also be settled in the third country mutually agreed upon by both Parties.

16. Laws Application: The formation of this Contract, its validity, termination, interpretation, execution and settlement of any disputes arising thereunder shall be governed by the laws of People's Republic of China.

17. This Contract shall be signed by authorized representatives of both Parties. The Contract shall come into force from the signing date. This Contract is made in 2(two) original copies, one copy to be held by each Party in witness thereof.

THE BUYER	THE SELLER
(signature)	(signature)

Part B Key Terms

Contract 合同

Consideration 对价

Cause 约因

Exclusion clause 免责条款

Recital clause (Whereas clause) 申明条款/鉴于条款

Quote 报价

Conditions 条件

Part C Exercises

Ⅰ. Translate the followings from Chinese to English

(1)对价;(2)书面合同;(3)进出口合同;(4)确认书;

(5)约尾;(6)鉴于条款;(7)品质异议;(8)友好协商;

(9)法律约束力;(10)商业纠纷;(11)免责条款

Ⅱ. Reflection question (answer in English)

(1)What is the definition for contract? Why do the trading parties usually prefer a written contract?

(2)Does the establishment of a contract mean its coming into effect?

(3)Describe the layout of a general contract.

Ⅲ. Complete the following sentences by translating the part in Chinese into English

(1) Enclosed (Attached) please find ____________________ (发票一式两份,保险单一式三份).

(2)Shipment will be effected ____________________ (一旦收到贵方购货确认通知书).

(3)Party B shall effect shipment ____________________(签字之日一个月内),i.e.,no later than December 15th.

(4) The consignor shall ____________________ (负全责) for any damages caused by the above consignment to the ship and/or to any other consignments on

board.

(5) Shipment: ____________________ (收到不可撤销的信用证一个月内船运).

Ⅳ. Fill in the Sale Contract in English with the particulars given below

(致大卫公司)敬启者:

很高兴从您6月25日的来信中得知您已接受我方6月14日的报盘。作为答复,我方确认向贵公司出售2 000打男士均码T恤,每打港币135元香港CIF价,每打装一纸盒,每10盒装一大纸箱,由卖方按发票金额110%投保一切险及战争险,2007年8月从内地港口运往香港,唛头由我方决定,以不可撤销的、保兑的即期信用证付款,信用证必须在装运前30天到达我方。按照惯例,信用证议付有效期为最后装运期后第15天在中国到期。

兹随函将我方7月2日在北京所签第290号合同寄予你方,望查收。请会签并退回我方一份。

此致

敬礼

中国纺织品进出口公司

经理:×××谨上

SALES CONTRACT

No. 290

Sellers: China Textiles Import and Export Corporation

Buyers: Messrs. David & Co.

This Contract is made by and between the Buyers and Sellers, whereby the Buyers agree to buy and the Sellers agree to sell the under-mentioned commodity according to the terms and conditions stipulated below:

(1) Commodity: ____________________

(2) Specification: ____________________

(3) Quantity: ____________________

(4) Unit Price: HKD ____________ Hong Kong

(5) Total Value: HKD ____________ (SAY ______________________________)

(6) Packing: ____________________

(7) Insurance: ____________________

(8) Time of Shipment: August, 2007

(9) Port of Shipment: China Port

(10) Port of Destination: Hong Kong

(11) Shipping Mark: at Sellers' option

(12) Terms of Payment: By confirmed, ____________________, to reach the Sellers ____________________ and remain valid for negotiation in China till the 15th day after the latest date of shipment as specified in the covering L/C.

(13) Arbitration: All disputes in connection with this contract or the execution thereof shall be settled through friendly negotiation, in case no settlement can be reached through negotiations, the case under dispute shall be submitted for arbitration to the China Economic and Trade Arbitration Commission Beijing in accordance with the provisional rules of procedures promulgated by the said arbitration commission. The award of the arbitration shall be final and binding upon both parties for revising the decision. The arbitration fee shall be borne by the losing part.

(14) Force Majeure: The Sellers shall not be held responsible for any delay in delivery or non-delivery of the goods due to Force Majeure. However, the Sellers shall advise the Buyers immediately of such occurrence and within fourteen days thereafter, shall send by airmail to the Buyers for their acceptance a certificate issued by the competent government authorities of the place where the accident occurs as evidence thereof. Under such circumstances, the Sellers however, are still under the obligation to take all necessary measures to hasten the delivery of the goods.

THE BUYER: (signature)

THE SELLER (signature)

第十一章

国际商务合同

很久以前人们发明了“互换承诺”作为一种引导其他人讨价还价的方法。这种“互换承诺”演变成了我们现在众所周知的“合同”，并且逐渐在人们的生活和商业活动中变得非常重要。一个承诺产生了具有强制性的法律责任。一个合同可短可长，可正式或非正式，可以简单或复杂，可以口头或者书面，但最流行的是书面并已印刷好的合同。

合同的重要性在国际商务交易中同样不可低估。买卖双方进行国际贸易的商务活动归根结底就是和双方签订国际贸易的买卖合同，以及履行国际贸易买卖合同的过程。这份合同通常是双方在法律约束范畴下提及各自清晰的责任、出现争议时的解决方法等的文件。同时它也是维持双方所定义的关系的一种“存在证明”。

第一节　合同的成立

1. 合同的定义

国际贸易合同是指营业地处于不同国家或地区的当事人之间所订立的货物买卖契约，合同双方都可受益。合同是对有关当事人规定了约束性责任的一种协定。这种协定可以是正式的或非正式的，也可以是书面的或口头的，应明了易懂。有些合同需要以书面形式确定以便执行。从广义角度来看，国际贸易合同包括协议的各个方面及双方的义务，根据该契约，一方有义务向另外一方支付一定数额的货款,或必须履行某种义务,或可以免除某种义务。从狭义上来看,合同就是两个或者两个以上的当事人,以发生变更或者消灭民事法律关系为目的所达成的协议。

2. 合同成立的时间

合同自成立时生效。但是,合同成立与合同生效是两个不一样的概念。合同成立的判断依据是接受是否生效;而合同生效是指合同是否具有法律上的效力。在通常情况下,合同成立之时,就是合同生效之日,两者在时间上是同步的。但有时,合同虽然成立,却不立即产生法律效力,而是需要其他条件成立时,合同才开始生效。

根据《公约》的规定,受盘人接受发盘并在发盘有效期内将接受送达发盘人,合同即告成立。在实际业务操作中,合同成立的时间以订约时合同上所写明的日期为准,或以收到对方确认合同的时期为准。

3. 合同生效的要件

根据各国合同法规定,一项合同,除买卖双方就交易条件通过发盘和接受达成协议外,还需具备以下要件,才是一项有效合同、一项有法律约束力的合同。

(1)合同当事人必须具备签订合同的行为能力

签订合同的当事人因是自然人或法人。自然人必须是精神正常的成年人,未成年人、精神病人等订立合同必须受到限制;如果当事人是法人,各国法律一般认为,必须通过其代理人,在法人的经营范围内签订合同,即越权的合同不能发生法律效力。

(2)合同必须有对价或约因

对价(Consideration)是英美法的概念,是合同成立的一个重要因素,英美法称之为对价,法国法称之为约因(Cause)。所谓对价,是指当事人为了取得合同利益所付出的代价。“合同一方得到的某种权利、利益、利润或好处,或是他方当事人克制自己不行使某项权利或遭受某项损失或承担某项义务。”

约因是指当事人签订合同所追求的直接目的。按照英美法和大陆法的规定,合同只有在有对价或约因时,才是法律上有效的合同。

(3)合同的标的物必须合法

合同涉及的货物必须合法。货物应是政府允许自由进出口的商品,如果属于政府管制的,应先取得有关许可证或配额;合同内容必须合法,包括不得违反法律,不得违反公共秩序或公共政策,以及不得违反善良的风俗习惯或道德三个方面。

(4)合同必须符合法律规定的形式

《公约》原则上对国际货物买卖合同的形式不加以限制,但允许缔约国对此提出声明予以保留。

(5)合同当事人的意思表示必须真实

在国际贸易中,买卖双方必须在自愿和真实的基础上达成协议。任何一方采取欺诈、威胁或暴力行为与对方订立的合同无效。

4. 签订书面合同的意义

在交易磋商的过程中,一方发盘经另一方接受后,交易即告成立,买卖双方就构成了合同关系。双方在磋商过程中的往返函电,就是合同的书面证明。但根据国际贸易习惯,买卖双方还要签订书面合同,以进一步明确双方的权利和义务。

签订书面合同不是合同有效成立的必要条件。《公约》规定:“销售合同无须书面订立或书面证明,在形式方面也不受任何其他条件的限制。销售合同可以用包括人证在内的任何方法证明。”但是,在国际贸易实践中,在当事人双方经过磋商一致,达成交易以后,一般均须另行签订一份具有一定格式的书面合同。因为签订书面合同具有以下三个方面的重要意义。

(1)书面形式的合同可以作为合同生效的要件

根据相关法律法规规定,合同生效的要件必须包括人证和物证材料。对于一份通过信件、邮件或传真形式而磋商订立的合同,提供书面材料证明此份合同生效是毫无问题的。然而,对于一份经过口头磋商订立的合同,我们必须找到相应的材料证明其有效性。往往会出现这样的情况,口头订立的合同因为很难通过书面文件查实,所以很有可能并不被法律所保护,甚至被判定无效。因此,在实践过程中,口头合约很有必要以书面形式订立,以确保其效力。

(2)书面形式的合同可以作为合同成立的依据

尽管在磋商期间当事双方已在所有交易条款上达成一致,但只要一方坚持合同必须以书面形式订立,那么,直到正式书面合同签订,所有条款才被视为有效。在这种情况下,签订书面合同被视为合同成立生效的依据。

(3)书面形式的合同可以作为合同履行的依据

不管交易是通过口头磋商还是书面形式达成,具体的贸易条款必须以清晰、完整和条理化罗列的特定形式加以订立,对于当事人双方而言,在整场交易中明确各自的职责和义务,并定义良好的履约基础是非常有必要的。

第二节　合同的结构

1. 书面合同的结构

在国际贸易中,进出口贸易书面合同的名称和形式,均无特定的限制。经常出现的名称有合同、确认书、协议书和备忘录,其中合同和确认书最为常见。

合同和确认书可以由当事人双方的任何一方起草,分别称为售货合同/确认书、购货合同/确认书。不管它们有怎样的叫法,对双方都有约束力。另外,虽然合同和确认书的法律效力差不多,但两者的结构形式和书写内容会有差异。销售或购货合同比销售或购货确认书更为正式,并且含有更多的细节。前者通常包含商品名称、规格、数量、包装、唛头、价格、运输、装运港、目的港、付款方式以及有关保险、商检、索赔、仲裁和不可抗力等条款,而后者只包含几项主要条款。此外,售货合同或购货合同对价值和数量较大的交易较为合适,因为合同制订了详细的条款以避免产生争议。如果数量不大或交易是通过代理或独销协议来进行的话,人们就经常使用销售或购货确认书。

2. 合同的一般内容

贸易合同是一份具有法律效力的协议书。它可以是正式的,也可以是非正式的,但在国际贸易活动中采用的贸易合同则是正式的文字合同。一般来说,一份正式的合同通常由约首、约文和约尾三部分组成。

(1)约首

约首是一份合同的最初部分。它通常包括合同名称、合同编号、缔约的当事人双方、当事人双方的主要营业场所或者居住地址、签订合同的日期和地点这些内容。

有时候,“鉴于条款”(whereas clause)也经常见诸一些合同中。“申明条款”(recital clause)又称为“鉴于条款”,它的内容包括陈述合同签订的背景、目的等事实。它由数个以“Whereas”字样开头的句子所组成,在约首后被陈述,表示当事人是基于对这些事实(例如订约的背景、目的、原由等)的共同认识,订立此合同。它被视为合同主体的基础而存在。为了更清楚地说明这种文体,以下摘录了一则补偿贸易合同的“鉴于条款”。

鉴于乙方拥有用于生产钢丝绳的机械设备,愿向甲方出售该机械设备;

鉴于乙方同意购买甲方用乙方所供应的该机械设备生产的产品、钢丝绳来补偿该机械设备的价款;

鉴于甲方同意从乙方购买该机械设备;

鉴于甲方同意向乙方出售产品、钢丝绳,以补偿乙方机械设备的价款。

(2)约文

约文是整个合同最主要的部分,通常包括货物名称、品质、数量、价格、货运、支付、检验、索赔、仲裁和不可抗力等条款的陈述。

①价格条款

当陈述合同价格条款时,款项的金额通常会用数字以及文字两种方式表达。在合同中明确有关货币单位也是至关重要的。在美国,法律和准法律文件中常见的一种模式是,当用文字和数字表述金额时,具体数值是用大写的。例如,总价56 053 800美元应该写成:USD56 053 800(伍仟陆佰零伍万叁仟捌佰美元)。另外最常见的用来陈述货物名称和规格、品质、单位、单价、数量的方式如下:

(1)货物名称和规格	(2)品质	(3)单位	(4)单价	(5)数量
总价值:USD56 053 800				

百分之_ 上下的溢短装属于合理范围。

总价值:伍仟陆佰零伍万叁仟捌佰美元。

②付款条款

在合同中说明付款条款是很重要的,它包括付款货币、付款方法、付款形式等内容的具体规定。在多种付款方式中,汇付、托收和信用证是三大最常用的方式。

汇付包括信汇(M/T)、电汇(T/T)和汇票(D/D)。在国际贸易中,如采用汇付,买方则应按照合同规定的条款和时间将货款通过银行主动汇给卖方。

托收是国际贸易中的另一种支付方式。在托收方式下,付款是通过银行付款交单(D/P)和承兑交单(D/A)这两种方式进行的。卖方开具汇票,随附装船单据,交给当地银行(如汇付行),并提出托收申请,然后委托该行在进口的代理行(如代收行)向进口人收款。

信用证是由银行担保买方的付款会被卖方准时收取且确保金额和数量的一种书面文件。它是最安全、可靠的付款方式,因为它同时为买卖双方的利益提供担保。因此它是多种付款支付方式中,凭借货运单据收取货款的最重要方式。

以下为合同中三种典型的付款条款示例。

- 汇付方式:买方应于 3 月 4 日前将全部货款以电汇方式预付给卖方。
- 托收方式:买方凭卖方开具的即期跟单汇票,于第一次见票时立即付款,付款后交单。
- 信用证方式:买方应在装运期前/合同生效后 10 日,开出以卖方为受益人的不可撤销的议付信用证,信用证在装船完毕后 15 日内到期。

③货运条款

货运条款是国际贸易中买卖双方合同中不可缺少的重要组成部分。货运是指卖方按合同规定的时间、地点和方式负责将货物装上指定的交通运输工具。通常,买方会坚持要求在指定的期限或时间间隔内进行货物装运。对于季节性商品、原材料和有待深加工的半成品来说,敦促卖方及时发货是很重要的事项。货运时间确定后,合同双方当事人在货运事项上的彼此责任也必须加以确定,这涉及随后各阶段的安排。这一过程中,一系列不可预见的事件可能会使情况变得更为复杂。因此,根据 CIF 交货规定,卖方在约定的时间内承担起装运货物的全部责任。FOB 将预定仓位、根据货物大小租赁载货船只等责任归为由买方承担。以下为合同中货运条款的示例:

卖方在货物装运后,应在两天内将合同编号、商品名称、数量、毛重、发票金额和起运日期用传真通知对方。当船舶按时到达装运港,由于卖方的失误导致没法顺利进行卸载时,空仓费以及滞仓费应由卖方承担。

④ 保险

国际贸易买卖存在各种风险,这些风险的发生将会给有关商人带来经济损失。比如,货物在运输途中会由于包装破损、破碎和火灾等原因而造成损坏。这些风险及其他一些风险都可以通过保险加以防范。虽然,每年都有一定数量的货物在运输途中不可避免地因遭受海上风险而被摧毁或受损,但灾难会降临到哪一批货上事先谁都无法预料。所有的货主都要冒货物灭失的危险。然而,从事国际贸易的商人可以通过保险来防止很多危险。保险的目的就是将风险分摊,这样风险发生时,就可以由所有的相关人员分摊而不是由直接遭遇方单独承担。在合同中一旦保险条款被制定,款项中必须明确因风险造成的损失该如何分摊,也就是说,条款应该明确何时何地发生的风险或损害,它的承担人应从出口商转为进口商。这样的话,出口商无需担心风险已经转嫁给进口商,进口商也无需担心在风险转嫁之后所发生的损害赔偿。下面来学习一下具体案例中的保险条款:

装配线与彩色电视机的买卖均在 FOB 基础上进行,其海运保险分别由甲方和乙方办理。在本合同期限内,装配线由甲方投保。如果发生损失或损坏,由甲方向保险人提出索赔并将从保险人处获得赔偿的一部分分付给乙方,这部分应与受损机械设备中甲方未支付的部分成比例。

⑤ 检验

有些时候,货品生产期内,买方会期望有权检验合同货品。通常,出口商在装运前会出具一份检验证明报告,报告内包含检验流程和检验方式。买方应做好事前准备来应对检验结果不符合要求的情况。以下是合同中检验条款的示例:

发货前,制造厂应对货物的质量、规格、性能和数量/重量做精密、全面的检验,出具检验证明书,并说明检验的技术数据和结论。货到目的港后,买方将申请中国商品检验局(以下简称商检局)对货物的规格和数量/重量进行检验,如发现货物残损或规格、数量与合同规定不符,除保险公司或轮船公司的责任外,买方得在货物到达目的港后 10 日内凭商检局出具的检验证书向卖方索赔或拒收该货物。在保证期内,如货物由于设计或制造上的缺陷而发生损坏或品质和性能与合同规定不符时,买方将委托中国商检局进行检验。

⑥ 索赔

错误总是在所难免。客户有时收到的货物尺码不符,或颜色不对;也可能收到的货物被损坏,或是有缺陷。他们可能付错钱,或没有按约定给予折扣;或是时令商品到货太迟,成了一堆没有用的东西。在这些情况下,客户有权向供应商提出索赔。所谓索赔,就是指争议发生以后,遭受损害的一方向违约方直接或间接提出赔偿的要求。买卖双方通常会在合同中写明索赔的办法以及有关商检和索赔的条款。索赔条款实例:

品质异议须于货到目的港之日起 30 天内提出,数量异议须于货到目的港之日起 15 天内提出,并均须提供经卖方同意的公证行的检验证明。如果货物已经过加工,买方即丧失索赔权利。如责任属于卖方,卖方收到异议 20 天内答复买方并提出处理意见。

⑦ 仲裁

仲裁是解决对外贸易争议的一种重要方式。所谓仲裁,就是指买卖双方在争议发生之前或之后签订书面协议,自愿将争议提交双方所同意的第三者予以裁决,以解决争议的一种方式。由于仲裁是依照法律所允许的仲裁程序裁定争端,因而仲裁裁决具有法律约束力,当事人双方必须遵照执行。此外,一旦争议双方决定以仲裁的形式解决争端,双方不得向法院起诉。这就是仲裁最重要的作用,即排除法院对争议案件的管辖权。

在合同中制定仲裁条款时,我们需要考虑以下四个问题:其一,仲裁地点。仲裁地点不同,适用的法律也可能不同,对双方当事人的权利、义务的解释就会有差异。因此,交易双方都会争取在自己比较了解和信任的地方仲裁。其二,仲裁机构。在国际贸易中,争议可以由当事人在仲裁协议中规定,在常设仲裁机构进行,也可以由当事人双方共同指定仲裁员组成临时仲裁庭进行仲裁。目前,世界上的大多数国家和一些国际组织都有它们的常设仲裁机构专门解决商业纠纷。其三,仲裁规则的适用。在买卖合同中,应定明进行仲裁的所在国以及适用的仲裁规则。最后是仲裁的裁决。仲裁的裁决一般是终局的,但仍应规定:仲裁裁决是终局的,对双方有约束力。以下为仲裁条款实例:

凡有关本合同或执行本合同而发生的一切争议,应通过友好协商解决,若协商不成,则应申请中国国际经济贸易仲裁委员会按照中国国际经济贸易仲裁委员会规定的仲裁规则在石家庄进行仲裁。该仲裁委员会的裁决是终局的,买卖双方均应受其约束,仲裁费由败诉一方负担。任何一方不得向法院或其他机关申请变更该条款。

⑧ 不可抗力

不可抗力又称人力不可抗拒。它是指在买卖合同签订后,不是由于合同当事人的过失或疏忽,而是由于发生了合同当事人无法预见、无法预防、无法避免和无法控制的事件,以致不能履行合同或不能如期履行合同,发生意外事件的一方可以免除履行合同的责任或推迟履行合同。因此,不可抗力是合同中的一项免责条款,也是一项法律原则。合同中不可抗力的范围包括由自然力量引起的,如水灾、火灾、冰灾、暴风雨、大雪、地震等,也包括由社会力量引起的,如战争、罢工、政府禁令等内容。

为避免因不可抗力事件而引起不必要的纠纷,防止合同当事人对发生不可抗力事件的性质、范围做任意解释,或提出不合理的要求,或无理拒绝对方的合理要求，故有必要在买卖合同中订立不可抗力条款，明确规定不可抗力事件的性质、范围、处理原则和处理方法，以利于合同履行。以下是合同中不可抗力条款的实例：

由于水灾、火灾、地震、干旱、战争或合同一方在签约时无法预见且无法控制、避免和克服的其他事件导致不能或暂时不能履行全部或部分合同义务，该方不负责任。但是，受不可抗力事件影响的一方须尽快将发生的事件通知另一方，并在不可抗力事件发生后 15 天内将有关机构出具的有不可抗力事件的证明寄交给对方。如果不可抗力事件持续 120 天以上，任何一方有权终止合同。

(3) 约尾(合同的结尾部分)

约尾是合同的最后一部分，包括合同的生效日期、合同的文字效力、当事人的签字和认证、合同的份数等内容。以下为实例：

本合同中英两个版式具有同等效力，但中英文本如有解释不一致处，以英文为准。本合同应由双方的授权代表签署，自签署之日生效。最后，本协议一式两份，每方各持一份作为副本。

买方：	卖方：
(签字)	(签字)

样本 11-1 **销售合同**

Contract No.: HNJK13107
Date: 2013-12-12

CONTRACT

The Buyer: QingDao Glory Unit Trade CO., LTD.
Address: 88#, AnShan Road, SiFang Distract, QingDao, ShanDong, China
Tel: 0532-88009672

The Seller: SenSo International Limited
Address: Laubacher Strabe 44, 14197 Berlin, Germany
Tel: +49 753188 -3688

The Buyers agree to buy and the Sellers agree to sell the following goods on terms and the conditions as set forth below:

1. Descriptions of Commodity

Commodity	Specification	Quantity	Unit Price
PCR	345×250×270 (L×W×H)	3 sets	USD 1 619
Total Value: USD 4 857			

10% more or less of shipment is allowed.

Total Value: Say US Dollars Four Thousand Eight Hundred Fifty Seven

2. Packing: To be packed in standard export packing that suitable to long distance sea/air transport, and being in accordance with inspection requirements for import packing material issued by China CIQ.

3. Shipping Marks: The Sellers shall mark on each package with fadeless paint the package number, gross weight, net weight, measurement and the wordings: "KEEP AWAY FROM MOISTURE", "HANDLE WITH CARE", "THIS SIDE UP", etc..

4. Time of Shipment: Within 60 days after receipt of T/T.

5. Port of Loading: Munich airport of Germany.

6. Port of Destination: Qingdao Liuting International Airport.

7. Payment: 100% value to be paid by T/T.

8. Insurance: To be covered by the Buyer for 110% of the invoice value against ALL risks and WAR risks.

9. Documents: The seller shall present the following documents required to the bank for negotiation.

(1) Airway bills marked "Freight to Collect" consigned to and notifying the buyer.
(2) Manually signed Invoice in three original and three copies, indicating Contract No..
(3) Packing list in three original copies.
(4) Certificate of Quality and Quantity in two original issued by the Manufacturer.
(5) Certificate of Origin in one original issued by the Manufacturer.
(6) Shipping advice in one original copy.
(7) Declaration of no-wood packing material or declaration of wood packing material indicated IPPC mark.

10. Shipping Advice: The Seller shall, within 48 hours after the shipment is effected, advise the Buyer by fax of the contract number, name of commodity, quantity, gross weight, invoiced value, car number and contact person.

11. Guarantee of Quality: The Seller shall guarantee that the Commodity hereof is made of the best materials with first class workmanship, brand new, unused, and corresponds to all respects with the quality, specifications and performance stipulated in this Contract.

12. Inspection and Claims: Within 90 days after the arrival of the goods at destination, should the quality, specifications, or quantity be found not in conformity with the stipulations of the Contract except those claims for which the insurance company or the owners of the vessel /airline company are liable, the Buyer shall, on the strength of the Inspection Certificate issued by the Inspection Bureau, notify the Seller promptly in writing of any claim for damages or for compensation, and all inspection charges shall be borne by the Buyer.

13. Force Majeure: The Sellers shall not be held responsible for any delay in delivery or non-delivery of the goods due to Force Majeure. However, the Sellers shall advise the Buyers immediately of such occurrence and within fourteen days thereafter, shall send by airmail to the Buyers for their acceptance a certificate issued by the competent government authorities of the place where the accident occurs as evidence thereof. Under such circumstances, the Sellers, however, are still under the obligation to take all necessary measures to hasten the delivery of the goods.

14. Late Delivery and Penalty: In case of delayed delivery ,except for force majeure cases, the Sellers shall pay to the Buyers for every week of delay a penalty amounting to 0.5% of the value of the goods whose delivery has been delayed .Any fractional part of a week is to be considered a full week. The total amount of penalty shall not, however, exceed 10% of the total value of the goods involved in late delivery and is to be deducted from the amount due to the Sellers by the paying bank at the time of negotiation, or by the Buyers direct at the time of payment.

15. Arbitration: All disputes in connection with this contract or execution thereof shall be settled through friendly negotiations. Should no settlement be reached, such dispute or claim may then be submitted to China International Economic & Trade Arbitration Commission (CIETAC) in accordance with the rules of procedures of the said Arbitration Committee. The Arbitration shall take place in Beijing. The decision of the Arbitration Committee shall be final and binding upon both Parties; neither Party shall seek recourse to a law court nor other authorities to appeal for revision of the decision. The arbitration fee shall be borne by the losing Party. The Arbitration may also be settled in the third country mutually agreed upon by both Parties.

16. Laws Application: The formation of this Contract, its validity, termination, interpretation, execution and settlement of any disputes arising thereunder shall be governed by the laws of People' s Republic of China.

17. This Contract shall be signed by authorized representatives of both Parties. The Contract shall come into force from the signing date. This Contract is made in 2(two) original copies, one copy to be held by each Party in witness thereof.

THE BUYER	THE SELLER
(signature)	(signature)

Chapter 12

Implementation of Import and Export Contract

Part A Text

Once a contract is concluded, both the seller and the buyer should honor their obligations. The seller must deliver the goods, hand over any documents relating to the goods and transfer the property in the goods, as required by the contract and the Convention. The buyer must pay the price for the goods and take delivery of them as required by the contract and the Convention. It is the mutual responsibility of both parties concerned to fulfill the contract. A timely and excellent fulfillment of a contract concerns the rights and obligations of both parties as well as influences the reputation of the enterprise and the image of the country.

Section One Performance of Export Contract

In the export business of our country, the trade term of CIF or CFR and the payment by L/C are adopted usually in an export contract. The general procedures to fulfill an export contract are as follows: preparation of goods, urging the importer to apply for L/C, examination of L/C, amendment of L/C, booking vessel, going through the export inspection, making customs declaration, making insurance, loading goods, the arrangement of shipping documents and the settlement of payment. All above could be summarized as four sections: goods (the preparation and inspection of goods), L/C(urging, examination and amendment of L/C), shipment (booking vessel, insurance and customs clearance), and payment settlement (making documents and settlement of payment). Therefore, following we will concentrate on studying the procedures for carrying out CIF and L/C transaction.

1. Ensure the Issuance of L/C

After signing an export contract with the payment by L/C, the exporter shall make sure of the issuance of L/C firstly. And ensure the issuance of L/C covers the following three sections: urging the L/C, examination of the L/C, and amendment of L/C.

(1) Urging the L/C

For the business with L/C payment, especially the business in large amount or the business of commodities made to order, the timely issuance of L/C upon the agreement is the basis of the sellers' fulfillment of contract. It is very important for the buyers to issue the L/C timely, otherwise the seller has not enough time to arrange for the production or get supply of goods. In the business practise, some importers abroad will put off the issuance of L/C, or not open the L/C on purpose due to the market fluctuation or the capital shortage. Therefore, the seller shall remind the buyer to open the L/C in time to ensure the smooth fulfillment of contract.

In the following cases, the seller may urge the buyer to open the L/C:

①The buyer fail to issue an L/C within the time stipulated in the contract.

In this case, the buyer breaches the contract. However, if the seller still does not want to break off the transaction, he may urge the buyer to open the L/C. The seller, though, reserves the right to claim against the buyer.

②In the case that the goods are ready for shipment, the seller may also urge the buyer to open the L/C in order to advance shipment

Urging can be made by sending the relative banking information to the buyer such as the beneficiaries' full name and address, the sales contract numbers, telephone numbers etc. and the beneficiaries' bank details. The seller may in the meantime request the buyer to ask his bank to try to choose seller's banks as the advising banks and negotiating banks if possible. All these information materials must not be in handwriting, in which slips of the pen and misreading often occur, and may finally interfere with our work. The seller especially inform the buyers of the exporters' name and address, only to prevent the clients from mixing them up. Some necessary repetition can play a role of reminder and confirmation.

(2) Examination of the L/C

After receiving a letter of credit, the seller must check the L/C immediately and thoroughly to ensure that the terms and conditions stipulated in the L/C are correct and conform to the sales contract, and that he can comply exactly with the L/C requirements. Otherwise, the seller must immediately ask the buyer to amend the L/C. If any terms and conditions of the L/C are not complied with, no matter how small, a discrepancy is said to occur and it can delay or prevent the payment.

In the business practice, the L/C issued will be different from the contract clauses due to the reasons such as the work neglect, the mistakes of telegram transfer, the different usual practices in trade, market changes or the importer's deliberate addition of the beneficial clauses to him; or there are some soft clauses in the L/C which cannot be met by the exporter and so on. In order to ensure the safe settlement of payment and smooth execution of the contract, and avoid the loss brought to us, we shall look through the L/C in the following aspects:

①Examine the political background and financial standing of the issuing bank

If issuing bank is domiciled in a country which has friendly relations with China, but its nationality is not acceptable, this credit is not accepted. If the issuing bank is a very small bank with a very poor financial standing, this credit is unacceptable, too.

②Examine the nature of the credit and the liabilities of the opening bank

Credit with a word like "revocable" is not acceptable. The undertaking clause of the issuing bank should be included. Sometimes although there is the word "irrevocable" in the L/C, some "limitation clauses" regarding the undertaking of the issuing bank also include such clauses as "This credit is not effective until we receive the notification of import licenses". Credits with such clauses are not acceptable.

③Examine the classification of L/C

According to the *UCP* 600, L/C is usually irrevocable. Moreover, we shall make sure whether the L/C is confirmed or not. If the L/C is confirmed, the confirming bank's name, the relevant expense and payer shall be verified.

④Examine the credit applicant and beneficiary

The information of the applicant of a credit shall be examined carefully to avoid a wrong delivery. Meanwhile, the information such as the name and address of the beneficiary shall be correct and consistent; otherwise it will influence the settlement.

⑤Examine the credit currency and sum

The currency adopted in the L/C shall be consistent with the currency stipulated in the contract. If they are not consistent with each other, the money shall be converted into the contract's sum of money according to the foreign exchange list of BOC and no less than the contract's sum of money. The credit sum shall be in accordance with that of the contract, and the sum in Arabic numbers shall conform to the sum in words. If there is more or less clause in the contract, the credit sum shall include the sum of more or less part.

⑥Examine the expiry date and expiry place of credit

It is stipulated in the Art.6 of *UCP* 600: A credit must state an expiry date of presentation. An expiry date stated for honor or negotiation will be deemed to be an expiry date for presentation. The place of the bank with which the credit is available is the place for presentation. The place for presentation under a credit available with any bank is that of any bank. A place for presentation other than that of the issuing bank is in addition to the place of the issuing bank.

The expiry date of acceptance or payment means the deadline of the acceptance or payment upon the requirement of the beneficiary against the issuing bank or the specified paying bank in the credit through the bank of the export country; the expiry place is usually the place of the issuing bank or the specified paying bank. The expiry date of negotiation means the deadline of the presentation and negotiation made by the beneficiary to negotiation bank; the expiry place is usually the export country. In case that the expiry place of negotiation stated in the credit is not in our country but at abroad, the relevant documents for presentation must be dispatched to the issuing bank or the specified paying bank before the expiry date, with the risks of post delay and loss to be taken by our foreign business company. Therefore, for the credit with the expiry date of negotiation at abroad, we shall require the counterpart to amend it.

⑦Examine the description of thc goods

The details of the goods described in the L/C shall be examined carefully, including the commodity, quality, specification, quantity, package, unit price, ports, insurance, etc.. It also shall be checked whether some extra special clauses or reservation clauses are added, for instance, the ship company is specified for the shipment or the commercial invoice, or the certification of origin shall be issued or stamped by the embassy or consulate abroad. Depending on the specific situation, the relevant policy shall be made to accept or revise the credit.

⑧Examine the shipping time and validity of credit

A shipping time is the time stipulated in a credit for the shipment, consistent with that of the contract in principle. In case that the credit reaches the beneficiary so late that the shipment cannot be effected on time, the beneficiary shall inform the credit applicant abroad to extend the shipping date by telegram; for the reasons like production arrangement or vessel, the shipment is delayed, the beneficiary also may require the credit applicant to make extension of credit. There shall be a reasonable interval between the validity of credit and the latest shipping time, so that the beneficiary has enough time to make documents and settle payment after shipment. If the validity in credit is the same date as the latest shipping date, which is called "double expiry date credit", it is not reasonable, thus the beneficiary shall ask the credit applicant to make amendment depending on the specific situation.

If the clause like partial shipment or shipment in installment is stipulated in contract, then it shall be confirmed whether the enough intervals between shipments are remained. According to the usual practice, for a contract with partial shipment clause, if any shipment is delayed, then the shipment and the following shipment under the credit are all taken as a failure to the fulfillment of contract. So we shall pay much attention to it. As for the transshipment, it shall be checked if any extra special limitation or requirement is added to the transshipment clause, such as specified transshipment place, vessel name or shipping company if the transshipment is allowed in contract. For the special limitation, we shall consider whether we can reach them, otherwise inform the applicant to make amendment in time. For others, such as port, and insurance, we also need to examine carefully according to the contract.

⑨Examine the payment

There are four types of payment through bank: payment in sight, deferred payment, payment with the acceptance of draft or negotiation. All credits must indicate clearly the payment types.

⑩Examine the shipment documents for presentation and special clauses

The documents for presentation shall be examined carefully including the types, copies and filling ways, etc.. For the improper requirement or stipulation, it shall be amended. As for the special clauses, it is not advisable to accept the special clauses of credit unless the exporter can reach the requirement stated in them.

...

All above stated are the key points which shall be examined by the negotiating banks and the exporter. In conclusion, the examination of the L/C shall be subject to the contract signed by both parties and the credit shall be checked carefully word by word. Once any unacceptable discrepancy is found, we shall ask the credit applicant to make amendment.

(3) Amendment the L/C

Amendment describes the process whereby the terms and conditions of a documentary credit may be modified after the credit has been issued. There are two reasons for the amendment of L/C. One reason is due to the beneficiary; for all the contents in the L/C which are not complying with the sales contract or unfavorable to the safe settlement of proceeds, the exporter shall ask the importer to make amendment of L/C. The other reason is due to the credit applicant, and the applicant is forced to amend the L/C because of the situational changes. During the credit amendment, the following points shall be paid attention to:

Firstly, in case that several places of a credit need to be amended, the beneficiary shall try to inform the applicant to make amendment for once in order to save time and expense. For each amendment, the L/C applicant will have to pay amendment fee to the opening bank, and the beneficiary also will have to pay some notification fee to the notifying bank, so it shall be avoided to make amendment for several times, which will influence the reputation as well as the fulfillment of contract.

Secondly, for contents amended in the credit, the beneficiary shall examine them carefully too. Once the amended contents are found to be unacceptable yet, the beneficiary shall notify the applicant to refuse them and require the amendment once more.

Finally, according to *UCP* 600, "Partial acceptance of an amendment is not allowed and will be deemed to be notification of rejection of the amendment." Thus, for the amendment of two items or more in the L/C, we shall notify the applicant to accept all of them or refuse at all; the partial acceptance is not acceptance.

The examination and amendment of a credit from abroad is an important basic element for the smooth fulfillment of contract and safe settlement of proceeds. We must pay much attention to it and do it well. After receipt of the amendment to the L/C, the sellers can formally make sure of the supply of goods and arrange the production.

2. The Preparation of Goods

According to the requirement of contract or L/C, the exporter purchases materials, arranges for production, and gets the goods ready in the agreed quality and quantity. It is the basic obligation for seller.

For different types of the exporters, the ways of preparing goods are different accordingly. For a foreign trade company, it shall contact the domestic manufacturers and place a purchase order with them. For manufacturing exporters, preparing goods covers the following details: deliver the production order sheet to the production or storage department to manufacture, process, check, pack, and write the shipping marks, then get through export inspection to obtain the export approval certificate, and so on. The production order sheet is the evidence for preparing goods, shipment and making documents. The exporter shall take care of the following items during the preparation:

(1) Quality, description and packing requirements

In determining the quality and description of the goods, the requirements in the contract will prevail: the overriding source for the standard of conformity is the contract itself. So we should check them according to the requirement of contract and process or revise if necessary to make sure that the quality and specification reach the standard stipulated in the contract or credit.

In many cases, lack of conformity is often caused by the inadequate packing of the goods. During the preparation of goods, the inner and outer package and upholster (including trade mark, logo and sticker) shall be checked and examined carefully.

For poor or damaged package, it shall be replaced or repaired in time in order to get clean bill of lading and settle the payment smoothly. In addition, the way in which the goods are packaged has to be sufficient to protect and preserve the goods after they were handed over by the seller to carrier, the goods have to be packaged in a way in which is suitable for the carriage of those goods, also in case of any delay, and which will last until the goods are handed over to the buyer at their destination.

(2) Quantity of goods

The sellers must deliver the exact quantity goods to the buyers stipulated in the contract. And the quantity of the goods prepared shall be a little more to replace or adapt to the space in case of the loss or damage during the transportation. So parties to international sales contracts frequently state the quantity of the goods to be delivered as approximate amount, leaving a margin as to the exact quantity to be delivered by using words such as "more or less", "not less than", "about". By such a stipulation, the seller gains some latitudes as to the amount he can deliver and still fulfill his obligation of delivering the goods that conform to the quantity.

(3) Preparation time

The schedule shall be arranged on basis of the stipulated shipping time in the credit or contract to catch the vessel.

3. Inspection

For all the commodities which are required by government or stipulated in contract to go through the inspection of China Entry Exit Inspection and Quarantine Bureau or the local branches, the exporter shall apply for inspection after the goods get ready. The customs will not release the goods before the goods are inspected and proved by the local Entry-Exit Inspection and Quarantine Bureau. The goods are not permitted to be exported if they fail to pass the inspection. The general inspection procedures are as follows:

(1) Making application

Fill in the application form of CIQ, and submit the application to the local Entry-Exit Inspection and Quarantine Bureau. After the application, in case that the contents in the application form are found to be wrong, or the goods are changed due to the credit amendment, the exporter shall ask for the modification of the application form and make explanation for the modification reasons.

(2) Inspection

The local inspection bureau inspects the commodities by sampling according to the relevant law or the inspection standard stipulated in the contract. The inspection contents include the quality, specification, quantity, weight, packing and the grade of safety, health and so on.

(3) Issuance of inspection certification

The inspection bureau will issue the inspection certification after the commodity passed the inspection. The exporter shall make shipment within the validity of the inspection certificate. In case that the shipment has exceeded the validity, the exporter shall apply for the extension of inspection and re-inspection. The validity of the inspection certificate keeps in effect for two months from the issuance of the inspection certificate, two or three weeks for fruits and eggs, three weeks for plants. The re-inspection shall be effected when the validity is over before the shipment.

4. Shipment, Insurance and Customs Clearance

The exporter shall arrange for the shipment, insurance and customs clearance when preparing the goods.

(1) Shipment

In arranging shipment, the seller (the shipper) shall fill in the shipping note to book the shipping spaces in a liner. If the shipping company accepts the order, it will then issue a shipping order (shipping permit) to the shipper with a confirmed space booking, authorizing the receiving clerk (cargo checker) at the container terminal or dock to receive a specified amount of goods from the named shipper.

A shipping order (S/O) typically contains the space booking number, names and addresses of the shipper and customers broker or forwarder, vessel and voyage number, sailing time, delivery date and location, customs closing date, and number and type of packages.

After receiving the S/O from the shipping company, the seller may start to ensure the loading of the goods. The seller should supervise the loading process. After the goods being loaded on board the vessel, the Captain or the Mate will issue a receipt, which is known as *the Mate's Receipt*. The seller shall exchange it for the bills of lading from the shipping company after making payment of the freight.

(2) Insurance

Once the time of shipment and name of vessel are confirmed, the exporters should apply to an insurance company for insurance covering the goods to be transported in an attempt to protect the goods in transit against damage or loss. The exporter fills in the insurance application sheet with the details such as commodity, insurance sum, shipment route, departure date, coverage of insurance and so on. The insurance company will issue the insurance policy or insurance certificate after the exporter paying the insurance fee.

(3) Customs declaration

Customs declaration covers the whole procedures that the exporter has to go through with the customs including customs declaration, customs clearance before the goods are shipped. The procedures of customs clearance are as follows: before the shipment, the exporter must fill in the export customs declaration form, then makes declaration to customs together with the commercial invoice, packing list, inspection certificate, exporter approval certificate, etc., and the involving contract if necessary, credit copy. After the customs check and verify the goods and documents with stamping "RELLEASE" on the shipping order, the goods may be shipped on board with it. The exporter may go through customs clearance by itself or through professional customs clearance service or international forwarder.

5. Documentation

After the goods have been exported, the exporter shall prepare the full set of documents upon the request of credit. Within the validity of credit, the exporter shall present the documents to the bank for the negotiation and payment.

(1) Quality requirements for documents

The quality of documents should meet the following general requirements:

①Accuracy: In handing the documents the doctrine of strict compliance must be observed. It should be noted that the documents have to comply with the terms of the credit and the documents themselves ought to be consistent with one another.

②Completeness: All detailed requirements for documents such as types of documents, numbers of originals and copies, items for each document in the credit should be met.

③Promptness: Make sure the documents are ready when they are needed to avoid any delay or confusion.

④Conciseness: No redundant words or expressions should be used.

⑤Cleanness: No correction should be made on the documents.

(2) Period of time for presentation of documents

The beneficiary must present not only the right documents, but also at the right time, namely, within the period of time for presentation laid sown in the credit and rules in the *UCP* 600. The time limit for presentation of documents is determined by the following three factors:

①The expiry date of the credit

UCP 600 Art.6 (d)(i) provides that "A credit must state an expiry date for presentation. An expiry date stated for honour or negotiation will be deemed to be an expiry date for presentation". After this date, the credit will cause to exist and can no longer be drawn on. Therefore, documents must be presented on or before the expiry date in the credit.

②The period of time for presentation specified in the credit

Credit may specify date for presentation as being ×× days after the date of shipment. In such case, the date for presentation is deduced according to the date of shipment. But in any way, it should not be later than the expiry date of the credit.

③21 days after the date of shipment

If, however, no such period of time for presentation is specified, the presentation must be made not later than 21 calendar days after the date of shipment, but in any event not later than the expiry date of the credit.

(3) Types of documents required by the credit

①Bill of Exchange (Draft)

A bill of exchange (or draft as it is sometimes called) is a written, dated and signed instrument that contains an unconditional order from the drawer(出票人) that directs the drawee(受票人) to pay a definite sum of money to a payee(收款人) on demand or at a specified future date. Simply put, a bill of exchange is a written order by the drawer to the drawee to pay money to the payee.

A draft is a useful instrument because it allows one party (the drawer) to direct another (the drawee) to pay money either to himself, to his agent, or to a third party. Of course, the order is valid only if the drawee has an underlying obligation to pay money to the drawer. This can arise in situations where the drawee is holding money on account of the drawer (i.e., the drawee is a bank), where the drawer lent money to a drawee (i.e., the drawee is a borrower), or where the drawer has sold goods to the drawee and the drawee owes the sale price to the drawer (i.e., the drawee is a buyer).

The following items shall be paid attention to during the preparation of a hill of exchange.

- Payer: Under the payment by L/C, the payer of a bill of exchange shall be written according to the stipulation of credit, who is usually the opening bank or the paying bank.

The special term "Drawn on ×××" is used to indicate the name of the payer in a draft, the name of the payer is written following the words "drawn on". In *UCP600*, it is stipulated that "a credit must not be issued available by a draft drawn on the applicant". The stipulation keeps the credit's issuing bank undertaking of payment at the first place.

- Payee: Usually the words such as "Pay to the order" are followed by the name of payee.
- Draw Clause: Under L/C, the clauses shall be written according to the stipulation of the credit. In case that there is no stipulation about it in credit, the name, place, credit number and the issuing date shall be indicated in the bill. For instance, "Drawn Under ××× bank Irrevocable L/C NO.××× Dated ×××." Under collection, the contract number shall be indicated in the bill.
- Bill Expiry Date: It is calculated from the next day whether using the word "from" or "after"; while the presentation expiry date is calculated according to the shipping date, the day is included with the word "from".
- Bill is usually issued in duplicate with the equal effective force, the other one is invalid if one is honored.

②Commercial Invoice

Commercial invoice is a list issued by the seller indicating the name of goods, quantity, price and the like details, which is taken as the key document for the delivery of the goods and payment between the buyer and the seller, as well as one of the necessary documents for the tariff declaration. There is no unified form for a commercial invoice in our country, but the main contents are the same, including Name and address of the seller, name and address of the buyer, date of issuance, invoice number, order or contract number, quantity and description of the goods etc..

It is crucial that the descriptions of the goods in the commercial invoice correspond precisely to the description of goods in the credit. The invoice amount should match exactly (or at least should not exceed) the amount specified in the credit. Banks have the right to reject invoices issued for the amount in excess of the amount stated in the credit. However, if a documentary credit specifies "about" in relation to the currency amount and quantity of the merchandise, then the invoice amount can be equal to ten percent more or less of the amount in the credit.

The invoice also states shipping details, weight of the goods, number of packages, shipping marks, terms of delivery, payment, among others, as required in the sales contract or L/C.

③Bill of Lading(B/L)

A bill of lading is a transportation document issued by an ocean carrier to a shipper with whom the carrier has entered into a contract for the carriage of goods. The bill of lading plays a vital role in international trade. There are three functions performed by the B/L:

- Receipt for goods: The bill of lading acts as a receipt for the goods received. A bill of lading describes the goods put on board a vessel, stating the quantity, and their condition. The form itself is normally filled out in advance by the shipper, then, as the goods are loaded aboard the ship, the carrier will check to see that the goods loaded comply with the goods listed. The carrier, however, is responsible only to check for outward compliance — that is, that the labels comply and that the packages are not damaged, If all appear proper, the appropriate agent of the carrier will sign the bill and return it to the shipper.

- Evidence of the contract of carriage: The B/L is an evidence of the contract of carriage between the shipper and the carrier. The bill becomes conclusive evidence of the terms of the contract of carriage once it is negotiated to a good faith third party (善意的第三方).

- Document of title (所有权) to the goods: The named consignee or the holder of a bill of lading, provided he has received it in good faith through due negotiation, has a claim to title and, by surrendering (交出) the bill, to delivery of the goods. The carrier is under obligation to deliver the cargo only against an original bill of lading, If the carrier delivers goods without the production of a bill of lading, he will be liable in contract or in tort to the bill of lading holder.

The following items shall be paid attention to during the preparation of a B/L:

Firstly, for a bill of lading, the consignee is very important as it is involved with the transfer of a B/L, which will be stated clearly in a credit. Secondly, the contents stated in a bill of lading (such as the types of B/L, the consignee, the names of the goods and packages, destination port, the statement about how to charge the freight, the numbers of the original B/L, etc.) must be complying to the credit. However, the description of the goods stated in B/L may be shortened so long as the shortened name of the goods is not conflicting against the description of goods in the L/C. Thirdly, we should pay attention to the numbers of the original B/L. In accordance with the stipulating of *UCP* 600, the bank accepts the sole original bill of lading or the full set of B/L issued in more than one original. For the bill of lading issued in more than one original, the force of each original is the same as the others, but the others become invalid once one original is used to take the goods. Therefore, it is stipulated in the contract or L/C that the exporter shall offer the Full Set or Complete Set of B/L, namely, all the originals of B/L issued by the carrier. Lastly, as to the freight indicated on a bill of lading, under the trade terms of CIF, CFR, CPT, CIP, "Freight Prepaid" shall be indicated on the B/L. Under the trade terms of FOB, FCA, "Freight to Collect" shall be indicated. The specific freight need not be written out on the B/L except it is stipulated in the L/C.

④Other documents

Other documents may be provided according to the stipulation of the credit. These documents may be prepared by the exporter, or provided by others at the request of the exporter. The common documents are:

- Insurance policy (or certificate)

The insurance policy (or certificate) is a document indicating the type and amount of insurance coverage in force on a particular shipment. In documentary credit transactions the insurance document is used to assure the consignee that insurance is provided to cover loss of or damage to cargo while in transit. A complete insurance document includes the following elements: name of the insurance company; name of the insurance document; number of the insurance document; description of the goods insured; description of risks covered and sum insured; name of place where claims are payable; means of transportation, name of vessel, loading port and destination port; issuing date of insurance document; signature of the insurer etc..

- Certificate of origin

This is a document evidencing the origin of the goods or the place of manufacturing. It may be issued by the China Council for the Promotion of International Trade, other competent inspection bodies or the exporter himself.

Certificate of origin is mainly classified as Certificate of Origin of the People's Republic of China (C/O in short) and Generalized System of Preferences (GPS in short). Certificate of Origin of the People's Republic of China is a legal document certifying the manufacture of the goods to be exported is in conformity with the *Rules of Origin for Export Goods of the People's Republic of China*, which is made in a uniform format by National Commercial Department. It is required by the countries or regions where the customs invoice or consular invoice is not used to set the duties on the imported goods. Generalized System of Preference (GPS in short) is a general, non-reciprocal, non-discriminative, preference system treatment granted by developed industrial countries to reduce tariff on the goods imported from developing countries, especially the industrial made-out products or semi-made products. For the time being, many countries including New Zealand, Australia, Japan, Canada and EU members have granted GPS treatment on the goods of China. For the goods exported to these countries, GPS certificate shall be furnished to the importer as the evidence of import tariff reduction.

- Inspection certificate

All kinds of inspection certificate are used to certify the nature, quantity, weight and sanitary situation of the goods respectively. In China, inspection certificate is usually issued by the Entry-Exit Inspection and Quarantine of the People's Republic of China. The certificate also may be issued by the exporter or manufacture depending on the specific situation if there is no specific stipulation in the concerning contract or credit. It shall be paid attention that the name of certificate and the listed items therein or inspection result must be in conformity with those stipulated in the contract and credit. The issuing date of inspection certificate must be no later than the issuing date of B/L.

Specimen 12-1 **Bill of Exchange**

BILL OF EXCHANGE

No. LD-DRGINV01

For US $ 18 825 600 SHANGHAI 27-May-01

(amount in figure) (place and date of issue)

At ×××××××××× sight of this FIRST Bill of exchange(SECOND being unpaid)

pay to BANK OF CHINA, SHANGHAI BRANCH or order the sum of

SAY UNITED STATES OOL_LARS ONE HUNDRED AND EIGHTY EIGHT THOUSAND HUNDRED AND FIFTY ONLY(amount in words)

Value received for 600 SETS (quantity) of TELECONTROL PACING CAR (name of commodity)

Drawn under CHEMICAL BANK YORK

L/C No. DRG-LDLC01 dated 14-Apr-01

To: CHEMICAL BANK NEW YORK
55 WATER SWREET, ROOM 1702,
NEW YORK, NY 10041

For and on behalf of
LIDA TRADING CO. LTD
×××
(signature)

Specimen 12-2 **Commercial Invoice**

江苏和泰股份有限公司

JIANGSU HOTIY CORPORATION

HOTIY BUILDING, 50 ZHONGSHAN, NANJING, CHINA

Commercial Invoice

No. TEST
April 28, 2000
Order No. 008001

Sold to: Torus Systems (Chicago) Inc.
201 Fifth Avenue, Suite 2001
New York, NY 10021
U.S.A

Shipment: Per sailing from SHANGHAI to NY on or about April 25, 2000

Payment: BY T/T

Insurance: For 110% of the invoice value against ALL risks and WAR risks.

Terms: CIF New York

Item No.	Description	Quantity	Price	Amount
PCR	Cloth doll pairs, 6.5". (Your item No.00001-C21030A) (Your Order No. 008001) (Our S/C No. S000225) (Bar Code: 78459632114)	1 200.00 pc	35.000	US $ 42 000.00
	Porcelian ducking pair, 6″(large). Each pair in a box. (Your item No. C00001-D10021) (Your Order No. 008001) (Our S/C No. S000225) (Bar Code: 74859321456)	500.00 pc	28.500	US $ 14 250.00
Total:		1 700.00 pc		US $ 56 250.00

Total Amount: U.S. Dollars Fifty-Six Thousand Two Hundred and Fifty Only.

Remarks: All merchandise shall be inspected by buyer's representative before shipment.

Torus Systems (Chicago). Inc.

(signature)

Specimen 12-3　　　　　　　**Bill of Lading**

<table>
<tr><td colspan="2">Shipper:
SHANGHAI GARDEN PRODUCTS IMP. AND EXP. CO.,LTD.</td><td colspan="2" rowspan="4">B/L No.:(1)SHYZ092234
承运人:Carrier

德威集装箱货运有限公司
DE-WELL CONTAINER SHIPPING CO.LTD.
OCEAN BILL OF LADING
ORIGINAL
RECEIVED in external apparent good order and condition except as otherwise noted. The total number of packages or units stuffed in the container. The description of goods and the the weights shown in this Bill of Lading are furnished by the merchants and which the Carrier has no reasonable means of checking and is not a part of this B/L contract.
(Terms of B/L continued on the back hereof)</td></tr>
<tr><td colspan="2">Consignee:
TO ORDER OF SHIPPER</td></tr>
<tr><td colspan="2">Notify party:
LAIKI PERAGORA ORPHANIDES LTD.,
020 STRATIGOU TIMAGIA AVE.,
6046,LARNAKA,
CYPRUS</td></tr>
<tr><td>Pre-carriage by</td><td>Port of loading
SHANGHAI PORT</td></tr>
<tr><td>Ocean Vessel Voy .No.:
LT DIAMOND V.021W</td><td>Port of Discharge:
LIMASSOL PORT</td><td>Place of Delivery</td><td>No. of original B/L
THREE</td></tr>
</table>

Marks and Nos Container& Seal No.	No. & kind of packages	Description of goods	Gross weight	Measurement
L.P.O.L. 186/09/10014 MADE IN CHINA NO. 1-325 1X 20' FCL,CY/CY CNO,:FSCU3214999 SNO,:1295312	325 CTNS	WOODEN GARDEN PRODUCTS	4 175KG	24.104CBM

<table>
<tr><td>Total No.of container or other pkgs or units (in words)</td><td>SAY THREE HUNDRED AND TWENTY FIVE CARTONS ONLY</td></tr>
<tr><td rowspan="3">For delivery of goods please apply to:
ABC Shipping Company
208 San Marding Street,
Limassol,Cyprus
Tel:02-33669812</td><td>Freight& charges
FREIGHT PREPAID</td></tr>
<tr><td>Place and date of issue:
SHANGHAI 12 FEB.,2009</td></tr>
<tr><td>Signed by:</td></tr>
<tr><td>Laden on Board the vessel:
Date:12 FEB.,2009
By:____________</td><td>DE-WELL CONTAINER SHIPPING CO.LTD.
As carrier:____________</td></tr>
</table>

6. Settlement of Export Proceeds in Foreign Exchange

Settlement of export proceeds in foreign exchange means the exporter sells its export proceeds in foreign exchange to the bank who pays it an equivalent amount in RMB according to the foreign exchange rate.

(1) Three ways of settlement of export proceeds in foreign exchange in China

According to the time when settlement is made (i.e. when the bank at the seller's side credits the beneficiary's account in RMB), there are three ways of settlement of export proceeds in foreign exchange in China, namely, "settlement after the payment from the reimbursing bank", "settlement on a fixed date" and "negotiation under L/C with shipment documents".

①Settlement after the payment from the reimbursing bank

After the examination of the shipment documents and making sure of the documents complying with the credit, the negotiating bank sends the documents together with the credit to the reimbursement bank abroad for the payment. In this way, the negotiating bank just transfers the sum of payment in RMB to the nominated account of the exporter in accordance with the spot RMB Forex rate after receiving the payment namely the Credit Note to the exporter's account from the reimbursing bank. Under this occasion, the negotiating bank takes no risk without prepaying any fund to the exporter, but the exporter may run into a hard time of capital running due to the late arrival of the payment.

②Settlement on a fixed date

This way means that after making sure that there is no discrepancy between the documents and the credit, the remitting bank shall dispatch the documents to the paying bank abroad for payment and shall then convert the seller's export proceeds in foreign exchange to RMB at the listed foreign exchange rate on a previously fixed day.

③Negotiation under L/C with shipment documents

After the exporter has shipped the goods and obtained all the documents under L/C, he may take the full set of shipment documents and the credit to the negotiating bank as the collateral for the application of the loan. After the examination of the documents, the negotiating bank may honor the draft of the beneficiary (exporter) or the shipment documents with a certain discount, deducting the interests and charges (calculating from the negotiation date to the future payment arrival date) from the sum indicated on the draft, pay the balance sum of payment to the exporter according to the spot RMB Foreign Exchange rate of the negotiating date. Thus, the negotiating bank turns into the draft holder after making payment to the beneficiary at advance, and claims for the payment against the payment paying bank with the documents. In this way, the negotiating bank gives capital financing to the exporter so as to speed up the capital running of the exporter.

(2) Remedy for the documents in discrepancies after shipment

For the documentation under L/C, the shipment shipping documents for negotiation are required to be in strict compliance with the credit and the documents. However, in practice, the documents in discrepancies cannot be avoided. According to a study conducted by the International Chamber of Commerce (ICC), Banking Commission, it shows that two-thirds of presentation of the documents against L/C deviate from the terms and conditions of the L/C on first presentation.

Commonly found discrepancies between the letter of credit and supporting documents include:

- Letter of the credit has expired prior to the presentation of draft;
- Bill of lading evidences delivery prior to or after the date range stated in the credit;
- Stale dated documents;
- Changes included in the invoice not authorized in the credit;
- Inconsistent description of goods;
- Insurance document errors;
- Invoice amount not equal to draft amount;
- Ports of loading and destination not as specified in the credit;
- Description of merchandise is not as stated in credit;
- A document required by the credit is not presented;
- Documents are inconsistent as to general information such as volume, quality, etc.;
- Names of documents not exact as described in the credit, beneficiary information must be exact;

- Invoice or statement is not signed as stipulated in the letter of credit.

When a discrepancy is detected by the negotiating bank, a correction to the document may be allowed if it can be done quickly while remaining in the control of the bank. If time is not a factor, the exporter should request that the negotiating bank return the documents for corrections, the exporter may handle the discrepancies in the following ways:

①Covering Suggestion

When the negotiating bank find minor discrepancies on the presented documents, the exporter may issue a guarantee letter to the negotiating bank requiring the negotiating with guarantee after receiving the approval of the importer. In this case, the remarks of discrepancies and the words like "negotiation under guarantee" are indicated on the covering schedule which is in company with the shipping documents.

②Telegraph Suggestion

When there are documents in discrepancies for negotiation, the negotiating bank may inform the issuing bank with the listed discrepancies through telegraph or fax, then, send the documents out after receiving the confirmation from the issuing bank. Through telegraph suggestion, the attitude of the issuing bank may be known as early as possible.

③Collection with Documents

For the presenting documents in discrepancies, the exporter may settle the payment by collection with documents in case that the negotiating bank is not willing to adopt telegraph suggestion or covering suggestion. Since the collection is concerning about the business under the credit issued earlier, the collecting bank still takes the issuing bank of the credit as the presenting bank to present the documents with draft to the importer for payment.

It shall be paid attention that the above-mentioned three remedy ways have changed a bank credit into a commercial credit, with the issuing bank free of the first undertaking of payment under L/C, which is unfavorable to the exporter. Therefore, it is not advisable for the exporters to adopt the above mentioned remedy measures unless it is inevitable. The exporters shall pay more attention to the documentation work with careful examination of documents so as to settle all the problems before the shipment and avoid any discrepancy on the documents.

Section Two Performance of Import Contract

In the import business transactions in China, most import contracts are concluded with the trade term FOB, if these contract are under the payment of sight L/C, the importer has to get through the following procedures: opening L/C, charter or booking vessel, loading, effecting insurance, examination of documents and making payment, customs declaration and receipt of the goods, making inspection, distribution etc.. All of these works have to be finished through the close co-operation of importer, carrier, inspection bureau, bank, insurance company and the client.

The operation of import business is similar to that of the export business. In the import business of China, it is more beneficial for the Chinese importer to conclude the contract with the trade term of FOB, so there are more deals conclude with the trade term of FOB. For the import business by L/C, the general procedures are as follows:

1. Issuance of L/C

It is one of the most important obligation for the importer to open L/C to the exporter abroad. The importer shall open the L/C within the deadline required in the contract, otherwise, it is a breach of contract. If it's stipulated in the contract that the L/C shall be opened after the exporter has obtained export licence or paid the deposit, the importer shall issue the L/C after receiving the exporter's notification that the export license is granted or the bank's advice that the deposit is received. If it is stipulated that the importer shall issue the L/C after the exporter has confirmed the delivery time, the importer shall issue the L/C after receiving the concerning advice from the exporter.

The importer applies for the L/C within the stipulated time in contract. The importer must have concluded trade financing contract and fill in the L/C application form in accordance with the sales contract, and pay credit opening charges to the L/C opening bank (the opening charges occupying 0.15% of the total L/C amount).

2. Charter and Book Vessel

Under the trade term of FOB, it is the buyer that in charge of chartering or booking vessel. After receiving "booking vessel confirmation", the importer shall inform the exporter of the vessel name, voyage and shipping date so that the counterparty may arrange for the cargo shipment. At the same time, in order to avoid the exporter's delay on cargo delivery, the importer shall supervise and urge the exporter to fulfill the contract timely, especially for the goods in large quantity or very important commodities, or nominate the local agent in the exporter's place to urge the exporter to fulfill the contract, or send for the concerning staff to supervise or inspect at the exporter site.

3. Effect Cargo Insurance

In China, the insurance for the imported cargo in transportation can be covered either for each shipment or open cover. For the insurance for each shipment, the buyer shall inform the insurance company to effect insurance once he receives the shipping advice from sheller. And the insured and the insurer must negotiate the terms for each shipment, including the type of coverage, cargo, and ship. On the other hand, open cover policies are commonly used in international trade, specifically by companies that are involved in high volume trade over a long period of time. Companies purchase this type of coverage because it precludes them from having to negotiate the terms of a new policy each time a shipment is made. Since the insured is agreeing to purchase a longer-term contract, it may be able to realize lower premiums. This is because the insurer does not have to spend time on repetitive negotiations, and because the insurer benefits from a having a guaranteed premium over a longer period of time.

4. Documents Examination and Payment

After receiving the draft and the shipment documents, the payment bank (usually the issuing bank) will check and examine them in accordance with the clauses of credit.

The issuing bank shall give the documents to the importer for recheck before making payment even though the bank has confirmed the documents are in compliance with the credit. According to the usual practice of Chinese banks, the issuing bank will fulfill payment at the request of the credit unless the importer doesn't agree. The payment of the issuing bank is without recourse. At the same time, the importer makes payment in RMB according to the listed Forex rate quotation to the issuing bank for the shipment documents. Then, the importer settles payment with his domestic client with the debit note issued by the issuing bank.

In case that the documents are found not complying to the credit, it shall be settled properly depending on the specific situation, including refusal to payment, payment on receipt of cargo and inspection approval, requiring the amendment of documents, holding the right of recourse for payment and so on.

5. Customs Clearance and Duty

The consignee of the imported goods or his agent presents the concerning shipment shipping documents to customs for customs declaration. Customs declaration must be operated by the enterprises which are registered in customs. The operator of customs declaration must be trained, assessed and approved by customs.

The procedures of customs declaration are as follows:

(1) Filling in import customs declaration form

After arrival of the imported cargo, the importer, his forwarder or his customs declaration agent shall fill in "Import Customs Declaration Form" based on the shipment shipping documents, then ask customs declaration with the form attached with the invoice, bill of lading, packing list, insurance policy, import license & other approval documents, import contract, certificate of origin and other documents required by customs; the inspection approval certificate shall be offer for the imported commodities subject to the legal inspection.

According to the stipulation of *Customs Law of the People's Republic of China*, declaration of the import goods shall be made to the customs by the consignee within 14 days of the declaration of the arrival of the means of transport; in case that the consignee fails to declare the import goods within the time limit prescribed above, a fee for delayed declaration shall be imposed by the customs which is 0.05% of the CIF price of the imported cargo per day; if the delay exceeds three months, the cargo will be sold off by the customs.

(2) Customs Examination

On receipt of customs declaration, the customs will carry out examination on the imported cargo to check and verify if the imported cargo is complying with the listed items on the declaration documents. The examination is carried out within the specified time at the site nominated by the customs, namely the warehouse or site of customs surveillance zone.

(3) Customs Duty Payment

According to *Customs Import and Export Tariff of the People's Republic of China*, the import tariff shall be levied on the imported cargo. Based on the stipulation of *Customs Law of the People's Republic of China*, the importer shall pay the customs duty levied in a certain amount to the nominated bank within even seven days following the issuance of the duty memorandum (except for Sunday and Saturday). In case of failure to meet this time limit, a fee for delayed payment shall be imposed by the customs, which is 0.1% of the levied amount per day.

(4) Customs Release (Customs Clearance)

After the customs examination and the importer's payment of duty, the customs declaration form and delivery order are signed and stamped, upon which the importer gets the cargo. For the bonded goods and the imported goods for processing, they cannot be taken by the importer immediately after being released, which are still under the control of customs until getting through the whole customs procedures.

6. Delivery

After going through the above-mentioned procedures, the goods may be delivered to the domestic client. The buyer arranges for transportation and warehouse with the domestic client making payment and taking goods.

Part B Key Terms

Mate's receipt 大副收据

Bill of exchange 汇票

Commercial invoice 商业发票

B/L 提单

C/O 一般原产地证书

GPS 普惠制

Insurance policy (or certificate) 保险单(保险凭证)

Part C Exercises

Ⅰ. Translate the followings from Chinese to English

(1)软条款;(2)大副收据;(3)汇票;(4)商业发票;(5)提单;(6)善意第三方;(7)贷记通知单;(8)电提;(9)凭保议付;(10)逐笔投保;(11)预约投保

Ⅱ. Reflection question (answer in English)

(1) What's the difference between O/C and GPS?

(2) What are the methods for the export documents for payment?

(3) What are the methods to process the discrepancy?

Ⅲ. Case & Analysis

(1) One of our trade companies establishes an export contract of Christian gifts with a foreign businessman. The contract stipulates that the delivery shall be on the CIF basis and the date of delivery is on or before Dec.1, 2001. However, the buyer doesn't stipulate the issuing date of the L/C in the contract. The buyer begins to urge for the establishment of the L/C at the beginning of November. After several urges for establishment, the L/C which is opened by the buyer reaches us on Nov. 25. We complete the shipment on Dec. 5 for the late L/C. When we offer the documents to the bank, the bank dishonors to us for the discrepancies of the L/C.

Questions: ①Is the bank's dishonor reasonable? Why? ②What are our mistakes in this case?

(2) One of our foreign trade companies exports a parcel of Motor on the basis of the irrevocable L/C available at sight. The shipment stipulated in the contract is in September 2006. After we sign the contract, the other party establishes the L/C on time, and we ship the goods timely according to the requirements in the L/C. However, when we make documents, the making member writes the name of commodity in the contract as "MACHINERY AND MILLWORKS, MOTORS" which is in accordance with that in the WC. But the general name of commodity should be "MOTORS" in the B/L.

Question: Can the paying bank dishonor the money for the above reason? Why?

第十二章

进出口合同的履行

一旦合同达成,买卖双方就应该履行各自的义务。卖方须按照合同及《公约》的要求交付货物及与货物有关的单据,并将货物所有权转移给买方。买方须支付货物价款,并按照合同及《公约》提货。履行合同是当事人双方共同的责任,按时、按质、按量地履行合同的规定,不仅关系到买卖双方行使各自的权利和履行相应的义务,而且关系到企业和国家的对外信誉。

第一节　出口合同的履行

在我国出口业务中,采用 CIF 或 CFR 贸易术语,并采用信用证付款方式的出口合同较为常见。履行出口合同的程序包括备货、催证、审证、改证、租船订舱、报检、报关、投保、装船和制单结汇等内容。归纳起来就是四大环节的工作:货(备货、报检),证(催证、审证和改证),船(租船订舱、办理货运手续)、款(制单结汇)。因此,接下来我们将着重讨论按 CIF 及信用证交易的履行。

1. 落实信用证

在签订出口合同后,如采用信用证作为付款方式,那么出口商首先要做的是落实信用证。落实信用证,主要包括催证、审证和改证三项内容。

(1)催证

在按信用证付款方式成交时,买方按约定的时间开证是卖方履行合同的前提条件,尤其是大宗交易或按买方要求而特定的商品交易,买方及时开证更为重要，否则卖方无法安排生产和组织货源。但在实际业务中，有时经常遇到国外进口商拖延开证；或者在行市发生变化或资金发生短缺的情况时，故意不开证。对此，卖方应结合备货情况，及时提醒买方开立信用证，以保证合同的顺利履行。

在以下情况中，卖方可以催促买方开立信用证：

①买方在合同规定的时间未能开立信用证。在这种情况下，买方构成违约。但是，如果卖方不想终止交易，他可催促买方开立信用证。不过，卖方保留向买方索赔的权利。

②如果货物已备妥待运，卖方也可催促买方开立信用证，以便提前装船。

卖方可以通过向买方寄送相关银行信息，比如受益人全称和地址、销售合同编号、电话号码以及受益人的银行详细信息来进行催证。在此期间，卖方还会要求买方在可能的情况下要求其银行选择卖方银行作为顾问和协商银行。所有这些信息材料都不应该是手写的，因为手写常会发生笔误和其他错误，并且最终影响到工作。在催开信用证的过程中，卖方会特别提醒买方出口商的名称和地址，以防买方混淆。一些必要的重复可以起到提醒和确认的作用。

(2)审证

收到信用证后，卖方必须立即全面地审核信用证，以确保信用证条款正确，并与销售合同规定一致，而且能完全满足信用证中开列的要求；否则，卖者必须立即要求买者改证。如果没有符合信用证条款的要求，那么无论差异多小，付款都可能被拖延或停止。

在实际业务中，由于种种原因，如工作疏忽、电文传递错误、贸易习惯不同、市场行情变化或进口商有意利用开证的主动权加列其他有利条款，往往会出现开立信用证条款与合同规定不符，或者在信用证中加列一些出口商看似无所谓但实际是无法满足的信用证付款条件(在业务中也被称为“软条款”)等。为确保收汇完成和合同顺利执行，防止我方造成不应有的损失，外贸公司审核信用证时主要看是否与合同一致，审核的项目一般包括：

①审核开证行的政治背景和财务状况

如果开证行所在国家与中国有良好的外交关系，但其国籍是不可接受的，那么，这种信用证不可接受。如果开证行是一家财务状况很糟糕的小银行，这种信用证同样不可接受。

②审核信用证的性质和开证行的责任

可撤销信用证不可接受，应该有开证行的保证条款。有些情况下，虽然信用证有“不可撤销”字样,但是,有关开证行责任的某些限制条款还是包括“此证在我们收到进口许可证通知后方可生效”这样的条款。载有这种条款的信用证不可接受。

③审核信用证的种类

信用证种类繁多,根据《跟单信用证统一惯例》第600号出版物的规定,信用证都是不可撤销的信用证。此外,还要审查来证是保兑的还是不保兑的信用证,如果是保兑,被哪家银行保兑以及保兑费用由谁负担都要审核清楚。

④审核开证人和受益人

要仔细审核开证申请人的名称和地址,以防错发错运。同时,受益人的名称和地址也必须正确无误,而且前后要一致,否则会影响收汇。

⑤审核信用证中规定的货币和金额

信用证采用的支付货币应与合同规定的货币一致。如果不一致,应按中国银行外汇牌价折算成合同货币,在不低于或相当于原合同货币总金额时方可接受。信用证的金额与合同金额应一致,总金额的小写和大写数字必须一致。如果合同定有溢短装条款,那么信用证金额还应包括溢短装部分的金额。

⑥审核信用证的到期日和到期地点

《跟单信用证统一惯例》第600号第六条规定:信用证必须规定一个交单的截止日期,规定的承付或议付的截止日将被视为交单的截止日。可在其处兑用信用证的银行所在地即为交单地点。可在任一银行兑用的信用证其交单地点为任一银行所在地。除规定的交单地点外,开证行所在地也是交单地点。

承兑或付款到期日是指受益人通过出口地银行向开证行或信用证指定的付款银行交单要求承兑或付款的最后期限,到期地点一般在开证行或指定银行所在地。议付到期日是指受益人向议付银行交单并要求议付的最后期限,到期地点通常在出口国。如信用证中的议付到期地点不在我国而在国外,那么有关单据必须在到期日前寄达开证银行或指定付款银行,我外贸公司要承担邮递延迟、邮件遗失等风险。所以,对议付到期地点在国外的信用证,一般应提请对方修改。

⑦审核信用证中有关货物的记载

审核来证中有关品名、质量、规格、数量、包装、单价金额、港口、保险等是否与合同规定的一致,有无附加特殊条款及保留条款,如指定由某轮船公司的船只运输,或者商业发票、产地证书须由国外的领事签证等,这些都应慎重审核,视具体情况作出是否接受或提请修改的决策。

⑧审核装运期和有效期

装运期是对货物装运时间的规定,原则上必须与合同规定的一致。如信用证到达太晚,不能如期装运,应及时电请国外买方延展装运期;如由于生产或船舶安排等原因,不能在装运期限内装运,也可要求对方延展装运期。信用证的有效期与装运期应该有一定的合理间隔,以便在货物装船后有足够的时间进行制单和结汇工作。如信用证的有效期与装运期规定在同一天,习惯上叫"双到期信用证",这种规定方法不太合理,受益人应视具体情况提请对方修改。

合同中规定分批、定期、定量装运,那么在审核来证时,应注意每批装运的时间是否留有足够的间隔。因为按照惯例,对于分批装运合同,若任何一批未按期装运,则信用证中的该批和以后各批均告失败,所以审证时要认真对待。对于转运,我们应该仔细审核在转运条款中是否加入了额外特殊的限制和需求,比如指定的转运地点、船舶名或运输公司。对于这些特殊的限定,我们应该考虑自身情况是否得以达成,不然就要及时修改相关条款。对于港口、保险等内容,我们也应该在合同中仔细检查。

⑨审核信用证的付款方式

银行的付款方式有四种:即期付款、延期付款、承兑汇票到期付款或议付。所有的信用证都必须清楚地表明付款属于哪一类。

⑩审核要求提交的单据以及特殊条款

要仔细审核来证要求提供的单据种类、份数及填制方法等,如发现不适当的要求和规定,应当做出适当处理。至于特殊条款,除非出口企业有把握做到,否则,我方一般不接受信用证特殊条款中的各种规定。

……

以上是银行和出口企业审证的要点。总之,审查信用证要以买卖双方签订的合同为标准,对信用证进行逐字审核。只要发现我方不能接受的不符点,就应要求对方修改信用证。

(3)改证

改证是指信用证开立之后,可能要对其中的条款进行修改的过程。信用证修改一般有两个原因。一是受益人的原因,凡是发现有不符合买卖合同或不利于出口方安全收汇的内容,就应立即要求进口商向原开证行申请修改信用证。修改信用证的另一个原因是开证申请人的原因,因为情况的变化迫使开证申请人认为有必要修改,有关信用证条款在改证中应注意以下几点:

首先,发现同一张信用证中有多处需要修改的地方,应尽量做到一次性向国外客户提出,以节约时间与费用。因为每次修改,国外客户都要向开证行交纳一定的手续费,受益人也要向通知行交纳一定的修改通知费,它不仅增加了双方的手续和费用,而且多次修改对外影响不好,也会影响及时履约。

其次,对于开证行根据客户申请发出的修改通知的内容,也仍然要认真地进行审核,一旦发现修改后的内容仍不能接受时,应及时向客户申明表示拒绝,并再次提请修改。

最后,根据UCP600的规定,"对同一修改通知中的修改内容不允许部分接受,因而对修改内容的部分接受当属无效"。国外开证行发来的修改通知中如包括两项或两项以上的内容时,我们对此通知要么全部接受,要么全部拒绝,不能只接受其中一部分而拒绝另一部分。

对国外来证的审核和修改是保证顺利履行合同和安全迅速收汇的重要前提,我们必须给予足够的重视,认真做好相关工作。而当收到修改后的信用证后,卖方就能正式确定货物的供应和安排生产了。

2. 备货

备货是进出口企业根据合同或信用证规定,向有关工厂企业或部门采购和安排生产的过程。按质、按量地准备好应交的货物,这是卖方履行合同的基本义务。

出口企业性质不同,备货的形式也有所不同。对于外贸进出口公司而言,备货就是要向国内有关生产企业联系货源,订立国内采购合同。对于自营出口的生产型企业,备货是向生产加工或仓储部门下达联系单,要求该部门按联系单的要求,对应交的货物进行清点、加工整理、包装、刷制运输标志以及办理申报检验和领证等各项工作。联系单是进出口企业内部各个部门进行备货、出运、制单结汇的共同依据。在出口备货时,要注意以下几个问题:

(1)品质、规格和包装的规定

确认货物的品质和规格,以合同要求为主:按合同本身判定是否符合标准最为重要。因此我们应该按合同要求核实货物的品质、规格,必要时进行加工整理,以保证其与合同或者信用证一致。

在很多情况下,货物不合格往往是由于货物包装不良造成的。在备货的过程中,要求对货物的内外包装和装潢(包括商标、贴头、标签)均进行认真核对和检查,如发现包装不良或有破损的情况,应及时进行修整或换装,以免在装运时取不到清洁提单,造成收汇损失。另外,包装方式应使货物从卖方交到买方之后，还能足以保护和保存货物。合适的包装需要适应运输条件，而且即使有任何延迟，也要确保货物完好地送到目的地交给买方。

（2）货物的数量

卖方必须向买方交付与合约规定一致的货物数量。另外，备货的数量应该适当留有余地，万一装运时发生意外或损失，以备调换和适应仓容之用。所以，国际贸易合同各方经常规定允许交付大约数量的货物，使用“多装或少装”、“不少于”或“大约”字样，限定实际交付的货物数量。根据这种规定，卖方对交付货物的数量有一定程度的自由，并且在该自由度下仍然能完成交付符合合同规定数量货物的义务。

（3）备货时间

备货时间应根据信用证规定，结合船期安排，以利于船货衔接。

3. 报检

凡属国家规定法检的商品，或合同规定必须经中国进出口商品检验检疫局检验出证的商品，在货物备齐后，应向商品检验局申请检验。只有收取商检局发给的合格的检验证书，海关才准放行。经检验不合格的货物，一般不得出口。报检的程序一般是：

（1）申请

凡需要法定检验出口的货物，应填制《出口商品检验申请书》，向商检局办理申请报验手续。申请报验后，如出口公司发现“申请单”内容填写有误，或因国外进口人修改信用证以致货物规格有变动时，应提出更改申请，并更改“申请单”，说明更改事项和更改原因。

（2）检验

商检机构对出口商品抽样，应当按照法律或合同规定的检验标准进行检验。检验的内容包括商品的质量、规格、数量、重量、包装及是否符合安全、卫生要求等。

（3）出证

商品检验合格后，即由商检局发给检验证书，进出口公司应在检验证书规定的有效期内将货物出运。如超过有效期装运出口，应向商检局申请延期，并由商检局进行复验，经复验合格，货物才能出口。对于检验证书的有效期，一般货物是从发证起 2 个月内有效，鲜果、鲜蛋类为 2~3 个星期内有效，植物检验为 3 个星期。如果超过有效期，装运前则应向商检局申请复验。

4. 装运、投保和报关

出口企业在备货的同时还必须及时办理装运、投保和报关等手续。

(1)装运

安排装运时,卖方(托运人)需要填写订舱单,预定班轮舱位。如果运输公司接受了预定,该公司会向托运人签发装货单确认预定的舱位,授权集装箱码头的点货员,从托运人处收取确定数量的货物。

订舱单一般包含订舱号、托运人及报关员或货代公司的名称与地址、船名和航次、开航时间、交货时间和地点、海关截止日期以及包装数量和类型。

从运输公司收到装货单后,卖方为了确保货物的装载,应监督装货过程。货物装船后,船长或大副签发收据,称为大副收据。支付运费后,卖方从运输公司处将大副收据换成提单。

(2)投保

一旦装船日期和船名确认后,出口商应及时向保险公司办理投保手续以备货物运输途中被损坏,造成损失。出口商要填制投保单,将货物名称、保险金额、运输路线、开航日期、投保险别等列明,办理保险手续,缴纳保费。保险公司接受投保后,即签发保险单或保险凭证。

(3)报关

报关是指进出口商品装船出运之前向海关申报的手续。报关程序为:出口公司在装船前,必须填写“出口货物报关单”,向海关申报,并应随附商业发票、装货单、商检证书、出口许可证等,必要时提供合同、信用证副本。海关对货、证核查无误后,在装货单上加盖“放行”章,即可凭以装船。出口公司可以自行办理报关手续,也可以委托专业的报关行和国际货运代理公司办理。

5. 制单

制单结汇是指出口货物装出之后,进出口公司即应按照信用证的规定,正确缮制各种单据。在信用证规定的交单有效期内,递交银行办理议付结汇手续。

(1)单据的质量要求

交付的单据,其质量要求需满足以下标准:

①准确:单据的处理要遵循严格相符的原则。需注意,单据必须与信用证的条款一致,而且单据之间应相互一致。

②完整：应符合对有关单据的所有详细要求，比如，信用证中有关单据的种类、单据原件和复印件的份数以及单据的每个项目的要求都应完整。

③及时：确保单据在需要时已准备好，避免任何推延或者混淆。

④简明：单据上没有冗余文字或用语。

⑤整洁：单据不能有修改的痕迹。

(2)单据的时间要求

受益人不但要提交正确的单据，而且要在正确的时间提交，也就是说，在UCP600规定的一定时间内交单。以下三个因素决定交单的时间限制：

①信用证的有效期

UCP600第6条(d)(i)规定，“信用证必须规定一个交单的到期日。规定的承付或议付的到期日将被视为交单的到期日”。这一日期之后，信用证将不存在，金额不再支取。所以，单据必须在信用证规定的到期日或之前提交。

②信用证规定的交单时间

信用证可以规定单据在货物装运后的××天后提交。在这种情况下，交单日期可以根据货物的装运时间推算。但交单时间无论如何不能迟于信用证的有效期。

③装船日期后21天

如果没有注明交单的确切时间，那么，交单就必须在货物装运日后的21个自然日内完成，但不能晚于信用证的有效期。

(3)信用证对单据种类的要求

①汇票

汇票是出票人出具的书面的、注有日期并署名的，要求受票人立即或在未来某个规定时间，支付一定金额给受款人的工具。简言之，汇票是出票人向受款人签发的，要求受票人向受款人进行支付的书面命令。

汇票是一种非常有用的工具，因为它使一方(出票人)向受票人发出命令，要求受票人向发票人自己、他的代理人或第三方付款。当然，该支付命令只有在受票人有向出票人付款的基础义务时才有效。该基础义务可能源于受票人代出票人掌管资金(例如，受票人为银行)，出票人借给受票人资金(即受票人是借款人)，或者出票人向受票人出售了货物，受票人欠出票人货款(即受票人是买方)。

在缮制汇票时，我们应注意以下问题：

- 付款人。采用信用证支付方式时，汇票的付款人应按信用证的规定填写,一般是开证行或付款行。

信用证规定付款人的专业术语为"Drawn on ×××",意为"以×××为付款人",所以介词 on 后的宾语即为付款人。UCP600 规定:"信用证不得规定汇票以开证申请人为付款人。"这个规定使得开证行信用证下第一性付款责任与其最终汇票付款人地位更为一致。

• 受款人。受款人也称为抬头。通常采用指示性抬头,例如,"付给背书人(卖方)或其指定人(Pay to the order of ×××)"。

• 出票依据,也就是汇票的"出票条款"(Drawn Clause)。如属于信用证方式,应按照来证的规定文句填写。如信用证内没有规定具体文句,可在汇票上注明开证行名称、地点、信用证号码及开证日期。例如:"凭×××银行×××号××××年××月××日不可撤销信用证开立"(Drawn Under ××× Bank Irrevocable L/C NO.××× DATED ×××)。如属于托收方式,汇票上则应注明有关买卖合同号码。

• 汇票到期日。无论用 after 还是 from,一律从第二天起算;而以运输单据日(有装运日记载的依记载,没有记载的依出单日)为依据计算交单日,用 from 的从当天起算。

• 汇票一般开具一式两份,两份具有同等效力,其中一份付讫,另一份自动失效。

②商业发票

商业发票是指卖方开立的载有货物名称、数量、价格等内容的清单,作为买卖双方交接货物和结算货款的主要单证,也是进出口申报关税必不可少的单证之一。我国各进口公司的商业发票没有统一格式,但主要内容基本相同,包含以下要素:卖方名称和地址、买方名称和地址、开票日期、发票号码、订单或合同号码、货物的品质和规格等。

商业发票中商品的描述与信用证中商品的描述一致这点非常重要。单价、总价及其他任何双方同意的费用,都要与合同和信用证一致。发票金额应与信用证一致(至少不能超过)。发票金额如果超过信用证金额,银行有权拒收发票,有一个例外,信用证上"大约"用于货物的货币金额及数量时,发票金额可以多于或少于信用证金额的10%。

发票上还包含合同或信用证所要求的装运明细、货物重量、包装件数、运输标志、交货条件、付款及其他所有信息。

③提单

提单是指由海运承运人向已与其订立了运输合同的托运人所签发的运输

单据，其在国际贸易中发挥着至关重要的作用。提单一般有以下三个作用：

- 货物收据：提单是签收货物的收据。提单描述已装船货物的情况，写明货物数量及状况。提单通常由托运人提前填好。在货物装船以后，承运人要负责检查货物，检查所装货物是否与提单列明的一致。但是，承运人只负责检查外表是否一致——即标签相符，包装是否损坏。如果一切正常，适合的承运人代理就会在提单上签字，并将提单退还托运人。

- 运输合同的证明：提单是托运人和承运人之间的运输合同的证明。一旦提单被转让给善意的第三方，提单便是运输合同条款的确凿证据。

- 货物所有权证明：通过正当转让，善意取得提单的指定收货人或提单持有人具有货物所有权，并通过交付提单，提取货物。承运人有义务凭正本提单交货。承运人如果在提单未出示的情况下交货，须对提单持有人承担合同责任或民事侵权责任。

另外说到提单缮制，我们必须对以下问题加以注意：

第一，在提单的缮制中，最关键的是提单抬头即收货人的填制，关系到提单所有权的转让方式，在信用证中，都会有明确的规定。第二，提单的各项内容（如提单的种类、收货人、货物的名称和件数、目的港、有关收取运费的记载、提单的份数等）一定要与信用证相符。但其中货物的描述只要与信用证的货物描述不抵触，可使用统称。第三，提单的签发份数。根据 UCP600 规定，银行接受全套正本仅有一份的正本提单，或一份以上正本提单。如提单正本有几份，每份正本提单的效力是相同的，但是，只要其中一份凭以提货，其他各份立即失效。因此，合同或信用证中规定要求出口人提供“全套提单”，就是指承运人在签发的提单上所注明的全部正本份数。最后，提单的运费项目，在 CIF、CFR、CPT、CIP 条件下，应注明“运费已付”；如为 FOB、FCA 条件，则应注明“运费到付”。除信用证另有规定外，不必列出运费的具体金额。

④ 其他单据

其他单据根据信用证中的规定提供。这些单据有时由出口商自己提供，或者由其他人应出口商的要求提供。常见的单据有：

- 保险单（保险凭证）

保险单（保险凭证）是表明特定货物的保险险别及保险金额的单据。在跟单信用证交易中，保险单据用于向收货人保证已经对货物运输中的灭失投了保。一份完整的保险单包含以下内容：保险公司名称；保险单据名称；保险单据号码；投保货物的描述；投保风险和投保金额；赔付支付地点；运输方式、船名、装货港和目的港;保险单据签发日期;承保人签名;等等。

- 原产地证书

这是证明货物原产地或者生产制造地的单据,可以由中国国际贸易促进委员会、其他有资格的检验机构或者出口商自己出具。

原产地证书主要分为一般原产地证书和普惠制原产地证书。一般原产地证书,简称"C/O 原产地证书",又称为"普通产地证书",简称"原产地证",它是证明本批出口商品的生产或制造符合《中华人民共和国出口货物原产地规则》的一种法律文件,是由商务部统一规定格式并印制,通常用于不使用海关发票或领事发票的国家或地区,以确认对货物征税的税率。普惠制是工业发达国家对来自发展中国家的某些产品,特别是工业制成品和半制成品,给予一种普通的、非互惠的、非歧视的关税减免优惠制度。目前,已有新西兰、澳大利亚、日本、加拿大和欧洲等国家或地区给予我国以普惠制待遇。对这些国家的出口货物,须提供普惠制原产地证书,作为进口国海关减免关税的依据。

- 商检证书

各种检验证书分别用以证明货物的品质、数量、重量和卫生条件等方面的状况。在我国,这类证书一般由国家出入境检验检疫局出具,如合同或信用证无特别规定,也可以根据不同情况,由进出口或生产企业出具。但应注意证书的名称及所列项目或检验结果应与合同及信用证规定相同,出证日期迟于提单日期的商检证书无效。

样本 12-1 汇 票

BILL OF EXCHANGE

No. LD-DRGINV01

For US $ 18 825 600 SHANGHAI 27-May-01

(amount in figure) (place and date of issue)

At ×××××××××× sight of this FIRST Bill of exchange(SECOND being unpaid)

pay to BANK OF CHINA, SHANGHAI BRANCH or order the sum of

SAY UNITED STATES OOL_LARS ONE HUNDRED AND EIGHTY EIGHT THOUSAND HUNDRED AND FIFTY ONLY(amount in words)

Value received for 600 SETS (quantity) of TELECONTROL PACING CAR (name of commodity)

Drawn under CHEMICAL BANK YORK

L/C No. DRG-LDLC01 dated 14-Apr-01

To: CHEMICAL BANK NEW YORK
55 WATER SWREET, ROOM 1702,
NEW YORK,NY 10041

For and on behalf of
LIDA TRADING CO. LTD
×××
(signature)

样本 12-2　　商业发票

江苏和泰股份有限公司

JIANGSU HOTIY CORPORATION

HOTIY BUILDING, 50 ZHONGSHAN, NANJING, CHINA

Commercial Invoice

No. TEST
April 28, 2000
Order No. 008001

Sold to: Torus Systems (Chicago) Inc.
201 Fifth Avenue, Suite 2001
New York, NY 10021
U.S.A

Shipment: Per sailing from SHANGHAI to NY on or about April 25, 2000

Payment: BY T/T

Insurance: For 110% of the invoice value against ALL risks and WAR risks.

Terms: CIF New York

Item No.	Description	Quantity	Price	Amount
PCR	Cloth doll pairs, 6.5". (Your item No.00001-C21030A) (Your Order No. 008001) (Our S/C No. S000225) (Bar Code: 78459632114)	1 200.00 pc	35.000	US $ 42 000.00
	Porcelian ducking pair, 6"(large). Each pair in a box. (Your item No. C00001-D10021) (Your Order No. 008001) (Our S/C No. S000225) (Bar Code: 74859321456)	500.00 pc	28.500	US $ 14 250.00
Total:		1 700.00 pc		US $ 56 250.00

Total Amount: U.S. Dollars Fifty-Six Thousand Two Hundred and Fifty Only.

Remarks: All merchandise shall be inspected by buyer's representative before shipment.

Torus Systems (Chicago). Inc.

(signature)

样本 12-3　　　　　　　　　　**提　单**

Shipper:
SHANGHAI GARDEN PRODUCTS IMP. AND EXP. CO., LTD.

B/L No.: (1) SHYZ092234
承运人: **Carrier**

德威集装箱货运有限公司
DE-WELL CONTAINER SHIPPING CO.LTD.

OCEAN BILL OF LADING

ORIGINAL

Consignee:
TO ORDER OF SHIPPER

Notify party:
LAIKI PERAGORA ORPHANIDES LTD.,
020 STRATIGOU TIMAGIA AVE.,
6046, LARNAKA,
CYPRUS

RECEIVED in external apparent good order and condition except as otherwise noted. The total number of packages or units stuffed in the container. The description of goods and the the weights shown in this Bill of Lading are furnished by the merchants and which the ***Carrier*** has no reasonable means of checking and is not a part of this B/L contract.

(Terms of B/L continued on the back hereof)

Pre-carriage by	**Port of loading**
	SHANGHAI PORT

Ocean Vessel Voy .No.:	**Port of Discharge:**	**Place of Delivery**	**No. of Original B/L**
LT DIAMOND V.021W	LIMASSOL PORT		THREE

Marks and Nos Container& Seal No.	**No. & kind of packages**	**Description of goods**	**Gross weight**	**Measurement**
L.P.O.L. 186/09/10014 MADE IN CHINA NO. 1-325 1X 20' FCL, CY/CY CNO,: FSCU3214999 SNO,: 1295312	325 CTNS	WOODEN GARDEN PRODUCTS	4 175KG	24.104CBM

Total number of container or other pkgs or units (in words)	SAY THREE HUNDRED AND TWENTY FIVE CARTONS ONLY

For delivery of goods please apply to:
ABC Shipping Company
208 San Marding Street,
Limassol, Cyprus
Tel: 02-33669812

Freight& charges
FREIGHT PREPAID

Place and date of issue:
SHANGHAI 12 Feb., 2009

Signed by:

Laden on Board the vessel:
Date: 12 Feb., 2009
By: ____________

DE-WELL CONTAINER SHIPPING CO.LTD.
As carrier: ____________

6. 出口结汇

出口结汇是指出口商将出口外汇收入按照外汇汇率卖给银行,银行向其支付等值人民币。

(1)我国出口结汇的三种方式

根据结汇时间(即卖方银行将人民币款额贷记受益人账户的时间),我国出口结汇有三种方法,即收妥结汇、定期结汇和议付结汇。

①收妥结汇

收妥结汇又称收妥付款,是指信用证议付行在审单无误的情况下,将单据寄交国外付款行索取货款的结汇做法。这种方式下,议付行都是待收到付款行的货款后,即从国外付款行收到该行账户的贷记通知单(Credit Note)时,才按当日外汇牌价,按照出口企业的指示,将货款折成人民币拨入出口企业的账户。在这种方式下,银行不承担风险,不垫付资金,但出口企业却可能因为收汇较慢而导致资金周转困难。

②定期结汇

这种方式是指寄单行在收到受益人提交的单据,经审核确认单据与信用证条款的规定相符合后,将单据寄给国外付款行索汇,并在预先规定的日期按当日外汇牌价,将卖方外汇收益折算成人民币,贷记卖方账户。

③议付结汇

议付结汇又称买单结汇,是指议付行在审单无误的情况下,按信用证条款贴现受益人(出口公司)的汇票或者以一定的折扣买入信用证项下的货运单据,从票面金额中扣除从议付日到未来收到票款之日的利息和手续费,将货款的余额按议付日外汇牌价折成人民币,垫付给出口企业。议付行向受益人垫付资金、买入跟单汇票后,即成为汇票持有人,可凭票向付款行索取票款。这种结汇方式实际上是议付行给出口企业提供了资金融通的便利,这有利于加速出口企业的资金周转。

(2)装船后单证不符的补救办法

在信用证项下的制单结汇中,议付银行要求“单、证表面严格相符”。但是,在实际业务中,由于种种原因,单证不符的情况会有发生。国际商会银行委员会所做的一项研究表明,有三分之二的单据在第一次交单时与信用证条款不符。

信用证和单证最常见的不符包括:

- 汇票提交前,信用证已过期;
- 提单标明交货时间先于或者晚于信用证中规定的时间;
- 过期单据;
- 发票改动没有得到信用证的授权;
- 商品描述不一致;
- 保险单据错误;
- 发票金额和汇票金额不一致;
- 装货港和目的港与信用证规定不一致;
- 商品描述与信用证不一致;
- 没有提交信用证要求的单据;
- 单据在有关体积、质量等一般信息方面存在不一致;
- 信用证中描述的文件名称不准确;受益人信息必须是准确的;
- 发票或声明没有按照信用证的规定签名。

如果议付行发现了单据的某个不符点,而单据还在银行手里,且不符点能很快更改,那么,可以允许修改单据。如果时间不是问题,那么,出口商就应要求议付行退回单据,然后进行修改。如果没有足够的时间修改,出口商也许会按下列方式处理不符点:

①表提

当议付行审单发现不符点时,如情节不严重,在征得进口商同意后,出口商可向议付行出具担保书,要求凭担保议付。这时,议付行向开证行寄单时,在随单据的表盖(Covering Schedule)上注明单证不符点和“凭保议付”字样。此种做法称为“担保议付”,也被称为“表盖提出”(简称“表提”)。

②电提

在出口商所交单据与信用证的规定存在不符的情况下,可由议付行先用电报或电传向开证行列明不符点,待开证行确认接受后,再将单据寄出。“电提”的目的是在尽可能短的时间内了解开证行对单证不符的态度。

③改为跟单托收

如出现单证不符,议付行又不愿意采用“电提”或“表提”的做法,出口商只能采用托收的方式,委托银行寄单收款。由于这种托收与原信用证有关,为了使进口商易于了解该项托收业务的来由,托收行仍以原信用证的开证行作为代收行,请其代为收款。

值得注意的是,以上三种处理方法,实际上已将银行信用改为商业信用,开证行已不再承担信用证项下的付款责任,致使出口商完全陷于被动状态。因此,除非万不得已,不要轻易采用上述三种补救措施,而是应该认真缮制单据,仔细预审单据,将问题解决在货物出运之前。

第二节 进口合同的履行

在我国进口业务中,进口合同多数是按FOB价格条件成交的,如果是采用即期信用证支付方式成交,履行这类进口合同一般要经过开立信用证、租船订舱、装运、办理保险、审单和付款、报关和纳税、检验、交接这些主要环节。这些环节的工作,是由进出口公司、运输部门、商检部门、银行、保险公司以及用货部门等各有关方面分工负责、紧密配合而共同完成的。

进口业务操作和出口业务操作原理是一样的。在我国进口贸易中,按FOB贸易术语成交,对我方更为有利,因此占的比例比较多。如果采用信用证支付方式,进口业务的一般流程为:

1. 开立信用证

及时对国外出口商开出信用证是进口商在进口合同下的最主要义务之一。进口企业一定要保证在合同规定的期限内开出信用证,否则就构成违约,使自己陷于被动。如果合同规定在出口方领到出口许可证或支付履约保证金后开证,则进口方应在收到出口方已领到许可证的通知,或银行通知保证金已照收后开证。如果合同规定在出口方确定交货期后开证,进口方应在接到出口方上述通知后开证。

进口方在合同规定的时间内申请开证。进口方必须与开证行订有贸易融资合同,根据买卖合同填写“开证申请书”,并向开证行缴纳开证手续费(约占开证金额的0.15%)。

2. 租船订舱

以FOB方式成交,由买方负责租船订舱。在收到“订舱确认”后,进口商应将船名、航次和装船日期通知出口商,以便对方安排货物运输。同时,为了防止卖方拖延交货,进口方还要注意做好催促工作,特别是对数量大的或重要的物资的进口,买方最好委托自己在出口地的代理督促外商履约,或派人员前往出口地点检验监督，以保证船货衔接。

3. 投保货运险

我国对进口货物运输投保一般采取逐笔投保和预约投保两种方式。对于逐笔投保来说，当收货人在接到国外出口商发来的装船通知后，直接向保险公司填写投保单，办理投保手续。参保双方将就每批货物的条款进行逐一磋商，包括保险范围、货物和船舶的类型等。另一方面，预约投保政策通常会在国际贸易中使用，特别会被从事数量大且历时久的贸易活动的公司所采用。公司采取预约投保，主要可以使得其避免重复多次就新政策的条款进行谈判磋商的困境。同时，如果投保方同意购买一份较长期的合同，则它可能会实现较低的保费。这是因为保险公司不必在重复的谈判上花费时间，同时也能使其在较长一段时间内享有保证保费的好处。

4. 审单和付款

银行收到国外寄来的汇票及单据后，对照信用证的规定进行审核。

如果开证行认为单据与信用证的规定相符，在向外付款前也要交给进口企业复审。按照我国习惯，如果进口企业在 3 个工作日内没有提出异议，开证行即按信用证的规定履行付款义务。开证行的付款是没有追索权的。同时进口企业用人民币按照国家规定的有关外汇牌价向银行买汇赎单。进口企业凭银行出具的“付款通知书”向用货部门进行结算。

如果审核国外单据发现单证不符，可根据具体情况做出适当处理。例如：拒付；货到检验合格再付款；凭卖方或议付行出具担保付款；要求国外改正单据；在付款的同时，提出保留索赔权等。

5. 报关和纳税

为了报关需要，进口货物的收货人或其代理人需要向海关交纳相关出货船务文件。报关必须由在海关办理过登记注册手续的企业进行。报关员须经海关培训和考核认证。

通常，报关手续由以下步骤组成：

(1) 填写进口货物报关单

进口货物运达后，由进出口公司、委托代理公司或其报关代理商根据进口单据填写“进口货物报关单”向海关申报，并随附发票、提单、装箱单、保险单、许可证及审批文件、进口合同、产地证和所需的其他证件。如果属法定检验的进口商品,还须随附商品检验证书。

根据我国《海关法》,进口货物的申报必须在运输工具申报入境之日起14天内进行,逾期未向海关申报的,由海关按日征收进口货物CIF价格0.05%的滞报金;超过3个月未申报的,货物由海关变卖。

(2)验查

海关受理申报后将对进口货物进行检验以核对其是否和报关单上罗列的款项一致。检验将在特定地点和场所进行,即在海关监管区域内的仓库、场地进行。

(3)纳税

海关按照《中华人民共和国海关进口税则》的规定,将对进口货物计征进口税。根据《海关法》的规定,进口商应在海关签发税款缴款书的次日起7天内(法定假期除外),向指定银行缴纳税款。逾期未缴的,将依法追缴并按滞纳天数征收应缴款额0.1%的滞纳金。

(4)放行(结关)

进口货物经海关查验并纳税后,由海关在报送单和货运单上签字和加盖"验讫"章,进口企业持海关签字、盖章的货物提单提取进口货物,任何单位和个人都不得将未经海关放行的货物提走。但对保税货物和加工贸易进口货物,海关放行后,还要对货物进行后续监管,直到办完海关手续为止,这批货物才能被提走。

6. 交接

办完上述手续后,货物将被运送给国内订货商。国内订货商安排运输和仓储并与国内直接用户进行付款和货物交接。

参考文献

1. Michael R. Czinkota 等. International Business(第一版)[M].北京:机械工业出版社,2006.

2. Charles W.L. Hill, International Business Companies (6ed). McGraw -Hill, 2007.

3. 国际商会编写. 中国国际商会/国际商会中国国家委员会翻译. 国际贸易术语解释通则 2010 中英文对照版[M]. 北京:中国民主法治出版社,2011.

4. 董瑾. 国际贸易理论与实务(第五版)[M]. 北京:北京理工大学出版社,2014.

5. 易露霞,方玲玲,陈原. 国际贸易实务双语教程(第 2 版)[M]. 北京:清华大学出版社,2010.

6. 易露霞等. 国际贸易实务双语教程[M]. 北京:清华大学出版社,2015.

7. 易露霞,方玲玲,陈原. 国际贸易实务双语教程(第三版)[M]. 北京:清华大学出版社,2011.

8. 易露霞,方玲玲,尤彧聪. 国际贸易实务双语教程(第 4 版)[M]. 北京:清华大学出版社,2016.

9. 易露霞,方玲玲,尤彧聪. 国际贸易实务案例教程(双语)[M]. 北京:清华大学出版社,2010.

10. 张素芳. 国际贸易实务双语教程[M]. 北京:对外经济贸易大学出版社,2013.

11. 黎孝先,王健. 国际贸易实务(第五版)[M]. 北京:对外经济贸易大学出版社,2011.

12. 吴国新,毛小明. 国际贸易实务(第二版)[M]. 北京:清华大学出版社,2011.

13. 杨春梅,赵宏. 国际贸易实务双语教程[M]. 北京:清华大学出版社,2014.

14. 傅龙海,丛晓明. 国际贸易实务双语教程[M]. 北京:对外经济贸易大学出版社,2001.

15. 傅龙海,丛晓明. 国际贸易实务双语教程(第二版)[M]. 北京:对外经济贸易大学出版社,2016.

16. 傅龙海,丛晓明,邵李津. 国际贸易实务双语教程(第二版)[M]. 北京:对外贸易大学出版社,2015.

17. 傅龙海,郑佰青,罗治前. 国际贸易理论与实务双语教程[M]. 北京:对外贸易大学出版社,2014.

18. 傅龙海等. 外贸英语函电实务精讲[M]. 中国海关出版社,2016.

19. 赵蕾,郭红蕾. 进出口贸易实务双语教程[M]. 北京:对外经济贸易大学出版社,2014.

20. 冷柏军. 国际贸易实务(第二版)[M]. 北京:中国人民大学出版社,2012.

21. 何泽荣. 国际结算教程[M]. 成都:西南财经大学出版社, 2007.

22. 高露华,顾颖茵. 国际结算[M]. 北京:清华大学出版社,2015.

23. 熊伟,陈凯. 国际贸易实务英语[M]. 武汉:武汉大学出版社,2015.

24. 王秋红等. 国际贸易实务[M]. 北京:清华大学出版社,2012.

25. 兰天. 外贸英语函电(第 7 版)[M]. 大连:东北财经大学出版社,2015.

26. 倪华. 外贸英语函电[M]. 北京:北京大学出版社,2013.

27. http://www.doc88.com/p-0486866678015.html.

28. https://wenku.baidu.com/view/c9d16459f78a6529647d5379.html.

29. https://wenku.baidu.com/view/7bcc2ffd0d22590102020740be1e650e53eacf5a.html.

30. https://wenku.baidu.com/view/3e6f1de1102de2bd96058862.html.

31. https://max.book118.com/html/2017/0707/120845441.shtm.

32. http://www.docin.com/p-1498383797.html.

33. https://wenku.baidu.com/view/7380c8f79e314332396893f6.html.

34. http://www.docin.com/p-1765977409.html.

35. https://wenku.baidu.com/view/63fdde95b14e852458fb5774.html.

36. https://baike. baidu. com/item/bill% 20of% 20exchange/3463841? fr =

aladdin.

37. http://www.torus.com.tw/product/et62/manual/images/Et611a.gif.

38. http://www.chinadmd.com/file/3t6piiieesixpwo3pruurtwc_1.html.

39. https://www.51wendang.com/doc/cc1d453e4689bda5d810d784.